Ex Libris

Tibetan Medicine

Tibetan Medicine

illustrated in original texts

presented and translated
by
the Ven. Rechung Rinpoche
Jampal Kunzang

UNIVERSITY OF CALIFORNIA PRESS
Berkeley and Los Angeles

UNIVERSITY OF CALIFORNIA PRESS
Berkeley and Los Angeles, California

ISBN: 0-520-03048-6
Library of Congress Catalog Card Number: 72-85513

California Paperback Edition, 1976

This work is also published in the United Kingdom
by the Wellcome Institute of the History of Medicine

2 3 4 5 6 7 8 9 0

Printed in the United States of America

Contents

Preface

THE CHIEF part of this book is a translation of the biography of the Elder gYu-thog Yon-tan mGon-po, the famous Court Physician of King Khri-sroṅ-lde-btsan who lived during the eighth century A.D. The Elder gYu-thog Yon-tan mGon-po visited India three times. He met and had discussions with many learned Pandits, and thus widened his knowledge of Buddhism and especially of medicine. On his return to Tibet he spread medical science throughout the country and shared his knowledge with many.

For the preservation of our Tibetan culture I had the great desire to translate books on Tibetan Medicine, as well as to translate the Biography of the Elder gYu-thog Yon-tan mGon-po, and thus approached Dr. F. N. L. Poynter, Director of the Wellcome Institute of the History of Medicine, with the idea. Dr. Poynter very kindly took a keen interest in my suggestion and placed it before the Wellcome Trustees. The Trustees most generously accepted my request and kindly made it possible for me to carry on my work by awarding me a Fellowship to start my research work.

The first block print of the Biography of the Elder gYu-thog Yon-tan mGon-po was made by Dar-mo sMan-pa bLo-bzaṅ Chhos-grags who was the Court Physician of the Fifth Dalai Lama. Dar-mo sMan-pa acquired the manuscript of the Biography of the Elder gYu-thog Yon-tan mGon-po from a descendant of the latter, whose name was Lhun-grub bKra-shis. Having corrected the manuscript, Dar-mo sMan-pa had the first block prints made during the seventeenth century. Until the Communist Chinese occupied Tibet the blocks were preserved at the Lhasa Zhol par-khang (printing house). This is the text used for the present translation (India Office Library Lhasa J 12). It is printed on both sides of 149 leaves, each 51.5 by 10 cm or 21.35 by 4.15 inches, with six lines on each side. A second print was later made in sDe-dge in the district of Kham. The date is unknown.

In the Introduction I have included the following:

(a) The History of Tibetan Medicine from its origin up to modern times, which has not been written in English before.

(b) A brief account of the Commentary on the bShad-rgyud, written by sDe-srid Saṅs-rgyas rGya-mTs'o, which is called *Lapislazuli Rosary*.

(c) A brief account of the two important chapters from the Phyi-rgyud; i.e. the examination of the pulse and the urine, forming the basis of Tibetan medicine and medical practice.
(d) A series of Anatomy diagrams.

First and foremost I owe my deepest gratitude to the Wellcome Institute of the History of Medicine for enabling me to achieve my wish to carry out and complete this work. The Wellcome Institute has contributed a great deal towards the preservation of Tibetan culture, since much has been lost since the occupation by the Communist Chinese of Tibet.

My greatest thanks go to Miss Marianne Winder, Keeper of Oriental Manuscripts in the Wellcome Institute, for her unfailing assistance and help throughout my work of translation. Miss Winder, a scholar, has knowledge of several languages including Sanskrit, Pali and Tibetan. I was very fortunate to have had her assistance, and it was indeed a pleasure to work with her.

My gratitude goes to the two Tibetan doctors, Dr. hJam-dbyaṅs Legs-pa'i bLo-gros from Ladakh and Dr. hJam-dbyaṅs Seṅ-ge from sDe-dge in Kham, whom I consulted in order to clarify my doubts and difficulties during the translation of the Commentary to the bShad-rgyud and the Phyi-rgyud.

I thank Rai Bhadur Densapa, a learned Buddhist scholar, for giving me the loan of his manuscripts from his vast collection of rare manuscripts for reference during my work.

I should also like to thank Rhenock Kazi Tse Ten Tashi, Sikkim, who has assisted me greatly in identifying the botanical names.

I thank the India Office Library, London, for lending the Wellcome Institute the block print of the Biography of the Elder gYu-thog Yon-tan mGon-po.

Last but not least I must thank Yapshi Pheunkhang Sey Gompo Tsering for his help and assistance in the collection of materials.

RECHUNG RINPOCHE
JAMPAL KUNZANG

PART I

Introduction

by

MARIANNE WINDER

THE BIOGRAPHY of the great physician-saint gYu-thog Yon-tan mGon-po is the first complete Tibetan medical work ever to be translated into a European language. The only other extant translations are parts of the rGyud-bzhi (Four Treatises) into Russian and five chapters out of 120 of Vāgbhata's work into English. Both these are originally Sanskrit works while gYu-thog's Biography is an original Tibetan work. It shows the poetic and imaginative features characteristic of Tibetan literature.

The Sanskrit original of the rGyud-bzhi was probably written about A.D. 400 but it was lost and only survives in Tibetan and Mongolian translations. The Mongolian translation was derived from the Tibetan. The translators into Tibetan were Vairochana and Zla-ba mṄon-dgah* in the eighth century A.D. The translation into Russian of the First Treatise published by Dambo Ulyanov in 1901 is stated by Korvin-Krasinski (see Bibliography) to be unintelligible. The translation of abridgments of the First and Second Treatises into Russian by A. Pozdne'ev was done from the Mongolian translation of the Tibetan translation of the Sanskrit, and was published in 1908. Klaus Vogel's edition of five chapters of Vāgbhata's *Ashṭāngahṛdayasaṁhitā* in Sanskrit and Tibetan and translation into English was published by the *Deutsche Morgenländische Gesellschaft* in 1965.

The History of Tibetan Medicine in the present volume has been culled from Tibetan sources and, while myth and legend is blended with it, as in western mediaeval history, the dates are precise as they are always related to the reigns of kings whose dates are known. This is very different from Indian medical history where the dates assumed by different historians vary by hundreds and even thousands of years. Furthermore, Tibet having been cut off from much of the rest of the world effectively for centuries, an uninterrupted tradition in medicine has been preserved, and it is fortunate indeed

* Skt. Candrābhinandana.

that the Venerable Rechung Rinpoche, himself the Incarnation of Rechungpa who told the story of the great Yogi Milarepa (A.D. 1140–1223), is able to pass it on to the West.

Racially the Tibetans resemble their Chinese and Burmese, and of course also Nepalese, Bhutanese, Sikkimese and Assamese neighbours but amongst themselves they vary considerably in shape of head, stature, build and so on. This is not surprising if one realizes that a population of three million people was scattered over 700,000 square miles divided by huge mountain ranges.

The earliest inhabitants we know of probably practised the shamanism prevalent in the whole of Northern Asia. The Tibetan form of this was called Bon religion. The small pockets of this preserved here and there up to the time of the Communist invasion were strongly influenced by Buddhism and are not likely to reflect much of the original practices. Conversely, Tibetan Buddhism has been influenced by the Bon substrate.

In the seventh century A.D. Buddhism was introduced into Tibet, and has had a tremendous influence on the population and its way of life ever since. For most of the time one-fourth of the male population have been monks. At the head of the government there have been successively fourteen Dalai Lamas, spiritual rulers, assisted by wordly and monastic government officials. Most of the districts and villages were governed by at least one monastic authority. The laity was devout and all its life was centred round its religion. Religious mantras like *Om Mani Padme Hum* could be seen chalked on the mountain sides. Stone heaps, prayer flags and chörtens dotted the countryside. A mantra is an invocation to a deity. The language used for invocations is Sanskrit and not Tibetan. *Om Mani Padme Hum* is the mantra directed to Avalokiteśvara, the divine protector of Tibet. A chörten is a bell-shaped monument built over the relics of a Saint.

Thus the history of medicine in Tibet is closely connected with the history of Buddhism. This was introduced mainly from India where it had flourished from its inception in the sixth century B.C. onwards. The Buddha Gautama Siddhartha, its founder, had collected round him the first community of monks. These had a large lay following, and the Buddha's teachings were preserved by oral tradition until the Fourth Buddhist Council in the first century B.C. By then it had spread to South East Asia, i.e. Ceylon, Burma, Thailand and Cambodia. When written down the Buddhist Canon comprised three main divisions: the *Vinaya* (monks' rules), the *Sūtras* or discourses of the Buddha in the form of stories, and the *Abhidharma* or philosophical and psychological treatises. The forms used here are the Sanskrit ones. The language used in the Southern School or *Hīnayāna* Canon, generally regarded as the earlier one, was Pali. In Pali *Sūtra* is *Sutta* and *Abhidharma* is *Abhidhamma*. For, though Pali Buddhism probably preceded Sanskrit or Mahāyāna Buddhism, the Pali language is a Middle Indian grammarians' language derived from dialects ultimately going back to Sanskrit. (*r* after consonants was assimilated to the preceding consonant in Pali.) About the first century B.C. the beginnings of the Northern or *Mahāyāna* School of Buddhism were probably taking shape in India. The Canon remained similar, with additions of a devotional and philosophical character. The Mahāyāna spread from India to Tibet, Mongolia, China and Japan. In the twelfth century A.D. it was driven out of India by advancing Mohammedanism and by other factors such as Hinduism resenting the equality given to persons of different walks of life and to women in Buddhism.

Just as the *Mahāyāna* had been an extension in metaphysical speculation and spiritual practice of the *Hīnayāna*, Buddhism when translated into the Tibetan language and mentality again underwent a change or, at least, an extension of range.

The Tibetan language belongs to the Tibeto-Burmese group but there is no longer much similarity with Burmese. Tibetan has many loan words from the Chinese. It is a chiefly monosyllabic language with agglutinative features such as a few word endings. It also shows what in Germanic languages is termed *ablaut* and *gradation*, i.e. vowel and consonant changes in different tenses of the verb. Its most conspicuous characteristic are the clusters of consonants at the beginning of most syllables. These are no longer pronounced and a system of pitches or tones has been introduced to distinguish words that have become phonetically homonyms through this. It is interesting to note that our knowledge of the structure and pronunciation of ancient Chinese is largely based on Tibetan, with its literary documents dating from the seventh century A.D.* These documents were transcribed in an alphabetic script based on the Sanskrit devanāgarī. From this and from rhymes scholars now conclude that Chinese has a disyllabic inflected past.

In the transliteration of Tibetan names and titles the usual method, derived from the customary spelling of Old Irish, has been adopted. The beginning of the stem of a word is shown by a capital letter while the preceding consonants remain in lower case. In compounds only the first stem is made to begin with a capital. The distinction between capital and small letters or the indication of compounds by hyphens does not exist in the Tibetan script as used in block prints. Every syllable is divided by a dot from the next, equally whether compound or not.

* Cf. F. Bodmer, *The Loom of Language*, 1941, p. 441.

The main extension of the Mahāyāna in Tibetan Buddhism is its ritualistic aspect, the Tantra. The practice of medicine by members of the Order of Monks has been discouraged in Hīnayāna Buddhism but in the Mahāyāna with its great stress on compassion it had become an important part of the curriculum, e.g. at Nālandā University in India. In Tibet, too, the great physician-saints were monks, and the giving and taking of medicine was always accompanied by prayers. The teaching and learning of a new medical text was accompanied or introduced by a ritual and a consecration.

The teachings are handed down from teacher to pupil and in the case of physicians' families, just as in ancient Greece, from father to son. There are, in this way, two types of lineage, to which can be added a third kind of continuity: rebirth in human form after death. There are six different realms where one can be reborn: that of the hells, the hungry ghosts, the animals, the human beings, the *Asuras* or titans and that of the gods. The final goal, Nirvāṇa, is to transcend all six realms. Rebirth is conditioned by *karma*, the law of cause and effect. Each action and each thought have their effect in the future. The Bodhisattva, the Saint of the Mahāyāna, is able to cause himself to be reborn where he is needed. In this way, gYu-thog reappears within his lineage several times and so do others of his relatives and teachers and pupils.

The technique used in the telling of gYu-thog's biography is that of prophecy and 'flashback' so that events do not always follow a temporal sequence and often are retold or recapitulated from a different point of view. Prophecies are often made in dreams, and it is interesting to remember that Galen's father destined him for the medical profession after Asklepios had appeared to him in a dream. Galen himself, too, when faced with a difficult medical decision, is reputed to have been given advice in his dreams.

A few recurring terms ought to be explained. They are translated in Sanskrit rather than Tibetan as they will be familiar in this form to some readers. The 'Three Jewels' invoked at the beginning of most ceremonies are the Buddha, the Teaching (Sanskrit *Dharma*) and the Community (Sanskrit *Saṁgha*) of Saints. The assembly listening to the recital of a medical text or sermon is usually composed of brahmins, rishis, spiritual heroes and ḍākinīs. The term *brahmin* has been taken over from Hinduism.

Rishis are wise ascetics living alone in the woods. Spiritual heroes are Bodhisattvas, that is Saints who undertake the dangerous and painful task of leading beings towards Nirvāṇa. They can take on any form they wish, human or non-human. Ḍākinīs are their female counterpart and they help those who meditate. They are recognizable by certain marks, and in gYu-thog's story we encounter a girl who is a ḍākinī without knowing it. This can be explained by the law of karma according to which somebody may be ready for a saintly career through efforts made in former lives.

There are also the great Bodhisattvas who are the embodiment of principles such as Avalokiteśvara of Compassion, Mañjuśrī of Wisdom, Vajrapāṇi of Power, and so on. These can send out innumerable emanations of their body, speech and mind, and also may appear momentarily in ordinary human beings while their consciousness is elevated to great heights.

Then there are gods and goddesses, ghosts and demons, all seen or otherwise perceived at certain stages of meditation or in certain states of consciousness. One of the chief protagonists among the ancestors of gYu-thog is the goddess Yid-hphrog-ma who planted the first medicinal herbs. She is comparable to the Greek Demeter who planted the first blade of corn and sent out Triptolemos to carry her gift to the farthest corners of the world. Both of them are connected with initiation ceremonies.

Another, even more archaic, aspect of Yid-hphrog-ma is the goddess rDo-rje Phag-mo (Sanskrit Vajravārāhī) who wears a sow's head at the side of her head, and she is worshipped together with the god rTa-mgrin (Sanskrit Hayagrīva) who wears a horse's head beside her own. Again one is reminded of Demeter to whom the pig was sacred and who was pursued by Poseidon, and to Poseidon the horse was sacred. It seems possible that in prehistoric times, in the region between Asia Minor and Central Asia, a cult of two such theriomorphic deities existed which spread to East and West.

While passages on pharmacology, surgery, medical ethics etc. are immediately intelligible to the Western reader, a word of explanation is perhaps needed on the philosophy underlying Tibetan medical thought. According to Aristotle, one of the fathers of Western science, matter is only potential unless impressed by form. Mahāyāna Buddhism goes further and says form, too, is empty of selfhood because it will always depend on something else: the eye of the beholder, the surrounding space, the mind that thinks it, etc. Therefore, all phenomenal existence is, as far as we can cognize it, Emptiness (Sanskrit *Śūnyatā*). About the Reality—of which Emptiness is the aspect intelligible to the human mind—nothing can be said.

Note on the transliteration of Tibetan words: ṅ is pronounced like ng in English 'ring'. zh was originally pronounced like s in English 'leisure', but is now pronounced like sh. The different spelling shows the etymological difference. ts' is pronounced as in English 'cats' home'. Sanskrit ś is pronounced sh. Where sh is used in Sanskrit it corresponds to a different character.

History of Tibetan Medicine

In the golden age when human beings had come into existence they, for a long time, did not have to eat material food but lived in *samādhi*.* There was neither sun nor moon nor stars for they themselves emitted light. There existed no words for night and day. They had miraculous powers, were able to fly through the air and had beautiful bodies. They lacked nothing and lived as if they were in heaven. One day one man ate the bitumen on the ground because of a habit acquired in a former life. Then he suffered from indigestion and suffered a great deal. He wailed and lamented. Brahma heard about it and felt compassion and thought: 'How could one cure this?' He remembered the medical text taught by the great Buddha Sha-kya Thub-chen† in which it is recommended to drink boiling water in order to cure digestive diseases. He taught the sick man to drink boiling water, and he was cured. Therefore they say that the first disease was indigestion and the first sick being was human and the first medicine was boiling water and the first doctor was Brahma.

After the passing of the Golden Age, when people had been alive for aeons, their span of life began to decrease and they met with an untimely death. The Devas assembled to discuss how one could find a method of preventing an untimely death. Brahma remembered the science of medicine and told them: 'In the Vedas it is said that Brahma churned the ocean and eight chalices of deathless nectar emerged from it. These were stolen by the Titans, and the Devas were downcast, and Vishṇu appeared as a beautiful woman and the Titans looked upon her as their ladylove and made her guard the chalices of nectar and went to disport themselves bathing. Then Vishṇu and Indra took the nectar to Indra's palace. When the Titans returned they could not find the nectar and searched for it everywhere, and they heard it had been taken by the Devas. At a carousal of nectar held by the Devas the Titan called Rāhu appeared as a Deva and took part in it. When he had drunk his share of nectar he fled. Chandra saw it and told Vishṇu: 'That is Rāhu!' They pursued him and Brahma threw his wheel and cut

* The bliss of deep absorption.

† In an earlier *kalpa* (aeon).

his head, but Rāhu did not die because he had partaken of the nectar and he threw the wheel back again and wounded Brahma's cheek and inflicted such pain on him that he fainted and remained unconscious for a long time. When he recovered he thought: 'What would be the best means to heal this wound?' At the time of the Buddha Kāśyapa he had heard him teach the science of Medicine and therefore the wound in his cheek emitted the sounds of the letters *a* and *tha*. These reminded him of the medicine the Buddha had taught in the world. Remembering it he composed the text called *gSo-dpyad hBum-pa* (100,000 ślokas on Medicine). He taught it to his disciple sKye-rgu'i bDag-po Myur-ba and to the two doctors amongst the Devas, Tha-skar-gyi-bu Ris-med and Lhag-bchas, the two divine physicians, sons of the Aśvinis. These two handed it down to Indra. Indra passed it on to rGyun-shes-kyi-bu who handed it on to Thaṅ-la-hbar, and he to dKah-gnyis sPyod, and he to Mu-khyud-hdzin, and he to bShol-hgro-skyed, and he to Me-bzhin-hjug, and he to Lug-nag, and he to rGya-skegs sna. Each of these great Devas wrote a commentary called *Tsa-ra-ka sde-brgyad*. Through these great Deva-Rishis the science of Medicine came gradually down from the gods into the human world, to the king of Benares, and the teaching was called the divine Brahma system. This is the first appearance of Medicine in the human world.

The Buddhist account of the origin of Medicine is as follows: We believe that, just as the third Buddha Kāśyapa taught Medicine in a past aeon, in this fortunate *kalpa* the Buddha Śākyamuni, the fourth of the thousand Buddhas, after delivering his First Sermon at Sarnath, taught the medical text called *Vimalagotra*. In the medicine chapter of the *Vinaya* the Buddha also said: 'A sick *bhikkhu** (monk) should consult a doctor and take the medicine given to him.' The third chapter in the Vinaya gives instruction in the downward-moving and a few other exercises. Moreover, while the Buddha was staying in the Jeta-grove and many bhikshus† were thin and pale from the autumn fever he asked them to take medicines. But they took them only at the prescribed times for meals and not out of turn. They did not recover and still looked pale and thin. Therefore he permitted them to take medicines at other times of the day and said: 'For this reason I will permit that bhikshus can take medicines at any time.'

The Buddha is said to have taught Brahma the *gCher-mthon Rigs-pa'i brGyud* in 3500 chapters. Others say he taught it in the coconut country to Śāriputra and Ānanda. According to the *gSer-hod Dam-pa*. he also taught Medicine. This deals with the subject of the body, the cause of diseases, diet, at

* Pali form.

† Sanskrit form.

what season what diseases are prevalent, during what season what medicines and what diet are to be used, and the time when the three diseases arise: those of air, those of phlegm and those of bile, how to treat them, the combination of two or three diseases, how to recognize combined and mixed diseases, and so on. Moreover, specially for the sake of the sick and of future disciples, he appeared as the Medicine Buddha and taught the *rGyud-bzhi* at lTa-na-sdug. But some people, for instance Bi-byi, say that the lTa-na-sdug where the Buddha taught Medicine is the same as Indra's palace in the King of the Mountains.*

sToṅ-mi Nyag-hug-pa gDoṅ-nag and his followers say: lTa-na-sdug is one part of the place of the Buddha which is called Gaṅs-chan mTs'o-skyes. But the majority believe that the stay in lTa-na-sdug refers to the four years the Buddha is reported to have lived in the medicine jungle† which must have been situated in Uḍḍiyāna. In that jungle there was a mountain plateau created by the Buddha, on which the Buddha created lTa-na-sdug. Countless Devas, Rishis, Buddhists and non-Buddhists surrounded him. He knew everything that went on in all his disciples. At the same moment when he intended that the Wheel of Medical Science should be turned he appeared as the Medicine Buddha and immediately fell into the *Samādhi* called 'Expelling four hundred and four diseases'. To herald in the appearance of his emanation, different coloured rays came out of his chest shining in all directions and drove away the diseases of all beings and then sank back into his chest. Then the rishi, called Lord Rig-pa'i Ye-shes, came out of his chest. He stayed in the sky in front of the Medicine Buddha and his attendants. Then he addressed them thus: 'Friends, all those who wish that people should be healthy and live a long life and if they fall sick that they should be cured ought to learn the Science of Medicine. Because health is of the first importance in any undertaking; all those, too, who want to meditate and reach Nirvāṇa and those who want wealth and happiness ought to learn the Science of Medicine.' Then rays of light issued from the Medicine Buddha's tongue and drove away the diseases of all beings and then sank back into his tongue. Then the great Rishi Lord Yid-las-Skyes appeared and made his obeisance to the Medicine Buddha and his emanation Rig-pa'i Ye-shes ('Wisdom of Knowledge'). He circumambulated them three times and then sat down in the sky in front of them, with his hands making the request gesture, and he said: 'Great Lord Rig-pa'i Ye-shes! You said one should learn the Teachings of Medicine. All these attendants here want people to be happy. So can you, please, tell us how we can learn it?' And

* Mount Meru.

† Mentioned in the Bye-brag bShad-mdzod Chhen-mo.

then he taught them the *rGyud-bzhi* with its 156 chapters, by the method of question and answer. While the deva attendants heard it as the medical text called *gSo-dpyad hBum-pa* (100,000 ślokas on Medicine) and the Buddhists heard it as the text *Rigs-gsum mGon-po* (About the Three Protectors of Knowledge) and the Rishis heard it as the medical text called *rTsa-ra-ka sDe-brgyad* (Sanskrit *Charaka-ashṭa-varga*) and the Hindus heard it as the text about Mahādeva: *dBaṅ-phyug Nag-po'i rGyud** (Treatise of Mahādeva), only Yid-las Skyed understood the meaning of the whole *rGyud-bzhi*. The other three heard it as the medical text commensurate with their knowledge. The perfect rGyud-bzhi was written down in 5900 ślokas with vaiḍūrya ink on sheets of pure gold. The original text is believed to be kept in the Ḍākinīs' place in Uḍḍiyāna.

The *rGyud-bzhi* consists of four treatises: the Root Treatise (*rTsa-rgyud*) which tells everything concisely, the *bShad-rgyud*, Commentary Treatise, which explains it in detail, the *Man-ṅag rgyud*, Information, which gives a detailed explanation and information on the practice, and the *Phyi-rgyud*, Last Treatise, which gives an explanatory account so as to make it easy to practise all the three.

In the History of Medicine written by Braṅ-ti during the turning of the third wheel, the Buddha Śākyamuni taught the medical treatise called *Shel-gi Me-loṅ* (Crystal Mirror) containing fifty chapters. The *hJam-dpal sNyiṅ-rje Zur-thig* (Essence of the Heart) says that the Bodhisattva Mañjuśrī composed a text on the treatment of head injuries called *mGo-bchos bDud-rtsi'i Lhuṅ-bzed* (Bowl of Nectar for Head Treatment) and a text on chest surgery and other medical treatises, and that the Bodhisattva Avalokiteśvara composed a treatise on general surgery called *dPyad-gches gzuṅ* (Precious Treatment) and others, and that the Bodhisattva Vaj-rapāṇi composed a treatise on anatomy and others, and that the Bodhisattva Tārā composed a treatise comprising 120 chapters on how to grow herbs and medicinal plants and another treatise on how to mix those herbs. Therefore they are called *Treatises According to the Bodhisattvas' Methods*.

In the same way it is said that the following *Treatises According to the Devas' Methods* were written: Brahma composed the medical text called *Gu-na sha-stra* and another text called *gSaṅ-ba'i sNyin-po'i Don-bsdus-pa* (Collection of the Secret Essence).

Among the Treatises According to the Rishis' Method is the *hPhrul-gyi Me-loṅ* (Mirror of Transformation) composed by the Rishi sKye-rgu-'i bDag-po (Skt. Prajāpati). The two sons of the Rishi Aśvinis, called Tha-skar-gyi Bu, composed the *Gches-bsdus* (Selected Essence) and the *Byaṅ-khog*

* Skt. Kṛshṇa-Īśvara-tantra.

Khrims-kyi Luṅ-hod hPhro-ba (Precepts Radiating from the Valley of Light on the Inside of the Body). The goddess of Medicine called Nor-rgyun-ma (Stream with Jewels) composed the *Rim-po-che hPhreṅ-ba* (Garland of Precious Stones).

The human Rishis were believed to have received the Teaching from the seven spiritual sons of a Deva-Rishi, a disciple of Indra. Their names were: rGun-shes* (Grapes of Wisdom) (Skt. Kratu), Hod-gzer-chan-ma (She with the Golden Light, Marīchi), Hod-yaṅ (Perfect Light, Aṅgiras), Yan-lag-skyes (Skt. Pulaha), lHa-min-hjoms (Conquering Gods and Men, Skt. Atri), mChhod-sbyin-chan (Honoured with Gifts, Skt. Vaśishṭa), gNas-bjog (Skt. Pulastya).

Later there were eight descendants of the Devas, with a human mother. Their names were: rGyun-shes-kyi Bu (Skt. Ātreya) (Son of the Stream of Wisdom), Me-bzhin-hJug (Skt. Agniveśa) (Fire Face), Thaṅ-la-hbar (Skt. Dhanvantari) (Blazing Steppe), dKah-gnyis-spyod (Double Accomplishment in Suffering), Mu-khyud-hdzin (Skt. Nimindhara) (Surrounding Boundary), hGro-skyoṅ-gi Bu (Son of the Protector of Beings), Nam-so-skyes (Born during the Seventh Lunar Mansion), and gShol-hgro-skyes (Born Walking behind the Plough). They composed one medical Commentary each which they had heard from Indra. The collection is called *rTsa-ra-ka*† *sDe-brgyad.*

The Rishi dPal-ldan hPhreṅ-ba wrote a commentary on the first part of the rTsa-ra-ka sDe-brgyad called *bsTod-hgrel-nyi Zla-sbar-bkab* (Clearer than the Moon and the Sun) and another commentary called *sMad-hgrel hPhrul-gyi lDe-mig* (Miraculous Key for the Commentary on the second part of the rTsa-ra-ka-sDe-brygad). Both together comprise 600 chapters.

Śālihotra, Legs-thos (Skt. Suśruta), Za-las-rgyal-ba and other Rishis living before and after the Buddha Śākyamuni have written and spread many medical texts. They came down to the famous and learned doctor of Taxila, whose name was rGyun-shes-gyi-bu (Son of the Stream of Wisdom) (Skt. Ātreya) who was the Court Physician of King Pad-ma-dpal. His disciple, hTs'o-byed-gzhon-nu, Sanskrit Kumāra-jīva, was born as the son of King Bimbisāra and a trader's wife. Grown up, he saw one day a group of white-clad men and he asked his father: 'Who are they?' He said: 'These are called doctors and they protect people from diseases.' As the result of his past karma hTs'o-byed-gzhon-nu was filled with the wish to become a doctor too and he asked his father for permission. He wanted to learn from Rgyun-shes-kyi-bu (Stream of Wisdom's Son). King Bimbisāra sent him

* Perhaps misprint of rGyun-shes (Stream of Wisdom, Continuing Wisdom).
† Tibetanized version of the name Charaka.

to Taxila with a letter to its King Pad-ma-dpal* (Glorious Lotus) asking him to help his son when learning under the guidance of rGyun-shes-kyi-bu. His teacher taught him the rudimentary part but hTs'o-byed-gzhon-nu learned very fast and soon learned more than what he was taught. Once accompanying his teacher on his round of patients, they came to one patient to whom the teacher gave a medicine. hTs'o-byed-gzhon-nu, knowing that he had not been given the right medicine and not wanting to say so in front of teacher and patient, went back afterwards and told the patient his teacher had asked him to give him a second medicine and not to take the first one. He used a diplomatic and polite way, avoiding offending the teacher or harming the patient. Later rGyun-shes-kyi-bu asked the patient how he was now and the patient answered: 'I am much better now'. The teacher said: 'You have still to go on taking the medicine', and the patient said 'Which one, the first or the second?' The teacher said, 'I have not given you two medicines. What do you mean by the first and the second?' The patient said: 'The first one from you and the second one from hTs'o-byed.' In this way the teacher found out that he had made a mistake and he was very pleased with hTs'o-byed and thought he was very learned. Since then he always took hTs'o-byed wherever he went.

Some other disciples were jealous and said: 'Our teacher likes only hTs'o-byed and not us.' And the teacher replied: 'hTs'o-byed is really very intelligent. Of whatever I teach him he understands the finer points. None of you does. hTs'o-byed has an excellent brain.' And he taught him everything except brain surgery. After some time a patient suffered from a brain tumour and hTs'o-byed made friends with him. When rGyun-shes-kyi-bu came to operate on him, hTs'o-byed was able to look on hidden in the house. After rGyun-shes-kyi-bu had taken off the scalp a tiny insect was found inside and the teacher wanted to take it out with a pair of pincers. But hTs'o-byed jumped forward and said: 'Don't do that! If you get hold of one of the legs, it may break off, leaving the insect inside, and damage may be done to the nerves. You should heat the pincers, then touch the insect for a moment; it will be numbed and you can take it out.' The teacher did this and the patient recovered. Then the teacher asked his pupil to leave the country because he himself was earning his living mainly from brain surgery, and advised him to practise abroad. hTs'o-byed bowed to him and left and soon he earned enough money to send sums to his teacher repeatedly, and he always showed him gratitude and respect.

As the result of his practice hTs'o-byed-gzhon-nu was crowned 'the king of doctors' three times. This meant being pronounced publicly as

* Rāja Padma Śrī.

such by the King. He is believed to be still alive because he achieved deathlessness.

His chief disciple Nāgārjuna was born in Beta, the coconut country in South India, in a Brahmin family, about 400 years after the Buddha's death. He was converted to Buddhism and became a great Buddhist philosopher. He wrote many commentaries on the Sūtras and Tantric texts and he improved medical education by writing the text *sByor-ba brGya-pa* (The Hundred Preparations) and *gChes-bsdus* (Precious Collection) and other texts.

His disciple dPa-bo was born in West Kashmir as the son of the brahmin Siṁhaguhya who was a great doctor. His mother's name was Ratnasiddhi. He became a great Hindu pandita and was converted to Buddhism by Āryadeva. His Buddhist name was Āchārya Aśvaghosha. He became a great Buddhist pandita and poet and wrote many texts on Buddhist philosophy, the Jātaka about the former lives of the Buddha Gautama, and the following medical texts: *Yan-lag brGyad-pa Chhen-po* (Great Eight Branches) and the *Yan-lag brGyad-pa-la hJug-pa* (Entering the Eight Branches) and *Yan-lag brGyad-pa'i sNyiṅ-po bsDus-pa* (Collection of the Essence of the Eight Branches) and a commentary to it, and especially when he wrote the latter there appeared many good omens all over the country for the spreading of medical science.

His disciple was a paṇḍita from Kashmir called Zla-ba mṅon-dgah (Abundantly joyful Moon). He wrote a commentary on the *Yan-lag brGyad-pa'i sNyiṅ-po bsDus-pa* called *Ts'ig-don Zla* (The Moon Ray of the Meaning of Words) and a dictionary of the names of the medicines mentioned in it called *Ts'ig-don sGra-sbyor* (The Meaning of Words and Syllables Illuminated), and others. He became so to speak the crown jewel of all doctors in India.

To Tibet during the reign of King Lha-mtho-ri gnyan-brtsan, the twenty-fifth king of Tibet, two doctors came from India: Doctor Bi-byi dGah-byed and Doctor Bi-lha dGah-mdzes, and taught the populace some branches of Medicine, for instance, how to diagnose diseases. Before the two Indian doctors came, the Tibetans had only known some dietary rules and simple instructions like how to stop bleeding by applying hot butter.

Three generations later King hBroṅ-gnyan Lde'u was attacked by a disease caused by demons. So he buried himself alive in a hole in the ground to prevent his descendants from contracting the disease caused by demons. His last words to his son, Prince Kon-pa Kra, were an injunction to worship the text *gNyan-po gSaṅ-ba* which had come down from the sky during the reign of his ancestor King Lha-mtho-ri gNyan-btsan. In this way the Buddhist teaching was believed to have appeared for the first time in Tibet. Kon-pa should invite a doctor from Ha-sha to operate on his eyes which were blind. The father also instructed him how to rule the country. The son did as he said and invited a very learned doctor who operated on his eyes with a golden instrument. Then he saw the demons living on sKyid-shod stag-mo-ri. Since then he was called Stag-ri gNyan-gzigs. During the reign of his son, King gNam-ri Sroṅ-brtsan, a medical and astronomical text was believed to have been brought from China, but it is not clear which text it was.

Under his son, King Sroṅ-btsan sGam-po,* the Tibetan alphabet was adapted from the Sanskrit Devanāgarī letters by Thonmi Sambhota who had gone to India and studied there. King Sroṅ-btsan sGam'po's Queen, a Chinese princess, brought the medical text called *Sman-dpyad Chen-mo* (Great Analytical Treatise on Medicine) from China, and it was translated into Tibetan by Ha-shang Mahādeva and Dharmakośa. He invited the following three great doctors to his Court: from India Bharadhaja, from China Han-wang-Hang and from Persia Doctor Galenos.† Each translated a book in their own way into Tibetan. The Indian doctor's texts were called *hBu-shag-ma Bu Chhe-chhung* (Big and Small Louse Gravel) and *sByor-ba Mar-gsar* (Preparation of New Butter), the Chinese doctor's text was called *rGya-dpyad Thor-bu Chhe-chhuṅ* (Treatise of Great and Small Scattered Chinese Surgery), the Persian doctor's were called *mGo-snon bsDus-pa* (Collection of Main Additions) and *The Treatment for Cock, Peacock and Parrot.* And from the discussion between the three doctors they composed a medical text called *Mi-hjigs-pa'i mTs'on-chha* (The Weapon of the Fearless One), comprising seven chapters, and presented it to the King. They received presents from the King, took their leave, and went home, except for Galenos who stayed behind as the King's Court Physician. He settled down in Lhasa, married and had three sons: the oldest one he sent to the upper gTsaṅ district where he married a member of the Bi-byi lineage, as a result of which it was continued from there. The middle one he sent south of Tibet, to gYor-po, which started the lineage of the Southern doctors. The youngest one stayed with his father and they called him Jo-roṅ and he continued the lineage at Lhasa.

At that time the King ordered a few Tibetan boys to learn Medicine and they were awarded two doctor titles: hTs'o-byed or sMan-pa, and he gave them twelve presents.

Braṅ-ti was a court official and physician of King Khri-lde gTsug-btan who became king in A.D. 704. His teaching was passed down through his family lineage, and later members of his lineage wrote his system down, and the ensuing book was called *Braṅ-ti-hi-Pod-khra-Pod-dmar.*

* Born in A.D. 605.

† Perhaps a Persian translator of Galen, or a pen-name adopted by a Persian doctor.

After that, the son of King Mes-'ag Ts'om, whose name was lJaṅ-ts'a, married a Chinese princess called Gyim-shang Kong-jo who brought with her medical and astrological texts which were then translated by Ha-shang Ma-ha sKyin-da and rGya-phrug Gar-mkhan and Khyung-po rTsi-rtsi and lChog-la sMon-hbar.

Simultaneously, Champashila, in Tibetan called Bi-byi, was invited with many disciples from Khrom, a province in Eastern Tibet. He translated the *rGyud Shel-gyi Me-loṅ* (Crystal Mirror Treatise), comprising fifty chapters, then he added forty-two chapters on the anatomy of the upper part of the body and twenty-five chapters on the anatomy of the lower part of the body. This was presented to the King. They covered it with silk and put it into a box studded with jewels and called it *The Treatment-Preserving Text.*

When Champashila was made Court Physician, the King ordered that the following six rules should be always observed: (1) The court physician should be on all occasions offered the seat of honour. (2) He should have the best cushions. (3) He should be offered the best food. (4) He should be taken and returned by horse. (5) His fees should be paid in gold. (6) Gratitude to him should be always remembered. Conversely, the doctors should treat their patients with compassion as if they were their own sons and not look out for food and other things in their patients' houses.

Later Champashila became regent of Tibet for some time. The descendants of Doctor Bi-byi increased in number. He had three disciples called Shaṅ lHa-mo gZigs, sToṅ-bsher Mes-po, and Braṅ-ti rGyal-mnyes. Later on they lived in Eastern Tibet to watch the Chinese border for four years. In return the King presented them with the medical text *rGyud Shel-kyi Me-loṅ* (Crystal Mirror Treatise), and the *rMa-bchos-ma Bu* (The Surgeon's Son) and other presents. He made them his Court Physicians and released them from the Army.

During the time between King Mes-'ag-ts'oms (flourished A.D. 710) and the coronation of King Khri-sroṅ-lde-btsan (A.D. 754), many texts were translated which have been preserved in Tibet. No names are given here as the list would be too long. King Khri-sroṅ-lde-btsan was thirteen years old when he was crowned. He invited Padmasaṁbhava and Śāntarakshita from India and built bSam-yas Monastery, the first monastery in Tibet.

Padmasaṁbhava also wrote a text called *bDud-rtsi'i sNyiṅ-po* (Nectar Essence) and other medical works. In Eastern India bStan-pa'i bLo-gros wrote a book on medicine called *Dri-med gZi-byid* (Pure Splendour). In Uḍḍiyāna the pandit Jinamitra wrote the *gSo-stoṅ dGu-bchu rTsa-gchig* (One Root Curing Nineteen Thousand). And during this time many others spread and preserved the teaching of Medicine also in India.

Padmasaṁbhava prophesied the birth of Vairochana whose father's name would be Pa-gor He-hdod and whose mother's name would be Bran-ka-bzah sGron-skyid, and who would become a great translator. He would be found in the district where the rivers gTsaṅ-nyaṅ-chhab and gTsaṅ-chhab meet. The king sent out his messengers and they found an eight-year-old boy fitting the description, and when he was nine years old he was brought before the king. They trained him and he learned Sanskrit from Padmasaṁbhava and Śāntarakshita till he was fifteen and he became very learned and became a novice in the Order of Monks. Then he was sent to India with all the equipment and bars of gold necessary for the journey in order to bring the Teaching to Tibet. He met twenty-five panditas on the way and had religious instruction from all of them, especially from pandit Zla-ba mṄon-dgah from whom he learned the rGyud-bzhi and other medical texts and brought them to Tibet. And he translated them all into Tibetan and presented them to the King and to Padmasaṁbhava. But Padmasaṁbhava said: 'This is not the time to teach these great life preservers. People are not ready for them. It would be better to hide them for a later age. Let us hide them in the chalice-shaped pillar on the rooftop of Samye Monastery.' And they prayed that in the future the right person should find them in the pillar, take them out and study and spread their teaching.

King Khri-sroṅ-lde-btsan thought: 'Before my time a system of medicine was created by my ancestors. Now that I have all the medical texts which have not yet been translated into Tibetan, I should develop this further and have them translated. He sent messengers with gold out to bring doctors from different countries: from India came Śāntigarbha, from Kashmir Guhyavajra, from China sToṅ-gsum Gaṅ-ba and Ha-sha Ba-la and Han-ti Pa-ta, from Persia Halashanti, from Guge Seṅ-mdo 'Od-chhen, from Dol-po came Khyol-ma Ru-tsi, from Nepal Dharmashala. Then he invited them to his palace and asked them to translate medical texts from their own language into Tibetan. Śāntigarbha translated the *Bas-sgrom sMug-po'i rGyud* and other texts, the Kashmir doctor translated the *dPyad-hphreṅ Sel-bar-byed-pa Mun-pa'i sGron-me* (A Wreath of Treatments as a Torch to Dispel the Darkness) and other texts. The Persian doctor translated the *mGo-bchos Mu-stegs-kyi sKor brGyad-pa rTsa-hgrel* (Commentary to the non-Buddhist Text on Head Treatment in Eight Sections). The Guge doctor translated the *Nag-po'i rGyud-gsum* (Three Black Treatises) and other texts. The Dol-po doctor translated the *Mi-hjigs-pa brGyad-kyi mTs'on-chha* (The Fearless eightfold System of Surgery). The Nepalese doctor translated the *hGram-pa-ti* (Treatment of Male and Female), the Chinese doctor translated the *sByor-ba'i hPhreṅ-ba* (The Wreath of Preparation) and so on. They put the translations into a box made of the wood of acacia catechu and said: 'These are the texts of the King's life preservers' and had a number of intelligent boys trained in medicine: from the upper part of Tibet Chher-rje Shig-po and Hug-pa Chhos-bzaṅ and Bi-chhe Legs-mgon, from Central Tibet gYu-thog Yon-tan mGon-po,* Mi-nyag Roṅ-rje and Braṅ-ti rGyal-bzaṅ, and from Lower Tibet gNyah-pa Chhos-bzaṅ and mThah-bshi Dar-po and sToṅ-pa Grags-rgyal. These became the nine learned Tibetan doctors, the King's court physicians.

King Khri-sroṅ-lde-btsan's chief physician was the Chinese doctor sToṅ-gsum Gaṅ-ba who had composed a medical text called *gSo-ba dkar-po lam-gyi sgron-ma* on the way from China and had presented it to the King. He cured the King's illness and was called mThah-bzhi-sToṅ-gsum-gaṅ-wa. The King, who so named him because he did the work of four foreign Doctors, gave him land called gYer-stod-j. He settled there and his descendants were called mThah-bzhi sman-pa (Foreign Doctors).

In the Tibetan religious tradition there was a break at the time of King gLaṅ-dar-ma who destroyed all religious institutions, and the teachings had afterwards to be brought back from abroad. The teaching up to gLaṅ-dar-ma was sna-dar (early propagation of the doctrine) and after gLaṅ-dar-ma, phyi-dar (late propagation of the doctrine). Such a break did not however occur in the Tibetan medical tradition which has been continuous from King Sroṅ-btsan-sgam-po until today. Therefore there is no distinction between the earlier and later teaching for medicine.

During king Lha-bla-ma Ye-shes-hod's reign in the latter half of the tenth century A.D., the Indian pandit Dharma Śrī Varma and sNye-bo lo-tsa-ba† dByig-gi Rin-chen and Mar-lo Rig-pa gZhon-nu and other lo-tsa-bas translated the Commentary on the medical text *Yan-lag Brgyad-pa'i Snyiṅ-po bsDus-pa* (Collection of the Essence of the Eight Branches).

After this, the great translator Rin-chen bZaṅ-po was born in Guge. When he was seventeen years old he went to India and stayed there for ten years. He received instruction from seventy-five panditas, amongst them the great pandita Nāropa. Rin-chen bZaṅ-po was the most influential religious founder and translator during the later period. He offered a hundred gold sraṅ to the Kashmir pandita Janārdana and learned from him 120 chapters of the *Yan-lag Brgyad-pa'i Snyiṅ-po bsDus-pa* and its commentary *Zla-ba-hi Hod-zer* (Moon Light), written by the pandita Zla-ba mṄon-dgah and by this he furthered the teaching of Medicine in Tibet greatly. He taught his chief disciple Zhaṅ-zhuṅ-pa Shes-rab Hod who taught rGya-ston Grags-pa

* The Elder (A.D. 786–911), the hero of the Biography.

† lo-tsa-ba = translator.

Shes-rab who wrote the medical commentary on the *rGyud-bzhi* called *gSer-gyi Baṅ-mdzod* and a history of medicine and some other works. He passed the teaching on to gYu-thog rGya-gar rDo-rje. gYu-thog rGya-gar rDo-rje passed it on to gYu-thog brJid-po who taught mGar-po from whom subsequently the teaching of medicine was carried on.

Among Rin-chen bZaṅ-po's many disciples were Myaṅ-hdas Seṅ-ge Sgra, Stag-bri Ye-shes, also called Shag-khri Ye-shes, hByuṅ-gnas, 'Oṅ-sman 'A-ye and Maṅ-mo Maṅ-btsun. These four were called the four great Ṅari doctors as they came from the district of Ṅari. The most learned and famous of them was Maṅ-mo Maṅ-btsun, and from all parts of Tibet people flocked to learn from him. Though he had many pupils there was one whom he taught all the theory and practice of medicine, and that was Chher-rje-ti-pa who passed the teaching on to Chher-rje Shaṅ-ston Shig-po who wrote a history of Tibetan Medicine and a medical book called *bKah-ts'om*. His disciple gTsaṅ-stod Dar-ma mGon-po wrote a medical work called *Zin-tig* and another one called *Yaṅ-tig*, and during his presence the Bo-doṅ district flourished.

Since the start of the lo-tsa-ba Rin-chen bZaṅ-po's lineage, the teaching of Medicine increased more and more all over Tibet. Some time later the central and the northern districts harboured the following nine famous doctors: gYo-ru, gYah-gyoṅ-po, Su-ma-sman from sTod-luṅ, gYu-thog rGya-gar rDo-rje, Mi-nyag Zla-grags, Braṅ-ti rGyal-po, Chhos-rje Lhun-ne, Hug-spa Chhos-seṅ and Chher-rje Stag-la-dgah.

They practised lo-tsa-ba Rin-chen's method, and many Tibetan medical texts based their teaching on that of lo-tsa-ba Rin-chen bZaṅ-po. But the two doctors Shaṅ-ston gZi Brjid-hbar from Yar-luṅ and sTod-ston dKon-chog Skyabs from Ts'a-luṅ were not satisfied with learning from a Tibetan doctor and went to India. Shaṅ-ston gZi Brjid-hbar went to Nālandā, and the paṇḍita Chandrasīha* taught him medicine. The way he had met him was as follows: After arriving in India he asked who was the best teacher and was given the name of the Rishi Chandravi. He went and sat down in a grass hut in front of Chandravi's door for seven days. When the great teacher asked him why he sat there, he said he wanted to be taught medicine, and the Rishi taught him the *Yan-lag brGyad-pa* from his own knowledge, without the aid of books. Then Shaṅ-ston gZi Brjid-hbar asked him to teach it to him once more, this time with the book, and to teach him the essence of the instructions and the practice. He taught him everything and asked him to write about medicine and to help the sick. And he returned to Tibet and wrote many books.

* Also called Chandravi.

Later gTer-ston Graṅ-pa mṄon-shes took the rGyud-bzhi out from the central pillar in Samye Monastery as had been prophesied by Padmasaṁbhava, and he taught dbUs-pa Dar-grags and the teaching was handed down through his lineage to the Second gYu-thog Yon-tan mGon-po. And sTod-ston met Shintipa and became very well versed in the text *Yan-lag Brgyad-pa*. Shaṅ wrote the commentary called *Zla-ba Hod-gser* on the *gZhuṅ-dri-med gZi-brjid*, and many scholars descended from his teaching in an uninterrupted line. sTod-ston wrote the *Sa-bched bsDus-don Rin-chen phreṅ-ba* and notes on the *gZuṅ Dri-med gZi-brjid*. It was he who later taught gYu-thog Yon-tan mGon-po.

The Second gYu-thog Yon-tan mGon-po* was born in gTsaṅ as the son of Kyuṅ-bu rDo-rje and Pad-ma Hod-ldan. At his birth the great rishis and the medical goddesses and many other gods appeared in the sky and they poured nectar over him and washed him, and rainbows enveloped him. As soon as he was born he recited the Medicine Buddha's mantra and displayed the activities of a bodhisattva. When he was three years old he kept playing 'doctor' with the other children and took their pulse, examined their urine, diagnosed diseases and collected medicinal plants and minerals. Wherever he went, the place smelt of medicinal plants. His religious knowledge was very good, especially the branch dealing with the teachings of Medicine. He became like the Medicine Buddha himself, and people called him hJam-dbyaṅs (gentle-voiced) gYu-thog Yon-tan mGon-po (the Excellent Protector). After he had reached the age of eighteen, he went to India six times, and learned a great number of medical texts from the ḍākinī dPal-ldan hPhreṅ-ba, and also to Ceylon to learn their version of the rGyud-bzhi from the rishi gSer-gyi Go-chha and many other medical texts, and he was protected by the ḍākinī from all troubles. When he came back, Medicine began to flourish in Tibet and he himself wrote a great number of medical texts, as for instance the *rGyud-kyi Chha-lag bChos-brgyad*. He taught it to the chief disciple amongst his many disciples, whose name was Sum-ston Ye-shes Zuṅ. He died at the age of seventy-six and ascended to lTa-na-sdug without leaving his body. After his death his lineage flourished for some time.

His disciple Ye-shes-zuṅ composed a very secret history of gYu-thog's life and teachings and a commentary on the *hBum Chhuṅ gSal-sgron* and on the *bShad rGyud* (Explanatory Treatise), a part of the *rGyud-bzhi*, and other medical texts.

In the fourteenth century there were two famous doctors, Byaṅs-pa and Zur-mKhar-pa. Byaṅs-pa was born as the seventh in the lineage of King

* i.e. the Younger gYu-thog who lived during the eleventh century, a descendant and reincarnation of the hero of the Biography, cf. p. 34.

Mi-nyag Se'u rGyal-po, as the son of Guṅ-chhos Grags-dpal-bzaṅ and hBum-skyon rGyal-mo, the daughter of Se-tu Chhos-rin in the wood pig year of the seventh rab-byuṅ.*

When he was small none of his activities were like those of ordinary children. His teacher was Lo-chhen Byaṅ-chhub Rtse-mo and his blood relative bsTan-pa'i rGyal-mts'an. He became very famous during the reign of the Second Dalai Lama dGe-hdun rGya-mts'o (1391–1475), who discussed many questions with him. He composed medical texts called *gSo-rig sNyiṅ-po bsDus-pa*, comprising 120 chapters, and a commentary on the *bShad-rgyud*, and one on the *Phyi-rgyud*. He put new life into Medicine by the teaching, discussing and writing of medical works. He lived for eighty-one years and had many disciples. Among them was the court physician Byams-pa dKon-chog Rin-chhen who, descended from Sroṅ-btsan sGam-po, in the line of kings of Tibet, had many teachers and became very learned in science and philosophy and was especially learned in all Tibetan medical texts. His son bKra-shis dPal-bzaṅ was also learned in medicine, having been taught it by his father. He wrote a commentary on the *bShad-rgyud*, called *Legs-bshad Nor-bu*, and a commentary on the *Phyi-rgyud*, and a history of Tibetan Medicine, and a commentary on the whole of the *rGyud-bzhi*.

The teaching remained mostly that of the original *Yan-lag brGyad-pa* up to the time of sTod-sman hTs'o-byed gZhon-nu. Then it declined a little. Lha-btsun bKra-shis dPal-bzaṅ and other doctors wrote commentaries on medical texts, and in this way the teaching recovered. The doctors founded a new system called the Byaṅ-lugs. Doctor Zur-mKhar-ba mNyam-Nyid-rDo-rje wrote a commentary on the *rGyud-bzhi* and other medical texts. He had eight chief disciples and many others. His system was called after him *Zur-lugs-pa*. The *Byaṅ-lugs* and the *Zur-lugs* continued for a long time uninterruptedly. But during the Fifth Dalai Lama's reign (1617–1682) there was a decline.

The Fifth Dalai Lama's first institution of a medical school was at dGah-ldan pho-braṅ† in the hBras-spuṅs monastery. There he put Nyi-thaṅ Druṅ-chhen bLo-bzaṅ rGya-mts'o in charge. Then he started a medical school in a country house called bsam-grub tse.

The regent, sDe-srid‡ Saṅs-rgyas rGya-mts'o (1653–1705), wrote a commentary on the *rGyud-bzhi* called the *Vaiḍūrya sÑon-po* (Blue Lapislazuli), and other texts. He practised the *byaṅ-lugs* and the *zur-lugs*. At that time the

* Sixty-year cycle.
† hall, palace.
‡ sDe-srid = regent.

Fifth Dalai Lama had as a court physician Dhar-mo sMan-rams-pa bLo-bzaṅ-Chhos-grags,* who saw to the printing of the life story of the first and second gYu-thogs and composed some other texts.

But the Fifth Dalai Lama wanted to build a suitable complex of buildings for a medical college and a hospital. To find a suitable place, sDe-srid Saṅs-rgyas rGya-mts'o circumambulated Lhasa by order of the Dalai Lama. When he came to the place called lChags-po-ri,† he sat down to take a rest. Suddenly he had a vision of the place looking like lTa-na-sdug.‡ He went to the Fifth Dalai Lama and told him all about his good omen for a suitable place to build a medical college on. The Dalai Lama was very pleased and, for the sake of all Tibetans, he gave the permission to build it on the mountain of lChags-po-ri.

Then sDe-srid Saṅs-rgyas decreed that from that time onwards each bigger monastery near Lhasa and in each district should receive from that medical college a doctor of its own. These were the beginnings of Public Health in Tibet. Medicine flourished there since that time until 1959.

In his *Medical History of Tibet*, sDe-srid Saṅs-rgyas rGya-mts'o says that in the *Biography of gYu-thog* the story of the rope between heaven and earth and the coming down of Dam-pa Tog-kar and the story of the wheels and the twenty-one-headed raksha king, and the distance of lTa-na-sdug from Buddhagayā are of the same character as the myths in the Vedas; but that from the account of the life of Duṅ-gi Thor-chog-chan onwards, everything is true.

Under the Thirteenth Dalai Lama (1895–1933) Tibetan medicine flourished because during his reign the new medical college at Lhasa, called sMan-rtsis-khaṅ (House of Medicine and Astronomy), was built by mKhyen-rab Nor-bu.§ mKhyen-rab Nor-bu was born in the Lho-kha region south of Lhasa in 1882. As a boy he became a monk at the Lṅa-mchhod Dra-ts'aṅ Monastery south of Lhasa. Within two years he learned reading and writing perfectly. At the age of fourteen he went with his parents on a pilgrimage to Lhasa. During their visit to the lChags-po-ri Medical College, he felt the strong wish to stay there and study medicine. He asked for and received permission to become a student there. Within two years he learned the complete *rGyud-bzhi* by heart and passed his examination. Then he studied the *rGyud-bzhi* under His Holiness's court physician Thub-bstan rGyal-mts'an. With his teacher he went through the *rGyud-bzhi* page

* Cf. colophon of gYu-thog's Biography.

† Pronounced Chakpuri.

‡ Celestial city.

§ Cf. Plate. No. 18.

by page and had every word explained to him, and within four years he gained complete comprehension of it. Surrounded by teachers, doctors and students, he passed his final examination without making the slightest mistake. With his own hands, His Holiness's court physician presented him with a scarf and his doctor's degree certificate. Congratulating him, he said: 'You will most certainly become a shining light in medical science!' He also learned Sanskrit, grammar, astronomy, and became extremely knowledgeable and well-versed in Buddhist literary tradition and history. He thought: 'Now I ought to found a college of medicine and astronomy. In this way I would be of great benefit to the Tibetan people, the Buddhist religion and also the Tibetan government.' He wrote to His Holiness's Cabinet asking for the permission and funds to build a college and halls of residence for students and a grant for books, apparatus etc. His Holiness, the Thirteenth Dalai Lama, was very pleased with this idea and granted everything needed. He commended the building of the college to the protection and attention of his Government. At the age of thirty-three, mKhyen-rab Nor-bu was able to start building the sMan-rtsis-khaṅ College in bsTan-rgyas-glin near the gTsug-lag-khaṅ,* the most famous temple in Lhasa, which had been built by Sroṅ-btsan sGam-po's queen in the seventh century. The College contained lecture halls, a hospital, living quarters for teachers and students, laboratories, store rooms, and so on. The Government issued a decree permitting the college to receive one student from each provincial monastery, altogether 150 students, and also any private students who wished to study there. It was given the name of Medical and Astronomical College. The College was of great benefit to many people. mKhyen-rab Nor-bu was given the rank of las-ts'an-pa (government official) and later promoted to that of mkhan-chhun for his successful work.

The College produced the first official calendar and sent it every year all over the country. Before, there had only been private calendars composed by private astronomers and astrologers. mKhyen-rab Nor-bu was always ready to learn more and learned the Sūtras and the Tantras from many different teachers during his whole life time.

The college routine was as follows: at three o'clock in the morning a bell woke the students up and they foregathered in the main lecture hall and recited a prayer to Mañjuśrī, the Bodhisattva of Wisdom. Then they learned medical and astronomical texts by heart and recited them till six o'clock. At six o'clock they did physical exercises like running and gymnastics. At eight o'clock they went back indoors and had breakfast and prayed a prayer for the Lineage of the medical teachings and other prayers. Then the more

* Pronounced Tsuklakang.

advanced students had instruction from mKhyen-rab Nor-bu or his assistant who explained the teaching of the rGyud-bzhi. The less-advanced students had instruction from two teachers, one on medicine and one on astronomy. All students learned both subjects. New students learned first of all grammar, reading, writing, and poetry. After lunch, at one o'clock, the students had to learn lus-thig (body measurements), rtsa'i hgro-staṅs (the pathways of the nerves and veins), and sman-ṅos hdzin-staṅs (how to recognize medicinal plants). New students had to learn mathematics and geometry and the history of medicine. This took them to about five o'clock in the afternoon. Lectures were finished at five, and they went to their own rooms and had tea and supper. At about seven they assembled in the main lecture hall and all teachers were present. Advanced and new students had to discuss and debate medical and astronomical subjects. Then they prayed for His Holiness, the Government and the increase of the Teaching. This ended about nine o'clock.

On the afternoon of the fourteenth and the whole of the fifteenth and the afternoon of the twenty-ninth and the whole of the thirtieth day of the month they were free. On the mornings of the fourteenth and the twenty-ninth day they had examinations. They had to be able to recite a certain number of pages of medical and astronomical texts by heart. Advanced students had to explain the texts and to compose a poem. New students were also examined in grammar and mathematics. Once a year there was a great examination on what they had learned during the whole year. The course lasted six years. If students were not able to pass within six years they were allowed to extend their studies until they passed. Two teachers were the examiners during the written and oral examinations and they showed their reports to the head of the college, who, if they were satisfactory, awarded the degrees.

When a student had passed, the Government gave him a doctor's diploma and sent him to that part of the country where a doctor was needed. In the place of this student the college accepted a new student from the same monastery from which the one before had come, and college officials brought him from the monastery.

Once in each season every year, practically the inhabitants of the whole college went up into the mountains to gather medicinal herbs and plants. The spots they chose were in the region of the gSaṅ-yib and the Neu-chhuṅ-ri mountains. They took it in turns with the medical school at lChags-po-ri to go once a year to Brag-yer-pa, the place where, in the past, the great paṇḍita Atīśa (eleventh century A.D.) and his chief disciple Brom-ston-pa, the incarnation of Avalokiteśvara, and other disciples had lived.

In order to go and gather plants at Brag-yer-pa they left Lhasa about the first of July. Before leaving they had sent a letter with a government seal asking the villages where they would stay to arrange and prepare for their arrival. The teachers and students wore new clothes, and over their left shoulders they wore beautifully folded patterned wild silk or cotton cloths to wrap themselves in when it rained, and medicine bags made from the same material. First they went in single file from the College through Byaṅ-chhub Byon-lam to the gTsug-lag-khaṅ to make obeisance to the Jo-bo Rimpoche, the famous image of the Buddha Śākyamuni that had been brought from China, and other sacred images. Then they went to the Ra-mo-chhe gTsug-lag-khaṅ with the Jo-bo image brought from Nepal, to pay their respects there. The townspeople came and watched this beautiful procession intently. When they arrived in the villages, the mayor and the representative of the district governor were waiting to greet them. For thirteen days they gathered plants in the mountains. On the twelfth day mKhyen-rab Nor-bu, the head of the College, came to join them. On the thirteenth day they went into the Brag-yer-pa Monastery where the villagers had carried all the gathered plants, and the teachers separated over 200 species of plants and had them laid out as a preparation for an examination. On the fourteenth day all inmates of the College gathered together in a tent and the students had to recognize each plant. Those students who were able to recognize over 200 plants and to describe their locale, their taste and their action were awarded the first prize, those with 180 the second prize. There was also a third prize for between 160 and 130 plants. Many visitors came to watch the examination and the prize-giving ceremony. On the fifteenth of July the festival of the Monastery was celebrated with the monks dancing. All College Staff went to the monastery temple and they performed the ritual of the Medicine Buddha. Then they spent a few days' holiday at the Monastery, after which they returned to Lhasa.

TREATMENT OF PATIENTS

Every morning at eight o'clock, all the doctors assembled for a prayer meeting at which they prayed for the Lineage of the medical teachings. There were about seven surgeries in the College. There each doctor examined and treated a number of patients one after the other, from nine o'clock to twelve o'clock. All this was a free gift from the Government for high and low. From one o'clock till five o'clock the surgery was continued. All medicines were free of charge and there were no doctors' fees. But sometimes people showed their gratitude by giving donations to the College. During the hours when the College was closed, emergency cases were always admitted. The country districts had their own doctors sent there by the Government in order to look after the sick. There were also many private doctors who charged for their services but never asked for a definite price to be paid for a medicine. It was left to the patient to pay as much as he wanted or could pay. Private doctors, too, would never take a fee from poor patients and would treat them for nothing.

NOTES ON PRACTICES CONTINUED IN TIBETAN MEDICINE UP TO THE PRESENT

Cupping

The copper bowl can be used on any part of the body. Take a small piece of paper, light a fire on it and place it four fingers' distance from wherever the pain is. Then clap the copper bowl down on it and keep it there for an hour. Then take the bowl off and cut the place with the bloodletting knife. Do this again. When you take the bowl off the second time, blood and pus will come out. Notice the amount of blood coming out and the amount of pain left. On this depends whether you do it three, four or more times. Used for pleurisy and air diseases.

Bloodletting

The little knife is used for this. You have to know for what diseases you ought to let blood. You can do so when there is high blood pressure or diseases caused by high blood pressure or if the blood does not circulate properly (the heart–lung circulation was known in Tibetan medicine since at least the eighth century A.D.), when blood pressure has caused a general infection of the body, etc. It is not to be performed if the patient is under the age of sixteen or pregnant or suffering from air diseases, i.e. nervous complaints. But if the patient has a disease where one can bleed, one has to see whether it is the right time for bleeding. Three days before bloodletting, a medicine to purify the blood is to be given, which separates good and bad blood. If the pain is in the head, the patient should be bled above the eyebrows, where the vein called gser-mduṅ dṅul-mduṅ is situated. For eye diseases, the eye veins should be bled. For someone who suffers from an issue of blood or from stricture of the urethra, the vein at the groin should be bled, also for most other diseases of the abdomen. There are specific veins for specific diseases.

Moxa

The golden needle should be used for moxa. For nervous diseases (air diseases) it should be used only on the crown of the head. Put the needle into a small amount of vegetable tinder and place it on the head. Put the tinder about an inch along the needle and light it at the upper end. Keep the needle on the crown of the head until the tinder has been burned away, i.e. until the fire just touches the head for a moment, then take the needle away. This helps against a nervous breakdown.

The air which has gone the wrong way is, through the heat, directed into the right channels. Broken nerves and pathways are joined together again. The moxa does not harm, because the material the needle is made of is gold.

Moxa can be performed on other parts of the body for digestive diseases, convulsions, dropsy, diseases caused by air and phlegm, but not those caused by bile. It is good only for cold diseases and not for fever or jaundice. The doctor has to measure a certain distance for each different disease and then put the heated instrument on a vein connected with the affected organ for a moment, and then the place becomes red and bursts.

All these medicines are still used today

(1) glaṅ-chen bcho-brgyad. Medicine with eighteen ingredients: yellow pigment taken from a concretion in an elephant's head or in the entrails of other animals,* camphor, coriander seed, olive, black aloewood, bitter re-skon, red sandalwood, white sandalwood, saffron, blue water lily, aquatic insect, medicinal climber, costus speciosus, justicia ganderussa, gold flower, bitumen, chiretta, cloves. A different quantity of each ingredient is specified. When mixed, it helps against convulsions, choleric cramps, swellings and lupus. One teaspoonful should be mixed with boiling water and taken after meals.

(2) srog-hdzin-bchū-dug, which has sixteen ingredients: cloves, black aloewood, nutmeg, a mineral drug called sho-sha, costus speciosus, saffron, frankincense, sandalwood, lime, rush, yellow pigment, shaṅ-dril, sha-chhen, salt, ginger, piper longum. It is used against nervous diseases and melancholia. To be taken in beer, or about one teaspoonful of hot water.

(3) tsa-tsi rdo-sbyor, which has ten ingredients: scopolia praealta Don., saffron, sulphur, sman-chhen, myrobalan, rush, asafoetida, musk, black aloewood, white and black hawthorn. Used against syphilis. To be taken with melted butter.

* Cf. bezoar stone.

(4) sga-lo, which has seven ingredients: herb whose root is used for purple dye, soma plant, justicia ganderussa, camphor, costus speciosus, olive, in appropriate quantities. Used against tuberculosis. To be taken in a spoonful of boiling water.

(5) bdud-rtsi-gsum-sbyor, which has three ingredients: soma plant, syrup, camphor. These three, mixed together, should be taken with beer. Used for vomiting, against bone fractures, tuberculosis and leukorrhoea.

(6) nor-bu-bdun-thaṅ, which has seven ingredients: myrobalan, olive, Solanum jaquinia, Terminalia belerica, Sophor Flavescens, Inula Helenium, Hedychium Spicatum. Three spoonfuls of these should be mixed together and boiled in a pint of water until the water is reduced to two-thirds, and then drunk. Used against high blood pressure, fever, colds and influenza.

(7) gser-mdog bchu-pa, which has ten ingredients: some plant, myrobalan, liquorice, bitumen, ginger, pomegranate, cardamom, piper longum, erycibe paniculata, rock salt from Sindh in Western India. Used against diphtheria and high blood pressure. One spoonful to be taken in boiling water.

(8) gser-mdog-bchu-gsum, which has thirteen ingredients: piper longum, saffron, blue lily, creeper, olive, justicia ganderussa, costus speciosus, salt, camphor, soma plant, low-growing rhododendron, iron filings, snake meat. It should be made into a tablet the size of a small bean, which should be taken with boiling water. Used against high blood pressure and jaundice, tumours, indigestion, stomach trouble and fever.

Tibetan Medicine

CHAPTERS FROM THE SECOND BOOK OF THE RGYUD-BZHI, CALLED BSHAD-RGYUD

CHAPTERS FROM THE FOURTH BOOK OF THE RGYUD-BZHI, CALLED PHYI-RGYUD

Chapters from the Second Book of the rGyud-bzhi, called bShad-rgyud

I ANALYSIS OF THE BSHAD-RGYUD

THE PRINCIPAL source from which benefits for the world and Nirvāṇa can be derived is the science of medicine. A short exposition of it can be divided into four parts:

1. The subject of the treatment.
2. The antidote.
3. How to treat.
4. The healer.

Under (1), the subject can be either of two things:

(a) The diseases.
(b) The parts of the body attacked by the diseases.

Under (2), the antidote can be divided into four parts:

(a) Daily activities or way of life.
(b) Diet.
(c) Medicine.
(d) Treatment.

Before starting to treat, one should know how the body is constituted. According to the second chapter of the *rGyud-bzhi* which is an explanation of its first chapter, there are seven main topics in the building of the body:

1. How to build a body.
2. Similes for every part of the body.
3. (a) The right amount of components needed by the body at different stages of development.
   (b) The connection of the veins.
   (c) The essential parts of the body.
   (d) The circulation of fluids in the body.

4. Qualities.
5. Explanation of the diseases and where they strike the body.
6. Enumeration of the parts of the body.
7. Signs of decay of the body.

II EMBRYOLOGY

Just as the combination of three things together (that is, dry soft wood, tinder, and their preparation) causes a fire, so three things are needed for the formation of a body: perfect semen without any flaw caused by diseases, menstrual blood, and the mind of the intermediate (bar-do) state driven by the right karma. The nature of all the five elements* is necessary for its continued existence: this is the cause of conception. It depends on the likings of the mind whether its body is going to become male or female. If it identifies itself with the semen and is attracted by the mother and dislikes the father, it is going to be born as a boy. If it identifies itself with the mother's menstrual blood, which must be in its right time and flawless, and if anger is felt with the mother, then a girl is going to be born. But it is essential that attraction to one parent and hatred of the other is felt in order that a new body should be born. If neither of these feelings takes place, there occurs no conception and no birth. If the mind emerging from the bar-do state is unfortunate, it is, apart from the feelings of like and dislike, beset by many different feelings. One of the strongest is fear, because it is under the illusion that there is rain and cold and thunderstorms and that people drive it, and it seeks shelter in the mother's womb as if it was entering a leafy hut or an earth hole or a cave or a clearing in the jungle. If it is a fortunate mind, it is also afraid of rain and so on but has the feeling that it is escaping into a well-appointed house where it is going to sit on a throne and ascend the roof and it enters it. When the mother feels very satisfied and a little heavy and, after trembling, feels suddenly very languid, then this is a sign that she has conceived a baby. The mixture of semen and blood is retained in the vagina for some time. On the right and left of the vagina, the ovaries go up to the womb, and through karma they are connected when conception takes place. The essence of the food eaten by the mother rises through the umbilical cord and feeds the embryo through its navel. Therefore no monthly periods take place because the blood carries food essence upwards instead of flowing down, like water irrigating a field through a canal from a pool at a distance. The two ovaries are connected by the baby's umbilical cord and placenta. During

* Earth, water, air, fire and sky (ether).

thirty-eight weeks, the embryo gradually changes through the influence of air (rluṅ).

From the moment of conception, through karma, the embryo's mind spreads the *srog-rluṅ* (breath of life). First week: through the srog-rluṅ of the father's semen and the *kun-gzhi rnam-shes* (consciousness) in the mother's blood every particle is thoroughly mixed like milk when churned into curds. Second week: the second rluṅ, *kun-tu sdud-ba* (gathering everything together) hardens the mixture and the embryo comes into being. Third week: *mdzod-ka-rluṅ* (treasury rluṅ) curdles the embryo into an even harder substance.

During the third week one can still influence the future child's sex. In general, births and subsequent fates are dependent on karma, but sometimes one can influence them by additional causes (*rkyen*). If someone wishes for a son, during the third and fourth week the method of 'changing the centre' can be practised. It can only be practised before the child's sexual organs have developed. It can even be done during the first or second week. This method is very efficacious, and the centre is quite suddenly changed where the karma most certainly destines the child to become a girl, and quite easily where the karmic chances for a boy or a girl are equal. For anyone who wishes to have male descendants it is very important to practice this method. The best day is that on which the star rGyal and Jupiter meet,* but at least it should be a day ruled by the star rGyal.† On that day a perfect smith should make a good image of a baby boy four fingers high, either from one kind of black male iron or from three or five kinds of male inferior iron. On a subsequent day ruled by rGyal, one should heat the little figure in a charcoal fire for a little while, just until it changes its colour. Then one should take two handfuls of milk of a cow that has male calves and pour this into a vessel. One dips the little figure into the milk, once if it is made of one kind of iron, three times if made of three kinds of iron, and five times if made of five, always just so long that it makes a hissing sound. The husband takes one handful of this milk and gives it to his wife to drink. Then one takes equal amounts of blood from a virgin girl and semen from a virgin boy and mixes them in molasses. If these cannot be procured, red *lhad-ts'er* (alloy application) and quicksilver, pulverized by burning, grinding and pounding, can be used instead. Equal amounts of each should be ground between mill stones and thoroughly mixed, then mixed with the molasses and eaten. Following this, one should take wool from the right shoulder of one, three or five sheep, depending on how many kinds of iron were used for the figure. Then a virgin boy should make a rope with three strands of the wool and

* When Jupiter is in the lunar mansion of rGyal.

† When the moon is in the mansion called rGyal.

make either one, three or five knots in it, according to the number of sheep used. The mother should tie this round her waist so that the two ends hang from the spot where her navel is. The figure should be wrapped into a female calf's skin and tied to the mother's rope, taking care to keep it always upright. The combination of all these circumstances and materials specified, planets and constellations meeting together will certainly ensure a positive result.

The *Vaiḍūrya sŇon-po* mentions that some ancient Chinese medical texts such as *Somarāja* and others say that on the first day the rluṅ is called srog-rluṅ (breath of life), and during the first week each day a different rluṅ is prevalent and helps the two substances to permeate each other. From the second week till the forty-third (*sic*) week, each day different rluṅs contribute to the growth of the embryo. But this does not agree with the *rGyud-bzhi* and other texts.

During the first three weeks, the vein of life is developing between the chest and the navel. It is formed like a fish. The branches have not yet grown at that stage. During the fourth week, the combined semen and menstrual blood, which had been of the consistency of curd up to that time, now change and become either hard and round, or soft and oval, or of a narrow shape. The first is becoming a son, the second a daughter, and the third a hermaphrodite. During this time, while the baby's sex is being determined, the mother will know that she is bearing a baby. Her buttocks are feeling heavy and she is getting suddenly thinner; she lacks appetite, she often yawns and feels a certain lassitude and has an acute pain in the knee-joints; her breasts are getting fuller, and she likes to eat many different and unusual types of food, often sour food, through the influence of the baby. If she is not given the food she wants, the baby may die or it may be born blind or dumb or hunchbacked. It is therefore important to give the mother this food, and even if it causes her sickness one should mix a little of it in her food for the sake of both baby and mother.

During the fifth week, on the day of *mkhraṅ-hgyur-gyi shag* (hardening of stone) the embryo turns harder and develops at the navel the basis of the vein system, that is the life vein with its branches, from which comes semen and rluṅ. The life vein is as fine as a hair, and one can see it only with difficulty; but it can be distinguished even in a dead foetus. The life vein is also called middle artery. At the right of the sixteenth vertebra one can see the indistinct form of a plexus consisting of four veins. During the sixth week, the middle artery is moving upwards, sixteen times the width of the embryo's fingers. On its upper end develops the heart plexus, which is situated at the eighth vertebra. During the seventh week it rises eleven fingerwidths, and a plexus of four veins is formed on the first vertebra of the neck. During this time (end of the seventh and beginning of the eighth week) the vein rises to the crown of the head and forms a plexus and the outlines of the eyes. From this, at the end of the eighth week, the shape of the head is formed. At the same time as the neck plexus, another plexus is formed ten fingerwidths down from the navel. The plexus at the crown of the head is called 'wheel of bliss', the neck plexus 'wheel of enjoyment', the heart plexus 'wheel of dharma', the navel plexus 'creative imagination wheel' and the plexus near the sexual organs 'the preservation of happiness wheel'. The growth of the plexus is caused mainly by the vital air. From the vital air issue other rluṅs, such as *yaṅ-dag-par sdud-pa*, *rGya chhen-po*, *hkhyil-pa* and so on.

During the ninth week, the upper and lower parts of the body are almost shaped, but there are as yet no extremities. Through the power of the vital air and the *yaṅ-dag-par sdud-pa*, the upper and lower parts of the body grow and it becomes like a fish. During the tenth week, the upper arms and the hip bones first appear. During the eleventh week, the nine openings of the body are formed. During the twelfth week, the following five organs are formed in outline: the heart, the lungs, the liver, the spleen and the kidneys. During the thirteenth week, the six vessels are formed: gall bladder, stomach, the small and the large intestine, urinary bladder, spermatic vessels in males or uterus in females. During the fourteenth week, the upper arm bones and thigh bones are coming through. During the fifteenth week, the lower arms, the palms of the hands and the legs and body of the feet are formed. During the sixteenth week, the ten fingers and ten toes are growing. During the seventeenth week, the veins visible from the outside and countless veins inside, which cannot be seen, come into existence. At this time the five limbs are formed, and the body looks like a tortoise. Therefore this is called the tortoise period.

During the eighteenth week, another air, called *dri-ma med-pa*,* spreads from the vital air. Flesh and fat are slowly coming into existence. During the nineteenth week, another rluṅ, called *shin-tu phra-ba* (infinitely subtle), comes into existence and the large and small glands and the sinews and tendons are formed. During the twentieth week, the *shin-tu brtan-pa rluṅ* (intensely firm air) is spread from the vital air, and the different bones and their marrow are formed. During the twenty-first week, the *yaṅ-dag-par bskyad-pa rluṅ* (perfectly formed air) is formed, and the skin begins to form, like the skin on the top of boiling milk.

During the first week of the sixth month, the *kun-tu rgyal-ba rluṅ* (all-conquering air) is spread, and the five sense organs and the nine openings

* Pure.

are completed. During the second week of the sixth month, the *yaṅ-dag-par hdzin-pa rluṅ* (perfectly gathering air) is spread, and during this week the hairs of the body and the nails are formed. In the third week, the *kun-tu hphyo-ba rluṅ* (all-swelling air) is spread, and all the forms are becoming distinct. The embryo begins to have emotions, such as suffering or feeling happy. In the twenty-fifth week, the *gron-khyer hdzin-pa rluṅ* (gathered city air) is spread, and airs are coming through the nine openings. During the twenty-sixth week, the *skyil-ba mṅon-par grub-pa rluṅ* (evidently perfectly retained air) is spread, and the mind gets very clear. During this period the embryo can remember its former life. During the first week of the seventh month, the twenty-ninth and the thirtieth week, the *sman-yon chen-po* (great excellent healing), *me-tog hdzin-pa* (gathered flower) and *me-tog hphreṅ-pa lchags-gyi sgo* (iron wreath door) airs are spread. Then everything is completed. During the thirty-first to thirty-fifth weeks, the *me-tog sdud-pa rluṅ* (accumulation of flowers air) is spread. This air causes the baby to grow. According to the tastiness of the food ingested, the mother's healthy looks alternate with those of the baby. When the baby looks unhealthy the mother looks healthy, and vice versa. During this time, it is hardly possible for a baby to be born, but sometimes, through an additional cause, it happens. During this time the baby eats even unclean things in its surroundings. Therefore this is called the pig's period. From the thirty-sixth week onwards, the baby feels oppressed by the bad smell, darkness, and unclean surroundings and it wants to get out. During the thirty-seventh week, the baby wants to turn a somersault. During the thirty-eighth week, the *thogs-pa'i rkyen rluṅ* (delayed contributory cause air) is spread in the baby and turns it upside down, so that it moves downward.

Three things cause birth to be postponed: (1) if too much blood flows, the baby's health is unable to improve and it is not ready to be born, (2) if the mother is too fat, the vagina is too narrow to let the baby out and (3) a downward wind (rluṅ) through the rectum shuts the road for the baby, preventing it from coming out. The signs that most probably a boy is going to be born are that the baby comes on the right side of the belly, facing the mother's backbone, that the right side of the belly is high, and that the milk starts coming in the right breast. The mother's body, when she is moving about, feels lighter than if it is going to be a girl. For the prognosis of a girl, all this applies to the left side, and when born it faces the front. If the middle of the belly feels lower than the two sides, twins will be born. The mother's abdomen feels heavy and she has pains there, and her lips feel dry and her gums are irritated. Through the downwards-driving rluṅ, the baby now straightens its arms and it is born with its arms straight. If through the baby's bad karma it has to die in the mother's womb, it cannot stretch its arms or legs and cannot turn itself upside down.

After the thirty-eighth week, although the attendants have prepared the softest materials for the baby to be laid on, contact with anything at all is very painful for the baby, and at birth it feels like a cow that is flayed alive and as if stung by a wasp, and when it is bathed the touch of warm water gives it a feeling as if it was beaten.

IV PHYSIOLOGY

There should be a balance between the three humours: phlegm, bile and air, and between the seven constituents of the body: blood, saliva, bone, marrow, fat, flesh, and semen, and between the three excrements: sweat, urine and faeces. The usual quantity of air in the body should be neither more nor less than what would fill each person's urinary bladder. The quantity of bile should be as much as would fill the scrotum. The quantity of phlegm should be six handfuls. The quantity of blood should be fourteen handfuls. The quantity of faeces should also be fourteen handfuls. The quantity of urine and white blood corpuscles should be eight handfuls. Suet and fat should be four handfuls, men's semen and women's blood two handfuls each, brain two handfuls, flesh 500 fistfuls for men and 520 for women, because of ten more fistfuls for breasts and ten more fistfuls for thighs. This is the average, but allowance should be made for different heights and so on.

There are 360 bones in the body: five kinds of head bones: skull, back of neck, nasal, tooth sockets, chin; nine kinds of trunk or rump bones: hip, shoulder, collar, chest, rib, pelvis, sacral, spine, small of back: three kinds of upper extremity bones: upper arm, lower arm, fist; five kinds of lower extremity bones: thigh, knee, heel, ankle, toe. The last kind is that of the sockets for finger and toe nails. This makes twenty-three kinds altogether.

In detail the bones are counted as follows:

4 skull bones
8 back of the head bones
2 back of the neck bones
32 tooth bones
32 tooth sockets
2 collar bones
28 spinal bones plus vertebrae
15 chest bones

24	ribs
2	small ribs
2	hip bones
1	small of the back bone
2	sacral bones
6	arm bones (2 shoulder, 2 elbow, 2 wrist)
50	hand bones
60	finger and toe bones
20	nail sockets for fingers and toes
70	leg bones
360	bones altogether

There are sixteen sinews: two at the back of the ankles, two at the back of the knees, two at the back of the elbows, two at the back of the wrists, two right and left of the spine, two inside the spine, two flat sinews in the neck and two in front of the neck.

There are 900 fibres in the body: 300 from the hole under the Adam's apple* to the top of the head, 300 from 75 on each arm and leg, and 300 in the rest of the body. On average there are 21,000 hairs on the body. There are 7,000,000 pores between the Adam's apple and the top of the head. On the rest of the body there are 14,000,000 pores. On each arm and leg there are 3,500,000 pores, that is 14,000,000 altogether.

There are five inner organs: heart, lungs, spleen, liver and kidneys. There are six vessels: stomach, gall-bladder, kidney bladder, small intestine, large intestine, generative organ. There are nine openings in a man's body: two nostrils, two ears, two eyes, one mouth, one anal and one urinary. There are twelve openings in a woman's body, the preceding nine and two breasts and one generative organ.

Bodies in our world should measure three and a half cubits between outstretched arms. If this is not balanced with the height, the figure is not good. But this depends on climate, type of country and the former karma of each person. The measurements given above are the average.

The veins. They can be divided into four kinds:

1. Thog-mar chhags-pa'i rtsa (First appearing vein).
2. Srid-pa'i rtsa (the vein of the world).
3. Hbrel-ba'i rtsa (the vein of union).
4. T'se-gnas-pa-yi rtsa (life-sustaining vein).

* Tibetan: og-ldom.

According to function, they can be divided into three kinds:

(a) All rluṅ rtsa (air veins) come from the dbu-ma (centre channel).
(b) All khrag rtsa (blood veins) come from the ro-ma (right-hand channel).
(c) All chhu rtsa (water veins) come from the rkyaṅ-ma (left-hand channel).

They all meet in the heart and the mental activities, emotions, etc. go through the chamber of the heart which causes the heart to beat. The veins, originating in the heart, carry blood and air together. Therefore they pulsate. They are of vital importance.

When the body comes into being in the womb, the first vein formed is the thog-mar chhags-pa'i rtsa (first existing vein) in the centre of the belly. From that, three other veins branch off. Through one goes the water element (moon) on the left side of the body through the heart, into the throat, to the centre of the wheel in the centre of the head. From its centre a white vein goes up to the top of the head and causes the brain to come into being. The brain produces mucus and is both a basic and an auxiliary cause of ignorance, mental darkness and gloom. Therefore sleepiness and gloominess are mostly felt in the head.

Cause, auxiliary cause and result exist in the upper part of the body. The 'blood or fire element' vein goes from the centre of the belly to the base of the liver and is there connected with the vein that draws out the essence of the food (daṅs-ma len-pa'i rtsa). From there, the vein goes to the tenth vertebra. There it becomes a (black) life vein with its branches. Blood is the cause of anger and from anger grows excessive bile. Therefore one can feel sudden anger rising from the middle of the body. From the navel, the right vein goes to the heart, then to the throat and to the wheel at the centre of the head.

Through the centre goes the air element vein, through the heart to the centre of the head. One branch goes down to the place of the generative organs, causing them to come into being. It causes semen, causing desire, and excessive desire becomes the cause of air diseases. Therefore cause, auxiliary cause and result exist also in the lower part of the body.

All veins, including those carrying the six sense consciousnesses, are dependent on the central vein (srid-pa'i rtsa-bo chhe).

Wherever the central vein and the right and left veins meet, a centre is formed, and from it issue four veins like the spokes of a wheel, at right angles to the central vein. From each centre also issue ten veins from the right vein and ten from the left. At each centre there are, therefore, twenty-four big veins. From each of the four veins which issue from the centre vein, twenty-five little veins branch off. From each of the twenty veins which issue from the right and left veins, twenty little veins branch off. Therefore there are altogether 500 little veins at each centre. Each centre serves a function for the health and development of the body.

There are twenty-four big veins for the purpose of sense perception: in the brain there is a vein called hkhyil-ba (winding vein), and connected with it are 500 branches and twenty-four veins with the function of sensation.

At the throat centre, there are twenty-four veins for tasting, together with 500 other veins.

Round the heart centre, called yid-bzaṅ-ma (good mind), there are twenty-four veins serving the consciousness of self, the six sense consciousnesses, memory, imagination and other functions, together with the 500 smaller veins mentioned earlier.

A red vein issues from the heart centre towards the front of the centre through which pass the five sense consciousnesses.* To the right of the yid-bzaṅ-ma issues a yellow vein serving the 'I' consciousness. To the left issues a blue vein from the yid-bzaṅ-ma, which serves mental activities. Towards the back of the yid-bzaṅ-ma issues a green vein, serving the sinful thoughts.

There are twenty-four veins serving the growth and preservation of the body, and these are placed round the navel centre (bsten-pa rtsa, 'reaction vein'), together with the other 500 little branches.

There are twenty-four veins near the generative organs, serving the preservation and continuance of the family, and these are placed round the centre called mts'an-nyid-chan together with the other 500 little veins.

Each of the veins in the body has a function and they are all connected with the central vein. All the veins perform their tasks rhythmically, in harmony with one another.

From the black life vein branch off all those veins through which blood flows. The black vein grows from the centre of the spleen vein, which causes all veins to be filled with blood by the agency of the ro-ma.† This is the auxiliary cause of flesh and blood, therefore it is called life vein (srog-rtsa). Its thickness is like that of a medium arrow. It starts at the first vertebra and is straight and parallel with the spine. From it, twenty-four veins branch off, going through the neck. Their purpose is to increase flesh and blood. There are eight important veins connected with inner organs. From a place in the black vein near the third vertebra branch off two veins, one going into

* That is, not counting the mind consciousness.

† See p. 39.

the heart, the other to the anterior lobes of the lungs. A vein branching off the life vein at the ninth vertebra is connected with the liver, while another at the eleventh vertebra goes into the spleen. At the thirteenth vertebra a vein branches off into the seminal vessel, and from a place near the fourteenth vertebra branch off two veins, going one to each side of the kidneys. These are called the secret veins, because they cannot be seen from the outside of the body.

There are sixteen visible veins: there are two carotid arteries, two in the chest, two near the heart, two connected with the liver; from the life vein two branch off to the hands and two to the legs, two connected with the heart and two in the generative organ.

From these issue:

In the head and neck:

1	gser-mduṅ (golden spear) on the forehead
2	veins at the back of the head
1	dṅul-mduṅ (silver spear) on the forehead
1	vein at the fontanel
2	rtse'u chhuṅ (vena jugularis externa) below the back of the head
1	thoṅ-rtsa in the middle of the forehead
2	lche-rtsa veins in the tongue
2	mur-goṅ hphar-rtsa veins in the cheeks
2	mig-rtsa veins in the eyes
1	sna-rtsa, nose vein
2	rna-rtsa, ear veins
2	ltag-ral, in the cleft at the back of the neck
2	so-rtsa, tooth veins
21	veins altogether

In the body, arms and hands:

2	dpuṅ-rtsa, shoulder veins
2	snod-ka rtsa, hand veins
2	gru-mgo, elbow veins
2	sgaṅ-rtsa, veins in the arms and hands
2	ru-thuṅ, veins in the arms and hands
2	mkhris-pa gshah-riṅ, veins in the arms and hands
2	bad-kan gshah-riṅ, veins in the arms and hands
2	glo-snyiṅ hdoms-rtsa, veins in the arms and hands

2 mchhin-mkhris hdoms-rtsa, veins in the arms and hands
2 skyor-goṅ, veins in the arms and hands
2 phran-bu, veins in the arms and hands
2 rgyab-rtsa drug-hdus, veins in the arms and hands
2 srin-lag rgyab-rtsa, veins in the arms and hands
8 veins between the fingers

34 veins altogether

In the legs:

2 big veins
2 sgab-rtsa
2 rta-mthur
2 byin-gshugs
2 loṅ-rtsa
2 gdoṅ-rtsa
2 yob-goṅ rtsa
2 byin-skyog rtsa
2 rgyu-rtsa

18 veins altogether

In the male organ there are:

2 pho-mts'an hgram-rtsa

Around the stomach there are:

2 pho-ba'i ra-rtsa

Altogether 77 main bloodletting veins, plus another:

4 at the ear

plus:

2 glo-mchhin hdom-rtsa
2 chhu-ser gshah-riṅ
4 mkhris-rtsa phran-bu
1 gzhug-rtsa

Thus there are altogether 90 veins for bloodletting.

V CHARACTERIZATION OF THE BODY AND ITS DISEASES

There are seven principal constituents which help to sustain life:

1. Saliva.
2. Blood.
3. Bone.
4. Marrow.
5. Flesh.
6. Fat.
7. Sperm.

Nutrition derived from food helps to improve the flesh, bone marrow, fat, sperm, etc. The blood is the most vital element, which sustains life. The function of the flesh is to cover the frame of the body. Fat maintains smoothness and natural texture of the body. The bones help to hold the flesh together. The marrow increases semen in the body. The semen enriches colour, complexion and gives lustre to the body.

In the human body there are five types of bile secretion. If bile secretion is rich and strong, it produces energy and helps to protect the body from diseases. The bile secretion called hJu-byed has its chief seat below the stomach and above the intestines. hJu-byed enables digestion, separating the digested food into two parts: the nutritious portion is maintained in the body and the rest is excreted in the form of stool and urine.

Effective digestion takes place when the bile hJu-byed is strong, thus strengthening the seven constituent elements. If it is not strong and effective, digestion is affected with the result that one suffers from swelling of the abdomen, excessive purging of the bowels, etc.

This is how the bile hJu-byed helps in digestion: after the food is masticated in the mouth, the air* called Srog-hdzin-rlung (vitalizing air) helps to push the food down the gullet to the stomach. The liquid taken helps to soften and mix the food in the stomach. The air Me-mnyam-gyi rlung (heat equalizing air) strengthens and heats hJu-byed, the bile secretion, assisting digestion of food in the stomach. After digestion has taken place, the digested food is separated into two: the nutritious part of the food is maintained in the body and the sediment is sent down to the intestines, where it undergoes another separation, liquid from solid; the liquid passes through the colon into the urinary bladder and is excreted as urine, the solid is sent into the

* There are five kinds of subtle air in the body (see below).

Black Intestines (small intestines) and finally excreted in the form of stool. The nutrition from the food passes through the vein daṅs-ma-len-pa'i-rtsa to a vein in the liver and then to the seminal vesicle. In the liver, assimilation is carried out with the help of bile (choler), phlegm and wind (air). The nutrition derived from food forms blood. Blood may be divided into two kinds: refined blood, which is distributed in the body and enables growth of flesh, and unrefined blood, which increases bile. The refined part of flesh forms fat, and the unrefined is excreted from the body through the nine orifices. The refined part of fat, called ts'il-lu' i-daṅs-ma, assists the growth of bones, and the unrefined maintains grease in the body and sweat. The refined part of bones enables growth of marrow and the unrefined helps to form teeth, nails and hair, covering the human body. The refined part of marrow promotes the growth and increase of sperm and menstrual blood; the unrefined part helps the growth of flesh around the anus. The refined part of sperm is preserved in the heart. Refined sperm, called mdaṅs, makes long life possible and enriches the complexion. The unrefined sperm is excreted at the time of intercourse. It is also necessary for conception.

The duration of time taken for the formation of sperm is not known exactly. Roughly the formation of sperm takes about seven days: on the first day after digestion, the nutrition from food forms blood; on the second day blood becomes flesh; on the third day flesh becomes fat; on the fourth day fat becomes bone; on the fifth day bone forms marrow, and on the sixth day marrow forms sperm. Sperm can be increased if flesh of the snow lizard is taken. Milk and meat soups also help to increase sperm.

There are three principal humours* in the body, as follows: Phlegm, Bile (choler), and Air. If the three humours remain balanced, they are good for the body, but should they become unbalanced various diseases result.

There are five main kinds of Air:

1. Srog-hdzin; air which assists breathing.
2. Gyen-rgyu; air which assists speech.
3. Khyab-byed; air which assists muscular motion.
4. Me-mnyam; air which assists digestion.
5. Thur-sel; air which assists excretion.

There are five kinds of Bile:

1. hJu-byed; bile assisting digestion.
2. Mdaṅs-bsgyur; 'making bright'.

* Tibetan ñes-pa, Sanskrit dosha, originally 'fault'.

3. sGrub-byed; 'making perfect'.
4. mThoṅ-byed; 'causing to see'.
5. mDog-gsal; 'clear colour'.

There are five kinds of Phlegm:

1. rTen-byed; 'causing the basis'.
2. Myag-byed; 'causing decomposition'.
3. Myoṅ-byed; 'causing taste'.
4. Ts'im-byed; 'causing satisfaction'.
5. hByor-byed; 'causing readiness'.

Phlegm, Bile and Air help to increase the sperm and menstrual blood. The three humours are spread all over the body. Principally, the seat of Air is below the abdomen, the seat of Bile in the region between the heart and the abdomen, and the seat of Phlegm in the area above the chest.

Of the five kinds of Air, (1), Srog-hdzin-gyi-rlung, is the first and the most important. Its seat is in the brain. It assists respiration, movement of the limbs and maintains good eyesight. This Air also assists the excretion of rejected food in the form of stool and urine. It assists belching and hiccup.

(2) Gyen-rgyu, is found mainly in the region of the chest, but it travels to the nose, tongue and gullet. It assists speech and is the source of strength, perseverance and good memory. It also enriches the complexion.

(3) Khyab-byed-rlung, is found mainly in the heart, but travels to all parts of the body. It enables bodily movement, movement of limbs, closing and opening of the eyes, mouth, etc.

(4) Me-mnyam-rlung, is found mainly in the abdomen and travels to all parts of the intestines and the stomach. This Air assists digestion, extracts nutrition from food and transforms the same into blood, enriching the seven constituents.

(5) Thur-sel-rlung, is mainly found around the area of the buttocks, but travels to the intestines, upper and lower urinary bladder, sexual organ of men, and thighs. The function of this Air is to regulate the passing of stool, urine, etc. It causes sexual urge and regulates the passing of the sperm and menstrual blood.

Of the five types of bile secretions, (1), hJu-byed, has been discussed in p. 43.

(2), mKhris-pa-mdaṅs-bsgyur, is found principally in the liver. Its function is to supply brightness to the sperm and menstrual blood.

(3) mKhris-pa-sgrub-byed, is located mainly in the heart. Its function is to give confidence, pride and wisdom.

(4) mKhris-mthoṅ-byed, is principally located in the eyes and assists good eyesight.

(5) mKhris-pa-mdog-bsal, is found in the skin and its function is to supply it with natural colour.

Of the five kinds of phlegm, (1), Bad-kan-rten-byed, is situated principally in the chest. It strengthens the other four phlegms and prevents excessive thirst.

(2) Bad-kan-myag-byed, is situated mainly in the digested part of the food in the upper part of the abdomen. It dissolves solid food.

(3) Bad-kan-myoṅ-byed, is situated in the tongue and its function is to give different flavours to food in the mouth.

(4) Bad-kan-ts'im-byed, is found principally in the head. Its function is that it develops the various sense organs, viz. eyes, nose, ears, body (skin) and tongue.

(5) Bad-kan-hbyor-byed, is principally situated in between the joints all over the body. Its function is to enable bodily movement and maintain and strengthen the joints.

The various kinds of bile, phlegm and air are all named after their respective functions in the body.

Nature of Air, Phlegm and Bile

Air. The nature of perfect Air is soft, light, cold, subtle, volatile and pungent.

Bile. The nature of Bile is oily, hot, light, violent, slightly unctuous, musty, liquid and flowing.

Phlegm. The nature of Phlegm is cool, sticky, heavy, sluggish, soft, slimy and solid.

Diseases are due to unbalanced Phlegm, Air and Bile, or to a combination of unbalanced Air and Bile; Phlegm and Air; Bile and Phlegm.

VI THE TYPES OF BODY AND THEIR FUNCTIONING

Air. Those persons born under a strong influence of Air have crooked bodies and are thin and bluish in complexion. Their joints produce a cracking sound during movement. Such people are easily susceptible to cold breezes; fond of singing, laughing, arguing and fighting; they are fond of bitter and sour foods.

Bile. Persons born with the maximum bile secretion in their constitution feel hunger and thirst at frequent intervals. The colour of their skin and hair is yellow. They are of medium size and height, intelligent and proud.

Phlegm. Persons born with the maximum phlegm secretion in their constitution do not have the required warmth. They are fat and have pale complexions. Such persons live long, become rich, are jolly, helpful by nature and are fond of sour food.

Those persons born under a strong influence of Air and Bile are usually short in stature; those born under a strong influence of Air and Phlegm are of average height, and those under a strong influence of Phlegm and Bile are tall.

Good health does not always depend solely on physical reasons. It also depends on the noble or bad deeds of one's previous life. To maintain a long and healthy life, one must take nutritious food, practise good habits, take proper medicines and say prayers.

VII TOKENS OF APPROACHING DEATH

Signs to be noticed by the Doctor

If the messenger from the patient's house is a priest or a sage, or one who has no physical defects, with clean habits; if he has journeyed on horseback and is well attired, then all this signifies that the patient is going to recover.

If the messenger be a eunuch, an unclean person or has some physical defect; if he has journeyed to call the Doctor either on a donkey, camel or buffalo; if he comes with great anxiety rubbing a stone or stick in between his hands; if he has a name with an ill meaning; if he carries a knife, stick or red flower in his hand and is gossiping or crying, all this signifies that the patient is not going to recover.

If at the time when the messenger comes to deliver the message from the patient's house, the Doctor is found to be in a bad mood, breaking things, talking nonsense, praying for the dead, not being in a mood to visit the patient, then all this is a sign that the patient will not recover.

If on the way to the patient's house the Doctor encounters weeping and wailing women, or people suffering from burns, or objects breaking while he is passing by, then all this is a bad omen and a sign that the patient will not recover.

But if the Doctor on his way to the patient's house sees grain heaped up, vessels filled with curd and millet drink, pretty women carrying children, images in white attire; if he hears the sound of bells, all this is a sign that the patient is going to recover.

Upon the Doctor's entering the house of the patient, if he meets people coming out of the house with grain, rice, jewellery or items that are supposed to bring luck, then this is a bad sign and signifies that the patient will not recover.

Dreams. If the patient dreams of riding on a rat, monkey, lion, or jackal, this signifies death. If he dreams of riding south on a horse, pig, buffalo, donkey or camel, all these are bad signs.

If the patient dreams of a tree growing from his forehead, where a bird's nest has formed; or of falling from a precipice, or of sleeping on a cremation ground; if he sees himself surrounded by crows, hungry ghosts, or drowning, or feasting with the dead, or wearing red clothes and a red flower necklace, this kind of dream signifies death. If persons of good health have such a dream, it is a bad omen.

Dreams to be taken into consideration are those that are dreamt early in the morning, when they are fresh on one's mind.

It is good to dream of: Images, gods, priests and holy people, kings and famous men, a big fire, people in white attire, religious objects, climbing on high hills, riding on horses or elephants, crossing oceans or big rivers, escaping from dark places or prison, overcoming enemies, being praised by parents. To have such dreams is a sign of prosperity, longevity and wealth.

Signs of death that can be noticed in a healthy person. Such persons for no reason will speak ill about others, about their own Doctor and priest. At times such persons look well in appearance, become very pleasant, suddenly acquire wealth; at other times they look ugly in appearance, their mind gets disturbed easily and for no reason, and they make friends with those who were considered enemies before; when they have a bath, the water poured on their body dries up quicker near the area of the heart than other parts. Such persons, no matter how they try to improve their health by taking nourishing food, deteriorate instead of improving; their nature and character change suddenly; when looking into a mirror they sometimes fail to see their reflection, or see their features distorted.

Sometimes bad dreams are dreamt due to illness; should bad dreams continue even after the illness is over, then this is a bad sign: a sign of death, but not immediate. Signs of immediate death can be, among others, forgetfulness, odd noises heard while belching, new parting in hair or eyebrows, sweat forming in the shape of the moon on the forehead and lips, breathing out heavily; the five elements merge together, finally resulting in death. When the earth element merges with water, the sign is that one is unable to see the various forms, e.g. houses etc. When water merges with fire, the symptom is that the nine orifices of the body, i.e. eyes, nose, ears, and so on, start to shrink and shrivel up. When fire merges with air, the symptom is that there is no warmth in the body. When air merges with sky, the symptom is that one is unable to inhale air.

All symptoms must be known to the Doctor, to enable him to judge as to whether the patient will live or not. Having bad dreams is not always an ill sign: such dreams can be overcome by prayer, meditation, charity, etc.

VIII THE CAUSES OF DISEASES

The causes of diseases may be divided into two kinds, immediate causes and long-term causes. The long-term cause is ignorance. Ignorance gives rise to anger, desire and mental darkness. Anger, desire and mental darkness are the three poisons of the mind according to Buddhist Philosophy, and are the causes for increase of Bile, Air and Phlegm in the constitution.

The origin of Air, Bile and Phlegm according to the Vedas is as follows:

Air. According to the Vedas, there was a God of Air, named Rdo-rje-hbar-ba, who went to the ocean to bathe. The goddess of Air, Nor-bu-hdzim-pa, beautifully adorned, happened to be near the ocean. They met and made love. While they were disporting themselves, the leather bag containing Air was left on one side by the God of Air. In the meantime a little Air escaped from the bag, and ever since that time the diseases due to unbalanced Air in the constitution came into existence.

Bile. According to the manuscript 'Bdud-rtsi-mchhog-gi-lung' (Tanjur), Brahma invited Maheśvara to attend an offering ceremony. In the seating arrangement, Maheśvara was given the last seat, with the result that he became very annoyed. In his anger he refused to accept the offering made by Brahma and instead he destroyed it, and from the eye in the centre of his forehead he sent out many diseases caused by unbalanced Bile in the constitution.

Phlegm. Many years ago, there lived a King by the name of Gyal-ba'i-miṅ-chan and his Queen, Ramaya. The Queen had an affair with one of the King's Ministers. The King, learning about this, grew very angry and cast them both to drown. The Queen and the Minister prayed a great deal and put a curse upon the King, that he might suffer from diseases due to unbalanced phlegm. The King in his anger threw a handful of dirt at them; some particles of this fell in between the feathers of an eagle. The eagle was in due course caught and eaten by some men, with the result that diseases of phlegm spread all over the kingdom.

Origin of hot diseases

Changes of climate and excess of heat give rise to diseases of bile. Diseases of fever, or hot diseases, arise when there is excess of heat in the seven constituents. Normally the seat of bile is in the lower part of the body, but when it is disturbed and unbalanced it travels upwards and gives rise to fever.

Air travels to all parts of the body. With respect to all bile diseases, air aggravates and worsens these diseases.

Origin of cold diseases

Diseases due to unbalanced phlegm usually start from the upper portion of the body and travel downwards. Phlegm is cool, heavy, akin to earth, and its tendency is to travel downwards. Various diseases of cold arise from unbalanced phlegm.

Air aggravates and worsens diseases of phlegm.

IX THE ACCESSORY CAUSES OF DISEASES

The immediate cause for diseases is change of time and climatic conditions: for instance, the summer temperatures being either higher or lower than usual, or the winter being either more or less severe than average, or the weather being warm when it should have been cold and vice versa—all such climatic conditions give rise to various diseases.

Diseases are also due to overworking of the five sense organs, e.g. eye diseases arise from reading under dim light and strain.

Diseases of phlegm, bile and air have their respective times for accumulation, outbreak and subsiding:

Air. Diseases of Air accumulate during the spring, break out during the summer and subside during the autumn.

Bile. Bile diseases accumulate in the summer, break out in the autumn and subside in the winter.

Phlegm. Phlegm diseases accumulate in the winter, break out in the spring and subside in the summer.

People born during springtime, when the land is dry, dusty, barren and unpleasant, have a light body and are hot-tempered. If, in addition, their diet is of little nutritional value, their constitution suffers from an accumulation of Air. Diseases due to unbalanced Air do not break out during the winter, since the land is then light and cool. Heat and cold being opposites, the cold prevents diseases of Air from breaking out. During the summer, diseases of Air break out due to excess heat and the coming of rain and wind. In the autumn, after the rains and strong winds are over and the weather is perfect, diseases due to unbalanced Air subside.

In persons born under the *influence of Bile*, during summer due to heat and the hot, warm and greasy food taken, diseases due to unbalanced bile accumulate. These diseases break out during the autumn, because the weather is then warm and moist and the wind is strong and effective. The summer rains cool the climate and prevent diseases of bile from breaking out. During winter, such diseases subside due to the cold.

In persons born under the *influence of Phlegm*, diseases of Phlegm accumulate during the winter, when the land is cool and moist. Heavy, oily food increases phlegm. During winter phlegm becomes frozen and solid, but with the coming of spring and increasing heat, it starts to melt and hence there are outbreaks of diseases of phlegm. In the summer, diseases of phlegm subside due to the strong light air.

Diseases are also due to bad diet, bad habits and wrong medicines.

X WAYS OF CONTRACTING DISEASE

There are four different ways by which disease is contracted:

(a) Period—spring, summer, autumn, winter.
(b) The three hundred and sixty evil spirits attacking living beings with diseases.
(c) Food.
(d) Habit and behaviour.

If Bile, Air and Phlegm are disturbed by any of the above four causes, diseases of Bile, Air and Phlegm arise. The seven constituents of saliva, blood, flesh, fat, bone, marrow and sperm are disturbed and affected.

Though Bile, Air and Phlegm are spread everywhere, their activity takes place chiefly as follows:

Bile—chiefly in the blood and sweat.
Air—chiefly inside the bones.
Phlegm—chiefly in the flesh, fat, marrow and sperm, faeces and urine.

XI SYMPTOMS

When a person is about to contract a disease of Air, the following symptoms appear: one craves food harmful for diseases of Air, having no desire or appetite for food such as meat, millet drink and sweet-flavoured things, which are good for diseases of Air. One desires to be lightly clothed instead of keeping warm, becomes active instead of keeping calm. The skin dries and darkens in colour. The body requires warmth, as it feels cold and shivers due to the disease. The stomach swells, one suffers from insomnia, giddiness, weak eyesight and restlessness.

For Bile diseases, the symptoms are that the stool, bile, skin and eyes turn yellow in colour. One feels much hunger, suffers from hypersomnia, excessive purging of bowels, swelling of the abdomen, excess of sputum and difficulty in respiration.

The bile Hju-byed is the main cause for either improvement or deterioration of the seven constituents. If it is too strong and effective, the nutritious portion of food after digestion tends to dry due to excess heat, with the result that the seven constituents are affected. If it is too weak and ineffective, the heat necessary for digestion is not produced with the result that the seven constituents are again affected. Since digestion suffers, it causes swelling of the abdomen, excessive purging of bowels, vomiting, etc.

Symptoms of excess of blood in the constitution: this causes a dry itch on the skin, diseases of spleen, leprosy, sores on the face, pimples, tumours, sore eyes, makes the colour of urine and skin turn red, etc.

Symptoms of excess of flesh in the constitution: this results in the growth of goitres, overweight, etc.

Symptoms of excess of fat in the constitution: one feels tired quickly; the breasts become larger, etc.

Symptoms of extra bones in the constitution: the appearance of double teeth, extra fingers and toes, etc.

Symptoms of increase of marrow: one feels heavy, the joints widen, etc.

Symptoms of excess of sperm: stones develop in the kidneys, there is increased discharge and increased attraction to women.

Symptoms of excess of faeces in the body: this causes swelling of the abdomen, pain in the intestines, etc.

Symptoms of excess of urine in the body: this causes water to accumulate in the system, frequent passing of urine, etc.

Excess of sweat causes bad odour, itching, etc.

Symptoms of a deficiency of Air in the system: one feels bodily weakness, dullness of mind, and one becomes less active.

Symptoms of a deficiency of Bile in the system: the skin turns a pale colour, there is less warmth in the body, etc.

Symptoms of a deficiency of Phlegm in the system: the brain is affected; there is giddiness and heart palpitation, joints become loose, etc.

Symptoms of malnutrition: one becomes thin, finds it difficult to swallow food; the skin becomes coarse, etc.

Symptoms of a deficiency of blood: one becomes soft and lifeless, likes remaining cool, takes to sour food; the skin becomes coarse, etc.

Symptoms of a deficiency of flesh: one becomes thin, the skin dries out, etc.

Symptoms of a deficiency of fat: the skin turns yellow, one suffers from insomnia, loses weight, etc.

Symptoms of a deficiency of bones: one's teeth and hair fall out.

Symptoms of a deficiency of marrow: the thigh bone becomes hollow; giddiness, hollowness in the eyes.

Symptoms of a deficiency of sperm: this causes the passing of blood from the male organ during intercourse.

The Doctor detects diseases due to unbalanced Air, Bile or Phlegm by examining the patient's urine and pulse.

Symptoms of diseases of Air. The pulse feels hollow and spurts up and down; the urine is bluish in colour; the patient feels tired and uneasy, giddy, his tongue turns red and rough with a feeling of dryness; his mouth tastes bitter, he suffers from aches and pains all over the body and shivering; his limbs become stiff, he vomits and becomes short-tempered.

Symptoms of diseases of Bile. The pulse feels hard and pulsates fast. The urine is reddish yellow in colour, with a bad odour. The patient feels warm, his head aches, his mouth tastes bitter-sour and furry substances form on the tongue; the tip of the nose becomes dry, the eyes turn reddish; he suffers from aches and pains all over the body, a vomiting sensation, thirst, excessive purging and excessive sweating.

Symptoms of diseases of Phlegm. The pulse seems low and pulsates at a very slow pace. The urine is whitish in colour, with not much odour or vapour. The patient's taste sensation is affected; his tongue and gums turn a pale colour; mucus and phlegm increase, his body becomes heavy and tired and he has no appetite. The digestive system is affected, the body swells, there is vomiting and dullness of mind, limbs and joints become stiff and the skin itches.

XII DIVISION OF DISEASES

Diseases can be divided according to: (a) the cause, (b) the individual, and (c) the kind of disease.

(a) *With respect to the cause*

(1) Diseases caused by unbalanced phlegm, air or bile.
(2) Diseases due to sinful actions (Karma) in one's previous lives.
(3) Diseases due to a mixture of both (1) and (2).

Diseases due to unbalanced humours are expressed as diseases caused by indulgence in irregular habits, by poison, by weapons and by demons.

Diseases due to sinful actions in former lives may at first appear as minor attacks, but turn out to be very serious indeed and result in death.

(b) *With respect to the individual*

These diseases can afflict men, women, children and old persons of every description. There are several diseases peculiar to each.

(c) *With respect to the kind of disease*

There are stated to be 404 kinds of common diseases. There are 101 diseases due to unbalanced humours, of which 42 are due to Air, 26 to Bile and 33 to Phlegm.

XIII EVERYDAY CONDUCT

To maintain good health and to be free from diseases, one must take good food and practice good habits. One should not impair the five sense organs. One should suspend the activities of body, speech and mind before fatigue. One should not board a dangerous ship, just as one should not go swimming in dangerous waters. One must think before doing anything.

Insomnia is due to excess of Air in the constitution. One who passes a sleepless night must make up for the lost sleep during the day. Those suffering from ill health, alcoholism, old age, fatigue or weariness must take rest in the afternoons, especially during the summer months, to prevent Air in the system from increasing. If those in good health take a nap in the afternoons, this is sometimes productive of phlegm, causing diseases of Phlegm, swelling of the body, headaches, dullness, cold, etc. Those feeling sleepy day and night can overcome the sleepiness by taking medicine to cause vomiting. Constant drowsiness is due to excess of Phlegm in the constitution; vomiting gets rid of the excess phlegm. For those suffering from insomnia, the taking of hot milk, soups, curd and nutritious food is essential to help overcome the disease. A little heated oil put into the ear enables one to sleep soundly.

One should not indulge in intercourse with animals, nor with wicked or dishonourable persons, pregnant women, weak women or women during the period of menstruation. During winter one can indulge in intercourse twice or thrice daily, since sperm increases in winter. In the autumn and spring there must be an interval of two days, and during summer an interval of fifteen days. Excessive intercourse affects the five sense organs.

One should anoint one's head and body with oils, and massage one's limbs, thus assisting the dissolution of excessive fat, easy bodily movement and good digestion. Massage is most essential for persons suffering from diseases of Phlegm. To prevent diseases of Phlegm and dissolve fat, after oiling the limbs one must rub on some powder made from peas. This powder enriches the complexion and dissolves fat.

Regular baths are essential for good health, good complexion, for the prevention of skin diseases and for the increase of sperm. They also prevent thirst. Washing the lower parts of the body with warm water is good for the body, but washing the head with hot water affects the hair and eyes. Those suffering from fever, loose motion, swelling of the abdomen or indigestion should refrain from bathing during the course of the illness. One should refrain from bathing immediately after meals.

The body may be affected suddenly with headache, pain in the throat, cholera, etc.; therefore one should always keep the necessary medicines in hand.

Those observing a noble conduct attain long life, health, happiness and fame.

XIV CONDUCT DURING THE SEASONS

To maintain a long and happy life, free from disease, one's conduct must be regulated according to the seasons.

There are six seasons in a year, divided into twelve months, as follows:

The year starts with the first month of the first part of winter, namely Smin-drug-zla-ba. The second month of the first part of winter is called Mgo-zla-ba. The first month of the second part of winter is rGyal-zla-ba and the second mChhu-zla-ba. The first spring month is dBo-zla-ba, the second Nag-pa-zla-ba. The first summer month is called Sa-ga-zla-ba and the second sNron-zla-ba. Then follows the first monsoon month, called Chhu-stod-zla-ba, and the second, Gro-bzhin-zla-ba. The first autumn month is Khrums-stod-zla-ba and the second dByu-gu-zla-ba.

The months are named after the respective stars which determine night and day during each calendar month. E.g., the first month of the first part of winter, sMin-drug-zla-wa, is so called after the constellation of sMin-drug, the Pleiades, because during this time sMin-drug determines nightfall.

With its appearance in the sky, dusk commences, and it remains in the sky till dawn.

Calculations of time. The smallest conceivable division of time is the 120th part of one moment or Skad-chig-ma (time required for the sound of snapping one's fingers); sixty such Skad-chig-ma or moments make one Thaṅ; thirty Thaṅ make one Yud-tsam (a small portion of time stated to vary from eight seconds to one and a half minutes); thirty Yud-tsam make a day and a night, or one Nyin-shag;* thirty Nyin-shag make one month or Zla-ba; two Zla-ba make a season, and six seasons make a year.

During summer, the days lengthen gradually until the climax is reached, after which the days begin to decrease in length; this climax or turning point is called Nyi-ldog (Summer solstice). The reverse phenomenon occurs in winter and the corresponding climax is called dGun-Nyi-ldog (Winter solstice). The winter and summer solstices of any particular year occur eleven days later than the Nyi-ldog or solstices of the year immediately preceding it. After the winter solstice the sun travels from north to south, and after the summer solstice it travels from south to north.

Three months after both the winter and the summer solstice, the length of the night equals that of the day. There is therefore one such day in the spring and one in the autumn.

In the period between the winter and summer solstices, the sun and the wind become exceedingly violent, hot and rough because of the nature of the Solar path, destroying the soma-like (moon-like) qualities of the earth. Then the rough, bitter, astringent and pungent flavours are great in strength. During this time (northern course of the sun) the sun absorbs the strength of man every day.

After the summer solstice, during the southern course of the sun, the strength of the sun declines. Beginning with the monsoon, the strength of man is revived; the moon is then strong because of its coolness, the heated earth is tempered by cool clouds, rain and winds. The flavours sour, salt and sweet are strong during this time.

The strength of man is great in winter. The digestive fire is strong, because it has been concentrated by the cold, which causes the pores of the skin to contract. This fire (Me-mnyam-rlung, the wind which assists the digestive process) being strong and effective assists easy digestion. Because of this, one is liable to feel hungry at dawn and since there is no food in the stomach for the fire to act upon, the seven constituents are affected. To remedy this one must oil one's body, take nutritious food and keep warm.

* If one Nyin-shag equals twenty-four hours, then one Yud-tsam equals forty-eight minutes, and one Thaṅ is one minute and thirty-six seconds, and one Skad-chig-ma is one and three-fifths of a second.

During winter phlegm accumulates, and in the spring, with the warm sun, the digestive fire becomes weaker with the result that diseases of phlegm break out. As a remedy against diseases of phlegm, one should eat bitter, pungent and astringent food. Meat of animals of high altitudes, boiled water, honey and ginger soup are recommended. Plenty of exercise is essential.

During summer the food taken must be sweet flavoured, light and cool. One should avoid staying for long under the sun, wrestling or eating bitter, pungent or astringent food. Bathing in cold water and wearing light clothing are recommended.

During the monsoons the land is wet, moist and cool. During this time one should eat sweet, sour and salty flavoured food in order to strengthen the digestive fire. The food taken should be light, warm and oily. Alcohol may be consumed in small quantities, to give warmth to the body.

During the autumn, diseases of bile break out. As a remedy against these diseases one should eat sweet, bitter and sour flavoured food.

XV AVOIDANCE OF OBSTRUCTING NATURAL IMPULSES

He who wishes for a long life, virtue, wealth and happiness should not suppress the natural urges of hunger, thirst, sputum, vomiting, wind, stool, urine, sperm, yawning, sleep, sneezing, cough, tears, panting with fatigue.

If hunger is not satisfied with food, the result is that the body becomes weak, one's appetite is disturbed, one's strength diminishes, one feels pain and one's head spins. In this case a little light, fat and warm food should be taken.

Through restrained thirst one's mouth gets dry, one's head spins, one becomes stuporous and forgetful, and heart diseases develop. In this case cool food should be taken.

As the consequence of suppressed vomit there may be loss of appetite, obstruction in breathing, swelling of the lower part of the body, and the skin may be affected in various ways ranging from itching eyes to erysipelas and leprosy. An inhalant of sandalwood and aloewood, a gargle prepared from the extracts of sandalwood and aloewood, and a purgative are recommended in this case.

By suppressing hiccup the five sense organs are affected. Headaches, stiffness of the limbs and distorted cheeks develop. In this case an inhalant prepared from sandalwood and aloewood is recommended; looking at the sun would also help.

By suppressing yawning the five sense organs are again affected, with the same results as fron suppressed hiccup. Every wind-destroying food and medicine is helpful in this case.

Suppressing breathing, especially just after exercise or fatigue, results in tumours, heart diseases and dullness of mind. In this case one should rest and take every wind-destroying food.

The results of restraining sleep are yawning, heaviness of head, weakened eyesight and digestion. In this case one should have rest, eat fat, light and warm food, meat soups, etc. Massage is also helpful.

The restraint of sputum results in obstruction in breathing, loss of weight, hiccup, and loss of appetite. A medicine prepared from the extracts of piper longum, ginger and raw sugar is recommended.

Catarrh, pain in the eyes, head, and heart, head spins and loss of appetite result from suppressed tears. In this case sleep, liquor and cheerful words are helpful.

Stoppage of the downward wind results in visceral induration, dry secretions, gripes, pain, dull weariness, tumours, weak eyesight, poor gastric heat, indigestion and heart diseases. In this case it is recommended to apply lubricants and consume wind-promoting food and drink.

Suppressed faeces result in cramps, colic, headache, pain, dull weariness, tumours, impaired vision, disturbed digestion, heart diseases, outflow of stool from the mouth and vomiting. The remedies are administration of enemas with mild medicines, oiling the body, soaking in medicinal water, bathing and taking vitamins.*

Retention of urine causes stones in the kidneys, gripes, pain, tumours, weak eyesight, heart diseases, disturbed digestion, urinary diseases, sickness in the body and the bladder. The remedies are soaking the body in medicinal water and administration of oil in enemas.

Suppression of sperm results in its outflow, penile diseases, cutaneous swelling, fever, throbbing of the heart, pain in the limbs, swelling of the testicles, difficulty and obstruction in passing urine, gravel and impotence, affected eyesight as well as the other sense organs. In this case milk, meat, fat food and millet drink should be taken.

XVI FOOD AND DRINK

One must be careful of one's diet. Food taken should be nutritious. One must know what is good and what is harmful for the body.

* Tib. Stobs-skyed, literally 'producing strength'.

Food has been classified as follows:

1. Grain.
2. Oil.
3. Meat.
4. Green vegetables.
5. Liquid diet.

1. *Grain*

Grain is classified into (a) cereals and (b) leguminous plants.

(a) *Cereals.* Rice, millet, buck wheat, barley, thick shelled barley (used for fodder), un-husked paddy. The above-mentioned grains are in general sweet in taste and gentle in digestion. The intake of such grains increases sperm and they are wind-destroying, but cause the growth and increase of phlegm.

Cereals are by nature cool, but while rice and buckwheat are light, millet, wheat and barley are heavy. The digestion of rice is smooth and that of buckwheat is rough. Rice diminishes phlegm, bile and wind, increases sperm, and stops loose motion and nausea. Millet is recommended in the case of fractured or cracked bones, but to be avoided if there are sores in the body, because it may aggravate them and increase the inflammation.

(b) *Leguminous plants. Peas* are by nature sweet, bitter, cool and light. They cause diseases of phlegm combined with fever and constipation; stop diarrhoea; produce blood, bile and fat. Rubbing the body with a powder made from peas is recommended to regulate the blood, bile and fat in the body.

Soya beans taste bitter as well as sweet. They increase bile, phlegm and air and cure pains in the joints, sores, and diseases of the blood.

Sesame (black and white) is by nature heavy and cold; it increases sperm and cures air diseases.

Any grain less than one year old causes diseases of phlegm. Grain over a year old is nutritious.

2. *Oil*

The varieties of oil are (a) oil from the stones of apricots, (b) oil from oleaginous seeds, rape seed oil, (c) oil extracted from marrow and (d) oil extracted from fat.

By nature the above oils taste sweet, heavy and cool. They cause a little loose motion (diarrhoea) and help digestion. If used for massage as well as consumption, they combat air diseases and diarrhoea, increase sperm, prevent the skin from becoming coarse and are essential for children, the aged, weak persons, and for those losing a lot of menstrual blood.

Oil derived from butter is by nature cool; it increases sperm, improves the complexion, creates energy and combats phlegm and fever diseases.

Old butter, however (about a year old), causes madness, forgetfulness, fainting and sores which take a long time to heal.

Slightly old butter increases strength and promotes longevity.

3. *Meat*

Meat of animals of high, dry land is by nature cool, light and rough; it combats diseases of phlegm combined with fever.

Meat of animals of low land is by nature warm, heavy and oily; it combats stomach-aches and back-aches.

Meat of animals of moderate altitude combats diseases of phlegm combined with fever and rheumatism.

Meat of wild animals and birds is by nature light and rough; it strengthens the digestive fire, combats tumours, kidney diseases, rheumatism and produces fat.

Fresh meat is cool; slightly old meat is nutritious; dry and frozen meat strengthens the digestive fire and cures air diseases. Meat of middle-aged animals is nutritious, but meat of dead animals is poisonous.

4. *Green vegetables*

Green vegetables are by nature warm and light if grown in dry land and cool and heavy if grown in wet land. Vegetables grown in dry land combat kidney diseases and rheumatism; those grown in wet land combat fever.

5. *Liquid diet*

Liquid diet regulates thirst, air, bile and phlegm; it stops diarrhoea, increases heat in the body and relaxes the veins.

Milk is sweet in taste and in digestion and oily; it increases vitality and the seven constituents, enriches the complexion, gives lustre to the skin, increases sperm and combats bile and air diseases. Its nature being cool and heavy, it produces phlegm.

Cow's milk is a vitalizer and elixir. It is wholesome for pulmonary consumption, stimulates the mind, invigorates and produces breast milk; combats fatigue, giddiness, intoxication, coughs, excessive thirst, hunger, gonorrhoea, a disease of the kidneys whereby urine is frequently and involuntarily discharged, and haemorrhage.

Goat's milk is light and removes obstruction in breathing; it combats fever, haemorrhage and diarrhoea.

Sheep's milk is sweet in taste and in digestion; it produces bile and phlegm, combats air diseases and generates firmness.

Milk of mares and asses eliminates air in the extremities and generates dullness in the brain and numbness.

Raw milk produces phlegm and is heavy and cool. Milk that has been excessively boiled is very heavy. Milk which is still warm from milking is like nectar. Pure milk is sometimes difficult to digest.

Difference between types of water. There are seven types of water (listed in order of goodness):

1. Rain water.
2. Melted snow water.
3. River water.
4. Spring water.
5. Well water.
6. Sea water.
7. Forest water.

Of the waters listed above, although *rain water* is vitalizing, refreshing, pleasing to the stomach, thin, satisfying, stimulating to the intellect, of indistinct taste, savoury, light, cool and nectar-like, touched by the sun, moon and wind while falling, its wholesomeness or unwholesomeness depend largely upon the time and the place.

To determine whether rain water is as pure and beneficial as Gangetic water, it should be collected in a bowl and mixed with unstained rice pap. If the mixture does not become discoloured or putrid, the rain water is wholesome.

Rain water is good when it is unspoiled, collected on wide open land hit by plenty of sun, moon and wind. One should not drink water that is turbid, covered by mud, tape-grass, grass and leaves, unseen by sun, moon and wind, nor celestial water that is unseasonable,* possessed of foam and insects, warm or unbearable to the teeth because it is excessively cold.

Mountain water that comes down with plenty of force and that is unspoiled and hit by the sun, moon and wind is good water, but if it comes down at a slow pace and is not hit by the sun, moon and wind in its flow, then it causes worms, elephantiasis, heart diseases and diseases of the stomach, throat and head.

It is said that any water be taken during the autumn months, since during

* Rain water not fallen during the right season.

that period the light of the star Rishi (Constellation of the Great Bear) kills poisons and germs in the water.

Cold water combats the influence of alcohol, stupor, nausea, spinning head, thirst, haemorrhage and poisoning. Hot water promotes and activates digestion, is easy to conduct through the throat, light on the stomach and purges the bladder. It cures urinary diseases and is recommended for hiccup, flatulence, new fever, cough, wind and phlegm.

Water that has been boiled and cooled down produces no phlegm, is light on the body and wholesome for persons affected with bile diseases. Water which has been boiled but which is a day old is bad for the health.

Alcohol is digestive, appetizing, violent, warming, generative of satisfaction and plumpness. It kindles the digestive fire, penetrates and purifies the apertures of the body and causes a little purging; in digestion and taste it is slightly sweet, sour, bitter and pungent. Alcohol is wholesome for those suffering from insomnia or hypersomnia; drunk moderately, it is wholesome for lean, very rough and very delicate people. Old alcohol, taken in limited quantities, aids the elimination of air and phlegm and is good for the body. Fresh alcohol is heavy and produces excessive air, bile and phlegm: in one word, it is like poison.

XVII DIETARY RULES

One must refrain from having certain types of food such as poisonous food, and food that is harmful to the body.

Poison may be classified into three types:

(a) Poison applied prepared as a mixture.
(b) Substances that have been converted into poison.
(c) Natural poison.

Food containing poison can be detected through taste and colour; the taste of such food and its colour are different from normal. If poisoned food is burnt on fire, the smoke is of rainbow colour, being more on the bluish side. The flame tends to bend on one side instead of being upright. The sparks from the fire travel far. Poisoned food is pleasing to the eyes of peacocks and crows. If given to dogs, it is usually vomited out.

Meat, raw or cooked, will not stick to a red-hot iron if it is poisoned. Such meat, boiled in alcohol, produces a steam that causes a burning sensation in the eyes.

Poisoned food must be done away with either by burning or burying deep under the earth.

There are certain combinations of food of two or more types which, taken together, sometimes have a poisonous effect, such as: curd taken with new wine; fish with milk; milk with walnuts; peaches with other fruit; eggs with fish; peas with curd together with molasses; chicken meat with curd; honey with oil; mushrooms fried in white and black mustard oil; melted butter and water.

Over-eating and an unregulated diet are harmful to the body.

Grain and meat of animals of the hills and dry land are light and produce strength and warmth; such food can be taken to one's full satisfaction. Heavy and cool food must be taken in small quantities, so as to assist easy digestion.

To facilitate digestion and to strengthen the digestive fire, food should be taken in reasonable quantities; many diseases affecting the stomach arise from indigestion. But on the other hand if the required quantity of food is not taken, health is affected causing loss of strength and colour, weakness and diseases of the bile, air and phlegm.

Indigestion causes blockage in the passage of the air called Me-mnyam-kyi-rluṅ (equalizing air or digestive fire), thus stopping heat from spreading all over the body. Persons whose digestive fire is not very strong should have a little wine after meals. For those suffering from swelling due to indigestion, boiled water, taken hot, is recommended.

XVIII RIGHT QUANTITIES OF FOOD AND DRINK

Food should be taken in proper quantities.

Grain and meat of animals of dry land, which are energy-producing and not heavy, should be preferred.

The quantity of food taken in the morning should be such that one is able to digest it by the afternoon, and the quantity taken in the evening such that one can digest it before dawn.

Food taken in moderate quantities strengthens the digestive fire and fortifies the body against diseases. If the food taken is inadequate, one's health is affected and one can contract many diseases. If more than the required quantity is taken, the digestive fire is affected and this in turn affects digestion and gives rise to chronic diseases.

XIX TASTE AND DIGESTIVE QUALITIES OF MEDICINES

Medicines prepared from herbs may be classified, according to taste, into six varieties: sweet, bitter, sour, astringent, acrid and salty.

Medicinal plants and herbs originate from the five elements of earth, water, fire, air and sky.

(a) The earth forms the base of the plants and herbs.
(b) Water moistens them.
(c) Fire generates heat and causes growth.
(d) Air causes movement, thus assisting growth.
(e) The sky allows sufficient space for growth.

Although all herbs and plants follow the same system in their growth, having the nature of the five elements, their individual tastes and effectiveness differ, owing to the differences between the seeds, and to the effectiveness and strength of the respective elements in each case.

Herbs and plants growing where the elements of water and earth are stronger than the other elements taste sweet; where fire and earth are strongest, they taste sour; where water and fire are strongest, they taste salty; where water and air predominate, they taste bitter; where fire and air are strongest, their taste is acrid and where earth and air, it is astringent.

Earth. Herbs and plants having the nature of the element earth are in quality heavy, strong, smooth, pungent and firm; they produce energy and combat air diseases.

Water. Herbs and plants having the nature of the element water are in quality cool, heavy, smooth, oily, soft and moist, and have no pungent smell. They help to unite the atoms* of the body; they oil, moisten and smoothe the system and combat bile diseases.

Fire. Herbs and plants having the nature of the element fire are in quality sharp, hot, light, rough and oily. Their smell is not pungent and their taste is indefinite. They produce warmth in the body, strengthen the seven constituents, enrich the complexion and combat phlegm diseases.

Air. Herbs and plants having the nature of the element air are in quality light, unstable, cold, rough, strong in texture, whitish in colour. They give strength to the body, facilitate bodily movement and the distribution of the nutritious portion of food throughout the body. They combat diseases of phlegm combined with bile.

Sky. Herbs and plants having the nature of any of the elements listed above also have in them the nature of the element sky. But there are also plants and herbs whose nature is chiefly that of the element sky: they are usually hollow, and combat diseases of bile, phlegm and air.

Medicines which have a tendency to travel upwards when consumed possess more of the nature of the elements fire and air, because these elements, being light, have this tendency.

* Tib. rdul, lit. 'speck of dust'.

Medicines which tend to travel downwards possess more of the nature of the elements water and earth, which are heavy and therefore tend to travel downwards.

The castor-oil plant acts as a purgative; although it possesses the nature of earth and water, its flavour is not sweet.

Medicines prepared from plants and herbs picked at the wrong time or season or not ground or mixed properly produce the opposite effect, e.g. a medicine taken to cause purging would cause vomiting instead, and one taken to cause vomiting would cause purging. This is sometimes the case with the castor-oil plant which, being rough by nature, requires good grinding. If not carefully ground into powder it can cause vomiting, although it is a laxative. Therefore if one wishes to use it as a laxative it should be well ground, and if one wishes to use it as an emetic it should be less well ground.

Poisonous plants and herbs may also be used in making medicines. Such medicines are made up by mixing poisonous plants and herbs with medicinal ones. Medicines can be prepared from every substance on earth.

The tongue is the organ of taste. When sweet food is taken, the sweetness lingers on and this taste, being pleasant, makes one wish for more sweet food. Salty food produces a lot of saliva in the mouth. Bitter-flavoured food reduces appetite and removes bad odour from the mouth. Pungent or acrid food causes a burning sensation in the mouth. Astringent food has a lingering taste.

Plants and herbs as medicine ingredients are classified as follows according to taste:

Sweet-flavoured

Bamboo-manna (substance secreted in the joints of bamboos), Sambucus Sibirica (bark), grapes, saffron, carrot, sugar, molasses, honey, meat, butter, etc.

Sour-flavoured

Pomegranate, Hippophae (berry), Cydonia sinensis (fruit), Crataegus pinnatifida (its fruit minus the kernel), jujube (seed), Cotoneaster melanocarpa (fruit), curd, butter-milk, yeast, millet drink, etc.

Bitter-flavoured

Gentiana chiretta (stalks growing in the Himalayas, used as an antidote against fever and liver complaints), Aconitum fischeri (flower, leaves and stem), Hemerocallis minor (fruit), Scutellaria baicalensis (root, leaves and stem), musk, bear-bile, Berberis sibirica (bark), Odontites serotina (the shrub itself), Gentiana macrophylla (root only), Gentiana pneumonanthe (flower, leaves and stem), Potentilla multifida (flower, leaves and stem), etc.

Acrid-flavoured

Mesua roxburgii (fruit), dried ginger, Piper longum (fruit), Caesalpinia sepiaria (substance secreted from the tree), Pulsatilla patens (flowers only), Alisma plantago-aquatica (flower, leaves and stem), onion, garlic, etc.

Astringent-flavoured

Santalum album (tree), Terminalia chebula (fruit minus kernel), Crataegus sanguinea (fruit minus kernel), Aquilegia parviflora (flower only), Padus asiatica (black pepper), Gingro biloba (acorns), Myricaria dahurica (leaves), etc.

Air diseases are combatted by food tasting sweet, sour or astringent, but aggravated by bitter and acrid food.

Phlegm diseases are combatted by sour, salty or astringent food, but increased by sweet and bitter food.

Bile diseases are combatted by bitter and astringent food, but aggravated by sour, salty and acrid food.

For instance, the Crataegus pinnatifida (fruit minus kernel) is sour and destroys phlegm and air, but increases bile.

There are always exceptions, such as that of old grain and the meat of animals reared on dry soil, which is sweet but does not increase bile, or the Terminalia chebula (fruit), which is astringent but is not effective against phlegm or air diseases. Again, Allium sativum (root) and Piper longum (fruit), though acrid, do not increase bile.

XX ACTION OF MEDICINES

Medicines can be classified by quality into heavy, smooth, cool, soft, light, rough, warm and sharp.

Medicines which are smooth and heavy combat air diseases; cool and soft medicines combat bile diseases and light, rough, acrid and sharp medicines combat diseases of phlegm.

Light, rough and cool medicines increase air; bile is increased by warm, sharp and smooth medicines; phlegm is increased by heavy, smooth, cool and soft medicines.

Medicinal plants and herbs grown in areas where the sun is hot are naturally warm. Those grown where the effect of the moon is strong are cool in nature, and generally the nature and quality of plants and herbs depends on climatic conditions.

VARIETIES OR TYPES OF MEDICINE

1. Metallic and organic drugs.
2. Mineral medicines.
3. Medicinal stones.
4. Medicinal trees.
5. Medicinal oils (Tse-sman).
6. Decoctions (Thaṅ-sman) from medicinal fruit and flowers.
7. Vegetable medicines, specially the leaves of medicinal plants.
8. Animal medicines.

1. *Metallic and organic drugs*

Their ingredients are: (a) red and yellow gold. The red-coloured gold is found in the sands of the ocean. Bells made out of this gold produce excellent sound. Yellow gold is also to be found in the ocean sands. Gold can also be reddish-yellow or whitish-yellow. The taste of all types of gold is bitter. Medicines containing gold should be taken in cases of poisoning, as they prevent poison from affecting the organs of the body by causing it to slide down like water poured on flower petals does.

(b) Silver, of which there are many varieties. Silver obtained from copper and lead ores is of poor quality. Silver obtained from earth and trees has a taste and effect like those of gold. Medicine containing silver dries and stops the flow of pus and blood.

(c) Copper, the best being natural copper. Other varieties are copper obtained from melted ore, which is reddish in colour, and soft red copper. Medicines containing copper taste sweet and have a cooling effect. They dry pus and cure fever in the lungs and liver.

(d) Iron, the varieties of which are magnet, iron obtained from animals, and white and black iron. Medicines with an iron content taste sour and have a cooling effect. They extract poison from the liver, cure eye diseases, dropsy, swelling of the body and stomach.

(e) Turquoise, which is either reddish-blue or whitish-blue in colour. Medicines containing turquoise cure fever of the lungs and liver.

(f) Pearls, of which the reddish coloured pearl is the best in quality, and the best of all metallic and organic drugs. (The Buddha and Bodhisattvas having transformed themselves into shellfish, red pearls were produced in their stomachs which came to be known as Rakta Mutig.*) It is said that there are other types of pearls obtainable from the brains and tusks of elephants, from the brains of cobras, and from the leaves of trees growing in South India. Medicines containing pearls cure brain diseases and extract poison, Medicines containing oyster-shell or mother-of-pearl also have the same properties.

(g) Shells, of which the best is the white conch shell with its coil reverting to the right. There is also a conch shell of reddish colour, the coil of which reverts to the left. Medicines containing shell dry pus, cure swelling, bone fever and bad eyesight.

(h) Coral, which is found growing near the rocks of the ocean. There are two types, one being red on top with a white base and the other blackish in colour; the former is superior in quality. Medicines containing coral cure liver fever, vein fever and fever due to poison in the system.

(i) Sapphire, one type of which is studded with particles of gold and the other is plain, the former being of superior quality. Medicines made from sapphire cure leprosy and extract poison from the system.

There are various other metallic and organic drugs. Relics of Buddhas are also used as ingredients for medicines.

When preparing medicines, it is essential to grind these ingredients very thoroughly into powder and to use the appropriate quantity of each in order to ensure the effectiveness of the medicine.

2. *Mineral medicines*

These are: (a) Salt-petre, which is white and clear in colour. Medicines prepared from this cure or dissolve stones in the kidneys and ease the passing of urine.

(b) Lead, of a reddish-yellow colour. Medicines containing this ingredient cure fever of the veins and sores.

(c) Brim-stone, which is found near hot springs. The colours available are yellow, white and black, of which the first two are superior in quality. Medicines containing brim-stone ease the flow of blood and pus and reduce swelling.

(d) Vitriol, which cures air diseases and fever.

(e) Bitumen, which cures fever and stiffness due to unbalanced air, diseases of the stomach, liver and kidneys.

* Literally 'Brahmin's blood', probably through association with the Sanskrit muktā, 'pearl'.

3. *Medicinal stones*

(a) Load-stone, which comes in two varieties. The superior quality is found in China and attracts ten needles at a time; the dull blackish-coloured load-stone is of inferior quality. Medicines containing load-stone help to extract bullets from the body, cure vein and brain diseases and help to put together dislocated joints.

(b) Haematite of ore (a kind of stone on which silver is tested). This is of a dullish colour on the outside and silver-coloured inside. On melting it, silver is extracted. Medicines made from this stone dry pus.

4. *Medicinal trees*

The most important of these are: (a) Paris quadrifolia, a tree of yellowish colour with big green leaves and vermilion flowers. A white sticky substance extracted from the tree is used in medicines.

(b) Santalum album, a tree of whitish colour with green leaves. To identify this tree, soak a piece of bark in hot butter, when the butter should become frozen. Medicines with this ingredient cure fever of the heart and lungs.

(c) Pterocarpus santalinus, a reddish tree with leaves of a glittering green and buds and flowers reddish in colour and slightly hairy. This is a heavy, strong tree and medicines made with this ingredient cure fever of the blood.

(d) Aloewood: the good quality aloewood tree is of a dark colour, with leaves green and fern-like. Its flowers are bluish and its roots are strong. There are one or two other kinds of aloewood tree. Medicines with this ingredient cure fever and particularly heart fever.

5. *Medicinal oils* (*Tse-sman*)

These are: (a) a yellow or purple pigment concretion found in the entrails of some animals. The best concretion is extracted from the liver of elephants: the next best comes from the liver of pigs and sheep. The purplish-coloured pigment is superior in quality to the yellowish one. Medicines containing this ingredient cure liver fever, extract poison from the system, and cure infectious diseases, typhoid fever, etc.

(b) Bamboo-manna, a substance secreted from the joints of bamboos. It is of a whitish colour. Medicines containing this cure inflammation of the lungs and sores.

(c) Flower of Crocus sativus (saffron). This is a herb of reddish-yellow colour. It cures liver diseases.

(d) Fruit of Amomum amarum. The tree is of a darkish colour and the pod is three-sided and whitish in colour. Medicines with this ingredient cure kidney diseases.

(e) Fruit of Myristica fragrans. The tree is whitish in colour with green leaves and yellow flowers, and the fruit is purplish with a strong smell. Medicines with this ingredient cure diseases of the heart and air.

(f) Fruit of Eugenia caryophyllata. Medicines containing this cure air diseases, diseases of the throat and rheumatism.

6. *Decoctions* (*Thaṅ-sman*)

These are prepared of the following: (a) Flower of Aquilegia parviflora. This flower comes in a variety of colours such as red, yellow or white, it has a green stem and the edges of its leaves are sharp and hairy. It cures lung diseases and fever of the liver.

(b) Dry buds, anthers and petals of Quisqualis indica. The tree and its leaves resemble a walnut tree; it has thorns and its flower buds turn to one direction. Medicines made with an anther ingredient cure liver fever, those with a petal ingredient cure heart fever and those with dry buds cure lung fever.

(c) Fruit of Lactuca scariola. This has narrow leaves with sharp edges, white flowers shaped like an umbrella and fruit resembling that of the Carum buriaticum. Medicines prepared with this ingredient cure lung fever.

(d) Fruit of Allium anisopodium. This has a long and hollow stalk, roundish oily leaves and small bluish flowers, and the fruit is three-sided and dark in colour. Medicines with this ingredient cure cold in the liver.

(e) Fruit of Conioselinum vaginatum. This has a short stalk and small leaves, and the fruit resembles that of Anisum vulgare but is slightly smaller and has a pungent smell. Medicines containing this ingredient cure stomach diseases and colds.

7. *Vegetable medicines*

These are prepared from the following: (a) Scutellaria baicalensis. This has bluish flowers and four-petalled, hairy leaves. The plant and its roots are used as ingredients in medicines that cure fever due to overwork and fatigue, lung, liver and heart fevers, spleen and kidney fever and air diseases and purify the blood.

(b) Saussurea alata or amara. This plant, which has big leaves with a bitter taste and white flowers with long stems, is used as an ingredient in medicines that protect against contagious diseases.

(c) Saussurea salicifolia. A plant found in grassy lands, pleasant-smelling, with short and hairy stem and slim hairy leaves, which is used to prepare medicines that cure chronic fever, extract poison and protect against contagious diseases.

(d) Potentilla multifida. A yellow plant with pleasant smell and bitter taste, whose flower is used as an ingredient in medicines that purify the blood, cure fever of the veins, convulsions and choleric cramps and stop diarrhoea.

(e) Flower, stem and leaves of Gentiana macrophylla. This plant grows in grassy land and has white flowers, green stems and blackish fruit with a bitter taste and rough texture. Another variety has bluish-coloured flowers and stems. Medicines with these ingredients cure lung fever and destroy bile.

(f) Leaves, stem and flower of Gentiana aquea. The flowers of this plant are yellow and have a smell akin to that of lotus flowers, and its leaves are green, roundish and shallow. Medicines with these ingredients cure fever due to unbalanced bile and liver fever.

(g) Dracocephalum argunense. All of this herb is used as an ingredient in medicines to cure liver fever and stomach upsets.

(h) Fruit of Gentiana amarella. This plant has reddish flowers and green leaves with a bitter taste. Its fruit is used as an ingredient in medicines that cure fever due to unbalanced bile.

(i) Stellaria dichotoma. A herb with purplish leaves and stem and white flowers. It is used in medicines that cure fever of the lungs.

(j) Arctostaphylos uva-ursi. A herb with fine stem, small leaves and bluish flowers, which is used as an ingredient in medicines to cure diseases due to unbalanced bile.

8. *Animal medicines*

Their ingredients and qualities are:
(a) Horns, claws and shell.
(b) Bones.
(c) Flesh.
(d) Skin.
(e) Blood.
(f) Fat.

(a) *Horns*. The horn of rhinoceros dries pus and purifies the blood; antelope's horn is used in medicines that stop diarrhoea; wild yak's horn cures tumours and gives warmth to the body; the horn of argali (Asiatic wild sheep) protects against contagious diseases; wild sheep's and Saigo antelope's horn assist easy birth. Crocodile's claws cure bone fever. Snail's shell cures dropsy and stomach diseases.

(b) *Bones*. Human skull dries pus and matter; human bone powder cures chronic fever; human spine cures ulcers and cancer. Dragon's bone dries sores and prevents internal rotting of infected parts; pig's bone cures phlegm diseases and convulsions; sheep's bone cures air diseases, and monkey's bone assists easy birth.

(c) *Flesh.* Deer's and stag's meat dries pus and purifies the blood; human flesh dries sores, cures bone infection, extracts poison and protects against infectious diseases; the flesh of birds of prey increases warmth in the body and extracts poison. The latter can also be achieved by eating peacock's flesh which, in addition, destroys excessive bile. The flesh of the night-hawk cures nausea, and sparrow's meat increases sperm. Snake's meat prevents constipation and eye diseases, while lizard flesh cures kidney diseases. The liver of the following animals is of medicinal value: otter's liver prevents obstruction in the passing of urine, marmot's liver helps the healing process of broken and cracked bones, and goat's liver cures eye diseases: fox's and swallow's liver cure lung diseases. Wolf's stomach increases warmth and assists digestion. Using the tongue of the following animals is helpful: dog's tongue dries sores, wolf's tongue cures rheumatism and donkey's tongue prevents diarrhoea. Animal's brains, too, can be used for cures: goat's brain for infection of the nerves, sheep's brain for giddiness, the brain of wild animals to prevent diarrhoea, rabbit's brain for intestinal pain. Human brain cures swelling and dries pus and matter.

(d) *Skin.* Snake's skin cures leucoderma and the skin of the ox and the rhinoceros cure smallpox.

(e) *Blood.* Stag's blood cures blood diseases and prevents the excessive flow of menstrual blood; goat's blood cures smallpox and extracts poison; wild yak's and antelope's blood prevent diarrhoea: pig's blood extracts poison and cures phlegm diseases: donkey's blood cures rheumatism and removes unwanted matter collected in the eyes and joints.

(f) *Fat.* Snake's fat helps to extract bullets from the body.

XXI PHARMACOLOGY

In the Tibetan medical text called bShad-rgyud not much is said about medical compounds and so reference has been made to the medical text called Phyi-rgyud.

FORMS OF MEDICINE

1. Decoction: extraction of essence of medicine by boiling down (Thaṅ-sman).
2. Powder medicine.

3. Pills.
4. Syrups.
5. Oily medicine.
6. Ash-like medicine (Thal-sman).
7. Concentrated medicine (Khan-da).
8. Medicinal wine.

1. *Decoctions*

An old soft weather-beaten human skull + dragon bone + Gentiana barbata (herb): the three combined, well ground into powder, should be boiled in a container with three tumblerfuls of water until the mixture boils down to one tumblerful. It should then be left to cool before being taken. This mixture cures diseases of air, bile and phlegm as well as sinus trouble.

Iron filings + Berberis sibirica (lining of bark) + Terminalia chebula (fruit) + Crataegus sanguinea (fruit) + Crataegus pinnatifida (fruit): these should be ground into powder and boiled together, then cooled before being taken. This decoction cures eye diseases.

Berberis sibirica (lining of bark) + Artemisia integrifolia (herb) + bear's bile: these should be ground into powder and boiled. Prevents bleeding from the nose.

Aconitum fischeri (flower, leaves and root) + Glycyrrhiza uralensis (root) + Gentiana algida (flower) + Bamboo manna + raw sugar: these should be ground into powder and boiled together. Cures sores and pain in the throat, and all throat infections.

Santalum album (tree) + Myristica fragrans (fruit) + Sterculia alata (fruit): these to be ground into powder and boiled together. This decoction cures heart fever.

Stellaria dichotoma (flower and leaves) + Glycyrrhiza uralensis (root) + lac + Bergenia saxifraga (root): to be ground into powder and boiled together. Cures lung diseases.

Eugenia caryophyllata (fruit) + Hemerocallis minor (fruit) + Terminalia chebula (fruit): to be ground into powder and boiled. This cures fever in the spleen and swelling of the stomach.

Terminalia chebula (fruit) + lac + Rubia cardiofolia (tree) + Eriobotrya japonica (leaves): to be ground into powder and boiled together. Cures fever of the intestines, fever of the kidneys and fever affecting the lower parts of the body.

Antitoxicum sibiricum (fruit) + Aconitum fischeri (root, flower and leaves) + Bergenia crassifolia (root): these should be ground together and then boiled. This decoction cures fever of the intestines and kidneys.

Tribulus terrestris (fruit) + Malva silvestris (fruit) + crab meat: should be well ground, then boiled. Eases the passing of urine and cures urinary diseases.

Paeonia albiflora (root) + Sambucus sibirica (tree) + Sophora flavescens (creeper tree) + Hedychium spicatum (root): must be well ground and boiled. Cures phlegm and air diseases, also blood pressure irregularities.

Gentiana barbata (herb) + Scutellaria baicalensis (root, leaves and stem) + Crataegus pinnatifida (fruit) + Odontites serotina (herb): to be well ground and boiled. Cures irregularities of blood pressure and purifies the blood.

Terminalia chebula (tree) + Athyrium crematum (herb) + Aconitum fischeri (flower, stem and leaves): should be well ground and boiled. Salt should be added after boiling. Extracts poison taken with food or applied.

Terminalia chebula (tree): to be boiled, and Hedychium spicatum (ginger) to be added after boiling. This decoction cures jaundice and tumours.

There are in all about fifty-four varieties of decoction (Thaṅ-sman), for the cure of fevers affecting the various organs or parts of the body, listed in the medical text Phyi-rgyud, and more in the book entitled sByor-ba-brgya-pa written by Nāgārjuna.

All these preparations must be concentrated by boiling down to one-third of the original volume. In cases of fever affecting any organ or part of the body the decoction should be cooled before being taken, but for diseases of cold it should be taken hot straight after boiling. For cases of combined fever and cold disease, the decoction should be taken lukewarm.

2. *Powder medicine*

Paris quadrifolia (substance secreted in tree) + Santalum album (tree) + Aconitum fischeri (root, flower and leaves): these should be ground into powder and given to the patient mixed with cold water in which sugar has been added. Cures fever and acts as a preventive against contagious diseases. This medicine is called Ga-pur-gsum-sbyor (camphor preparation with three ingredients).

Ga-pur-gsum-sbyor + Carthamus tinctorius (flower) + Gi-waṅ (yellow pigment concretion found in the entrails of certain animals and in the neck of elephants): this cures fever, gives protection against contagious diseases and is called rGyal-blon-lṅa-pa (victorious prescription containing five ingredients, i.e. camphor preparation with three ingredients plus two more ingredients).

rGyal-blon-lṅa-pa + bear's bile + musk (the last two ingredients have a mild effect): this mixture cures fever, gives protection against contagious diseases, and is called rGyal-blon-bdun-pa.

Paris quadrifolia is very strong and increases air, but in combination with other ingredients its harmful effects are eliminated.

All above medicines should be taken with water, but for persons suffering from air and phlegm diseases it is advisable to take them with millet wine.

Paris quadrifolia (secretion in tree) + Santalum album (tree) + Gi-waṅ + Bamboo manna + Crocus sativus (flower) + Scutellaria baicalensis (root, leaves and stem) + Gentiana barbata (herb) + sugar: the first and last ingredients should be mixed in the ratio 1:4, the others in equal quantities. This cures backache and fever and is called Ga-pur-bdun-pa (camphor medicine with seven ingredients).

Paris quadrifolia (secretion in tree) + Bamboo manna + Crocus sativus (flower) + Eugenia caryophyllata (fruit) + Elettaria cardamomum (fruit) + Amomum medium (fruit) + Myristica fragrans (fruit) + Santalum album (tree) + rhinoceros bone + Aquilegia parviflora (flower) + Aloewood (root) + musk + Bergenia crassifolia (root) + Gentiana barbata (herb): these should be ground into powder amd mixed together. The mixture cures mental diseases, fainting due to ill health and dumbness due to sickness, and is called Rin-chhen shags-sbyor (gladmaking jewel).

There are many more medicines with Paris quadrifolia as the main ingredient.

Crocus sativus (flower) + Bamboo manna + Gi-waṅ + Myristica fragrans (fruit) + Aloewood (root) + Sterculia alata (bark) + Inula helenium (root): this powder cures heart fever and is called Gur-gum bdun-pa (wild saffron medicine with seven ingredients).

Crocus sativus (flower) + Bamboo manna + Gi-waṅ + Inula helenium (root) + Glycyrrhiza uralensis (tree) + Vitis vinifera (fruit) + Stellaria palustris (herb): this medicine is called Gur-gum-bdun-pa and cures lung fever.

Crocus sativus + Bamboo manna + Gi-waṅ + Aquilegia parviflora (flower) + Odontites serotina (shrub) + Dracocephalum ruyschiana (flower, leaves and stem) + bitumen: this powder cures liver fever.

Crocus sativus + Bamboo manna + Gi-waṅ + Hemerocallis minor (fruit) + Eugenia caryophyllata (fruit) + Terminalis chebula (fruit) + Piper longum (fruit): these ingredients combined as a powder cure fever of the spleen.

Crocus sativus + Bamboo manna + Gi-waṅ + Elettaria cardamomum (fruit) + bitumen + Juniperus communis (leaves) + Terminalia chebula (fruit): to be mixed and ground into powder. Cures fever of the kidneys.

Crocus sativus + Bamboo manna + Gi-waṅ + Aconitum fischeri (flower, leaves and root) + Antitoxicum sibiricum (fruit) + Bergenia crassifolia (root) + Akebia quinata (trunk): this powder cures fever of the intestines.

If Santalum album is added to any of the above Gur-gum-bdun-pa medicines, the resultant mixture is called Tsan-dan-brgyad-pa (sandaltree medicine with eight ingredients) and is suitable for fevers of a less serious type. There are in all about forty-two varieties of Gur-gum-bdun-pa listed in the medical texts.

Black calambac or aloewood + Myristica fragrans + Sterculia alata + Bamboo manna + Boswellia carteri (substance secreted from tree) + Inula helenium (root) + Terminalia chebula + Quisqualis indica (flower anthers and petals): these should be ground into powder and sugar added in the ratio 1:3. This powder cures heart diseases, mental illness, dumbness due to illness and pain in the breast and liver, and is called A-gar-brgyad-pa (A-gar medicine with eight ingredients).

Gi-waṅ + Crocus sativus + Aquilegia parviflora + Akebia quinata (trunk) + Gentiana barbata + red chalk + Inula helenium + Odontites serotina + Hemerocallis minor (fruit) + sugar: this cures diseases affecting the liver (e.g. excess of blood, swelling or fever) and phlegm diseases, and is called Gi-waṅ-dgu-pa (bezoar medicine with nine ingredients).

Terminalia chebula + Eugenia caryophyllata + Hemerocallis minor (fruit) + Valeriana officinalis (root and leaves) + Quisqualis indica + Piper longum + Amomum medium + sugar: this powder cures spleen diseases such as swelling, sores, pain and fever of the spleen.

Terminalia chebula + Crocus sativus + Elettaria cardamomum + red chalk + Gentiana barbata + Canavalia gladiata (fruit) + Eriobotrya japonica (leaves) + Galium boreale (root) + Vermilion Juniperus communis (leaves) + sugar: this mixture cures sores in the kidneys, swelling and obstruction in passing urine, pain in the waist, difficulty in walking, kidney fever and is called A-ru-bchu-pa (arura medicine with ten ingredients).

Red chalk + musk + Crocus sativus + Elettaria cardamomum + bear's bile + Aconitum fischeri + Dracocephalum ruyschiana + Terminalia chebula + Bergenia crassifolia + sugar: this cures bile diseases, disease due to affected liver and fever in the stomach, and is called Brag-zhun-dgu-pa (red chalk medicine with nine ingredients).

Medicines for all diseases of cold:

Punica granatum (fruit) + Cinnamomum cassia blume (lining of bark) + Piper nigrum (fruit): these mixed in equal quantities cure liver trouble, difficulty in breathing and indigestion and are called Se-hbru-gsum-pa (pomegranate medicine with three ingredients).

If Kha-ru-ts'va (black salt of fetid odour prepared by fusing fossil salt with a small amount of emblic myrobalan) is added to Se-hbru-gsum-pa, the mixture cures swelling and uneasiness in the stomach, indigestion causing vomiting, and is called Se-hbru-bzhi-pa (pomegranate medicine with four ingredients).

Punica granatum + Cinnamomum cassia blume + Piper longum + Elettaria cardamomum + Hedychium spicatum (root) + molasses: this powder cures bile upset causing indigestion, tumour in the stomach, air in the heart and kidney diseases and is called Se-hbra-lṅa-pa (pomegranate medicine with five ingredients).

Punica granatum + Cinnamomum cassia blume + Elettaria cardamomum + Piper longum + Myristica fragrans + Crocus sativus + Amomum medium (fruit) + Hedychium spicatum: this cures stomach diseases, liver, phlegm and air diseases and heart tumour, and is called Se-hbru-brgyad-pa (pomegranate medicine with eight ingredients).

There are about thirty varieties of pomegranate medicines, all used for cold diseases.

Rhododendron + Piper nigrum + Cinnamomum cassia blume + Elettaria cardamomum + Hedychium spicatum + Piper longum: this cures diarrhoea, vomiting, difficulty in respiration, piles, tumours, swelling of the body and lung diseases and is called Da-li-drug-pa (rhododendron medicine with six ingredients).

Lactuca scariola added to the above produces a powder that cures fever affecting the upper part of the body and is called Da-li-bdun-pa (rhododendron medicine with seven ingredients).

There are in all fourteen medicines falling under the category of Da-li-bdun-pa.

Galedupa arborea (fruit) + Hedychium spicatum + Capsicum annuum (root) + Equisetum arvense (fruit) + Terminalia chebula + Piper longum + sugar: this mixture cures swelling of the abdomen due to indigestion and strengthens the digestive fire, and is called Ka-ran-dza-drug-pa (pongamia glabra medicine with six ingredients).

There are many more medicines in powder form for the cure of cold diseases.

3. *Pills*

4 oz Terminalia chebula + 1 oz Inula helenium + $\frac{3}{4}$ oz Acorus calamus (root) + $\frac{1}{2}$ oz arsenic + $\frac{1}{3}$ oz musk: these ingredients should be pulverized and then made into pills. Cures sores, aches and pains and is called Khyuṅ-lṅa.

Neck of Lamago vulture + aquatic bird + any carnivorous animal + badger + wild yak + wild ass + Bamboo manna + Crocus sativus + Eugenia caryophyllata + Elettaria cardamomum + Myristica fragrans + Amomum medium + Hedychium spicatum + Piper longum + Piper nigrum + rock salt + sal ammoniac + black salt + Anisum vulgare (fruit) + Conioselinum vaginatum (fruit) + Allium anisopodium (herb): the above to be mixed together with molasses and made into pills. This cures tumour diseases and is called Za-phed-ril-bu.

Fruit of Pongamia glabra (known in Tibet as hjam-hbras) + Nelumbium nucifera (fruit) + Bamboo manna + Crocus sativus + Elettaria cardamomum + Terminalia chebula + Myristica fragrans + Conioselinum vaginatum + Piper longum + Hedychium spicatum + Aquilegia parviflora + Rubia cardifolia (tree) + Capsicum annuum + Citrullus vulgaris (fruit) + Gingro biloba (fruit) + Cotoneaster melanocarpa (fruit) + Punica granatum: should be powdered, mixed and then made into pills for the cure of air and phlegm diseases, dysentery, giddiness and indigestion. This medicine is called Gu-liṅ-hbras-ril-bu.

Zingiber officinale (root) + Piper longum + Piper nigrum + Potentilla salesovii (tree) + Capsicum annuum: to be ground and then made into pills for the cure of pains in the ribs, palpitation of the heart, heart trouble and loss of appetite.

Myristica fragrans + Terminalia chebula + Boswellia carteri (secretion from tree) + black Terminalia chebula (fruit) + Hedychium spicatum + Caesalpinia sepiaria (secretion from tree) + Bamboo manna + Crocus sativus + Eugenia caryophyllata + Amomum medium + Anisum vulgare + Santalum album + Pterocarpus santalinus + Melia toosendan (fruit) + Crataegus pinnatifida (fruit) + Sterculia alata (flower and leaves) + Rhamnus dahuricus (tree) + Allium sativum (root) + Bergenia crassifolia: to be ground together and made into pills to cure heart diseases, air in the heart, mental trouble, pains and aches, nervousness and fainting. These are called Bi-ma-mi-tra pills.

Black aloewood (root) + Cinnamomum camphora (tree) + grey aloewood + Santalum album + Pterocarpus santalinus (tree) + bamboo manna + Crocus sativus + Eugenia caryophyllata + Elettaria cardamomum + Myristica fragrans + Amomum medium + Terminalia chebula + Melia toosendan + Crataegus pinnatifida (fruit) + Paeonia albiflora (root) + Sambucus sibirica (tree) + Sophora flavescens (creeper tree) + Gentiana barbata + Scutellaria baicalensis (root, stem and leaves) + Hedychium spicatum + Odontites serotina + Kochela + Vatica lanceaefolia (dark secretion from tree) + musk + Carduus crispus (flower) + Aconitum napallus (root) + Quisqualis indica + Inula helenium + Inula britannica (flower, stem and leaves)+Senecio brylovii (flower)+Punica granatum+Stellaria dichotoma (flower and leaves): to be ground into powder and then made into pills to cure bile, air and phlegm diseases, backache and difficulty in respiration. These are called A-gar-so-lṅa pills.

Canavalia gladiata (tree) + Areca catechu (fruit) + black aloewood + Eugenia caryophyllata + Myristica fragrans + Caesalpinia sepiaria (secretion from tree) + Inula helenium + Sterculia alata (flower and leaves) + Aconitum napallus + fat of female yak + Zingiber officinale (root) + Piper nigrum + black salt + the heart of wild yak or vulture: to be ground into powder and made into pills the size of peas. Cures all diseases of air, mental trouble, deafness due to ill health, heart trouble and nervousness.

The medicines mentioned above can be taken either with water or millet wine, in the mornings or in the evenings.

4. *Syrups*

Abutilon theophrasti (fruit) + Terminalia chebula + Bamboo manna + Crocus sativus + Eugenia caryophyllata + Triglochin maritima (herb) + Glycyrrhiza uralensis (root) + iron filings: to be ground and made into a paste with sugar and fresh butter. Cures fever of the lungs and chronic fever. Can be taken with warm water. This medicine is called Lchags-phye-brgyad-pa (iron filings paste with eight ingredients).

Gentiana barbata + Hemerocallis minor + Aconitum fischeri + Paeonia albiflora + Piper longum + Akebia quinata (tree): to be ground and made into a paste with honey. This medicine cures lung diseases, diseases due to unbalanced bile and headaches and is called Tig-ta-drug-pa'i-lde-gu (gentian syrup with six ingredients).

Crocus sativus + Vermilion + bear's bile or bile of any other wild animal + Quisqualis indica: to be ground into powder and mixed into a paste with fresh butter. This medicine cures diseases of the lungs, liver diseases, excess flow of menstrual blood, and bleeding from the nose and is called mKhris-sna'i-lde-gu (bile and divers ingredients syrup).

Bitumen + Terminalia chebula + Odontites serotina + Crocus sativus: to be ground into powder and made into a paste with honey. This medicine cures diseases due to unbalanced blood in the liver (when blood turns impure in the liver) causing pain in the joints, gout, etc., and is called Brag-zhun-bzhi-pa-lde-gu (bitumen syrup with four ingredients).

Terminalia chebula + Hedychium spicatum + Rubia cardiofolia + Lithospermum erythrorhizon (root) + Bamboo manna + Crocus sativus + Eugenia caryophyllata + Triglochin maritima (herb) + Glycyrrhiza uralensis + Bergenia crassifolia: to be well powdered and mixed into a paste or thick syrup with either sugar, honey or fresh butter. This medicine cures lung diseases, blood and pus formed in the lungs, etc., and is called mDar-gsum-lde-gu (syrup with three red ingredients).

Terminalia chebula+Melia toosendan+Crataegus pinnatifida+Anisum vulgare + iron filings + Glycyrrhiza uralensis + a herb called Rtsa-a-wa in Tibetan: to be mixed in sugar and fresh butter after being ground into powder. Cures all eye diseases.

Punica granatum + Cinnamomum cassia blume + Elettaria cardamomum + Zingiber officinale + Piper longum + Piper nigrum + black salt + Inula helenium+Capsicum annuum+Tribulus terrestris (fruit): should be powdered and mixed with molasses, or boiled in water and honey until the water evaporates, left to cool and then stirred; can also be boiled with molasses and fresh butter following the same procedure, or boiled with sugar but the sugar should then first be ground into powder and mixed with buffalo milk before being mixed with the powdered ingredients. This medicine cures swelling due to unbalanced phlegm, excessive palpitation of the heart due to irregularity in flow of menstrual blood, kidney diseases, stomach aches and intestinal diseases and is called Se-hbru-bchu-pa (pomegranate syrup with ten ingredients).

5. *Oily medicine*

Gentiana barbata + Scutellaria baicalensis + Odontites serotina + Saussurea alata+Gentiana macrophylla (flower and leaves): these should be powdered and boiled in either cow's or buffalo's milk, then mixed with fresh butter; to this mixture should then be added powdered Quisqualis indica, Crocus sativus, sugar and honey and the whole made into an oily paste. This medicine cures eye diseases, swelling of the body due to unbalanced wind, skin diseases and chronic fever and dries pus and matter. It is called Tig-ta-dgu-ba'i-sman-mar (gentian oil with nine ingredients).

Rhamnus dahuricus (tree)+Gentiana macrophylla + Terminalia chebula + Melia toosendan + Crataegus pinnatifida + Boswellia carteri + Caragana microphylla (fruit) + Abutilon theophrasti (fruit) + Piper longum: boil water and honey together until the water evaporates, then mix in the above powdered ingredients, stir and make into pills. This medicine cures leprosy, gout and rheumatism and is called Seṅ-ldeṅ-dgu-pa'i-sman-mar (rhubarb oil with nine ingredients).

Black aloewood+Santalum album+Areca catechu+Sterculia alata+Vitis vinifera (fruit): boil sugar in water till water evaporates, then mix in the powdered ingredients and make into pills. This medicine cures heart fever and is called Sho-sha-a'i-sman-mar.

For sGog-skya'i-sman-mar (Garlic oil) see p. 85.

Hellebore (root)+Piper longum+hbri (female yak) butter: this mixture enables barren women to conceive and is called Ba-spru-sman-mar (hellebore oil).

6. *Ash-like medicine* (*Thal-sman*)

Pinus silvestris (tree) + Iris dichotoma (root) + yellow myrobalan + Terminalia chebula + Melia toosendan + Crataegus pinnatifida + Paeonia albiflora+ Ustilago (fruit)+Castor-oil plant+salt petre+rock salt+cinnamon +burnt salt +Piper longum +Capsicum annuum +Zingiber officinale + Piper nigrum: should be powdered and mixed with yak's milk, curd, butter, fat and marrow, and the mixture put into an earthen pot, well sealed and bedaubed with clay, and put in the fire until the ingredients inside are burnt into ashes. These ashes are then removed and used as a medicine to cure tumour, diseases of phlegm, dropsy and to enrich the digestive fire.

Gold dust (ash): pure gold is first beaten as thin as the wing of a fly, then cut into bits and ground into powder. To this powder is added brimstone powder, black sesame powder, Linum (stem, leaves and flower) powder and Tsa-la (a salt which is mixed with rock salt to colour it white). Then add water and make into pills, put these in a non-melting metal container, well sealed, and place into the fire until the contents are burnt into ashes. There are a number of varieties of gold dust medicines.

Copper dust (ash): copper is first burnt or heated in the fire, cooled, then beaten very fine, cut into bits and washed in water. Then a paste made of brimstone and Tsa-la soaked in millet wine is smeared on to the copper bits and the whole wrapped in cloth and placed inside a container which is put in the fire until the contents are burnt to ashes. There are a great number of medicines with a copper ash ingredient.

Iron filings dust (ash): mix iron filings with Tsa-la, Terminalia chebula and brimstone, then put this powder into a container and the container in the fire until the contents are burnt into ashes. (Brimstone and Tsa-la should be added in adequate quantities so as to assist burning.)

7. *Concentrated medicine* (*Khan-da*)

Bamboo manna + Crocus sativus + Eugenia caryophyllata + Santalum album+bear's bile (or bile of any other animal): pound the first four ingredients and then mix with the bile; boil the mixture in water for a long time, then strain through a fine cloth and reboil until it becomes concentrated, then make into pills. This medicine cures diseases of fever. There are many medicines made in this way for the cure of diseases of fever.

8. *Medicinal wine*

Mix 1 oz of honey with 6 oz of water and boil down to 2 oz. Then add 1 oz water, stir, add a little yeast and then some Elettaria cardamomum. The mixture should be wrapped in a warm cloth and left to ferment, after which powdered Piper longum, Zingiber officinale and Piper nigrum should be added. A spoonful of this medicine should be taken early in the morning or evening. Cures diseases due to menstrual trouble causing pain in the joints and bones, and diseases of air. There are other varieties of medicine made in this way.

XXII SURGICAL INSTRUMENTS

MODES OF TREATMENT

A. (i) Inhaling medicinal vapour.
(ii) Soaking the body in medicinal water.
(iii) Application of ointments.

B. (i) Bleeding (gtar-ga) or cupping
(ii) Burning (me-btsah).
(iii) Boring a hole (dbug-pa).
(iv) Slitting (hphral-ba).

C. (i) Cutting (gchod-pa).
(ii) Scraping (hdrud-pa).
(iii) Extraction (hbyin-pa).

INSTRUMENTS

1. Instruments used to help locate the afflicted part of the body (to diagnose diseases).
2. Pincers.
3. Sharp-edged small instruments for cutting (scalpels).
4. Spoons.
5. Miscellaneous.

1. *Diagnostic instruments*

There are various instruments used in locating and diagnosing diseases:

(a) For bone fractures: this is a fine, long instrument, about 6 inches in length, of even thickness end to end. (Cf. facing p. 130, diagram no. 16, i x.)

(b) For locating bullets: there are four instruments: (i) is 12 inches long, fine, rounded and of even thickness end to end, one end being shaped like a ball; (ii) is also 12 inches long, fine, rounded and of even thickness end to end, but has one end shaped like a buck wheat, three-edged, the tip being slightly bent on one side; (iii) is similar to (ii) except that the tip is slightly more bent on one side; and (iv) is similar to the others but has one end shaped like a snake's head bent to one side. All four instruments are slender, straight and strong. (Cf. ibid.)

(c) For testing swelling and determining whether the affected part is ripe: this is a square-shaped instrument 8 inches long, hollow, one side being pointed with a hole on the tip the size of the eye of a needle. If the boil or affected part is ripe, pus collects on the tip of the instrument. (Cf. ibid.)

(d) For detecting piles: this instrument is bottle-shaped, oblong, one end being nipple-shaped at the tip. The bottle is 3 inches long and the nipple tip ½ inch. The nipple-tipped end has a hole on the top big enough for a thumb to pass through, and two holes on either side nearer to the tip, large enough for a pea to pass through. The other end of the instrument is open for looking through to detect piles. The instrument is passed through the anus and, should a pile be detected, another instrument is used which has only one hole instead of two: the pile is put into this hole and cut with scissors passed through the open end of the first instrument; melted fresh butter is then applied to the sore. (Cf. ibid. i y.)

2. *Types of pincers*

(a) A broad, short instrument with one end shaped like a lion's head. (Cf. ibid. ii x.)

(b) An instrument with one end (4 inches long) shaped like the beak of a crane. (Cf. ibid.)

(c) This has one end shaped like the beak of a crow. (Cf. ibid.)

All pincers are 18 inches long, with eight-sided handles having the thickness of fingers, one shaped like a hook and the other like a loop. These are used for extracting bullets, etc. from in between bones.

(d) There is another instrument for extracting bullets from in-between the fibre and the skin: this has one tip 8 inches long and shaped like a wild duck's beak. (Cf. ibid. ii y.)

(e) For extracting matter from sores, there is a fine, long instrument, 12 inches in length and hollow throughout so that a wire can be passed through. (Cf. ibid.)

3. *Types of scalpels*

(a) Shaped like the feather of a sparrow, 6 inches in length, with one sharp-edged end: this is used for bloodletting from veins close to the skin. (Cf. ibid. iii x.)

(b) Similar to (a) but sharp-edged both ends: used for bloodletting from throbbing veins. (Cf. ibid.)

(c) Another 6 inch long instrument, with a rounded handle one end and the other end shaped like an axe: this is used for bloodletting from veins close to the bones. (Cf. ibid.)

(d) A similar instrument with a rounded handle and the other end shaped like a sickle, for letting blood from a swollen tongue. (Cf. ibid.)

4. *Types of spoons*

(a) A spoon with a rounded handle, hollow right through, the top shaped like a frog's head and with a hole in it: this is used to remove water from the heart and liver. (Cf. ibid. iii y.)

(b) Similar to (a) but with a top shaped like the tip of a pen: used to remove water from the body, e.g. in dropsy. (Cf. ibid.)

(c) A long spoon with a tip shaped like a bird's beak, slightly bent on one side and hollow right through: used to detect pus in the body. (Cf. ibid.)

(d) A spoon with a rounded handle, the top shaped like a grain of barley, without a hole: used for removing a tumour from the spine. (Cf. ibid.)

(e) A similar spoon but with a top shaped like the head of a frog and sharp, for removing a tumour from the liver, lungs and other organs. (Cf. ibid.)

5. *Miscellaneous instruments*

(a) For cutting bones: an instrument 10 inches long and 2 inches wide, with numerous teeth like a saw. (Cf. p. 130, diagram no. 16, iv x.)

(b) For cutting fibre and veins in sores, there is an instrument shaped like scissors.

(c) For extracting a dead child from the womb, a hook-shaped instrument two spans in length. (Cf. ibid. iv y.)

(d) For extracting stones from the urinary bladder, an instrument two spans in length, with a tip shaped like a snake's head standing erect.

(e) To enable passing of urine where there is an obstruction, an instrument 12 inches long and the thickness of a stem of barley, hollow right through. (Cf. ibid. v x.)

(f) For passing medicine through the anus, an instrument shaped like a trumpet, the base wide enough for a thumb to pass through, narrowing towards the top to an opening just big enough for a pen to go through. Midway around the instrument there is a band. (Cf. ibid. v y.)

(g) For removing bad blood and pus from affected parts of the body, a round copper bowl, 4 inches in diameter. (Cf. ibid.)

XXIII HEALTH RULES

For a long and healthy life, correct diet, good habits and proper medicines are essential. The observance of these rules is called Chu-liṅ in Tibetan. Some of them are given below:

One should live in clean and peaceful surroundings, free from robbers and evil spirits.

Sexual intercourse should be avoided.

The elixir drawn from flowers (i.e. honey) and that drawn from pebbles promote long healthy life and preserve the eyes and the other five sense organs* in good condition.

The following preparation is recommended for cleaning the stomach: Terminalia chebula (fruit) + Melia toosendan (fruit) + rock salt + Piper longum (fruit) + Zingiber officinale (root) + Menyanthes trifoliata (leaves, flower and stem) + Curcuma longa (root) + Equisetum arvense (fruit): these ingredients should be mixed with molasses and then soaked in water.

For curing all diseases of air, such as heart palpitation and mental trouble, thereby promoting good health and longevity, it is recommended to use the following medicine, called sGog-skya-bo'i sman-mar (garlic oil): 11 oz Allium sativum (root) to be pounded into powder and boiled in water until the water evaporates, then mixed with 21 oz of yak's butter, placed into a container and left to ferment for twenty-one days buried in grain.

A medicine which cures all diseases of phlegm, air and bile and promotes a long and healthy life is the following, called 'Bitumen oil' (Brag-shun-sman-mar): it consists of bitumen well ground and mixed with gold, silver and copper ashes and iron filings, and should be taken with food containing plenty of vitamins, such as all species of beans.

The following is good for strengthening the digestive fire and for health and longevity: Capsicum annuum (root), ground into powder and mixed with butter and honey.

One should refrain from eating stale, sour, mouldy or any other harmful food.

If one follows the instructions given in the medical text Phyi-rgyud, one will achieve perfect health within one year.

More details of bchud-leṅ are given in the text called Man-ṅag-rgyud, the third treatise of the rGyud-bzhi.

* Mind is in Buddhism the sixth sense organ.

XXIV DIAGNOSIS OF DISEASES

A doctor should be able to diagnose diseases from their symptoms.

At first the doctor should find out how the patient acquired the disease, e.g. whether he slipped, or something fell on him, or he got wet, or burnt, or spent the night in the open air, etc.

There are fifteen parts in an examination:

1. The five sense organs: ears, nose, tongue, eyes and body.
2. Sputum.
3. Faeces.
4. Vomit.
5. Urine.
6. Blood.
7. The doctor should examine the patient, noting his constitution, eyes, tongue, etc.
8. The doctor should feel the affected parts in the patient's body.
9. The doctor should question the patient as to the pain felt at the present moment in the affected parts.
10. The doctor should take the patient's temperature by feeling his pulse vein.
11. The patient should be asked whether he has suffered from the same disease in the past, and if so when.

XXVI DOCTOR, NURSE AND PATIENT

A good doctor must have knowledge of all five sciences, as well as spiritual knowledge; he should be able to diagnose diseases and perform surgery, and should know how to deal with patients; he should follow the example set by his teachers and must also have practical experience.

A doctor should not look for material gains and must treat all patients alike, without discrimination; he should take every possible care of his patients; the medicines he prepares should be of the best quality.

The person looking after the patient must be one who cares for the patient's welfare and who is able to follow the doctor's directions for the administration of medicine and food. Such a person should also have clean habits.

A patient who complies with the doctor's orders, who is frank with the doctor regarding his disease, who is not afraid of undergoing any treatment but has high hopes of recovering, such a patient has every chance of recovery.

XXVII GENERAL RULES FOR TREATING DISEASES

There are two ways of curing diseases, General and Particular.

1. *General*

When a symptom of any disease appears, one must try to prevent its spread right from the start by taking mild medicines in the form of decoction. If this first step should be overlooked, then the second step would be to take medicines to cause bowel emptying and vomiting, in order to bring out the disease. If one should neglect to take either of these two steps and the disease should become serious, giving rise to other diseases, then one should first take medicines to cure the more serious disease and then the less serious diseases. When on the way to recovery one should take mild medicines to guard against being infected by other diseases.

It is most essential to adopt good, healthy habits.

Each disease has its normal fixed times for accumulation, outbreak and cure, but occasionally a disease will appear at a time other than its usual, and in such cases steps must be taken to have it cured at once, or cure may become impossible.

Medicines should always be taken as prescribed and at the times specified by the doctor: some should be taken before meals, others during the course of the meal and yet others after meals.

2. *Particular*

Particular cures may be divided into three categories:

(i) Where the digestive fire becomes weak, affecting digestion, and is combined with diseases due to unbalanced humours resulting in the spread of disease all over the body: in such cases a medicine must first be taken to draw all the germs* together in one area, to facilitate diagnosis. If the infection is in the upper part of the body, medicine must be taken to cause vomiting, and if it is in the lower part then medicine should be taken to cause bowel emptying. One should not restrain the passing of stool nor suppress vomiting which comes naturally.

(ii) Where diseases due to unbalanced humours are in the course of accumulation before outbreak: in such circumstances proper food and good habits should be adopted to prevent outbreak; food and habits harmful to the condition will result in deterioration and bring about the outbreak of the disease.

* Tibetan: 'bru, literally seed, grain.

(iii) Where a person suffering from a disease due to unbalanced air is then attacked by a disease of phlegm: in such cases air travels to the area where the phlegm disease is accumulating, and vice versa, resulting in the disease becoming serious. If the disease of phlegm is the stronger of the two, then this should be cured first, and after it is cured the disease of air will subside.

XXVIII HOW TO BEGIN THE TREATMENT OF PARTICULAR DISEASES

How to diagnose a disease of air in case of doubt: the patient should be given a soup made of the ankle bone of sheep, bull, etc.; should he obtain some relief and comfort by this, the doctor then knows that it is a disease of air.

How to diagnose a disease of bile in case of doubt: a soup should be prepared from Gentiana barbata, ground and boiled, and given to the patient; if it should give relief, then it is a disease of bile.

How to diagnose a disease of phlegm in case of doubt: give the patient soup made from boiled rock salt, and if it gives relief, then it is a disease of phlegm.

To diagnose if a disease is due to air or blood pressure, should there be doubt, the patient should be given a medicine made up of Sambucus sibirica (tree)+Paeonia albiflora (root)+Zingiber officinale (root)+Sophora flavescens (tree creeper), powdered and boiled down to a high concentration. If this gives relief, the doctor will know the disease.

When the doctor is in doubt whether to give the patient a strong or a mild laxative, being uncertain of the strength of the patient's stomach, then the following laxative would be safe:

Terminalia chebula (fruit) + Melia toosendan (fruit) + Crataegus pinnatifida (fruit)+rock salt, ground into powder and boiled.

To determine whether or not to perform moxa (cautery), a cloth should be dipped in heated oil and placed on the affected part; should the pain be relieved, then it is necessary for the doctor to cauterize (by burning an iron rod till red hot and poking lightly the affected part with it).

To find out whether bloodletting is necessary, cold water or a cold stone should be placed on the affected part. If this gives relief, bloodletting should be performed.

There are various other ways of testing, but such tests should not be overdone and any medicines for testing should be given in small doses.

A doctor should not guess a disease without proper diagnosis. He should only disclose the disease to the patient when he is absolutely sure of his diagnosis. The patient must be told whether he is to recover or not.

It is not proper to give medicines with a cooling effect to a patient suffering from fever which has not yet ripened enough to burst out; such medicine given at this time would cause phlegm to erupt and the fever to worsen. A medicine called Ma-nu-bzhi-thaṅ (peony decoction with four ingredients) should be given to the patient first, to ripen the fever and cause it to burst out; its ingredients are powdered Sambucus sibirica (tree)+Paeonia albiflora (root)+Zingiber officinale (root)+Sophora flavescens. This should then be followed by a medicine with a cooling effect, to bring the fever down.

Bloodletting should not be performed before separating the pure from the impure blood; this is done by giving the patient the medicine called Hbras-bu-gsum-thaṅ which separates good from bad blood, and then bloodletting can be performed.

In cases of disease of phlegm, poison or fever, when the germs have spread all over the body, it is necessary first to administer medicine to gather the germs together, and follow this with another medicine to cure the disease.

XXIX HOW TO IMPROVE AND MAINTAIN GOOD HEALTH

1. By taking nutritious food, good medicines and vitamins.
2. By dieting.

1. A nutritious diet is suitable for people suffering from excessive wind in the constitution, the weak and aged, the under-nourished, those affected with lung disease or insomnia and diseases resulting from it. It is also recommended after excessive bleeding following delivery, and after excessive intercourse. It is particularly important to have a nutritious diet during the spring, when the body becomes weaker.

The types of food recommended are mutton, molasses, sugar, milk, curd, millet drink, etc. These must be complemented by vitamins, exercise and massaging the body with oil, good habits, plenty of sleep and peace of mind. If all these instructions are followed, they will increase the body's resistance to diseases.

An over-nutritious diet, on the other hand, can be harmful for the body and cause complaints such as ulcers, dullness of the mind, frequent passing of urine, phlegm diseases, etc. Medicines must then be taken to reduce excessive fat. Such medicines are:

(i) Vatica lanceaefolia (substance secreted from tree)+bitumen+Sambucus sibirica (tree): to be ground into powder, then mixed into a paste with honey.

(ii) Terminalia chebula (fruit) + Melia toosendan (fruit) + Crataegus pinnatifida (fruit): preparation as for (i) above.

(iii) Honey mixed with powdered salt petre, barley, Crataegus pinnatifida, Equisetum arvense (fruit) and ginger.

2. Dieting is recommended in cases of indigestion, bile diseases due to too much greasy food, stiffness of the limbs, contagious diseases, gonorrhoea, sores inside the stomach, gout, spleen diseases, brain diseases, fever, difficulty in passing urine, diseases of phlegm and bile.

Should one contract any of the above diseases during the winter, one should diet for three days. Persons with a weak constitution would need to diet for a longer period.

XXX HUMORAL PATHOLOGY

For *diseases due to unbalanced air*, the food taken should be heavy, oily and warm. The patient's room should be warm and cosy. Warm clothing and plenty of sleep are essential.

Medicines helpful to such diseases are prepared in the form of a decoction using various ingredients, e.g. butter, essence of meat, millet wine and molasses; or Asafoetida and rock salt, etc. Massaging the body with oil and performing moxa on the crown of the head and base of the neck are also part of the treatment.

Those suffering from *diseases due to unbalanced bile* should be given fresh butter made from cow's and goat's milk, fresh meat of animals found in the hills, curd, fresh vegetables and food without spices but light, cool and well cooked.

Relaxing in a cool place under shady trees, with plenty of fresh air, is also helpful, and so is massaging one's body with sweet-smelling herbs. Medicines taken should be cool, soft, sour and bitter in taste.

For those suffering from *diseases due to unbalanced phlegm*, the food taken should consist of fish, yak meat, flour made from old grain, millet wine and plenty of boiled water, as well as water with ginger added. The food should be light and warm and reasonable quantities should be taken in order to assist easy digestion.

Sleeping during the day is harmful, but sitting in the sun and near the fire is beneficial. Warm clothing should be worn. Medicines taken should be light, rough, acrid and sharp; medicine to cause vomiting in order to bring out the excess phlegm may also be taken. In serious cases of disease of phlegm, moxa is also performed.

XXXI REQUIRED QUALITIES AND DUTIES OF A DOCTOR

1. *Intelligence*

One wishing to become a good doctor must be intelligent, having a deep comprehension, quick understanding and a good memory. He must be able to read and write in order to learn all about medicine and master the medical texts. His teacher must be one who knows all about medicine and is able to explain everything, not hiding any knowledge from the student; an understanding and kind-hearted person and generally knowledgeable in every field. The student should obey and be patient with his teacher, and coordinate with his fellow-students to help one another in their studies and not be lazy.

2. *Compassion*

One wishing to become a good doctor must always think of being helpful to all beings. He must have a sympathetic mind and must not be partial, but treat all alike. He should wish happiness for all and have the desire to obtain enlightenment. One with such a good mind will have no trouble in his medical practice.

3. *Vows*

The eleven vows a doctor must take are:

(i) A person undergoing medical training must have great regard for his Teacher, considering him like a God.

(ii) He must believe in whatever his Teacher teaches him and have no doubt whatsoever in his teachings.

(iii) He must have great respect for the books on medicine.

(iv) He must keep good, friendly relations with classmates, having regard and respect for each other.

(v) He must have sympathy towards patients.

(vi) Secretions of patients he should not regard as filth.

(vii) He must regard the Medicine Buddha and other medical experts as the guardians of medicine.

(viii) He must regard medical instruments as holy objects and keep them properly.

(ix) He must regard medicine as something very precious, something that fulfils all wishes.

(x) He must regard medicine as a deathless nectar.

(xi) He must regard medicine as an offering to the Medicine Buddha and all the other medicine deities.

4. *Practice*

Doctors must have practical experience, being able to use all the medical instruments, and must be expert at, e.g.:

Passing medicine through the anus (Skt. niruha);
Bloodletting (Tib. gTar-ga);
Burning and cautery (Tib. Me-btsah);
Passing spoon inside the body to extract matter (Tib. Thur-ma);
First aid (bandaging affected parts, broken bones, etc.);
Operating.

5. *Bedside manner*

Doctors must have a pleasant nature and be understanding and able to give encouragement and confidence to patients. They must be well versed in medicine and able to diagnose diseases without difficulty. A doctor should be familiar with the customs and usages of the common man, know how to talk and behave, and have some knowledge of religion. He should not be selfish and should have pity for the poor. He should look after a patient well until the patient has fully recovered.

A doctor who has all the above qualities will attain fame, prosperity, etc. A good doctor is like a protector and deliverer of those who are helpless; he is like a representative of the Medicine Buddha and of the lineage of the Teachers of medicine.

6. *Criteria of a good doctor*

A doctor must be of noble birth, or else he will not be respected by people.

A doctor not having a thorough knowledge of the books of medicine will not be able to diagnose diseases, as a blind man cannot recognize gold.

A doctor lacking practical experience is like one taking an unknown road, not knowing where it will take him.

A doctor is no doctor if he does not know how to test urine, veins, etc. to detect diseases.

A doctor who is unable to instruct, advise and communicate with his patient is like a ruler who is unable to make a speech.

A doctor unable to prepare medicines and lacking the required medical instruments is like a soldier going to war without any weapons.

A doctor lacking the necessary qualities of a good doctor is like a demon, in that he takes away life.

Chapters from the Fourth Book of the rGyud-bzhi, called Phyi-rgyud

I EXAMINATION OF PULSE AND VEINS

There are many veins in the human body, but the ones to be examined are those that pulsate, which originate in the heart and carry blood and air together. These veins are like messengers between the doctor and the patient.

General rules for doctors and patients before examination of the vein

On the evening preceding the examination, the patient must refrain from having rich food such as meat, wine, etc. Neither must he exert himself or sit in the hot sun. He must be well rested and must have had light food so as to avoid disturbing the bile, phlegm and air in his constitution, to enable the doctor to make a clear diagnosis. The doctor in turn should be well prepared and relaxed before the examination in order to obtain good results.

If the disease comes suddenly necessitating an urgent examination, then both the doctor and the patient should try to relax just before the examination of the pulse takes place.

The pulse is examined at a spot one inch from the wrist joint. Pulsating veins can be felt at other parts of the body as well, but the wrist is used because it is closest to the vital organs of the body. The reason why the pulsating vein in the neck is not used is that the comparative proximity of the heart and lungs has such an effect on the pulse as to mask the effect produced by other organs. The pulsating vein in the leg is also unsuitable for examination because it is too far from the vital organs of the body.

In examining the pulse one should use the index finger, middle finger and ring finger. (The first is called mts'on, the second kan and the third chhag.) The fingers must be held in a line close to one another yet not touching each other. The index finger must not put too much pressure on the skin; more pressure should be applied by the middle and ring fingers.

Left hand of patient examined by the right hand of the doctor. When examining the pulse, (a) the tip of the index finger on the right side detects heart diseases and on the left intestinal diseases; (b) the tip of the middle finger on the right side detects diseases affecting the spleen, and on the left stomach diseases; and (c) the tip of the ring finger on the right side detects kidney diseases and on the left diseases affecting the seminal vessel.

Right hand of patient examined by the left hand of the doctor. (a) the right tip of the index finger detects lung diseases, the left tip diseases affecting the guts; (b) the right tip of the middle finger detects liver diseases, the left tip diseases due to unbalanced bile; (c) the right tip of the ring finger detects kidney diseases, and the left tip diseases affecting the urinary bladder.

The right-hand pulse should be examined first in the case of female patients, and the left-hand one in the case of males. The reason for this is that the tip of the female heart is tilted towards the right and vice versa with males.

The pulsating vein of the wrist is classified into three types:

(a) Pho-rtsa (male vein type)
(b) Mo-rtsa (female vein type)
(c) Ma-niṅ-rtsa (eunuch vein type, or neutral vein)

The first of these has a strong beat, the second a quick and mild beat and the third a slow, soft beat.

A male having a Mo-rtsa (female type) vein will live long and more daughters than sons will be born to him.

A female having a male type vein (Pho-rtsa) is supposed to acquire wealth, and more sons than daughters will be born to her.

If either one of a couple, or both, have Ma-niṅ-rtsa veins, the couple will have a long and happy life; they will not have children but will be less affected by diseases and will be popular in society.

If a couple both have a male type vein, they will have more sons than daughters, but if they both have a female type vein it will be the other way round.

The pulse must beat five times within the period of inhaling, exhaling and transition: two beats during inhalation, two during exhalation and one beat at the transition point.

The doctor must feel the pulse at length and if the beat remains steady all along, i.e. five beats during inhaling, exhaling and transition, then the patient's health is normal. Should there be more than five beats within the specified period, the patient is suffering from fever, the fever being higher in proportion to the additional beats above normal. If the number of beats reaches ten, the patient is said to be in a serious condition leading to death.

If the number of beats is less than five, the patient is suffering from a cold disease: the fewer beats, the more serious the disease. If there is only one beat, the patient is in a serious condition.

Sometimes it is possible for a normal person to have six, or four, pulse beats within the specified period: this depends on the place and the climatic conditions.

If the pulse feels stiff and hard, the patient is suffering from fever; if it feels hollow and relaxed, this signifies a disease of cold.

The pulse of a person suffering from a disease of cold feels big, and there is much pressure upwards while it pulsates. Even if it is pressed down, the pulse jumps up and down and feels hollow, with an uneven interval between each beat.

The pulse of a person suffering from bile diseases feels fine, hard and strong.

The pulse of a person suffering from a phlegm disease feels low, slow and has an indistinct beat.

The pulse of a person suffering from air and fever feels quick and hollow.

The pulse of a person suffering from phlegm and bile diseases feels as if the beat were coming from deep down, this being due to unbalanced phlegm, and the effect of stiffness is due to unbalanced bile.

The pulse vein of a person suffering from wind and phlegm diseases feels hollow due to unbalanced air, and slow due to unbalanced phlegm.

The pulse vein of a person suffering from high blood pressure feels filled up with a slow beat; the beat is slightly more relaxed than that of a pregnant woman.

The pulse of a person suffering from any virus infection feels as if the beat were oozing out, and the vein feels flat.

The pulse of a person affected with leprosy feels empty and shaky.

The pulse of a person suffering from fever due to overwork and fatigue feels big, with much pressure upwards while beating.

The pulse of a person suffering from fever due to contagious diseases feels quick, and the vein feels thin.

The pulse of a patient suffering from severe pain in the stomach feels as though it were beating at short intervals, it throbs.

The pulse of a person suffering from poisonous infection feels rough, embedded deep inside, which makes it difficult for the doctor because of the deep effect of the beat.

The pulse of a person suffering from meat poisoning feels stiff and quick; the beat comes from deep within.

The pulse of a person suffering from fever within the constitution that has not broken out yet feels thin, with a quick beat; the vein seems to be moving here and there on examination.

The pulse of a person suffering from inflammation of sores feels big, stiff and has a quick beat.

The pulse of a person suffering from hidden fever feels flat and has a deep, strong beat.

II EXAMINATION OF THE URINE

The diet of the patient on the evening before the examination of urine must be controlled: food taken must be mild and not rich; the patient should not restrain thirst. He should not exert himself, but have a good rest and sleep.

Urine passed before midnight should not be tested, since food taken during the day is digested just before midnight and causes the colour of urine to change, thus making it difficult to detect the disease. The first urine passed at dawn is suitable for examination, since its colour is not affected by digestion and by the colour the doctor can detect diseases.

The colour, steam and sediment should be tested. The urine should be kept in a plain container, so that the colour is not affected, and either a stick or straw of white colour must be used for stirring it during examination

On food reaching the stomach it is broken up by the phlegm Myag-byed; then the bile hJu-byed helps the process of digestion and assimilation and the air Me-rlung extracts the nutrition from food. The digested food goes into the white intestines, where it undergoes another process: the thick portion or sediment goes into the urinary bladder through the lower intestines, and the liquid or nutritious portion goes through the stomach to the liver, where it is transformed into blood. In the liver the blood separates into two: the nutritious portion becomes fat and the sediment goes into the gall bladder and becomes bile. The bile separates into two: one portion becomes serum and the sediment goes into the urinary bladder. Therefore sediment or Ku-ya originates from blood and bile.

The sediment in the urine of patients suffering from a disease of fever is thick and plentiful; in diseases of cold it is fine and of a small quantity.

The urine of a normal person free from any infection is white with a yellowish tinge like the colour of freshly-melted butter; it is light, with a bad odour; the steam is normal and remains for a moderate time after the urine is passed; the bubbles in the urine are moderate in quantity; after the odour has disappeared, the sediment is blue with a yellowish tinge, neither thick nor thin: the scum is fine and settles around the edges of the container after the steam and the warmth of the urine have disappeared.

The urine of those suffering from air diseases and of the aged is bluish; of those suffering from bile diseases it is yellowish and of those suffering from phlegm diseases it is whitish.

If the colour of the urine is reddish, this signifies a disease affecting the liver due to excess of blood. If it is indefinite and has a rainbow effect, the patient is suffering from poison.

If the steam or vapour is very dense, making it difficult to identify the colour of the urine, the patient is suffering from high fever; if the steam is not very dense but remains for a long time, this indicates chronic fever: if it is thin and disappears quickly, the patient is said to be suffering from diseases of air, phlegm and cold.

If the smell is rusty, the patient suffers from a disease of air; if it is like the smell of a burnt flower or butter, this indicates a disease of bile; if it has a stale odour, it is a disease of phlegm; urine having the smell of blood indicates blood infection; if the odour is very bad it indicates a disease of fever, and when there is little or no odour at all, this indicates a disease of cold.

If the bubbles formed on the urine are big and bluish, this indicates a disease of air; if small and bluish, a disease of phlegm and if the bubbles are few and quickly disappear this indicates a disease of bile: bubbles of a reddish colour indicate blood infection and rainbow-coloured bubbles indicate poison in the constitution.

If the sediment or Ku-ya looks as though it could be picked up when settled, this signifies a disease of air; if it looks sprinkled it indicates a disease of cold; if it settles on the top this means a disease affecting the heart and lungs, if halfway it indicates diseases affecting parts between the heart and the navel; if it settles below, this signifies diseases affecting the kidneys and intestines, etc.

Scum usually settles on top: if it is fine, it indicates diseases of cold; if thick, diseases of fever and if settled sparingly, tumour.

If the urine is reddish in colour with a smell of rotten leather, this indicates fever. If medicine is then given to cure the fever and has no effect, the colour of the urine remaining unchanged, this indicates death from fever.

If the urine is bluish in colour without smell, bubbles or sediment, this indicates a disease of cold. If the medicine given to cure the disease has no effect, this signifies death.

If the colour of the urine is dark blue, being deeper below than above, with waves on top, this indicates death resulting from a disease of air.

Bibliography of European Works on Tibetan Medicine

I BOOKS AND PAMPHLETS

1. Badmaev, Petr Aleksandrovich, *O sistemie vrachebnoi nauki Tibeta.* [Tibet's system of medicine.] Fasc. I. (No more publ.) St. Petersburg, 1898.
2. Badmaev, Petr Aleksandrovich, *Glavnoe rukovodstvo po vrachebnoi naukie Tibeta Zhud-shi v novom perevodie P.A. Badmaeva s ego vvedeniem, raz'yasnyayushchim osnovy tibetskoi vrachebnoi nauki.* [The principal textbook of Tibetan medicine rGyud-bzhi in a new translation by P.A.B. with his introduction explaining the basic ideas of Tibetan medicine.] St. Petersburg, 1903. [Contains abridged translation of first two books of the rGyud-bzhi.]
3. Badmajeff, Włodzimierz, *Chi—szara—badahan.* Warsaw, 1929.
4. Badmajeff, Włodzimierz, *Chi, Schara, Badahan—Grundzüge der tibetanischen Medizin.* Uebersetzt von Anna Koffler-Harth. Pfullingen, Johannes Baum, 1933?
5. Badmajeff, Włodzimierz, *Medycyna tybetanska, jej istota, cele i sposoby działania.* [Tibetan Medicine, its essence, aims and forms of practice.] Warsaw, 1933.
6. Bergemann, Hans Hugo, *Die philosophischen Grundlagen der lamaistischen Medizin in der Schau des Zahnarztes.* (*Abhandlungen und Aufsätze aus dem Institut für Menschen- und Menschheitskunde, Nr. 54.*) Augsburg, Institut für Menschen- und Menschheitskunde, 1958.
7. Brodowski, Feliks, Badmajeffowie—*Medycyna Tybetu w zetknieciu z cywilizacja zachodu.* [The Badmaevs—Tibetan Medicine in contact with Western civilization.] Warsaw, 1932, illus.
8. Burang, Theodor (pseudonym for Theodor Illion), *Tibeter über das Abendland.* Salzburg, Igonta Verlag, 1947. (pp. 139–210 are part III: Wie heilt der Tibeter Krankheiten?)
9. Burang, Theodor, *Tibetische Heilkunde.* Zurich, Origo Verlag, 1957.
10. Filchner, Wilhelm, *Ein Beitrag zur Geschichte des Klosters Kumbum.* Berlin, E. S. Mittler, 1906, illus. (pp. 90–2 on Medical College.)
11. Filchner, Wilhelm, *Kumbum Dschamba Ling. Ein Ausschnitt aus Leben und Lehre des heutigen Lamaismus.* Leipzig, F. A. Brockhaus, 1933, illus. (Chapter 18 on pp. 362–75: Von der Heilkunde und den praktischen Lebensregeln des Lamaismus; also Notes on pp. 519–28.)
12. Francke, August Hermann, *Tibetische Hochzeitslieder.* (*Schriften-Reihe Kulturen der Erde. Material zur Kultur- und Kunstgeschichte aller Völker. Abteilung: Textwerke.*) Hagen i. W. and Darmstadt, Folkwang-Verlag, 1923, illus. (On pp. 12, 45, 46, 51 and 52 verses on the worship of medicine gods.)

13. GAMMERMAN, Adel' Fedorovna and SEMICHOV, Boris Vladimirovich, *Slovar' Tibetsko-latino-russkikh nazvanii lekarstvennogo rastitel'nogo syr'ia.* [Dictionary of the Tibetan, Latin and Russian names of medicinal plants.] Ulan-Ude, Akademiia Nauk SSSR, Sibirskoe Otdelenie, 1963.
14. GOULD, Sir Basil, and RICHARDSON, Hugh, *Medical vocabulary. sMon dań nad la gtogs pa'i miń ts'ig dByin Bod shan sbyur ñer mkho bzhugs so.* Kalimpong, G. Tharchin, 1968.
15. HUARD, Pierre, *La médecine tibétaine.* Paris, Latéma, n.d., col. illus.
16. HUC, Évariste Régis, *Souvenirs d' un voyage dans la Tartarie, le Thibet et la Chine pendant les années 1844, 1845 et 1846.* 2 vols. Paris, A. Le Clerc. 1st ed. 1850, 2nd ed. 1853. (Vol. II, pp. 116, 142–3 and 178–81 in both editions describe medical education at monastery of Kumbum and botanical excursion.)
17. HUEBOTTER, Franz, *Beiträge zur Kenntnis der chinesischen sowie der tibetisch-mongolischen Pharmakologie.* Berlin–Vienna, Urban & Schwarzenberg, 1913, illus.
18. HUEBOTTER, Franz, *Chinesisch-tibetische Pharmakologie und Rezeptur.* Ulm-Donau, K. F. Haug, 1957, illus.
ILLION, Theodor—See Nos. 8 and 9.
19. KORVIN-KRASINSKI, P. Cyrill von, *Die tibetische Medizinphilosophie. Der Mensch als Mikrokosmos.* (*Mainzer Studien zur Kultur- und Völkerkunde, Band 1. Veröffentlichungen des Institutes für Völkerkunde an der Johannes-Gutenberg-Universität in Mainz/Rhein.*) Zurich, Origo, 1953, 2nd ed. with second introd. by W. A. Unkrig (1964), diagr. (Apart from the introductions, this book deals with Mongolian Medicine.)
20. LANDOR, Arnold Henry Savage, *In the forbidden land.* London, W. Heinemann, 1898, 2 vols, illus. (Vol. I, pp. 302–16 deal with Tibetan Medicine.)
21. LAUFER, Heinrich, *Beiträge zur Kenntnis der tibetischen Medizin.* Berlin, Unger; Leipzig, Harrassowitz, 1900, 2 vols.
22. POZDNEEV, Aleksei Matveevich, *Uchebnik tibetskoi meditsiny. S mongol'skago i tibetskago pereved A.P.* [Textbook of Tibetan Medicine. Translated from the Mongolian and Tibetan.] (Mongolian and Russian parallel translation of the first two books of the rGyud-bzhi.) St. Petersburg, Imperial Academy of Sciences, 1908, Vol. I, no more publ., illus.
23. REHMANN, *Beschreybung einer tibetanischen Handapotheke, ein Beitrag zur Kenntnis der Arzneikunde des Orients.* St. Petersburg, 1811.
24. TUCCI, Giuseppe, *To Lhasa and beyond. Diary of the Expedition to Tibet in the year MCMXLVIII with an Appendix on Tibetan Medicine and Hygiene,* by R. Moise (pp. 98–100, 163–76). Translated by Mario Carelli from the original *A Lhasa e oltre* of 1950. Rome, Istituto Poligrafico dello Stato, 1956, illus.
25. UKHTOMSKII, Esper Esperovich, *Prince, Puteshestvie Gosudaria Imperatora Nikolaia II na vostok v 1890–1891.* [Travels to the East of the Emperor Nikolai II during 1890–91.] Leipzig, F. A. Brockhaus, 1893–9, 6 vols. (In Vol. I, part 2, of 1894, on p. 285 illus. showing Tibetan doctors.)
26. UL'YANOV, Dambo, *Podstrochnyi perevod I-i chasti Tibetskoi Meditsiny 'Zavi-dzhyud'* [Interlinear translation of the first part of Tibetan Medicine rTsa-ba'i rGyud, i.e. the First Book of the rGyud-bzhi.] St. Petersburg, 1901, illus.
27. UL'YANOV, Dambo, *Pervaya chast' Tibetskoi meditsiny Zavi-dzhyud ili Malliga* [i.e. *Mālikā*] *chetki iz goluboi lazuri, raz'yasnyayushchaya chetyre razsuzhdenie, ukrashennyya mneniem Man-ly (Bud-dy) kommentatora Sang-dzhi-Dzhamtso* [First part of Tibetan Medicine rTsa-ba'i rGyud and pieces from the Lapis-lazuli Rosary explaining the Four

Treatises which are adorned by the explanations of the Master of Medicine (Buddha), the Commentator Saṅs-rgyas rGya-mts'o.] 2nd ed. St. Petersburg, 1903, illus.

28. VĀGBHAṬA, *Aṣṭāṅgahṛdayasaṃhitā. The first five chapters of its Tibetan Version.* Edited and rendered into English along with the original Sanskrit by Claus Vogel. (*Abhandlungen für die Kunde des Morgenlandes XXXVII, 2.*) Wiesbaden, F. Steiner, 1965, with 1 facsim.

29. VEITH, Ilza, Medizin in Tibet. Leverkusen, Bayer, 1960, col. illus.

30. WADDELL, Laurence Austine, *Lhasa and its mysteries.* London, John Murray, 1905, illus. (pp. 140–4 and 376–9 on Medicine; illus. facing p. 340 stone small-pox edict at Lhasa, facing p. 378 physician feeling three pulses.)

31. WISE, Thomas Alexander, *Review of the history of Medicine.* London, Churchill, 1867, 2 vols. (Vol. II, pp. 400–50 on Tibetan Medicine.)

II ARTICLES

32. BADMAJEFF, Włodzimierz, Tibetanische Medizin. Uebersetzt von Anna Koffler-Harth. *Atlantis* (Leipzig), 1935, **7**, 45–6.

33. BANERJI, Śārada Prasād, A note on the illustrations of the surgical instruments of Tibet. *J. Buddh. Text Soc. India* (Calcutta), 1894, **2**, Part 3, Proceedings, ix–x, illus.

34. BARBAROSSA, Carlo and BARTOLOMEI, Giovanni di, Gozzo endemico e trattamento della sifilide nel Tibet e nel Butan alla fine del 1700. *Pag. Stor. Med.*, 1970, **14**(2), 30–7.

35. BEIGEL, Hermann, Ein Beitrag zur Medizin des Tibetanischen Buddhaismus. *Wiener med. Wochschr.*, 1863, **13**, cols. 507–8, 523–4. (Extracts on Medicine from H. and R. Schlagintweit: Results of a scientific mission to India and High Asia, 1861.)

36. BERGEMANN, Hans Hugo, Manramba: Der tibetische Arzt, seine Ausbildung und seine Praxis. *Z.M.*, July–August 1943, 200–2, 219–21, illus. (The periodical is given by initials only even in Dr. Bergemann's own bibliography to item No. 6.)

37. BERGEMANN, Hans Hugo, Die Anatomie des Kopfes und der Mundhöhle in der tibetischen Medizin des 17. Jahrhunderts. *Blätter f. Zahnheilkunde*, (Zurich), 1967, **28**, 135.

38. BERGEMANN, Hans Hugo, A tibeti gyógyító tudomány történetéböl (Hungarian). [From the history of Medicine in Tibet.] *Orvosi Hetilap*, 1968, **109**, 1885–7, illus.

39. BRAMLEY, M. J., Some account of the bronchocele or goitre of Nipal, and of the Cis- and Trans-Himalayan regions. *Transactions of the medical and physical Soc. of Calcutta*, 1833, **6**, 181–264. (On Tibet pp. 207–8, 227.)

40. CAMPBELL, A., Notes on Eastern Thibet. *Phoenix* (London), 1871, **1**, no. 7, 83–4, 107–11, 142–5. (Paragraph on diseases on p. 145.)

41. CSOMA DE KÖRÖS, Alexander, Analysis of a Tibetan medical work (i.e. contents table of the rGyud-bzhi). *J. Asiatic Soc. Bengal*, 1835, **4**, 1–20.

42. DESGODINS, Abbé (Lithograph of Tibetan doctors in letter on his Notes Ethnographiques sur le Thibet), *Ann. Extrême Orient* (Paris), 1879–80, **2**, 10–12.

43. FRANCKE, August Hermann, Uebersetzung eines Briefes aus Turfan, wahrscheinlich aus dem 8. Jahrhundert, der von einem Krankheitsfall berichtet. *Sudhoffs Arch. Gesch. Med.*, 1925, **17**, 198–9. Original reproduced in A.H.F., Tibetische Handschriftenfunde aus Turfan, *Sitz. preuss. Akad. Wiss.*, 1924, 5–20, on plate III.

ILLION, Theodor, see No. 56.

44. JACQUOT, Félix, La Tartarie et le Tibet. Topographie et climat. Hygiène. Médecine. *Gaz. méd. de Paris*, 1854, 3e sér., **9**, 607–12, 643–9, 671–6; 1855, 3e sér., **10**, 421–7.
45. KIRILOV, N. V., The present importance of Tibetan Medicine as part of the Lamaistic doctrine (Russian). *Vestnik obshchestvennoi gigieny, sudebnoi i prakticheskoi meditsiny* (St. Petersburg), 1892, **15**, 95–121.
46. LALOU, Marcelle, Texte médical tibétain. *J. Asiatique*, 1941–2, **233**, 209–11, illus.
47. LALOU, Marcelle, Fiefs, poisons et guérisseurs. *J. Asiatique*, 1958, **246**, 157–201. (Tibetan text and French translation of a few fragments.)
48. LAUFER, Berthold, kLu 'Bum bsDus pai sÑiṅpo. Eine verkürzte Version des Werkes von den hunderttausend Nāgas. Ein Beitrag zur Kenntnis der tibetischen Volksreligion. *Mém. Soc. Finno-Ougr.*, 1898, **11**, i–vii (1–20), 1–120. (Religious work marginally concerned with Medicine.)
49. LEKARZ TYBETANSKI (Polish periodical) ['The Tibetan doctor'], 1932–6. Continued as: *Medycyna syntetyczna* [Synthetic Medicine], a quarterly journal edited by Włodzimierz Badmajeff, 1937–? (All in Polish except Nr. 3/4 (1938) which contains contributions in German, English and French, including a bibliography of 107 titles mainly on Indian Medicine.)
50. MASSELOT, F., La médecine thibétaine, vue par la père Huc, prêtre missionaire de la congrégation de Saint-Lazare (1842). *Presse médicale*, 1959, **67**, 800.
51. MORSE, William Reginald, Tibetan Medicine. *J. West China Border Res. Soc.*, 1926–9, **3**, 114–33, illus. (Extremely ignorant and biased.)
52. MUELLER, Reinhold Franz Gustav, Ueber Votive aus Osttibet (Kin-tschwan). *Anthropos*, 1923/4, **18–19**, 180–8, illus.
53. MUELLER, Reinhold Franz Gustav, Die Krankheits- und Heilgottheiten des Lamaismus. Eine medizingeschichtliche Studie. *Anthropos*, 1927, **22**, 956–91, illus.
54. MUELLER, Reinhold Franz Gustav, Die Heilgötter des Lamaismus. *Sudhoffs Archiv Gesch. Med.*, 1927, **19**, 9–26, illus.
55. MUKHERJEE, Girindra Nath, The Tibetan surgical instruments. *J. Ayurveda* (Calcutta), 1933, July Number, 5–15, illus.
56. NOLLING, Theodor (pseudonym for Theodor Illion), Lamaistische Zaubermedizin: Die drei Essenzen im menschlichen Körper und die vierhundert Heilpräparate des Tibet-Arztes. *Berliner illus. Ztg.*, 1943, Nr. 42, 499–500.
57. OLSCHAK, Blanche Christine, The art of healing in ancient Tibet. *Ciba Symposium*, 1964, **12**, 129–34, illus.
58. ROCK, J. F., Contributions to the shamanism of the Tibetan-Chinese borderland. (Includes descriptions of exorcisms of disease demons.) *Anthropos*, 1959, **54**, 796–818, illus.
59. ROCKHILL, William Woodville, The Lamaist ceremony called 'making of mani pills'. *J. Amer. oriental* Soc. (New Haven), Proc. f. 1888 publ. in 1890, **14**, Meeting Oct.–Nov. at Philadelphia, xxii–xxiv.
60. ROWNTREE, Cecil, Surgery in Thibet. *Ethnologica Cranmorensis* (Chislehurst Ethnological Museum), 1938, Nr. 3, 11–13, illus.
61. SAMSON, Otto William, Prints of popular gods in China and some parallels in Tibet and India. *Actes VIe Congr. int. Sci. anthrop. ethnol.* (Paris) (held in 1960, publ. in 1964), vol. **2**, part 2, 475–8.
62. SCHIEFNER, Franz Anton, Ueber das Bon-po Sutra: 'Das weisse Nāga-Hunderttausend'. (With a preface by W. Grube.) *Mém. Acad. Imp. St. Petersb.*, 1880, 7 sér., **28**, I–IV, 1–86. (Diseases as the result of evil deeds.)

63. SEMIČOV, Boris Vladimirovič, Die tibetische Medizin bei den Buryaten. Die burjatisch-mongolische Expedition des Botanischen Gartens der Russischen Akademie der Wissenschaften. *Janus*, 1935, **39**, 1–36, illus.
64. SUDHOFF, Karl, Die anatomischen Ganzfiguren in tibetanischer Ueberlieferung. *Sudhoffs Arch. Gesch. Med.*, 1914–15, **8**, 143–5, illus.
65. TERRACINA, S., Spunti medici in due resoconti di spedizioni nel Tibet e nel Nepal. (Expeditions by G. Tucci in 1950 and 1953.) *Riv. Stor. Med.*, 1960, **4**, 217–34.
66. TIBETAN anatomical chart. *Brit. med. J.*, 1923 (i), 530, illus.
67. TIBETAN trap for epidemics. *MD med. Newsmag.*, 1967, **11** (2), 161–3, illus.
68. UNKRIG, Wilhelm A., Ein eigenartiges Kapitel mittelasiatischer Lebensweisheit. Nach mongolischen Quellen. *Braunschweiger G-N-C-Monatsschrift*, 1928, **15** (9–10), 364–72, illus. (Contains translation of one chapter of the rGyud-bzhi.)
69. UNKRIG, Wilhelm A., Zur Gegenwartswertung der lamaistischen Heilkunde und über ihr Instrumentarium. *Medizinische Welt*, 1934, 139–43, illus.
70. UNKRIG, Wilhelm A., Das Kapitel vom praktischen Arzt. Eine Uebersetzung aus dem Mongolischen. *Fortschritte der Med.*, 1934, **52**, Nr. 16, 359–63.
71. UNKRIG, Wilhelm A., Zur Terminologie der lamaistischen Medizin, besonders ihrer Arzneien. *Forschungen u. Fortschritte* (Berlin), 1936, **12** (20/21), 265–6.
72. VOGEL, Claus, On Bu-ston's view of the eight parts of Indian Medicine. (Bu-ston was a Tibetan historian.) *Indo-Iranian J.*, 1963, **6**, 290–5.
73. WADDELL, Laurence Austine, Ancient anatomical drawings preserved in Tibet. *Asiatic quart. Rev.*, 1910, **30**, 336–40.
74. WADDELL, Laurence Austine, Ancient Indian anatomical drawings from Tibet. *J. roy. Asiat. Soc.*, 1911, (i), 207–8.
75. WALSH, E. H. C., The Tibetan anatomical system. *J. roy. Asiat. Soc.*, 1910, (ii), 1215–45, illus.

PLATE No. 1

In the body there are 77 main bloodletting veins, and 112 other veins which are not used for bloodletting (see pp. 37–42). The bloodletting veins shown in the diagram are Nos. 1, 2, 3, 5, 7, 8, 15, 16, 27, 31, 32, 38, 39, 41, 42.

Starting from the head

1. mTs'ogs-gsaṅ, 'concealed likeness?' vein
2. gSer-mduṅ, golden spear vein
3. lTag-ral, back of the neck hair vein
4. sMin-dkyel, middle space vein
5. Mig-rtsa, eye vein
6. hPhred-nyal, temple vein
7. mThoṅ-rtsa, chest vein
8. Mur-goṅ-hphar-rtsa, cheek moving vein
9. mDzod-spu chhuṅ, little fine hair vein
10. Myur-ba, swift vein
11. hPhar-rtsa, movement vein
12. Me-hi hkhor-lo, fire wheel
13. bLta-rtsa, examination vein
14. bLa-rtsa, life vein
15. sNod-ka, hand vein
16. sGaṅ-rtsa, hill vein
17. rLuṅ-rtsa-hi hkor-lo, air vein wheel
18. A-so-li-ka, (from Sanskrit Asurika) heart vein
19. Au-zur-kha-hkhal, thread vein
20. rNyul-hdu, silver vein
21. Duṅ-bud, perspiration junction vein
22. dÑul-gyi hbu-ru gzer-hdra, silver stud vein
23. gLo-bu zer-mgo, nail stud vein
24. gLo-bu zaṅ-ma rdo, lung vein
25. Nu-rtsa a-loṅ skor-hdra, round ear-ring breast vein
26. Srog-rtsa, life vein
27. Pho-rtsa, stomach vein
28. Pho-rtsa ka-ba, stomach pillar vein
29. sBrul-mig, snake's eye vein
30. mKhal-rtsa rus-zhen, kidney vein
31. Loṅ-rtsa, lower intestine vein
32. rGyu-rtsa, intestine vein
33. Sam-se-rtsa, seminal vessel vein
34. mKhal-rtsa rkaṅ-hdegs, thigh-yoke kidney vein
35. mChher-pa-hi rtsa nag, black spleen vein
36. gNyan-goṅ chhu-yi hkhor-lo, water circle vein
37. sGab-rtsa nag-po, hollow of the knee vein
38. gDon-rtsa, front vein
39. mKhris-rtsa skya-riṅ, yellow bile vein
40. gSer-rtsa ka-gduṅ, golden pillar vein
41. Loṅ-rtsa, bulging veins
42. Yob-goṅ, instep vein
43. Nan-loṅ-lchags-kyi sran-ma, iron pressure ankle vein
44. bZhag-hdra mthil-hdrog, sole vein

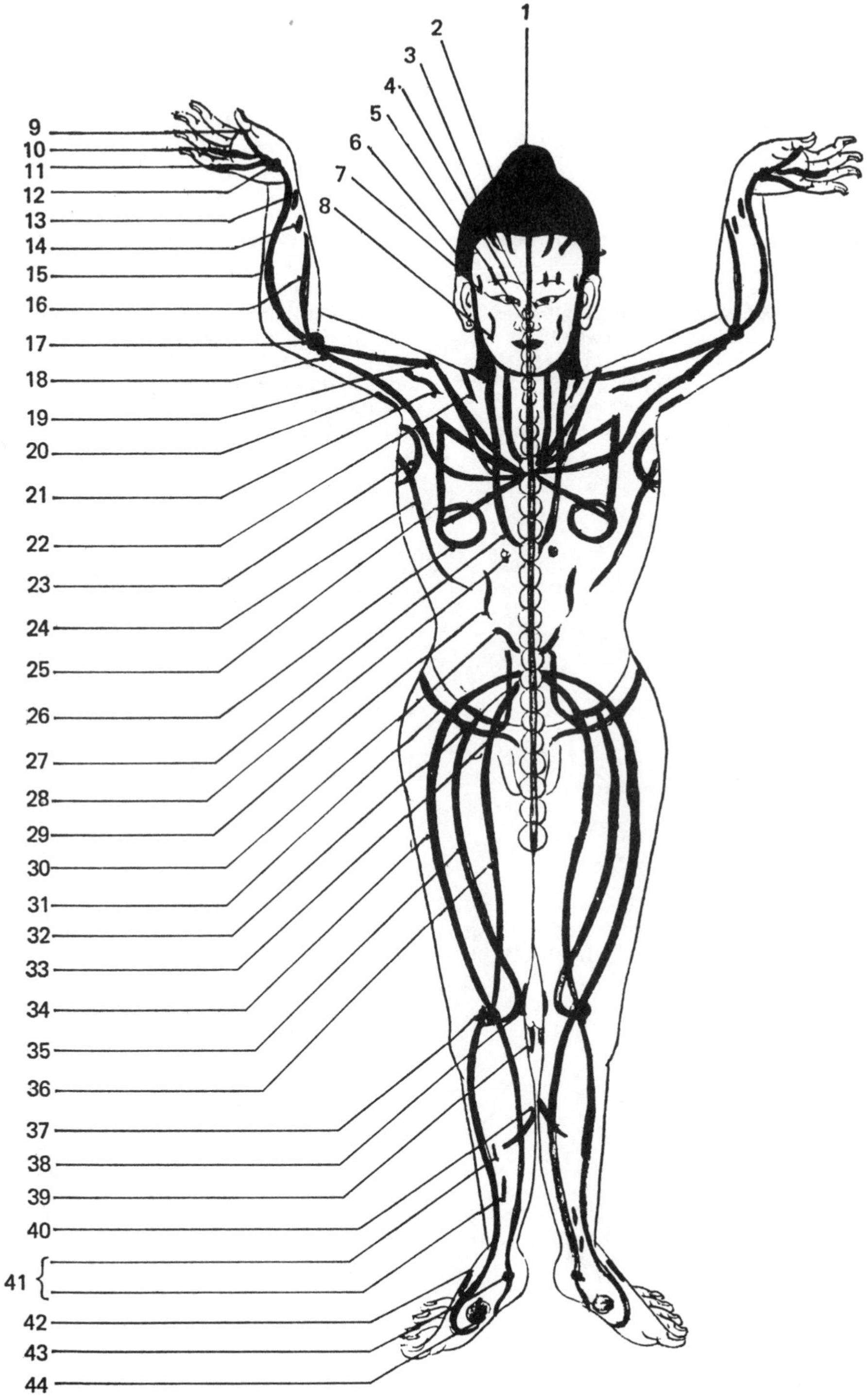

1
2
3
4
5
6
7
8
9
10
11
12
13
14
15
16
17
18
19
20
21
22
23
24
25
26
27
28
29
30
31
32
33
34
35
36
37
38
39
40
41
42
43
44

PLATE No. 2

The growth of the vein system from the central point at the navel and the growth of the various wheels (see pp. 32–7).

1. Ts'aṅ-pa-hi skud-pa, threads of Brahma
2. sPyi-bo-hi hkhor-lo, crown wheel
3. mGrin-pa-hi hkhor-lo, throat wheel
4. sNyiṅ-ga-hi hknor-lo, chest wheel
5. lTe-ba-hi hkhor-lo, navel wheel
6. gSaṅ-gnas hkhor-lo, private parts wheel
7. rKaṅ-pa-hi rtsa-bo-chhe, large thigh vein
8. Byin-kyog, calf bend
9. rTa-mthur, horse rein
10. gSer-rtsa-ka-duṅ, golden pillar vein
11. rGyu-rtsa, base vein
12. Yob-goṅ rtsa, instep vein

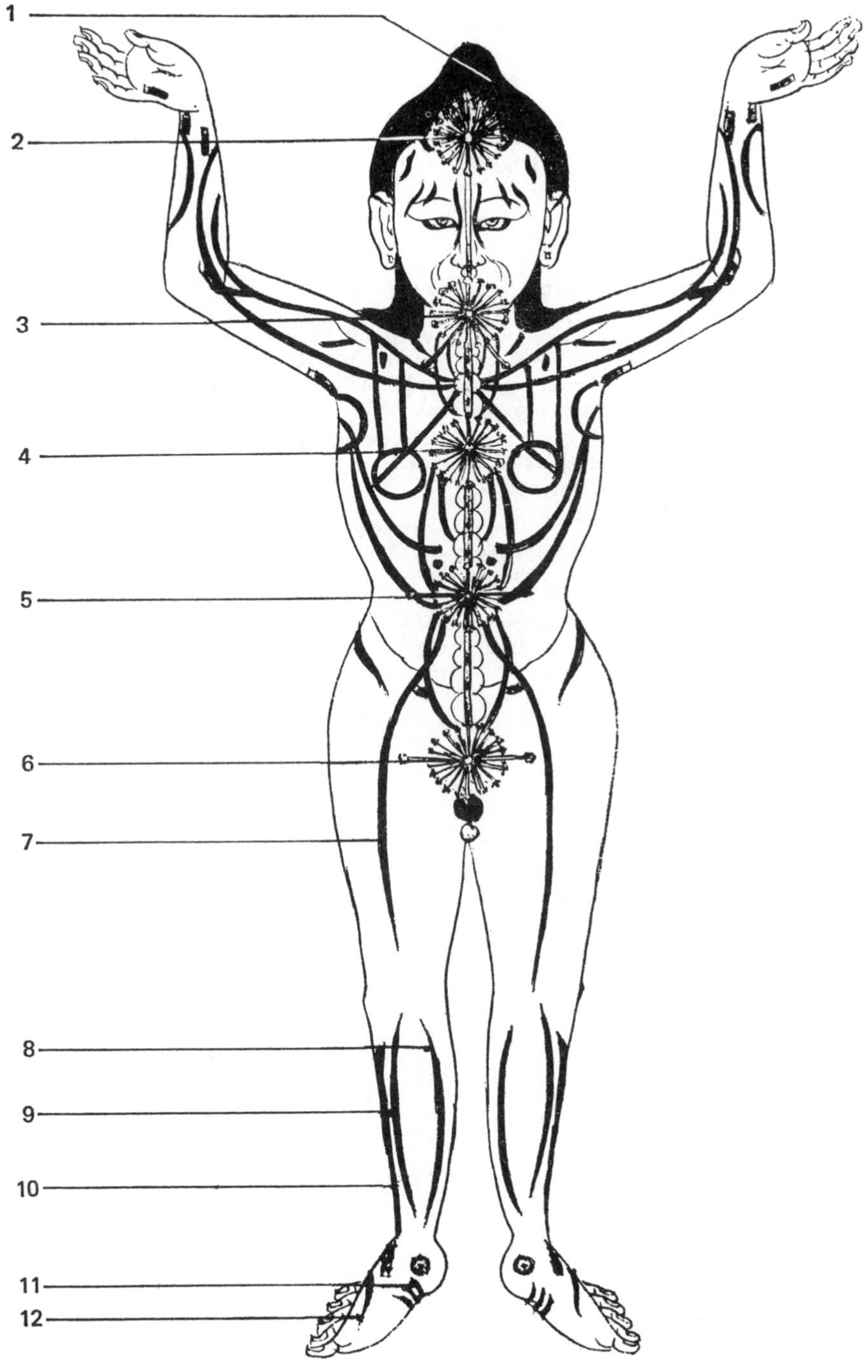
1
2
3
4
5
6
7
8
9
10
11
12

PLATE No. 3

Conciousness veins:

1. sGo-lṅa-hi rnam-shes rgyu-ba-hi rtsa, vein connected with the consciousness of the five sense doors
2. Nyon-moṅs-pa-hi-yid rgyu-ba-hi rtsa, vein connected with the consciousness of one's faults
3. Yid-kyi rnam-shes rgyu-ba-hi rtsa, vein connected with mental consciousness
4. Kun-gzhi rnam-shes rgyu-ba-hi rtsa, vein connected with the store consciousness
5. Yid-bzaṅ-ma rnam-shes rgyu-ba-hi rtsa, vein connected with transcendental consciousness

Each of these five veins corresponds to a certain type of consciousness. These five types of consciousness are also in the Tantric Teaching of the Kālachakra associated with these five veins. Tibetan Medicine and Religion have this association in common.

The sGo-lṅa-hi vein branches off to the front and corresponds to the five sense consciousnesses of seeing, hearing, smelling, tasting and touching. The Nyon-moṅs-pa-hi vein branches off towards the back and is connected with the ordinary, worldly ego-producing consciousness. The Yid-kyi rnam-shes rgyu-ba-hi rtsa branches off on the left and corresponds to the mind consciousness that registers incoming impressions. The Kun-gzhi rnam-shes rgyu-ba-hi rtsa branches off on the right hand of the subject, not as seen by the reader. This is true of all Tibetan drawings, probably because they are often connected with instructions to identify with the figure drawn. It corresponds to the Store Consciousness, Sanskrit Ālayavijñāna, a latent reservoir of all the memory traces of past lives. The Yid-bzaṅ-ma is the vein at the heart and corresponds to Transcendental Consciousness.

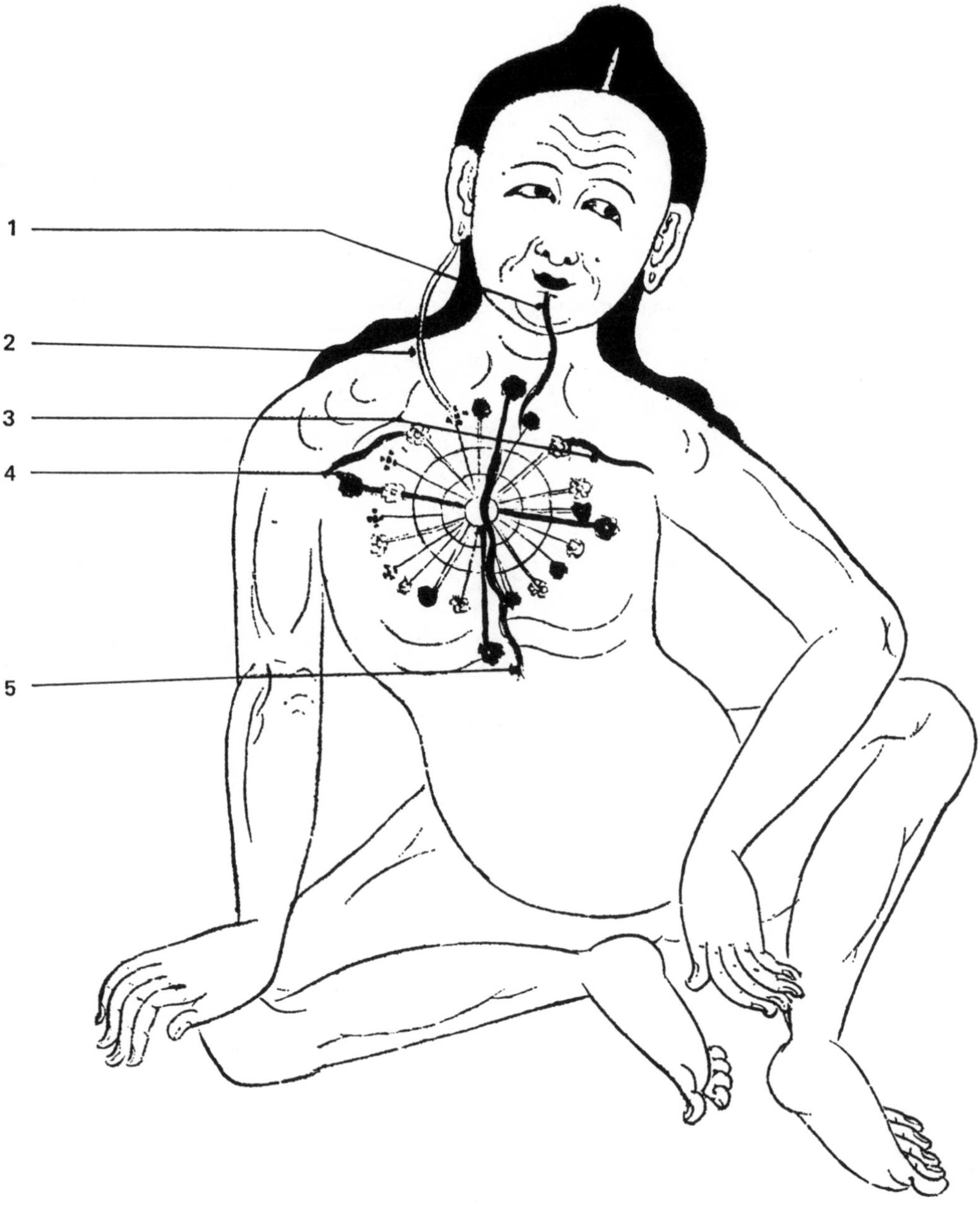

1
2
3
4
5

PLATE No. 4

The starting points and pathways of the veins from the vertebrae to the five principal inner organs and from there upwards and downwards to the rest of the body.

1. Re-thag bzhi, four rope vein
2. Au-zur khug-pa, upper edge section
3. Kun-rgyug, continuous running vein
4. mKhris-pa sha-riṅ, long bile vein
5. Ru-chuṅ, small horn
6. mKhris-rtsa gser-gyi ka-ba, golden bile pillar
7. gZer-mgo, ray-head
8. sṄon-bu, blue vein
9. gLo-ma-naṅ-rgyug, inner lung vein
10. mChher-rtsa-bya-rkaṅ, bird's leg spleen vein
11. gLo-ma grog-rked, lung vein narrow as an ant's waist
12. gLo-ma sge-dor, lung vein
13. mKhal-ma-hi rtsa-nag, black kidney vein
14. sNag-chhen, great vein
15. mKhal-rtsa rkaṅ-hdegs, thigh yoke vein
16. mChher-pa-hi rtsa-nag, black spleen vein

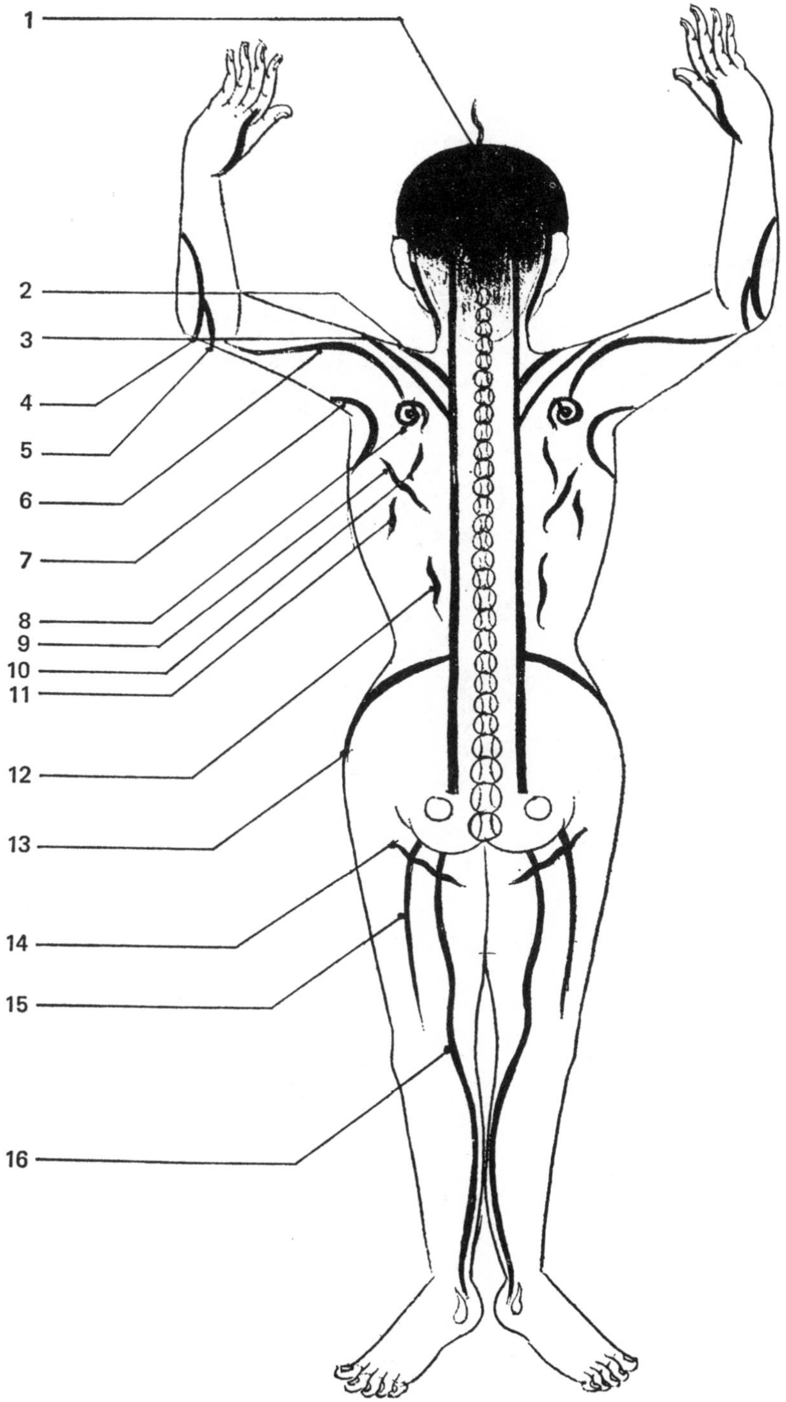

1
2
3
4
5
6
7
8
9
10
11
12
13
14
15
16

PLATE No. 5

The veins connected with the organs of the body:

1. sMin-dbus, mature centre
2. gSer-mduṅ, golden spear
3. sMin-hjug, mature entrance
4. rNa-rtsa, ear vein
5. Ratna, jewel vein
6. rTse-nag, black point vein
7. rTse-hdra, point-like vein
8. dPuṅ-rtsa, shoulder vein
9. Pho-ba-hi ra-rtsa, stomach vein
10. Pho-mts'an hgram-rtsa, male organ vein

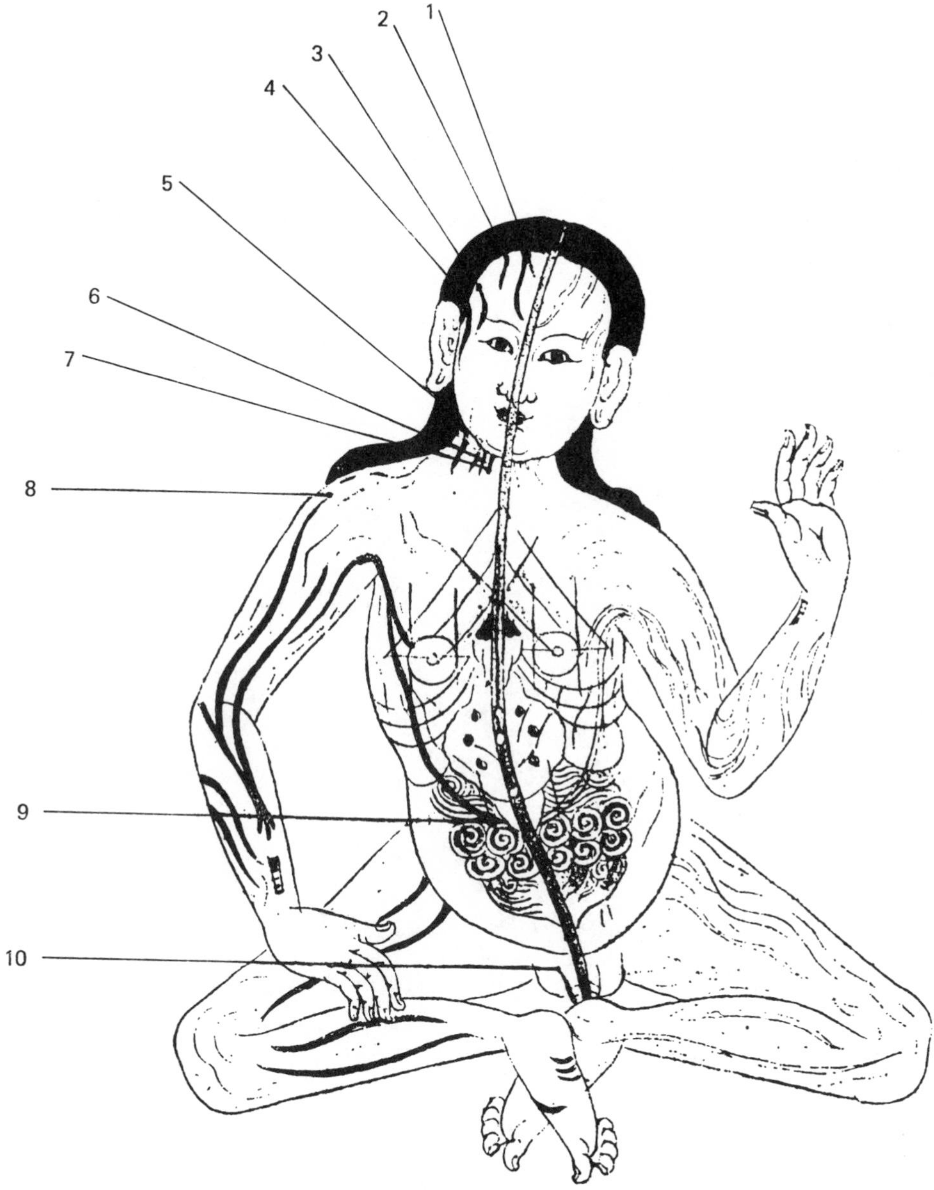
1
2
3
4
5
6
7
8
9
10

PLATE No. 6

The skeleton with the same veins as in Plate 5.

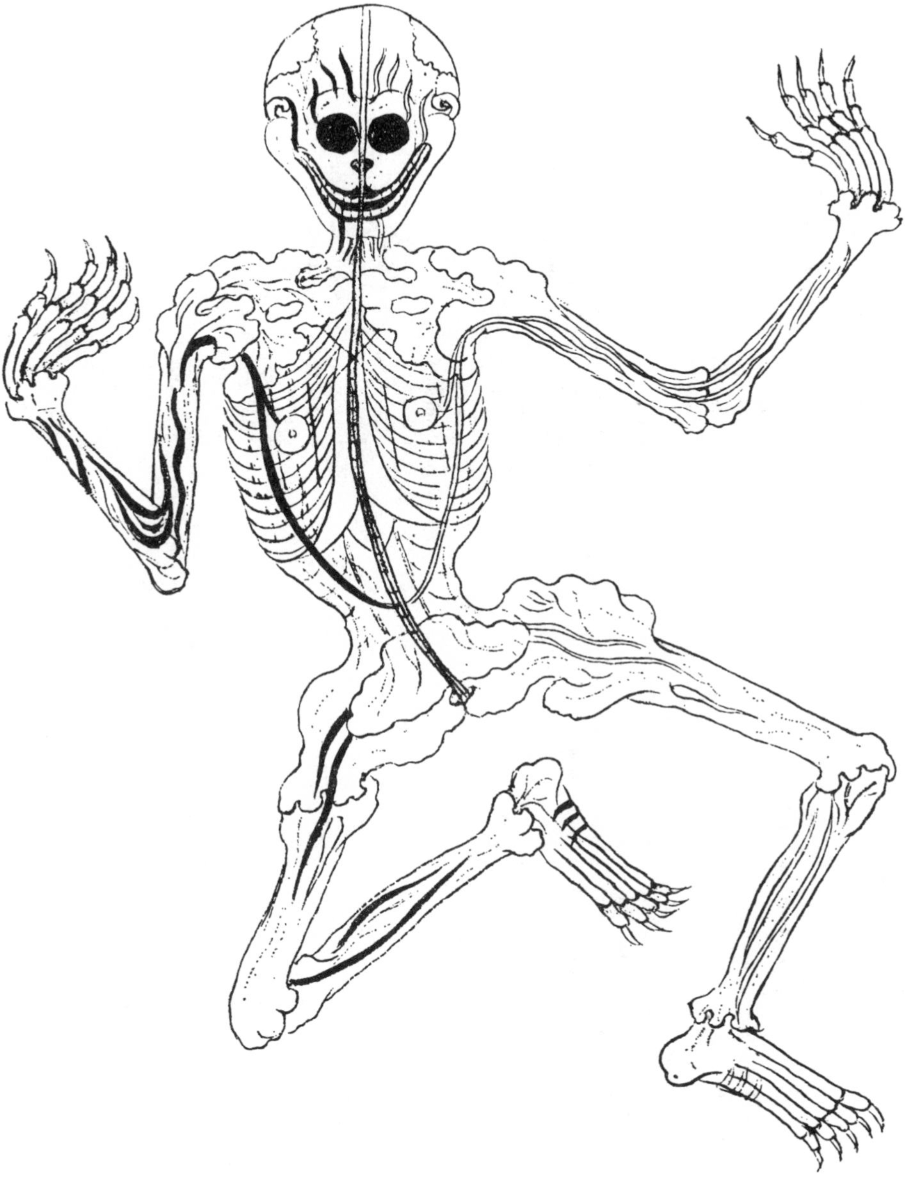

PLATE No. 7

Six bloodletting veins appearing at the back of the body:

1. rNa-ba-hi-G'on-Shiṅ, ear tree
2. lTag-ral, back of the head hair vein
3. Bad-kan sha-riṅ, long phlegm vein
4. mKhris-pa sha-riṅ, long bile vein
5. rGyab-rtsa grug-hdus, group-supporting vein
6. Byin-skyog, calf bend

PLATE No. 8

Front view of Plate No. 7: the most usual of the ninety bloodletting veins except 12, 18, 20, which are non-bloodletting veins.

1. dKral-rtsa, top vein
2. gSer-mduṅ, golden spear
3. sNa-rtsa, nose vein
4. Mig-rtsa, eye vein
5. lTag-rtsa, vein leading to the back of the neck
6. Mur-goṅ-hphar-rtsa, jaw-movement vein
7. rTse-nag, black point vein
8. mThoṅ-rtsa, chest vein
9. sGaṅ-rtsa, hill vein
10. Ru-thuṅ, short horn
11. dPuṅ-rtsa, shoulder vein
12. rNyul-hdu, perspiration vein
13. Pho-ba-hi ra-rtsa, stomach vein
14. brLa-naṅ rtsa-bo-chhe, large inner thigh vein
15. sGab-rtsa, shin vein
16. gDoṅ-rtsa, front vein
17. Byin-gzhug, calf vein
18. bZhag-hdra, inside of foot vein
19. rGyu-rtsa, base vein
20. mThil-hphrog, sole vein

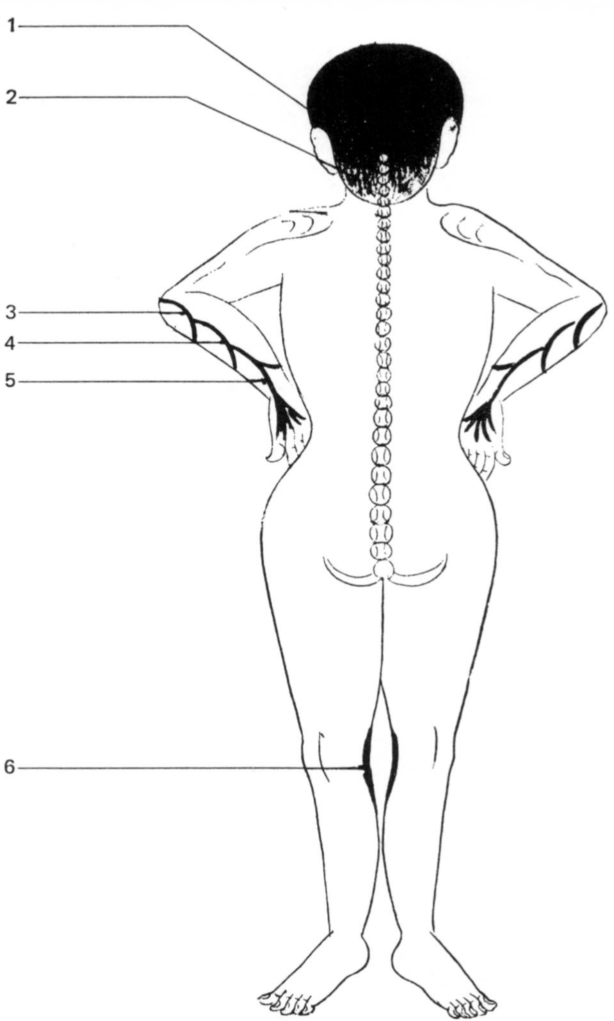
1
2
3
4
5
6

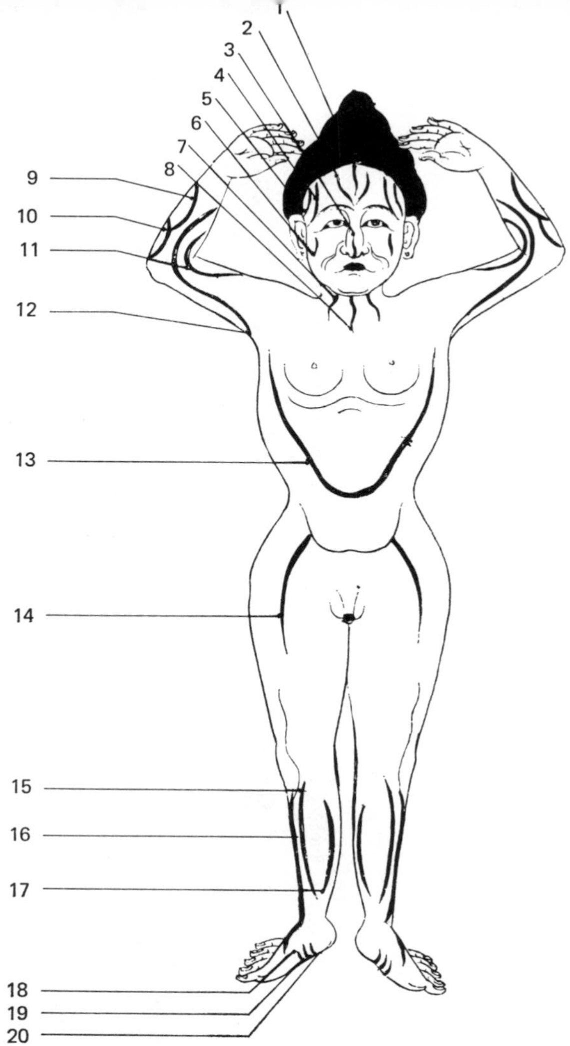
1
2
3
4
5
6
7
8
9
10
11
12
13
14
15
16
17
18
19
20

PLATE No. 9

Inner organs:

1. sNyiṅ, heart
2. gLo-bu, lung
3. mChhin-pa, liver
4. mKhal-gyas, right kidney
5. gLo-bu, lung
6. mChher-pa, spleen
7. mKhal-gyon, left kidney
8. sam-se-hu, seminal vessel

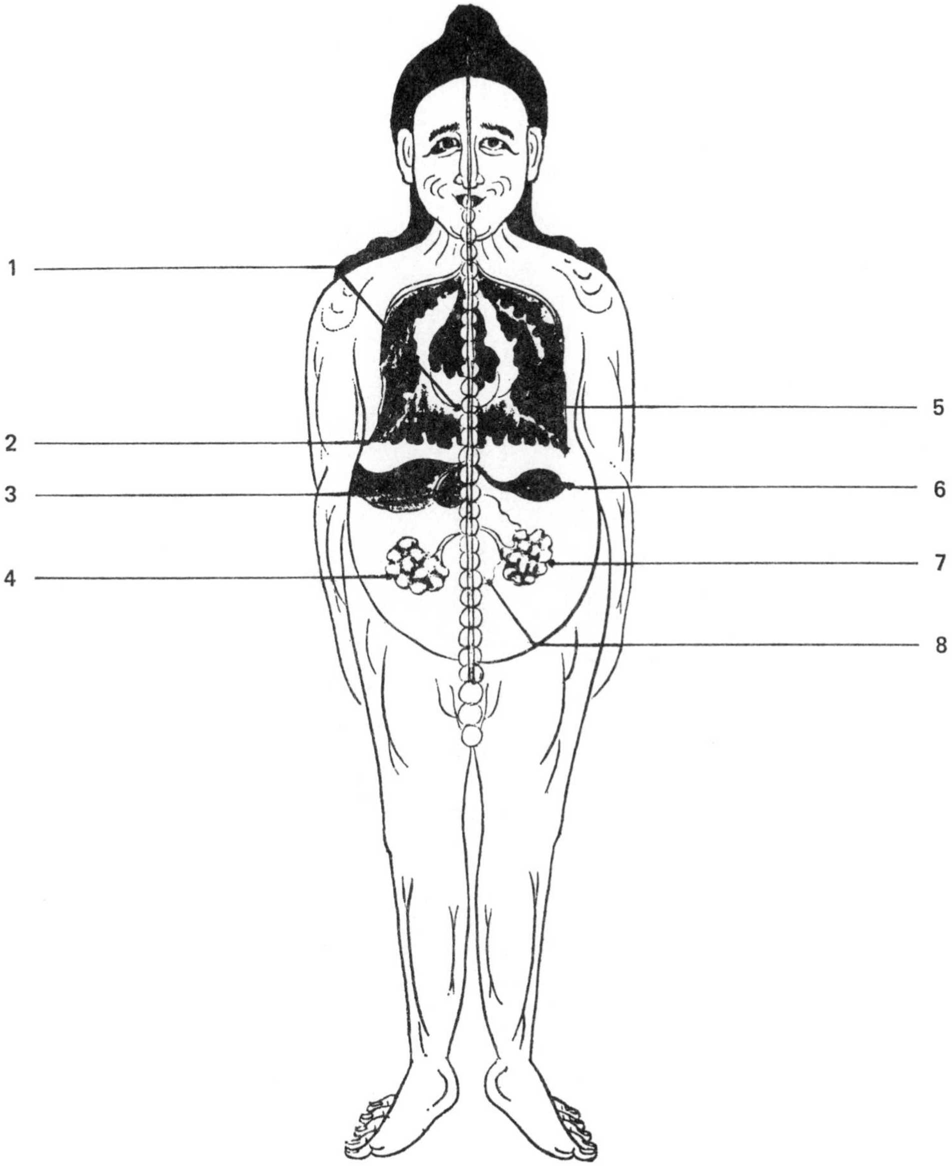
1
2
3
4
5
6
7
8

PLATE No. 10

Viscera

Left-hand figure:
1. mChhin-khri nag-po, seat of the black liver
2. mChhin-pa ldog-mts'ams, intermediary renewal liver
3. mKhal-ma gyas, right-hand kidney

Right-hand figure:
4. sNyiṅ, heart
5. gLo-bu, lung
6. mKhris-yul, region of the gall bladder
7. rGyu-loṅ, blind gut, appendix

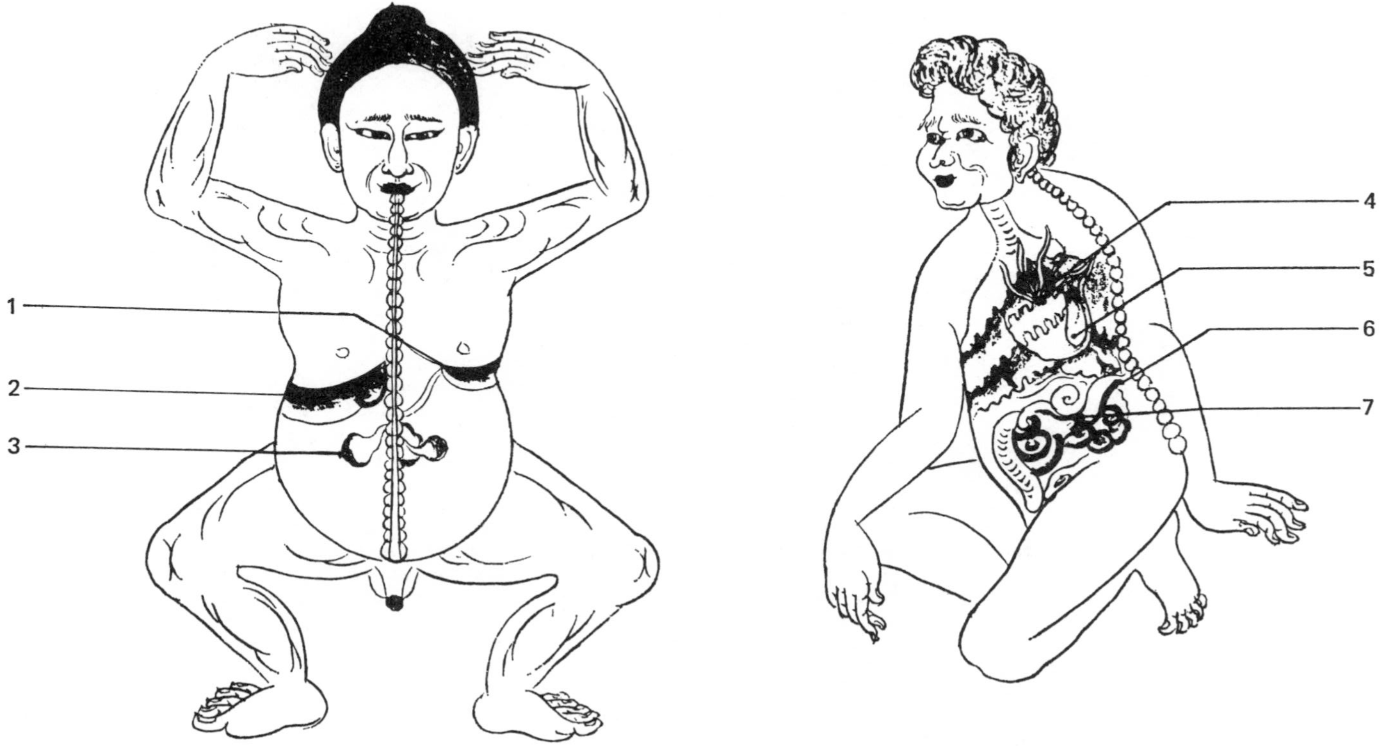
1
2
3
4
5
6
7

PLATE No. 11

1. Bu-gu-chan, increasing watery element
2. hJah-byed, causing rainbow
3. Ratna, jewel
4. Terminal point of Bu-gu-chan

There are six bu-gu chhen veins. There are nineteen veins causing the increase of the watery element in the body. Thirteen of them are connected with the inner organs and cannot be seen. Six are visible from the outside. No. 11 shows the six visible veins of the watery element coming out from the nape of the neck to one inch on each side from the centre going downwards and meeting at the fifth vertebra, then separating again and meeting at the eleventh vertebra where the seminal vessel vein and the kidney vein branch off. From the fourteenth vertebra issue four branches: two of them end at the hip and two run downwards to the feet. At the heels they are connected with other veins. The hJah-byed veins come out at the two sides of the back of the head and go down to the fourteenth vertebra from the point corresponding to the Adam's apple in the front and have four branches: two of them go down with the pulmonary veins to the fourteenth vertebra, go inside and come out at the hips and go through the front of the thigh and come out at the back of the knee. They go through the leg and meet with the pu-gu-chan under the heel. The two other veins go to the shoulder and go inside from there, then they go through the arms to the palms of the hands. The ratna comes out behind the ear lobes, goes through the clavicles, then goes inside, then from the armpits through the arms to the back of the hands, thence to the thumb and then they are connected with the hJah-byed in the palm.

PLATE No. 12

Pathways of the Ratna and hJah-byed veins:

1. End of Ratna in the palm
2. Ratna turning towards the back of the head
3. Ratna going into clavicle
4. The point to which the ratna goes from the earlobe
5. hJah-byed from hip to thigh in the front
6. hJah-byed going through the leg coming out at the heel
7. Bu-gu-chan going through the second toe to the heel and is connected there with the hJah-byed

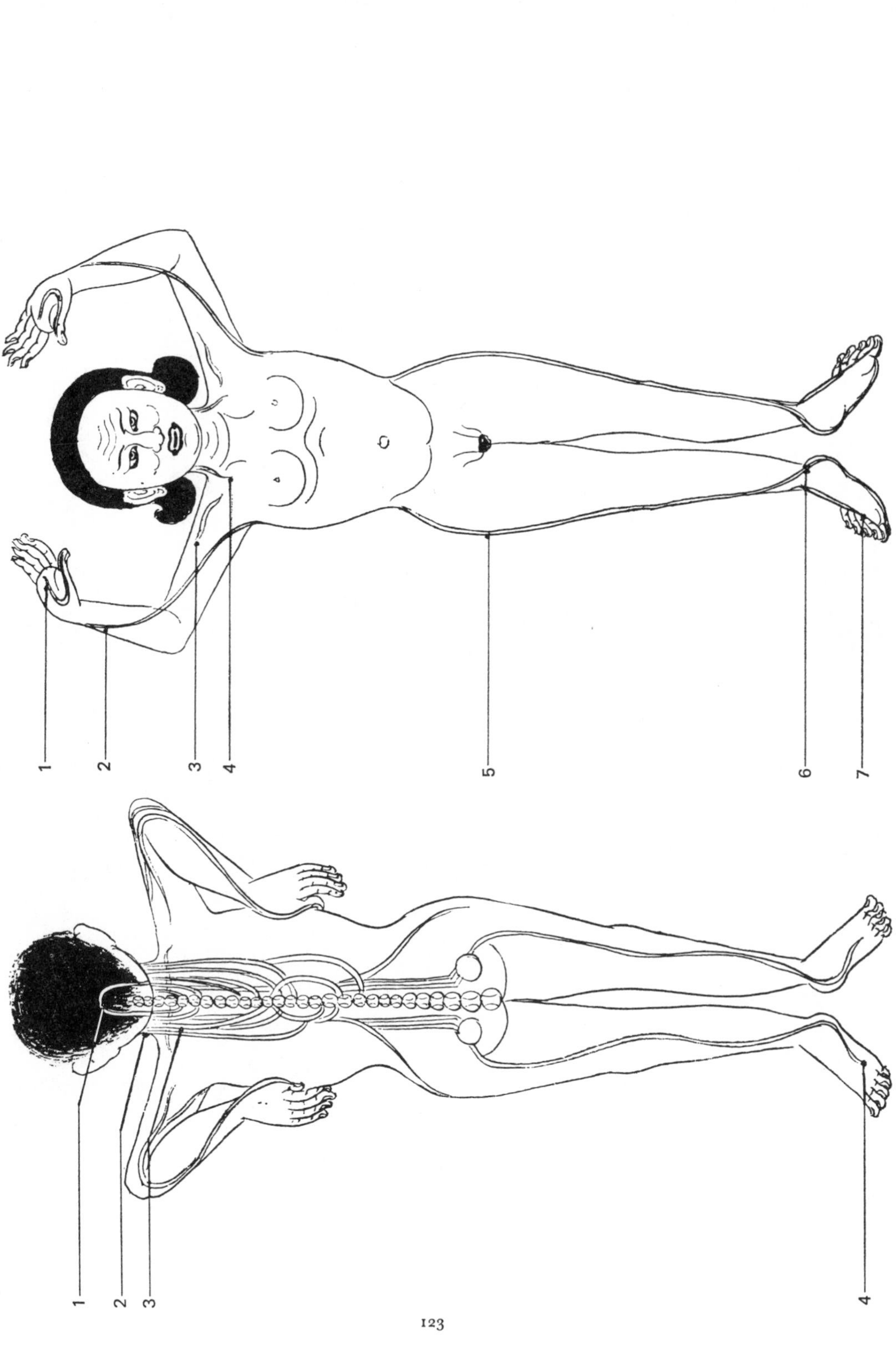
1
2
3
4
5
6
7
1
2
3
4

PLATE No. 13

Some points for Moxa given in the *Maṅ-ṅag rGyud*, the Third Book of the rGyud-bzhi.

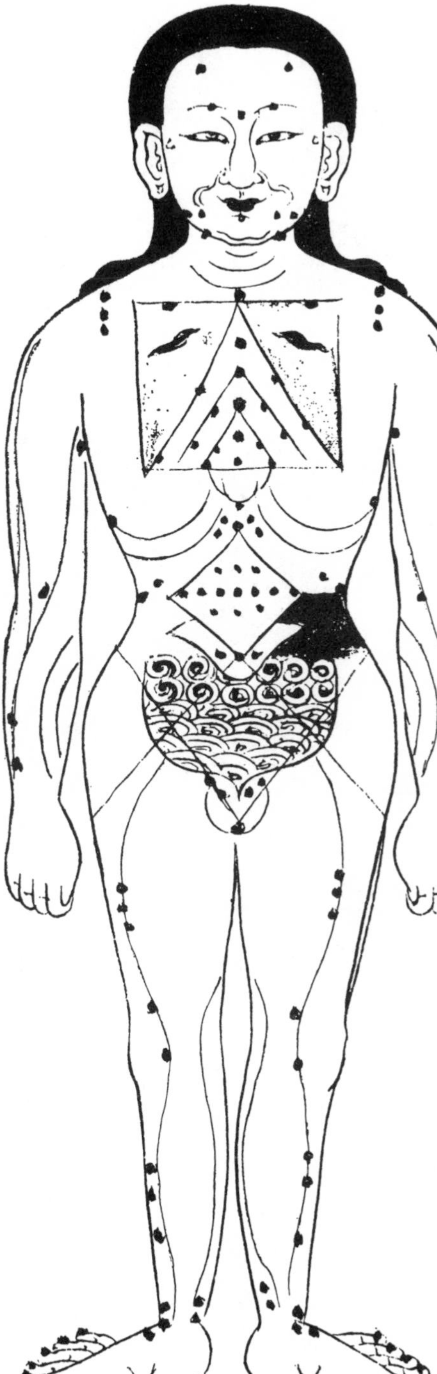

PLATE No. 14

Connection of veins with flesh and skin. According to the fourth chapter of the *bShad rGyud* there are twenty-three types of bones (see *Tibetan Medicine*, p. 37). The right-hand side veins are drawn in black because in them is a preponderance of the element of fire. The veins on the left-hand side are drawn white because in them water preponderates.

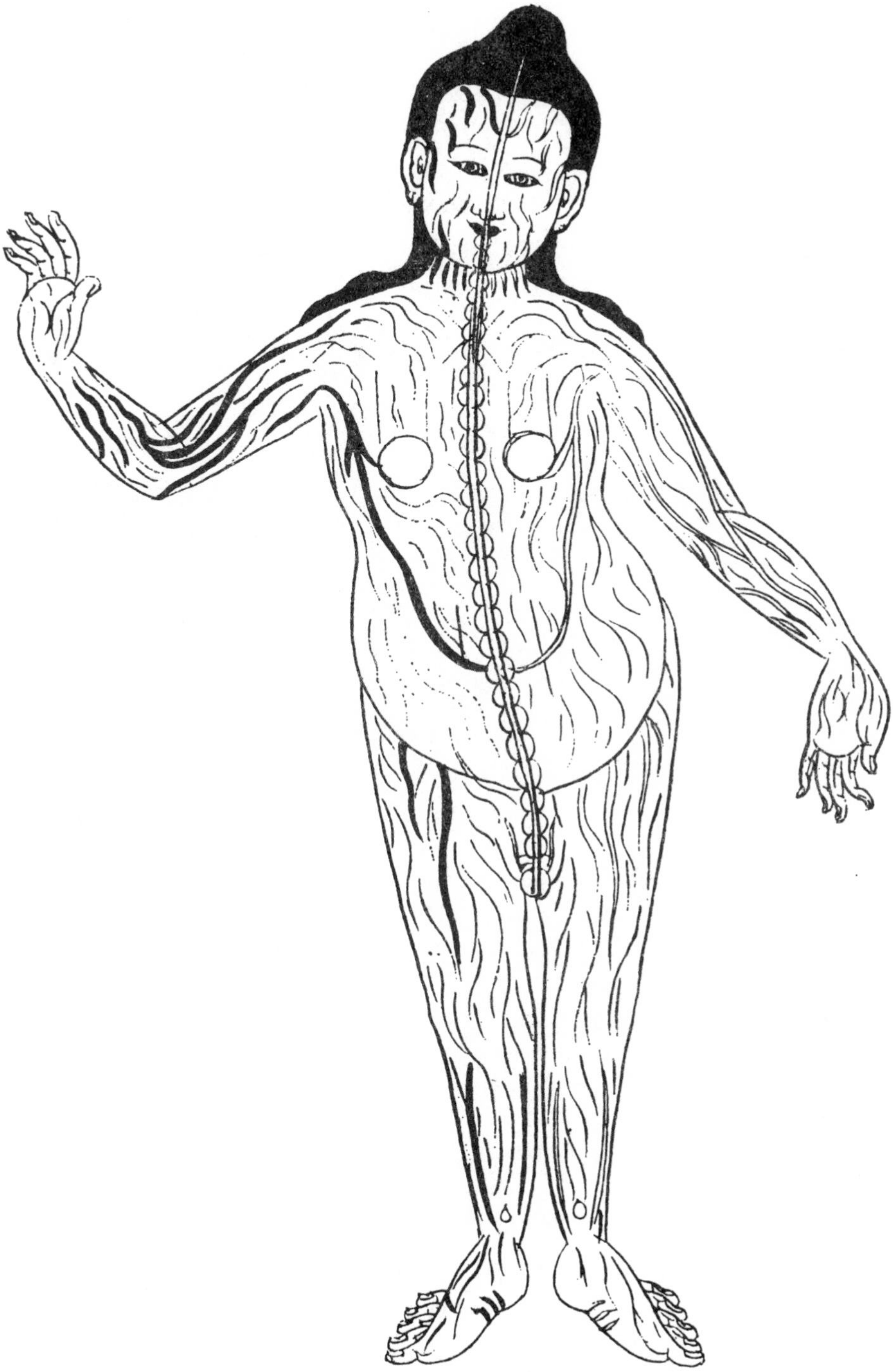

PLATE No. 15

Body measurements (see pp. 37–38)

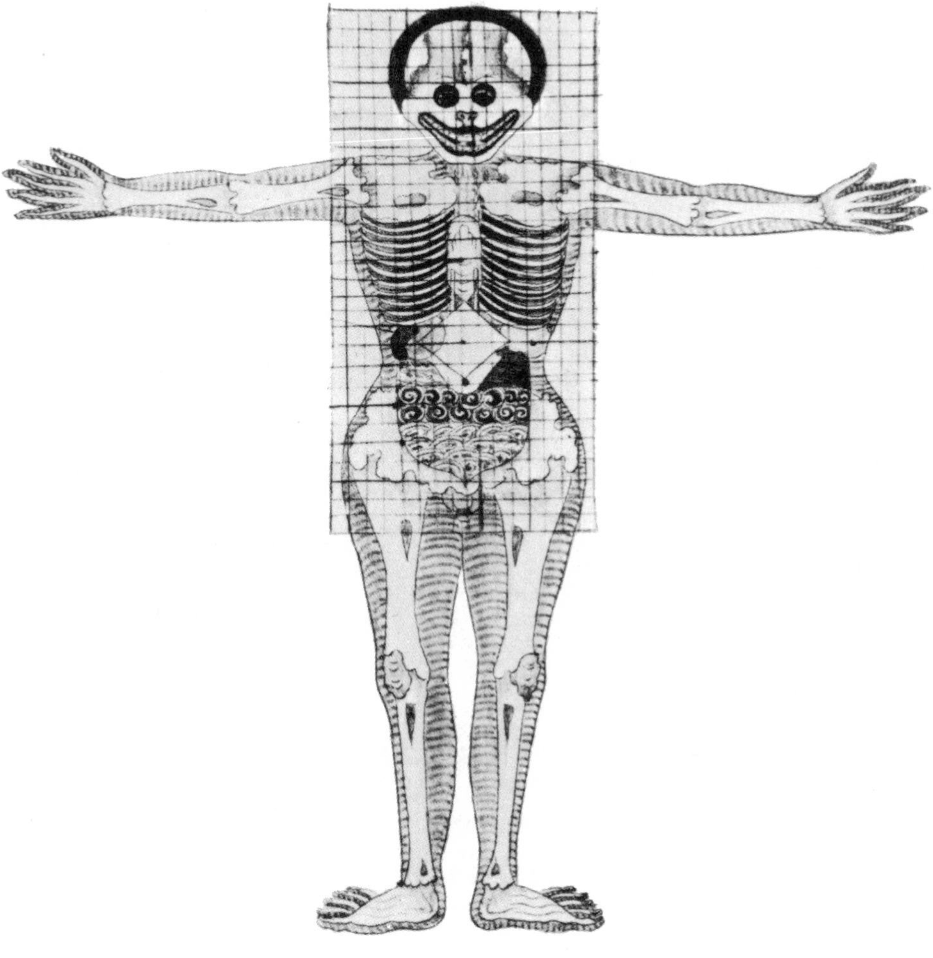

PLATE No. 16

Medical and surgical instruments (see Chapter XXII):

i x Diagnostic instruments (see pp. 82–3).

i y Instruments for detecting haemorrhoids (see p. 83). Long handle with oval ring: instrument for cutting off detected piles. Lion's head pincers belong to category in Section ii.

ii x Pincers, tongs, forceps (see p. 83).

ii y Eel's mouth blades for extracting bullets from deep wounds. Divided toungue instrument with hole running through centre for extracting pus. Sparrow's feather and five scallops lancets belong to Section iii (see p. 83).

iii x Scalpels and lancets (see p. 84).

iii y Spoons (see p. 84).

iv x Scraping instrument and saws (see p. 84).

iv y Trephines. Hook for removing pustules from ear, nose and throat. Instruments for extracting dead foetus from womb and for extracting calculus from bladder (see p. 84).

v x Catheters (see p. 84).

v y Trumpet-shaped instruments for passing medicine through the anus. Uroscopy bottle. Copper bowl for bad blood and pus (see p. 84).

vi x Inhalation apparatus: two tubes inserted into nostrils and, in the instrument with three, one into the mouth. Hot water is introduced through the pipe on the side.

vi y Vessel for cut-off shavings. Moon-shaped shaving mirror. Moxa instruments belonging to Section vii.

vii x Moxa instruments made of different metals. Each set consists of two rods, one plain and the other with a flower. The metal flower has a hole in the centre, which is put over the affected part which had been covered with powdered herbs. Then the second rod is heated with the tinder shown in vii y and put over the hole. This will cause the powdered herbs to burn exactly on the affected part.

vii y Double spoon for applying powdered herbs. Two types of tinder: one made of wood, the other of spunk.

viii x Spoon for applying eye medicine. Lancet case. Instrument for pressing the eye down. In the centre fire receptacle.

viii y Medicine container. Metal pipette for introducing medicine into the throat and cauterizing the uvula. Medicine sieve. Medicine brushes for ointments and powders.

i
ii
iii
iv
v
vi
vii
viii

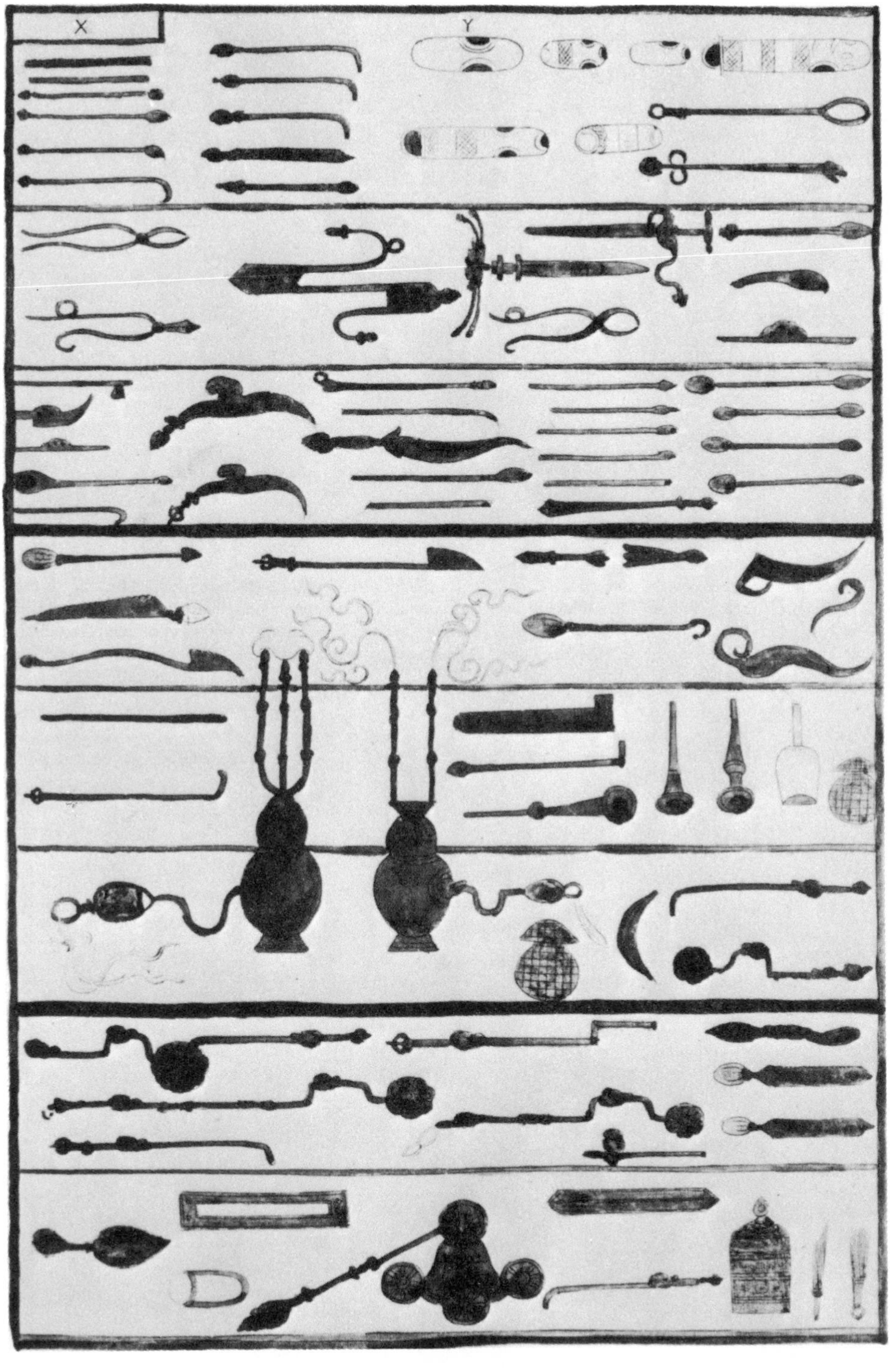

PLATE No. 17

A Tibetan doctor's medicine bag made of leather and silk brocade, where he keeps his medicines and instruments. Each powder is kept in a little leather bag with a bone label as shown. The bag in the Wellcome Library is 9 inches high and the diameter at the bottom measures 10 inches. It contains fifty little bags with powders. Spoon for measuring medicines. Instruments for taking off a cataract. An ox's horn used for cupping. Medicinal stone. A cow's horn with a small hole at the tip, through which the doctor sucks blood from the diseased area. The stone is a flint used for igniting tinder.

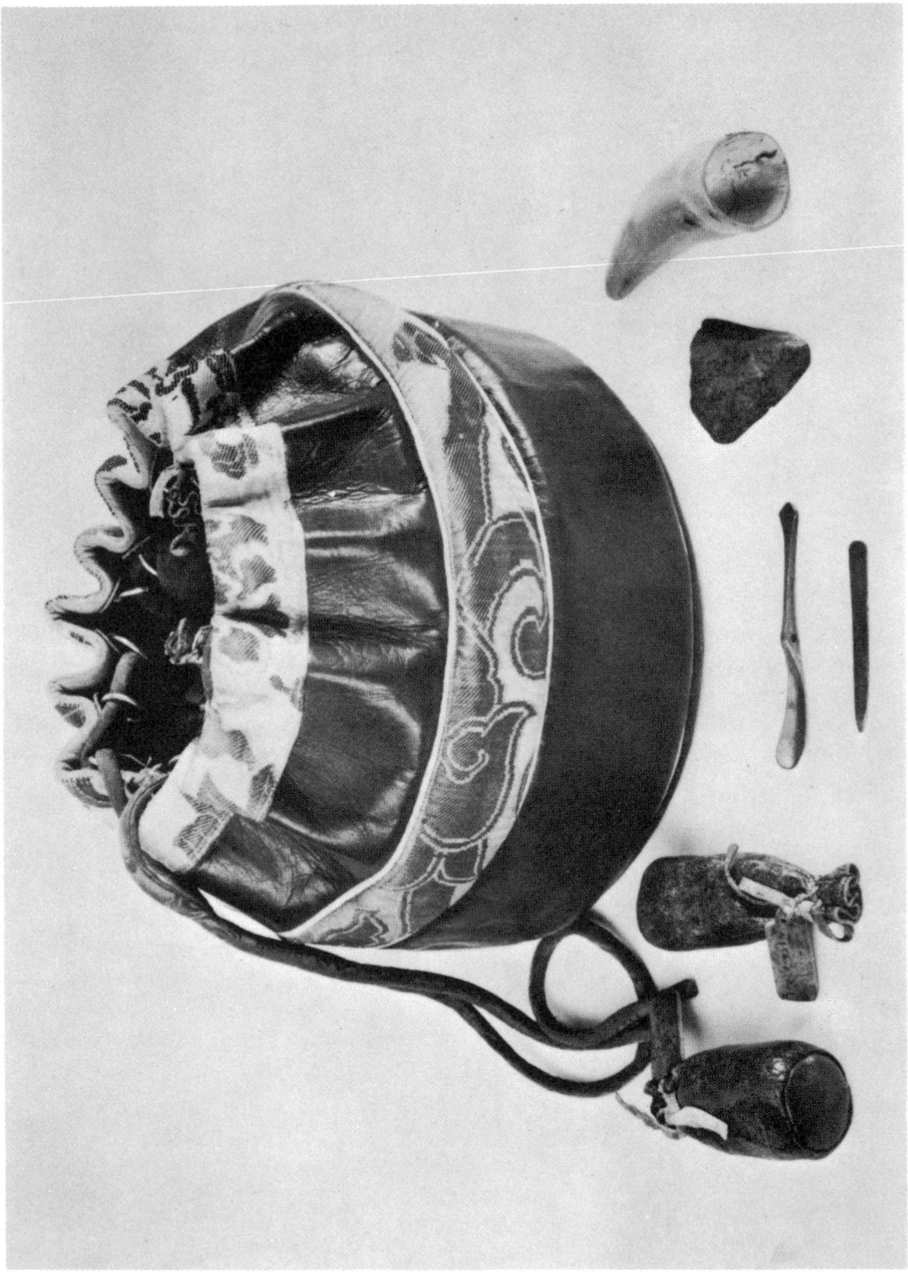

PLATE No. 18

mKhan-chhuṅ mKhyen-rab Nor-bu (born 1882), Head of sMan-rtsis-khaṅ Medical College (see History, pp. 22–3).

Younger head of Medical College, mKhan-chhuṅ Thub-tan Bhun-drub, with medicine bags, rosary and medical Scriptures.

(Photographs by courtesy of Rhenock Kazi Tse Ten Tashi, Sikkim.)

PLATE No. 19

Thaṅ-ka I

In the centre: gYu-thog Yon-tan mGon-po. Top centre: the Buddha Śākyamuni appearing as the Medicine Buddha. On his right: Yid-las-Skyes asking the Medicine Buddha to tell the *rGyud-bzhi*. On the left: Rig-pa'i Ye-shes telling the *rGyud-bzhi* as it comes from the Medicine Buddha; one can see the golden thread. Before each chapter of the *rGyud-bzhi* Yid-las-Skyes asks and Rig-pa'i Ye-shes making the preaching gesture tells a chapter. In the centre: hTs'o-byed gZhon-nu with four attendants; on the right: the four-faced Brahmā; on his left: a brahmin holding a jewel. On his left: the Buddhist Avalokiteśvara and on his left a deva. Underneath: the eight goddesses of Medicine. Bottom centre: the dharmapāla Shaṅ-blon. On the left: medicine bags; on the right: jewels, the four Medicine Mountains and medicinal plants. Left, higher up: medicinal trees.

PLATE No. 20

THAṄ-KA II

In the centre: Gyu-thog Yon-tan mGon-po Left top: gYu-thog's birth. Under it to the right: finding the woman with the turquoises in the river. Top centre: gYu-thog taking pearls to the king. Right top: Bodhgayā, gYu-thog learning from Indian pandits. Right centre: gYu-thog founds a medical college at Kong-po. Right bottom: disciples mourning the death of gYu-thog. Bottom centre: Bi-byi dGah-byed and the Indian lady doctor come to Tibet and see a girl carrying her mother out of the house to let the sick mother die in the wilderness. Left bottom: the Indian doctors take the mother indoors and treat her. Above that: the Tibetan king Lha-tho Tho-ri invites the two Indian doctors, puts them on the throne, and offers Lha-chen Rol-chha to them, who becomes the Tibetan ancestor of the gYu-thog lineage.

PART II

The Life of the Great Physician-Saint gYu-thog Yon-tan mGon-po

Translated from the Tibetan by the
Ven. Rechung Rinpoche Jampal Kunzang

Contents

Note

For reasons of internal evidence and to help the reader to understand the sequence of events, certain sections in the Biography have been transposed in this translation as follows: Chapter XLII was in the Tibetan block-print between the present chapters XXXII and XXXIV. Chapter XLVII there incorporated the present chapters XXXIII and XLI. Chapters LIV and LV were located between the present chapters XXVI and XXVII. It seems highly probable that the block-print followed a manuscript tradition that had got a little out of order during the course of the centuries.

M.W.

INVOCATION

I bow before the Lama (*Guru*) and the Tutelary Deities, the Dākinīs and the Buddhas, the Dharma, the Saṁgha and the men skilled in medicine, the Goddess of Medicine and the Protectors of the science of medicine. I bow before the great physicians of India, China, Khotan, Tibet, Kashmir, Mongolia and Iran, Garlog, Dölpo, Gru-gu* and all other countries. Excellent healers, curers of diseases, who can guide people in the teaching of medicine, who protect from diseases and destroy completely the root of the sufferings caused by diseases. I bow before the great doctors, the great physician-saints.

I KOṄ-PO'S REQUEST

Thus have I heard about gYu-thog Yon-tan mGon-po, the protector of beings of all realms, above, below and on earth, full of learning and spiritual power, the great king of physicians, and his lineage in the snow-fenced land of Tibet: Duṅ-gi Thor-chog, bLo-gros Chhen-po, bLo-gros mTs'uṅgs-med, bLo-gros Rab-gsal, bLo-gros rGyal-mzod, bLo-gros bShes-gnyen, the six doctors who lightened the darkness of Tibet, and after that hDre-rje Vajra, Khyuṅ-po rDo-rje, the Excellent Yon-tan mGon-po, mKhas-pa hBum-seṅ, Srā-lu and the elder gYu-thog. After that the teaching was handed down to Jo-sras dPal and Byams-pa and Thugs-rje dPal, Kun-chhog Bde-legs, Byams-pa bDe-legs who have improved the teachings of medicine. This has been the family lineage of gYu-thog the Elder. All of this lineage were very learned and saintly but the most learned and the greatest saint was called gYu-thog Yon-tan mGon-po.

There are four things on which I should like to base the life-story of gYu-thog, the most excellent learned of the learned who descended from the Indian king bLo-gros Chhen-po and was born at sTod-luṅ sKyid-sna.

1. The explanation of why the life-story should be true.
2. How gYu-thog's family came from India to Tibet.
3. How he went from Tibet to India.
4. How he spread the teaching of medicine in Tibet.

* Turkestan.

There are two subdivisions to the First Part, the explanation of why the life-story should be true: 1. The request for his life-story by the disciples, and 2: then gYu-thog's answer.

1. Once on the night of the anniversary of the death of gYu-thog hDre-rje Vajra Chhos-kyi rGyal-po, on the third day of the fourth month of the Iron Dog year, when gYu-thog Yon-tan mGon-po was staying at sTod-luṅ sKyid-sna, surrounded by about five hundred disciples, teaching medicine and attending to the sick, gYu-thog Yon-tan mGon-po's disciple called Koṅ-po bDe-rgyal had a vision of eight beautiful women holding medicine bags made of leather in their hands appearing to him and telling him to ask gYu-thog Yon-tan mGon-po to tell him his life-story, and then they disappeared. Then Koṅ-po went to gYu-thog Yon-tan mGon-po and said: 'Your Reverence! I saw eight beautiful women who told me to ask you to tell me your life-story, and then they disappeared. May I, therefore, request you to tell your life-story?' gYu-thog Yon-tan mGon-po replied: 'I have already told my life-story when I was the doctor hTs'o-byed Gzhon-nu hJigs-med Drags-pa. Now let this old man get on with looking after sick people!' And he did not grant him his request.

On the fifteenth day of the sixth month of the Iron Dog year, gYu-thog Yon-tan mGon-po and his disciples were gathered together for the consecration of the medicines, which turned them into nectar, and the consecration of eight nor suṅ gods and goddesses of Medicine and the lineage of brahmins. That night Koṅ-po had a dream: Three white-robed men led him to the palace of lTa-na-sdug. When they arrived the three men said to him: 'Look at this palace attentively! From the outside it has the appearance of the city of lTa-na-sdug. In reality this city exists inside your own body. Ask His Reverence, gYu-thog, about it,' and disappeared. The city had four gates, and each gate had a great king for its lord. Koṅ-po went to the east gate and asked king Yul-hkhor-sruṅ for permission to enter the city. Having received permission, he entered into the city by the east gate. Having passed through the outer gate, he came to the inner gate. There stood rTa-mgrin, and again he asked him for permission which was granted, and he entered the city. The palace of the city was square and had four gates with arches. The walls, in five layers of different colours, were fivefold and ornamented with balconies, half-lattice work railings and with a parapet on the roof. In the palace there are pharmacies and medicinal trees, lakes, pools and rivers of the eight kinds of water, peacocks, pheasants, parrots, ducks and many other water birds, elephants, bears and other wild animals living without anger, with compassion and looking very attractive.

There are sweet scents in the air dispersing all diseases. The palace is very large, and transparent from the outside to the inside and from the inside to the outside. It has sixteen thousand pillars made of precious jewels, with beams and rafters inlaid with many different jewels. It is not a place that can be reached by everybody; only those who have attained the goal of the Mahāyāna teaching can enter there. In the centre of the palace there is a throne made of precious vaiḍúrya, and sMan-pa'i rGyal-po, the Lord Buddha of Medicine, is sitting there. On the right there is the great brahmin rGyun-shes-kyi-bu and other Indian brahmin physicians. On the left hDre-rje mKhas-pa rGya-gar rDo-rje, an Indian, and great Tibetan physician-saints. These were the two outside rows. Flanking the throne there were two further rows, and in the right-hand row flanking the throne, were the great physician-saints of China and other countries, on the left sKyes-bu Me-hla and other Indo-Tibetan physician-saints. Three brahmins are making tablets and the eight goddesses are offering to the Buddha of Medicine. Moreover, there are many people in doctors' robes walking about and making medicines. Koṅ-po stood at one of the doors because he could not find a place suitable for him to sit down. Eight white-robed ladies holding leather medicine bags came to him and asked him: 'Why did you come here?' And he replied: 'I came to the city of lTa-na-sdug. I could not find any place to sit, therefore I am standing here.' Then they said: 'O those doctors who are treating their teacher with disrespect and do not understand the perfect meaning of the texts and instructions, who do not care about the welfare of their patients but about the reward, not meditating on the State of Enlightenment, but have selfish and proud thoughts, and who like women, drink, singing, dancing and ornaments and take little account of poor patients but make much of the wealthy and powerful ones, committing many sins and achieving little merit, prefer the Vehicles of the Śrāvakas and of the Pratyeka Buddhas, and inveigh against the Mahāyāna. Go away! This place is a celestial city, and unworthy disciples cannot enter here.' And they pushed him out of the door. At this moment he thought: 'All these people, when they were in the human country, achieved much merit, practised the essence of meditation, thought of the well-being of their patients, believed in everything their Guru said, those are able to be here, in the miraculous celestial city'.

Then he said: 'For a miserable person like me there is no chance to enter such a celestial city. Now, O Medicine Buddha, brahmin-saints and your lineage, look mercifully upon me!' There was a very high hospital nearby and he climbed on its roof and wanted to jump down from it. As he was on the point of jumping, a white-clad man with a medicine bag seized him and said: 'Venerable son, don't do that! This is the most excellent of all celestial cities. Therefore there is here no suffering nor mention either of suffering or happiness, a place beyond the illusion of subject and object. What is wrong with you?' Then Koṅ-po told him what had happened to him, and the white-clad man laughed: 'Ha, ha! This is the most excellent of all celestial places. Not everybody can enter it. You have to come with offerings to the Medicine Buddha and the brahmin-saints. Did you* omit to pray to the Medicine Buddha and the brahmin-saints or did you mix your medicines in a careless manner? Have you had no patience to drive away diseases and to cure people? Did you not keep your vow?' Then Koṅ-po fainted with fear and great shame. The white-clad man asked him: 'In whom have you got faith, you bad son?' Koṅ-po (came round and) said: 'I have faith in the Medicine Buddha and his Attendants.' Thereupon the man said: 'Very well then, I shall request the admission for you', and he went. After some time he came back with a smiling face and said: 'Come now, I have the permission.' Then Koṅ-po went with him and was motioned to take up a place without a cushion on the floor near the Medicine Buddha. At the same time they put a throne near the Medicine Buddha, which was made of sun crystal jewels. One of the crowd, attired in robes like those of the Medicine Buddha, made precious offerings and asked the Medicine Buddha: 'Who is going to sit on this throne?' The Medicine Buddha replied: 'hTs'o-byed-gzhon-nu is the Incarnation of my speech and gYu-thog Yon-tan is his Incarnation, and Koṅ-po bDe-rgyal has requested to hear gYu-thog's life-story, so he is going to sit there; ask him to come here.' Then the man robed like the Medicine Buddha put me on the throne and then asked the Medicine Buddha: 'Where is the learned gYu-thog staying at present, and for the sake of what beings is he working, and where will the excellent gYu-thog finally go?' 'At present he is staying in the human world working for the good of gods, demons and human beings. At the end he will come here and be the head of all of you,' said the Medicine Buddha. Then the man in the robes like the Medicine Buddha asked: 'What is the benefit derived from asking for his life-story, of writing it and of reciting it?' 'The person asking for gYu-thog's life-story will join the ranks of the brahmin-saints, and the persons writing and reciting it will become capable of following the Mahāyāna teaching. If a person prays to gYu-thog all the disease-causing demons will disappear from him. Even a person hearing gYu-thog's name will begin striving to acquire merit, and the power of his sins will decrease', said the Medicine Buddha.

* Printing error: Did you pray.

Then Koṅ-po thought: 'I must ask gYu-thog for his life-story. The Medicine Buddha said the person who requests the life-story of the Incarnation of his Speech will be speeded towards Liberation like a shooting star.' Immediately after this he woke up and thought: 'Alas, a person of such excellent learning and faculties as gYu-thog I have treated simply like a friend and with the contempt arising out of familiarity!' And, full of regret, he began to cry bitterly. Then he thought: 'Now, at dawn, I will go to gYu-thog and open my heart to him asking his forgiveness and request his life-story from him. It was because I did not see gYu-thog as a Buddha that I was sent away from the ranks of the brahmin-saints.' He prayed devoutly and afterwards felt very sorrowful and tears ran down his face. When the dawn had come he went to see gYu-thog who was in the midst of teaching many disciples. His tears ran down his face. gYu-thog asked him: 'What has happened to you?' He said: 'I have had a dream,' and told it to him and asked his forgiveness. Then he bowed and put gYu-thog's feet on his head and said: 'Your Reverence, please, may I request the whole story, your descent on both the father's and the mother's side? What deeds have you done for the sake of sentient beings?' gYu-thog replied: 'Koṅ-po, my son, don't be so rash! I have a life-story to tell, but who is going to listen to it, and who is going to believe it? Moreover, what is worse, for the foolish worldlings listening to it, it might become the cause of committing more sins. The people of the highest learning, with a perfect religious disposition, will disapprove of it. Think carefully and work for the weal of the sick! Meditate with compassion for sentient beings! Pray from the depth of your heart to the Guru and not only paying lip-service!' Then Koṅ-po said: 'We, from the Koṅ-po district, are obstinate and self-conceited people. If you don't tell your life-story, there is no other way out for me than to kill myself and cut the thread of a life which has no meaning for me any longer. Mind, I am serious! Are you saving the life of other people or taking it away? Bless me by letting me hear your story in my next life!' And he tried to jump into a deep abyss but the learned Don-yod, a disciple of gYu-thog, and some other disciples seized him. Then gYu-thog Yon-tan mGon-po said: 'Koṅ-po, my son, I, gYu-thog Yon-tan mGon-po, will tell you the life-story of gYu-thog. Listen to it! The family of gYu-thog had a turquoise roof on their house,' and then he laughed. Then Koṅ-po gave up his intention of killing himself and he bowed to gYu-thog's feet and asked him repeatedly: 'Please, tell your life-story. Please, tell it and protect me!' Then gYu-thog replied: 'Still you must think carefully because usually an Incarnation's story is a bag of lies. My descent from bLos-gros Chhen-po, the minister in charge of religious affairs of the Indian king, is also falsehood. There is no benefit in telling a story full of lies, rather listen to my advice!' And he gave his *Instruction consisting of seven jewels*:*

'Listen, my son Koṅ-po, bDe-legs rGyal:
Usually a life-story is a bag of lies;
gYu-thog-pa also tells many lies.
To open the bag will cause much shame.
Stop asking and work for the weal of the sick.
First, when you examine a disease,
Very flexible are the veins, like a dancer's hand:
The outcome of a disease is difficult to tell.
A stronger pulse comes from a fever,
A shallower pulse from a cold disease.
A urine like a rainbow is difficult to judge,
You can see it but it is difficult.
When the sediment of urine is thick, it comes from fever,
When it is thin, from cold diseases.
Take this essential instruction and don't open the bag of lies!'

Then Koṅ-po said: 'Great Lama gYu-thog, if you tell the life-story of the great Guru, the instruction will be implicit in it. Please, tell your life-story!' and he again begged him imploringly.

II LORD BA-NU-MA COMES DOWN FROM HEAVEN

'Koṅ-po, my son, and you other disciples, very well then, I shall tell my life-story. Rejoice now and listen to it! My ancestors came from the heaven of 'Od-gsal-lha.† Two kinds of ancestors can come from there: Ba-nu-ma and Ra-nu-ma.‡ My ancestors belong to the Ba-nu-ma. On my father's side, my ancestry is the same as that of the Buddha [Śākyamuni]. On my mother's side, from an inn-keeper's daughter called sKyes-pa'i Yid-phrog-ma. To tell it in detail: Once, in the land of the Āryas (India), there was a big country called the 'land of the lotus flower.' It consisted of nine districts: five large districts and four in between at right angles. The central district was called The Essence-of-the-Lotus-Flower, the Eastern district The-Planting-of-the-Lotus-Flower, in the South The-Ripening-of-the-Lotus-Flower, in the West The-Activity-of-the-Lotus-Flower, and in the North

* The purpose of this speech was to prevent Koṅ-po from asking further.
† Heaven where the inhabitants see by the light of their own shining bodies.
‡ Drinking cows' milk and drinking goats' milk.

The-Enjoyment-of-the-Lotus-Flower. In the North-East there was The-Planting-of-the-Blue-Water-Lily, the district in the South-East was called The-Ripening-of-the-Blue-Water-Lily, in the South-West The-Activity-of-the-Blue-Water-Lily, and in the North-West The-Holding-of-the-Blue-Water-Lily. Each district had six thousand and five hundred towns. To the central district called The-Essence-of-the-Lotus-Flower, once Lha-bu Dam-pa Tog-dkar-po came down from heaven into the human world. In the district of The-Essence-of-the-Lotus-Flower there was a red wishing-cow which went to wherever Lha-bu Dam-pa Tog-dkar-po was staying, and gave him milk. A dairymaid, when she went in search of her, saw that she gave milk to a man, and told a brahminī called Chhos-kyi bLo-gros about this. The brahminī also went to see it and saw the graceful, radiant, strong and handsome man, and she asked him: 'Where do you come from?' and the man pointed to the sky. He was able to see in the dark through his own brightness and, drinking nectar, he did not need any food. The brahminī asked, 'What is your name?' But he did not tell her. So the brahminī gave him the name of Lord Ba-nu ('Drinking Cow's Milk'). He became her lover and from their union two sons were born called Brahma rDo-rje Chhog-hbebs and Brahma Shes-rab Ral-gri. After some time Lord Ba-nu said: 'All of you three can come to heaven.' But the brahminī replied: 'Then the goddesses will be jealous.' 'All right,' said Ba-nu, 'then you stay in the human country, and I shall come back after seven days and nights to give their inheritance to my sons.' Then he climbed to heaven by the rope of the gods. After seven days and nights he came back and gave a chalice filled with gold to each son. Then he stayed incognito in the human country for some time. Later he went again up to heaven. The brahminī had an evil husband who brandished his sword and cut the rope which had connected men and gods. Ever since that time the link between gods and men has been severed. The brahminī gave each son as a hereditary portion a chalice with gold from their father.

III SHES-RAB RAL-GRI MEETS YID-HPHROG-MA

In the middle of the above-mentioned central district, called The-Essence-of-the-Lotus-Flower, there was a king called Lily-face who was an Incarnation of the Bodhisattva Kun-tu-bzaṅ-po. His queen, who was the reincarnation of 'Od-gzer-chan-ma (Sanskrit Marīchi), was called bLo-gros bDe-byed-ma. She was the daughter of brGya-byin (Indra). She had a gor-shi-sha sandalwood tree whose trunk, branches, leaves and flowers fulfilled all wishes.

In the district east of the centre, called The-Planting-of-the-Lotus-Flower, the brahminī's son Shes-rab Ral-gri lived together with his brother. This older brother took Shes-rab Ral-gri's gold-filled chalice by force from him. He had two wives and lived most of the time with the younger wife while he put the older one in charge of the two chalices and he weighed the gold every night. Shes-rab Ral-gri thought: 'Alas, my brother has taken the gold from me! Now I shall go to the monastery of Padmo'i Ts'al and become a monk and then I shall take revenge on my brother.' The enjoyment of beer and women is not permitted in that monastery. When you visit that monastery you have to go with a guide.

Once, when he went on an errand to the monastery, accompanied by a guide, he met a beautiful and charming woman on the road. Then he pondered in his mind: 'If I had a beautiful woman like this for my wife I should be very happy.' He asked her: 'My good lady, what is it you want?' She said: 'I am sKyes-pa'i Yid-hphrog-ma, a beer-seller's daughter, and I am looking for people who will buy beer.' He said: 'Can you sell me beer if I pay for it with gold out of a chalice I have got at my brother's house?' She said: 'That's all right with me.' Then he followed her. In India no beer seller was allowed to keep an inn on the second floor but she had a large inn on the groundfloor and in the basement. He went in and drank of 'the fools'water'. Then he thought: 'Where is she sleeping? I want to go there.' Yid-hphrog-ma prepared a bed for her assistant in a long chamber in the inmost part of the house and one for the brahmin in another chamber. She herself slept near the hearth. While the assistant was asleep the brahmin went to her and said:

'You charming, delightful, beautiful creature!
So gifted with wisdom and knowledge, so young!
The pleasure of your company increases all happiness.
Fulfil my wishes and give yourself to me!'

Yid-hphrog-ma replied:

'The pleasure of my company may increase happiness
But I'm afraid I'll be chastened by the king's punishment.
My mind would be troubled by the thought of people talking.
He who acts without having received a promise acts like a fool.'

He said:

'So young and with such a discerning mind,
What a charming and beautiful girl you are,
Who harbours love without anger.
Let us comfort each other and not trouble each other's mind!'

She said:

'Brahmin's son, whose knowledge is great,
I, charming sKyes-pa'i Yid-hphrog-ma,
If you do whatever I want,
I shall offer my body to you.'

Then they slept together and he said: 'I have a chalice filled with gold which my brother took by force, and he put his older wife in charge of it and weighs it every night on his scales. Is there any method by which I could get it back from him?' She said: 'Make friends with the older wife and find out what is the weight of the gold!' Then the brahmin's son went to the older wife, made friends with her, and found out what was the weight of the gold. The older wife had a chalice exactly the same as the one containing the gold. The brahmin's son asked her to give it to him and he gave it to Yid-hphrog-ma. She said: 'Get some iron ore from the sea-shore!' And he brought it and gave it to her. When he had given her the iron ore she said: 'Now, brahmin, you have got the gold!' She put iron ore the same weight as the gold into the chalice, covered it and sealed the cover on with molten metal. She said: 'Exchange the chalice with the iron ore against the chalice with the gold and ask your brother to give you his older wife!' He talked the matter over with the older wife and exchanged the chalice with the gold against the one with the iron ore he had brought along. Then he went to his brother and said: 'Instead of my gold chalice, may I have your older wife?' And the brother agreed and gave him the older wife. Then he gave the chalice and the older wife to Yid-hphrog-ma and went away to the monastery.

Some time later a group of monks were invited to a place near where Yid-hphrog-ma lived and the brahmin's son was amongst them. The monks were given an ox as a present and they did not go back to the monastery but went to Yid-hphrog-ma's house, and Yid-hphrog-ma offered them food at the prescribed time according to the monastic rules, before midday. Then the brahmin's son and Yid-hphrog-ma made love. The monks found out about it. Yid-hphrog-ma said: 'This is the law of the monastery! They will definitely expel you from the order of monks, and me they will throw into the water. There is no way out of this. Ask the monks for the little ox, and it will drop a khal of gold every day. Put the ox into a well-closed shed, collect the gold, and keep silent about it until I come back.' Then the brahmin asked her: 'Will you not die if you are thrown into the water?' She said: 'I shall not die and I shall return soon.' Then the brahmin asked the monks for the ox, and the monks gave it to him. Then they put Yid-hphrog-ma into a box, together with some rice and her ornaments and her clothes, and threw her into the sea, and the brahmin and the older wife stayed behind in Yid-hphrog-ma's house. He kept the gold yielded by the ox.

IV YID-HPHROG-MA AND THE RISHI SBA-MI-SBA

The box with Yid-hphrog-ma in it drifted on the waves of the ocean onto an island where a great rishi lived whose name was sBa-mi-sba and who, through constant truthfulness, had acquired the power to show forth miracles, and whatever he prayed for would come true. He sometimes went to the forest and sometimes to the sea-shore. One day he came to the sea-shore and saw the great wooden box sealed with molten metal. When he opened the box and looked inside he saw a beautiful and charming girl. The rishi asked her: 'Where do you come from and why were you put into the box?' Then she told him all about what had happened. Great compassion grew in the rishi when he heard this, but there is a law amongst the rishis that in day-time a rishi must stay a stone throw's distance from a woman and at night-time an arrow's distance and thinking he might otherwise lose his power, he went back to his hermitage.

Once a white man with a crystal eye on his forehead came from out of the sea and made love to Yid-hphrog-ma, and she asked him: 'Who are you?' He said: 'I am kLu Duṅ-skyoṅ. I will help you to meet kLu dKar-rgyal, our Guru of the Nāgas, face to face. You have to live with the rishi and request from him all his excellent wheels and secret teachings. Above all he has one made of two fathom-long pieces of sandalwood presented by kLu dKar-rgyal to him. Ask for it! Ask him also for every method of securing success!' And then he disappeared. Yid-hphrog-ma made beer out of rice, which was like nectar, the drink of the gods, having a hundred delicious tastes. She sprinkled a drop of this beer onto the tablets eaten by the rishi. Then the rishi ate one tablet, and it had the total effect of a hundred delicious tastes together. He ate all the tablets and became intoxicated. Then Yid-hphrog-ma put on her ornaments, took the rice beer, and went to the rishi, and the rishi made love to her. When he was sober again he felt great regret at what he had done but it had happened. Then he thought: 'Yet I have not lost my wisdom and shall indeed increase my knowledge of the Mahāyāna view of the state of mind which recognizes the essence of all things. The vow and instruction of the Hīnayāna is a possible, dispensable, and subsidiary cause of Buddhahood; but the certain and principal cause of Buddhahood is the Third Consecration. For the basis of the Third Consecration is the thabs-lam, the method of uniting Emptiness and Bliss. Now I shall offer the woman who is free from attachment, with the marks of the Ye-shes* Ḍākinīs, Kun-tu bZaṅ-mo, the Excellent Mother of All the Buddhas, to Bram-ze Chhen-po Yan-lag mDah-riṅ and Black Garuḍa, the King of Achara.' Then he addressed Yid-hphrog-ma:

'Kun-tu bZaṅ-mo, Great Mother of the Buddhas,
Woman free from attachment, who has wisdom,
The goddess who is the origin of the indescribable Bliss of Emptiness,
Appearing as Yid-hphrog Lha-mo:
I bow before bDud-rtsi-ma, the principal of the eight goddesses of medicine.'

He kept her for seven days as his consort for the growing of his Bliss of Emptiness. Then Yid-hphrog-ma said:

'You are appearing in a wrathful and a fearful mood,
You who are subduing the evil spirits,
In your right hand holding a Vajra,
In your left hand a snake noose,
Adorned with a necklace of snakes and jewels.
Great Hero who is wearing a loin cloth of tiger skin,
Sitting in a blaze of wisdom fire,
Please, give me your blessing and Supreme Wisdom!'

The rishi asked Yid-hphrog-ma: 'Will you prepare a sacrificial offering?' She prepared it and he said: 'Be of good cheer!'

Then he gave her an invisible-making charm protecting her from the wild men of the jungle,
And the wheel in which to spell-bind the power of kings,
And a wheel to work spells on courtiers,
A wheel to numb generals and make them immobile,
And spells to make kings crawl before you.
The courtiers will obey every nodded sign;
A wheel to keep the people in order,
A wheel to infatuate men
And a wheel to bind and to beat.
Wheels to ward off evil visitations,
To subdue your enemies;
The wheel of various magic articles and mantras,
The wheel to make obedient,

* Wisdom.

A wheel to make men follow you,
A wheel to make women follow you and to turn their minds in your favour.

Two fathoms of sandalwood he gave to her. Yid-hphrog-ma said: 'Instructions to bind the enemy?' Then he gave her two ropes made of his own hair, nine fathoms each, two strands of hair, about the thickness of a piece of sheep's dung. He said:

'Wise woman, believe in the teachings,
Go to the brahmin Yan-lag Mdah-riṅ and ask him for instruction.'

V YID-HPHROG-MA IN THE LAND OF THE NĀGAS

Yid-hphrog-ma put all her belongings in the box and used the two sticks of sandalwood as oars. She rowed to another island. There she searched for the brahmin Yan-lag mDah-riṅ and she saw a brahmin in a hut made of leaves. His hair, eyebrows and moustache, [the three] were all red; he had a sword in his belt and a dagger in his hand. The brahmin asked her: 'Where do you come from?' She said: 'I come from the brahmin sBa-mi-sba', and told him all about it. Then he laughed: 'Ha, ha! Ordinary people cannot go to that rishi sBa-mi-sba. I will examine you', and cut her trunk open with his dagger. Inside her trunk the palace of the Medicine Buddha became visible, and the lineage of the brahmins, the goddesses of medicine, and the lineage of the teachings. There the Medicine Buddha was teaching the gods and goddesses and brahmins, the attendant disciples, Buddhist and non-Buddhist. Many Buddhas and Bodhisattvas were offering to him, four great kings guarding the palace, Brahmā, Indra and demons were offering and officiating. He said:

'Beautiful, charming woman, free from attachment,
Excellent Mother who gave birth to the Buddha,
Reincarnation of the mind of the Medicine Buddha,
Woman, I bow before you, mDaṅs-ldan-ma,'

he said this, and kept her as a consort. Then Yid-hphrog-ma offered him a skullful of rice beer with a hundred tastes and said:

'With your majestic look and pleasing form,
Showing the marks of utmost perfection,
You are holding a sword for cutting ignorance and holding a book,*

* This shows that he is an emanation of the Bodhisattva Mañjusrī.

Able to dispel with your rays the darkness of ignorance.
Tutelary deity with wisdom and mercy,
It is you who can increase my knowledge.'

Then she prayed to him. And he replied: 'Prepare the sacrificial offering and pray!' And she prayed.

Then he gave her the wheel of victory
And the wheel to keep the wars away
And the wheel to protect from the enemy
And the wheel to drive out the enemy
And the wheel to turn the enemies against each other
And the wheel of fire for burning
And the wheel of air to cause explosions to the enemy
And the wheel of water to cause floods
And the wheel of iron for cutting
And the wheel of wood to bring to you
And the Hai hKhor-lo for breathing fire.

He said:

'Listen, Yid-hphrog-ma!
Keep this wheel on your body against Nāgas' poison
And go down into the country of the Nāgas.
There ask kLu dKar-rgyal for instruction!'

She left her belongings and other wheels with the brahmin and went to the sea-shore and called the kLu Duṅ-skyoṅ. He came and gave her saffron and he said:

'You human beings are so contaminated,
Wash yourself in this or else you'll get diseases.'

She washed all her body in saffron water. Then kLu Duṅ-skyoṅ took her on his back. And they reached the country of the Nāgas. He gave her two jewels and he said: 'My sister is a gate-keeper of the kLu dKar-rgyal, a Yoginī you can recognize by her whiteness. Give her the jewels from me and ask her to introduce you to kLu dKar-rgyal.' Then Yid-hphrog-ma came in front of the gate of a great palace. There were many Nāga girls and amongst them a white Yoginī. She walked up to her, and the beauty of the Nāga girls was outshone by the fair and charming body of Yid-hphrog-ma. The king of the Nāgas admired her then, and the Nāga girls became jealous and sent poison steam from their mouths which stayed for a day and a night; and kLu

Duṅ-skyoṅ saw the steam and he thought the Nāga girls would kill Yid-hphrog-ma with their jealousy. But Yid-hphrog-ma was not harmed and stayed sitting there in all her brightness. Then the Nāga girls were amazed and introduced her to kLu dKar-rgyal.

Yid-hphrog-ma was brought into the presence of kLu dKar-rgyal and presented a jewel to him. Then she said:

'Your body's colour is white and shining brightly,
With your excellent handsome form and young and beautiful appearance,
Please, give me instruction in the superior arts and the wheels.'
kLu dKar-rgyal replied:
'You are fair and beautiful and look like a goddess,
With a sweet fragrance like saffron and attractive,
Infatuating men and outshining the girls of Nāgas and gods.
I will fulfil all your wishes.'

He said this and gave her the wish-fulfilling wheel. Then he said: 'I will keep you as my female consort', and he did so. Then the Nāga girls offered her a thousand jewels and Duṅ-skyoṅ offered her ten thousand jewels.

VI THE THREE PROTECTORS' INSTRUCTION

Then she returned to Yan-lag mDah-riṅ, the great brahmin and offered him 500 jewels and told him:

'Will you, please, pay great attention!
Because of evil past deeds I have a bad body,
Of a low birth, born as a female.
I am passing through great suffering caused through my own fault by a great amount of the five poisons:*
I was attacked by the poisonous steam from the Nāga girls
But I did not die, through your kindness.
From now on, please, protect me, my Guru!'

Then he said:

"For anyone acquiring merit for the sake of even one being there will be no hell;
But above all for one who has made even one step to help the sick,
There is no hell,
And also it can cause great merit to be acquired
And the gaining of Enlightenment within one life.

* Greed, hatred, ignorance, envy, pride.

You have done great and difficult deeds,
You have been helped with sincerity and kindness;
You and all those who helped you, both will gain great and good rewards.
Do you remember why you had to do those things?'

She replied: 'No, I don't.' He replied: 'Tonight go to the Black Garuḍa, the King of Achara, and ask him for instruction. Tomorrow I and sBa-mi-sba will go to him for the sacrificial offering. If you ask him why you had to do all these things we will tell you all about it.' Then Yid-hphrog-ma turned her wish-fulfilling wheel, and immediately she came to Achara. Then Achara made a threatening gesture and said: 'Oṃ Maṇi Padme Hum. How I pity the beings who go through suffering and who commit sins! Please, look down on us, Great Buddha of Infinite Light!' Then he asked: 'Who are you?' Then she told him all about herself. Then he gave her a skullful of sanctified beer, and said: 'I am going to examine you'. She offered the beer up to the rishi and the brahmin and the great Achara and to kLu dKar-rgyal, and she drank all of it. Then Achara laughed: 'Ha, ha', and covered his head with his robe. Then Yid-hphrog-ma offered him a skullful of rice beer. Then King Achara said: 'What a splendid offering!' Yid-hphrog-ma acted as a Ḍākinī and, holding the skull-cup, he exclaimed: 'The consort free from attachment is the cause of knowing Perfect Reality! Thabs and Shes-rab—Method and Wisdom. The Consort without desire represents Śūnyatā.* The Wisdom which knows Śūnyatā together with the Bliss! One without the other, and Enlightenment cannot be experienced. Just as one hand cannot perform anything perfect and one wing cannot fly. By the strength of former prayers sick people are healed and the miseries of the poor are being dispelled. I bow before you, the immortal goddess of medicine!' And he drank it and took her as a consort. She said: 'Son of the Dhyāni Buddha of Infinite Light! Holding the lotus flower and the crystal rosary,† looking down on the six kinds of beings with mercy, above all the god of the snow-fenced land! Please, protect me with your mercy!' Then Achara said: 'I shall fulfil your wish and make the sacrificial offering.' Then he gave her the wheel to dispel maledictions and the wheel to undo magic wrought by heretics and the wheel of success in growing medicinal plants, and the wheel for the ripening of medicinal fruits. Then he made the threatening gesture to the four directions, beginning from the south, and from all four directions came inconceivable quantities of food and drink and medicines and nectar. Then Achara‡ blessed those foods and they were turned

* Emptiness, a philosophical term in Mahāyāna Buddhism.

† The attributes of the Bodhisattva Avalokiteśvara, the special protector of Tibet.

‡ Achara and the rishi and the brahmin are emanations of the three Protectors.

into nectar of five colours. The next day drums and many other noises were heard. Then Achara told Yid-hphrog-ma: 'Prepare an offering! The rishis Yan-lag and sBa-mi-sba are coming.' Then Yid-hphrog-ma prepared it and when she looked up she saw the rishi and the brahmin flying through the air towards Achara like birds. Achara made thrones composed of different jewels and precious stones, and the three of them sat there. Then they made the sacrificial offering with Yid-hphrog-ma officiating, and she offered them all her jewels and the beer of a hundred tastes. Then she said: 'I bow before Avalokiteśvara who has great compassion! I bow before Mañjuśrī who is the Light which dispels the darkness of ignorance. I bow before Vajrapāṇi who conquers evil spirits by his great strength. Please, look with compassion on me and on the six kinds of beings! Give me your blessing to enable me to work for the sake of future beings!' Then the great rishi (Achara) said: 'O Yid-hphrog-ma, a long time ago the great Buddha gSer-thub gave his blessing to you as Mother Kun-tu-bzaṅ-mo, and he gave you to dPal-chhen Heruka, and he commanded you to plant different medicinal plants in India, China, Nepal, Khotan, Tibet, and so on, for the sake of future beings. We three are to be a help for success, and King Utpala-gdoṅ, Queen bLo-gros bDe-byed-ma, and Paṇḍita Khrus-kyi sDoṅ-po, and above all the ministers bLo-gros Chhen-po and gSer Chhen-po, as prophesied by the wishing ox. Starting from Bodh Gayā and the above-mentioned places you have to plant as commanded by the Buddha. Do you remember that?' When he said this, at that moment she remembered it through the power of her former prayers. Then she prayed a great prayer before the three incarnations of the three gods, Avalokiteśvara, Mañjuśrī, and Vajrapāṇi, for success for the sake of all beings. Then she turned the wish-fulfilling wheel, and immediately she got with all her belongings to her home, and she met the brahmin Shes-rab Ral-gri. And Shes-rab Ral-gri was very glad and told her and said:

'Most beautiful are you,
Charming like a daughter of the gods,
With a pleasing fragrance and a handsome form,
He who looks upon you is never sated,
The Incarnate Goddess of Medicine!
I bow before the goddess Rigs-byed-ma.
It is a great joy to meet the friend of my heart,
Not destroyed by the sea,
Not troubled by sickness.
Is it a dream or reality?'

'As the result of my making offerings and praying to the little wishing ox I got a khal of pieces of gold for each night and day. I have sealed the door of the treasury where the gold is kept.' Yid-hphrog-ma said: 'Wise, acute and judicious man of brahmin caste, Incarnation of the Medicine Buddha, having found you is the dawn of good fortune for me. I have heard the prophecy from the Great Buddha Ser-thub that I would plant the seeds of medicine in Khotan, Nepal, Tibet, Eastern and Western India, China, etc. Please, go and bring me medicinal tree shoots from the country near the Eastern Ocean.' She gave him a wheel to keep the war away and a wheel to drive the war out and sent him to the country near the Eastern Ocean. Then the brahmin Shes-rab Ral-gri went to the Eastern king Pad-ma gDoṅ. He presented the two wheels to him and he brought from him snake's heart sandalwood and a thousand different kinds of shoots from medicinal trees. He brought them to Yid-hphrog-ma and told her: 'Charming Yid-hphrog-ma, please, take the thousand shoots of medicinal trees and the snake's heart sandalwood to make medicine which drives out the sickness and suffering caused by the three poisons. Plant them quickly!'

At that time Yid-hphrog-ma bore a son to the brahmin Shes-rab Ral-gri, called brahmin dGah-ba'i bLo-gros. Then Yid-hphrog-ma asked the brahmin: 'Where do they have more gold, in Eastern or Western India?' The brahmin went to find out. He said: 'There is a rich man called Much-gold who lives in the Forest Monastery.' Then Yid-hphrog-ma turned the wheel of attracting men to herself and Much-gold came to her. When Much-gold saw Yid-hphrog-ma he fell in love with her and felt great desire, and they became husband and wife. Then Yid-hphrog-ma turned the wishing-wheel, and all Much-gold's possessions came to her. Then Yid-hphrog-ma sent the brahmin Shes-rab Ral-gri to find medicinal plants and Much-gold to find more gold and they found it.

VII THE ABDUCTION OF THE QUEEN

Once the son of king Utpala-gdoṅ and queen bLo-gros bDe-byed-ma, whose name was mDzes-ldan, fell ill through some defilement. When the queen and her son were bathing in a swimming pool an ape-man of the jungle abducted them. Then the king suffered much grief so that, in his thin face, the eyes sank deeply into the sockets. The king attempted to vanquish the ape-man but without success. Yid-hphrog-ma gave the brahmin Shes-rab Ral-gri the wheel to drive away the enemy, to make him silent, to become invisible, and to protect from the ape-man, and sent him to snatch the king's son from the ape-man. Then the brahmin went to the ape-man's country. When the brahmin reached the ape-man's place the queen was sleeping with the ape-man and had put her little son into a box, and the brahmin snatched him away, and the queen awoke and put her hand out saying: 'My son, my son?' Then the ape-man also awoke and asked the queen: 'What happened?' Then the queen said: 'You took my son away!' The ape-man replied: 'If I have taken your son I am not the owner of the gold frog and the red sandalwood dagger.' Then the queen said, 'What should I do with your golden frog and red sandal dagger? I want my son!' Then the ape-man said: 'If I am without the golden frog and the red sandal dagger I will die.' Then she said: 'If you don't give me my son I shall kill the frog!' The ape-man said, 'You cannot kill the frog except with the help of the paṇḍita with magic power who can burn it with the sacrificial fire from the thorn bush. I am going to help you to search for your son.' He got up, and the queen said: 'No one but you can have taken my son. If I do not get him back I shall send the army of the king of India against you and I shall kill you.' He said: 'Oh, oh! Then I will eat human flesh!' The brahmin who had snatched her son gave him to Yid-hphrog-ma. Yid-hphrog-ma engaged three nurses for him and kept him in a secret place. After some time the king had a dream in which a white man appeared and told him: 'Your son has been snatched away!' Then he exclaimed: 'Now I believe my queen and my son are separated! What a suffering this world is! Now, if I cannot meet mother and son in this life any more, bless me, my Guru and Three Jewels, so that I meet them in the next life.' He cried aloud, 'My wife and son!' and wept. Immediately many ministers came to attend to him, and asked: 'Oh, what has happened?' And he told them his dream about the queen. Then he said: 'Listen, my ministers, all compounded things are impermanent. It is in the nature of things that those who have been together are separated again. I want to give up my kingdom and devote my life to the Dharma.* Who of my subjects, ministers or generals would like to buy my kingdom? I'll sell it at the price of 1,800,000 khals measured by Indian great Bre. If I sell it my mind will become free from the sense of possessions. Because even I do not know when I shall die it is better if I now give up the desire for property.' His ministers tried to restrain him but they were not able to. Then he sent out a proclamation about selling his kingdom and at what price. Yid-hphrog-ma heard about the decision of selling the kingdom. She went to see the king. Through his ministers she made it known that she was prepared to buy the kingdom for 1,800,000 khals measured out in great Indian bre. The king said: 'What does that generous lady look like?'

* Religion.

Then the ministers said: 'She is beautiful and charming, of gentle speech and whoever sees her wishes to look upon her forever more. She is rich in property, herds, gold and jewels, a son, and she is fortunate and would be well suited to be a queen. If you have her as a queen your joy and happiness will continue always, and with her you can gain more glory and fame, and it is improbable that you have ever seen so beautiful a lady.' Then the king replied: 'She cannot be compared to one hair of my queen bLo-gros bDe-byed-ma.' Then the ministers said, 'She outshines the girls of the gods, human beings and nāgas and she is more handsome than hundreds or thousands of bDe-byed-mas'. Then they called Yid-hphrog-ma to the king. The king's mind was very much taken with Yid-hphrog-ma but it also was very troubled by the loss of his queen and son. So he stepped onto the top of the palace, and Yid-hphrog-ma was in the middle of it. Then Yid-hphrog-ma turned the wheel and made the king's mind come and join her. Made powerless the king came to her. He made Yid-hphrog-ma his consort and declared her queen. She addressed the king and the ministers: 'Kun-tu bZaṅ-po appearing as king, and all your attendant Bodhisattvas appearing as ministers, I will offer you the prince mDzes-ldan. I will conquer the evil ape-man too. Before long I will offer you your queen too. If you promise me to fulfil one wish I shall do all this.' The king promised it and the ministers did not interfere. 'If you will keep,' she said, 'mDzes-ldan and my son dGah-ba'i bLo-gros like younger and older brother and make no distinctions between them.' Then the king was overjoyed. 'You have a beautiful form and sweet voice and a gentle voice and a kind heart; you have accomplished your mind's quest for knowledge, I bow before you who are the incarnation of the goddess sMug-bsel-ma with the smiling face, please, fulfil the wishes of suffering beings!' Then Yid-hphrog-ma turned the wishing-wheel, and all her property, her house, her wishing ox, and prince mDzes-ldan, the brahmin Shes-rab Ral-gri and her son dGah-ba'i bLo-gros and the rich man Much-gold, came and filled the king's palace, and the king and his ministers were very much astonished. Especially she offered them mDzes-ldan, and he told his story. The king made the brahmin Shes-rab Ral-gri the head of all officials of which his kingdom had about 1600 because he thought: 'This man is very wise and brave.' Then the king said: 'Until now your name was Shes-rab Ral-gri. From now on it is Great-minded Minister of the Indian King of the Dharma.' He asked his ministers and subjects to find out from the soothsayers which of the two, prince mDzes-ldan and brahmin dGah-ba'i bLo-gros, was better suited for worldly activities and which for religious activities. The soothsayers said: 'The brahmin's son is suited for the vocation of practising the science of medicine, prince mDzes-ldan is suited for religion in general.' Then the king said: 'Well now, which of the two will be the greater gain for my kingdom?' The soothsayers said: 'If dGah-ba'i bLo-gros rules the kingdom he will benefit it more.' Then king Utpala felt regret at the thought that another should come into the place of his own son and asked paṇḍita Khrus-kye sDoṅ-po again about this question, and the paṇḍita gave the same answer as the soothsayers. Then the king believed it and made mDzes-ldan a member of the clergy and to dGah-ba'i bLo-gros he gave the kingdom and gave him the name of King mDah-ba'i bLo-gros. Then the king told Yid-hphrog-ma: 'Now bring back my queen bDe-byed-ma from out of the hand of the ape-man and conquer the ape-man!' Then Yid-hphrog-ma said: 'Get me your Garuḍa* bird which eats human flesh, and I will try and find a method of bringing the queen here.' Then the king caught a young Garuḍa bird and gave it to Yid-hphrog-ma. Then Yid-hphrog-ma took human flesh from the cemetery and fed it to the young Garuḍa. She said: 'King of the birds with the powerful wings, when the strength of your wings is perfected fly to the place of the evil ape-man in the border city and bring queen bDe-byed-ma, the golden frog and the red sandalwood dagger to the palace. Come back with a great show of the strength of your wings and of your consummate skill!' Then the young Garuḍa nodded three times. Then Yid-hphrog-ma put the invisible-making wheel on the rich man Much-gold and sent him as a messenger to the queen. The wheel was prepared so as to make him invisible only to the ape-man. She sent a message as follows: 'Fair and well-favoured Queen, when you went to bathe in the swimming pool we lost you by the hand of the evil ape-man. The ape-man could not eat prince mDzes-ldan because the brahmin snatched him from you. From the separation of mother and son you suffered like one in hell. Prince mDzes-ldan has reached the king's palace. Now is the perfect moment. I am sending a powerful garuḍa to escort you home. Bind the golden frog and the red sandalwood dagger to this rope made of brahmin's hair and lay it on the garuḍa's back. You can ride on the top of it and come back to the palace without fear or suspicion.' With this message she sent the rich man Much-gold and he fulfilled his task well. Because of his successful errand he became Minister Much-gold. Then Yid-hphrog-ma instructed the bird as before and sent it to escort the queen back. When the ape-man was away the queen loaded the golden frog and the red sandalwood dagger on the garuḍa and she also rode back on it. The ape-man came running trying to catch her but he was not even able to catch the garuḍa's shadow. When the queen came back she met the king but because she had forcibly stayed with the ape-man and had had to eat

* Kind of eagle.

human flesh she had lost her good looks, and the king did not believe that it was her. The king invited paṇḍita Khrus-kyi sDoṅ-po who performed a ritual ablution on the queen, and she became as before. Paṇḍita Khrus-kyi sDoṅ-po burned the golden frog with the wood of the thorny bush. Then the ape-man became desiccated. The king and his ministers were rejoicing at having their prince and queen back and the ape-man conquered.

VIII THE PLANTS FROM HEAVEN

Then the king addressed Yid-hphrog-ma:

'Yid-hphrog-ma, beautiful as the autumn moon,
Your melodious voice is putting Brahmā's voice to shame,
You have the Perfect Mind of Wisdom which knows all of Reality whatsoever.
I bow before you as a great Medicine Goddess,
You are fulfilling the wishes of me and all beings,
Planter of medicine for the sake of all beings.
I am offering you this medicinal plant
Which is the cause of happiness.
Please, bless all six kinds of beings
To escape from sickness!'

He offered her the plant, the cause of happiness. Then the queen spoke:

'Beautiful Yid-hphrog-ma who wears the cloth of modesty
And is adorned with the ornaments of Wisdom,
Seated on the seat of faithfulness,
Wearing at her belt the sword for the cutting of doubt;
Who has overcome the three worlds
And who acts as a guide through the three worlds.
I pay homage to you with my body, my voice and my mind,
sMug-bsel-ma, the Goddess of Medicine,
For the sake of your protecting countless beings
Who have suffered from sickness
I also offer you this plant of sandal gor-shi-sha.
Please, take this plant and protect us from hot and cold diseases!'

She offered the gor-shi-sha plant borrowed from heaven with its root, branches, fruit and leaves.

The raksha Mahata heard about Yid-hphrog-ma's perfection. When Yid-hphrog-ma stayed with king Utpala and queen bDe-byed-ma surrounded by their ministers the raksha brought soldiers along. Yid-hphrog-ma gave the king the wheel for victory over the enemy, and to the ministers she gave the wheel to drive away the enemy. The wheel to catch and bind kings she gave to the minister bLo-gros Chhen-po and she also gave him the rope plaited from three plaits of a great rishi's hair. To the minister Much-gold she gave the wheel to catch and bind ministers and a rope made of a great rishi's hair. She gave the wheel to bind soldiers to King mDah-ba'i bLo-gros. Then Yid-hphrog-ma herself turned the wishing-wheel and fought with the raksha. Rakshas have often many heads and many hands. The king of the rakshas has twenty-one heads and forty-two hands and as weapons he uses bows and arrows and axes and spears and so on. One of the raksha's ministers called Khyab-pa Lag-riṅ had eleven heads and twenty-two hands and carried the same weapons as the king. King Utpala-gdoṅ and King mDah-ba'i bLo-gros stayed in the fortress and turned the wheel the way Yid-hphrog-ma had instructed them. The ministers bLo-gros Chhen-po* and gSer-chhen-po (Much-gold) acted as generals and fought with the rakshas. The king of the rakshas threw his weapons against the minister bLo-gros Chhen-po who threw the rope made of brahmin's hair against the king of the rakshas. The rope fell on his eleventh head and clasped it tight. When the raksha minister threw his weapons against minister Much-gold he also used the rope made of rishi's hair as a lasso and it encircled the sixth head which was a monkey's head. Then the rakshas lost their battle and went back to their own country. The king and minister of the rakshas were brought to the palace and given to Yid-hphrog-ma. Then Yid-hphrog-ma told them: 'Powerful strong king and minister, the two of you, you do not care about your future life and have destroyed the merit accumulated by you and your like making war because of your evil minds. Why did you act like this causing suffering to yourselves as well as harming other people?' The king and the minister of the rakshas answered: 'Beautiful and charming Yid-hphrog-ma, blemishless to behold from all directions, we did self-destroying deeds and those harming other people for the sake of getting you. Please, protect the life of the two of us!' Minister bLo-gros Chhen-po and minister Much-gold brought each a plait of rough matted hair of an ordinary person and they beat the raksha king and minister who suffered as if their bodies were alternatively burned in fire and dipped into cold water and they cried with pain. Then they requested Yid-hphrog-ma as follows: 'Yid-hphrog Lha-mo who knows how to do things, who has compassion: we will offer you these six good plants: nutmeg, cloves, saffron, cardamom, camphor and sandalwood with leaves and branches which can drive away diseases and

* New name of the brahmin Ral-gri.

pain, and another medicinal plant from which all medicines can be made. We are offering them to you. Please, make us into friends of king Utpala and protect our life!' Then Yid-hphrog-ma made king Utpala and his minister into friends of the raksha king and minister, and since that time the two countries have been helping each other.

The king sGra-chhen-zhen of the barbarians heard about Yid-hphrog-ma's perfection and he sent two brahmins to abduct her. When Yid-hphrog-ma went out to disport herself the two brahmins got hold of Yid-hphrog-ma and brought her before king sGra-chhen-zhen. Then the king of the barbarians conceived a great desire for her, and after some time the king made an offering to the heretic gurus and their disciples. And he asked Yid-hphrog-ma: 'Would you like to make some offering to them?' She said: 'Yes, I will also make offerings, and give me the necessary objects!' Then he gave her all that was necessary. Then the king offered to the heretics, and Yid-hphrog-ma invited the Buddha and his disciples in the sky and made an offering. The heretics grew angry. Then the king said to Yid-hphrog-ma: 'Would you like to see Mahā Deva?' Then Yid-hphrog-ma saw Mahā Deva and she made the gesture against the evil eye, and his figure disintegrated. Then the heretics got even angrier and used black magic against Yid-hphrog-ma. Yid-hphrog-ma turned the wheel to drive away the heretics' black magic. Once when Yid-hphrog-ma was staying with the king on the top of the palace she felt the impact of axes, spears, and other weapons hitting her which were sent by the black magic of the heretics. Yid-hphrog-ma turned the wheel and they could not harm her. The king was astonished and presented to her a stone from which all earthy medicines can be made and a water from which all watery medicines can be made and a fire from which all fiery medicines can be made and an air from which all airy medicines can be made and a wood from which all woody medicines can be made, one juice from which all syrup medicines can be made, one animal life from which all animal medicines can be made and one gum from which all resinous medicines can be made. He offered her a tree with these eight substances on it, with branches and leaves and fruit from which all conceivable medicines could be made. He said: 'Beautiful Yid-hphrog-ma, you were contemplating to plant for the sake of all beings and to drive away their diseases. This is a medicinal tree, the origin of all medicines. I present you with it for not having been harmed by the heretics.'

When king Utpala was unhappy because he was separated from Yid-hphrog-ma he told bLo-gros dGah-ba'i: 'Handsome young dGah-ba'i bLo-gros, you have received much kindness from your mother Yid-hphrog-ma since you were a small child. Your mind and that of your mother cannot even be separated for a short moment. Thinking and thinking, I keep remembering her.' Then king bLo-gros dGah-ba'i replied: 'Listen, I bear deep affection to my mother who has given body and mind to me. Because of her beauty which has proved to be fateful to her, she has been abducted by the king of the barbarians. The heart of a son without a mother is colder than water. O please, protect me today and forever more, Three Jewels!' Then queen bDe-byed-ma said to the kings: 'There is no need to be so worried about it. If you ask paṇḍita Khrus-kye sDoṅ-po he will find a method of getting her back.' They requested the paṇḍita, and the paṇḍita told them: 'On an Indian island lives a great rishi called sBa-mi-sba. I'll try and get a suggestion from him how to get her back.' The paṇḍita went to the rishi and told him what had happened. The rishi sBa-mi-sba turned the wheel of fire and burned all the heretics there while Yid-hphrog-ma and the king remained unharmed. Then king sGra-chhen-zhen took Yid-hphrog-ma to king Utpala, and the king of the barbarians became Utpala's subject. Then Yid-hphrog-ma sent some reviving nectar to the country of the barbarians, and the king of the barbarians instilled it into the burned bodies of the heretics. They all came back to life, and Yid-hphrog-ma also reformed once again the teachings of the heretics. The two kings and the queen were very happy to get Yid-hphrog-ma back and they were gratified that the king of the barbarians had become their subject. Paṇḍita Khrus-kye sDoṅ-po addressed Yid-hphrog-ma in this way: 'Beautiful and charming Yid-hphrog-ma! By your beauty you make people happy. Driving all diseases away you make people cross the four rivers.* I and all beings who have been one another's mother in past lives, bow before you, goddess who has obtained wisdom and siddhis† from now until we reach Enlightenment, look after us with your mercy and bless us and keep our lives free from sickness, enabling me to spread and preserve the teachings of medicine.'

IX THE PLANTING OF THE MEDICINES

When the time to die had come for the wishing ox he said to Yid-hphrog-ma: 'Yid-hphrog Lha-mo, appearing for the welfare of all beings! The power of your prayers has driven the diseases of all beings away. Out of your mercy you will plant the seeds of medicine. I bow before you, the goddess of medicine, 'Od-rjaṅ-ma. Indifferent to all the troubles you have taken upon yourself, you have gladly brought seeds from different places. Ask the brahmin

* The four sufferings of birth, old age, disease and death.

† Spiritual powers.

Achara rGyal-po and the paṇḍita and king Utpala-gdoṅ, queen bDe-byed-ma, the two ministers bLo-gros Chhen-po and gSer Chhen-po and prince dGah-ba'i bLo-gros to go with you to Bodhgayā and to help you with your prayer for successful planting. What all of you pray for together you will definitely succeed in. The place where you have to plant is one with four great medicine mountains: Between the mountains lies India, China, Khotan, Nepal and Tibet. What you have to plant is herbs, medicinal juices, medicinal trees, metallic medicines, medicinal liquids, medicinal resins, earth medicines, water medicines, fire medicines, air medicines, and animal medicines, that is manifold medicines curing all four kinds of diseases. Pray and plant them! In particular plant my flesh, bone, blood, veins, skin, nails, brain, hair, bile, horny and other parts of my body, and seal it by prayer! Start out from Bodhgayā and they will most certainly grow successfully through the power of places, the power resulting from prayers, the power of help-mates, the power of the natural cause and the power of compassion, and the power of concentration.' Yid-hphrog-ma replied: 'Wishing-ox, incarnation of Gaṇeśa, you have the attainment of all wishes abundantly like rain. Your speech is like a golden mountain. Please, open the lotus flower of my heart and reside there and give me the blessing of the perfect and the lower siddhis!'*

Then Yid-hphrog-ma asked the kings and their attendants as the ox had told her to: 'Incarnations, kings and attendants, you are very fortunate indeed, having accumulated both wisdom and merit. I, sKyes-ba'i Yid-hphrog, mDaṅs-ldan, mDzes-byed-ma, even I, Kun-tu-bZaṅ-mo, have been appointed, for the sake of future beings, to plant medicines: please, do your best to help me.' The king said: 'I bow before the incarnation of the Great Mother of the Buddhas. Whatever you need in planting medicines for the sake of future beings, we will most certainly help you. Please, give me your blessing!' She went to the paṇḍita Khrus-kye sDoṅ-po: 'Fatherless, motherless, born spontaneously from the stalk of the lotus flower in the limpid lotus lake, you are as the five Dhyāni Buddhas, they all exist in you. You are the Reality of them all and the Buddhas of the past, future and present, you are Chenrezi, the speech of the god of Mercy who has the five kinds of Wisdom and of bodies, who is called Padmasaṁbhava, as reincarnation of Avalokiteśvara, I bow before the paṇḍita Khrus-kye sDoṅ-po who has no equal in the three worlds, below the earth, on the earth, above the earth. For the sake of future beings I am planting medicines, praying for success. Please help me by the power of your mercy!' Then the paṇḍita, the king, queen and attendants and Yid-hphrog-ma, all went together to Bodhgayā. Then Yid-

* The lower siddhis are psychic powers.

hphrog-ma prayed: 'Gurus and Buddhas and Bodhisattvas who live in all the ten directions, Medical Buddha, and lineage of Rishis, and brahmins, goddesses and all the lineage of teachers of medicine, tutelary deities and Ḍākinīs, who are full of mercy and wisdom, and especially rishi sBa-mi-sba, brahmin Yan-lag mDah-riṅ, the Black Garuḍa king of Achara, paṇḍita Khrus-kye sDoṅ-po, king and queen and ministers and gods and nāgas who like the religion of the good. All of you, please, come here and help with my prayer for success, for the sake of future beings. Then she scattered a thousand Sraṅ of gold into the air, and wherever she offered it there the gods and tutelary deities found gold in their hands, and especially the three brahmins who were making a sacrificial offering, had much gold in their lap. Then the rishi sBa-mi-sba said: 'Let us go to help Yid-hphrog-ma with the success of her prayer for the sake of future beings!'

Then the three of them flew to Bodhgayā. Yid-hphrog-ma again offered a thousand Sraṅ up into the air and repeated her prayer as before. Yid-hphrog-ma rubbed the red sandalwood sword and sam-chog sandalwood half into powder, and the other half she cut into little pieces and planted them in the above-mentioned four great medicine mountains and also in the countries of India, Khotan, China, Nepal and Tibet; she planted all seeds of medicine and prayed: 'I, Yid-hphrog Lha-mo, am planting, as the wishing-ox had prophesied, seeds of medicine to drive out sicknesses caused by the three poisons,* in East and West India, Khotan, China, Nepal and Tibet. As I have planted them, so they will grow leaves and spread branches and fruit will ripen on them. May the physician-saints and brahmin-saints and other learned physicians of the lineage of the Medicine Buddha gain their medicines effortlessly and with them drive away all diseases, and may Enlightenment follow speedily!' After this the three rishis and brahmins returned home. Khrus-kye sDoṅ-po stayed in Bodhgayā praying for Yid-hphrog-ma's success in increasing the growth and efficacy of the medicinal seeds and plants and for their successfully destroying the pains caused by diseases. The king and queen and the ministers and their court went back to the palace.

X THE MEDICINE BUDDHA'S PROPHECY

Yid-hphrog-ma thought: 'Are the seeds planted with prayers for the sake of future beings succeeding or not?' At that moment the king said: 'Shall I request the paṇḍita Khrus-kye sDoṅ-po to find out whether the planting

* Hatred, desire and ignorance causing excessive bile, air or phlegm.

has been successful?' Then Yid-hphrog-ma invited the paṇḍita to come back to the palace and requested him: 'Incarnation, you who know very clearly the past, the future and the present, please, prophesy to me whether my prayers and plants are going to succeed or not, by looking with your wisdom eyes!' The paṇḍita said: 'Great Mother of the Buddhas who has accumulated a great mass of wisdom and merit. You are the goddess of Medicine who has succeeded in both her purposes, for your own sake and for that of others. You have both wisdom and compassion. Drive away the suffering of all beings! You have undertaken the planting with prayer and compassion; now I will see whether you have succeeded or not.' By his miraculous power he went to all the aforementioned countries and told Yid-hphrog-ma how they had succeeded. 'Goddess of bDud-rtsi-ma appearing as Yid-hphrog-ma, as you prayed when planting for the sake of future beings, so the blessings of Buddhas and Bodhisattvas together with the karmic results of all beings have ripened now. Listen with concentration and engrave it on your heart; the place where the nectar of medicine is growing is as I shall describe to you now: There is one dpag-ts'ad and half a rgyaṅ-grags* north of Bodhgayā a medicine mountain sPos-ṅad-ldan, a jungle of medicinal plants which can be smelled ten dpag-ts'ads away, and all medicines for curing any disease are growing there. The bleak part of the mountain and the rocky part and the grassy part were all celestial mountain parts, and the white mind-made incarnation of a white sandalwood Buddha was residing there, splendid with his physical perfections, and surrounded by his attendants who were all bodhisattvas. Ordinary people and the followers of the Hīnayāna cannot enter there. It can only be used by the Mahāyāna Āryas. One dpag-ts'ad from there was the city of lTa-na-sdug, beautiful and well-constructed, with sixteen thousand pillars made of jewels and arched buttresses, four gates and pediments, eight steps, five walls, the platforms for the offering goddesses and ornamental embroidered hangings, roof ornaments, parapets made of jewels, and covered galleries. In the centre of the celestial palace on a vaiḍūrya throne was the Medicine Buddha sitting in his shining splendour with thirty marks of perfection and eighty-four signs of beauty, surrounded by attendant gods, rishis and brahmins, Buddhists and non-Buddhists, the goddesses of medicine and their lineage of the teachings, and the three Great Protectors (Mañjuśrī, Avalokiteśvara, Vajrapāṇi) and Ānanda and hTs'o-byed gZhon-nu and other rishis and brahmins. All attendants were bodhisattvas, and the city was filled with celestial birds and animals. There were no pebbles and no gravel nor any other imperfections in this city. This was a perfect celestial city, only to be entered and used by those with

* One rgyaṅ-grags is five hundred fathoms. Five hundred rgyaṅ-grags are one dpag-ts'ad.

perfect knowledge and experience of the Mahāyāna. And the Medicine Buddha prophesied: 'Without a shadow of doubt, the medicine plants which you, paṇḍita Khrus-kye sDoṅ-po, saw planted by Yid-hphrog-ma will succeed.' Then the paṇḍita said: 'One dpag-ts'ad to the east from here there is, as you saw, the medicine mountain sPos-ṅad-ldan, remember all its excellence and how the plants are growing on it, as you have seen it, remember it and pray! Two dpag-ts'ads to the south there is the medicine mountain hBegs-byed. The jungle there is of red sandalwood and pomegranates and piper longum are growing there and all plants driving away diseases caused by cold. In that excellent mountain lives the celestial figure of the wisdom of the Medicine Buddha who came into being from sun crystal. His colour and his attendants are indeterminate, he is shining, the Medicine Buddha of great excellency, surrounded by attendants who are all Incarnations. Remembering him, pray! Six thousand dpag-ts'ads away to the West from there is the medicine mountain of Ma-la-ya. There is a jungle of gor-shi-sha sandalwood where the six good plants are growing: nutmeg, cloves, saffron, cardamon, camphor, and sandalwood which gives happiness to the people. On the grassy mountain-side saffron is growing and chick pea (cicer arietanum) and also mineral substances and metallic medicine, medicinal juice and trees, resins, medicines suitable for decoctions, herbs, animal medicine, and all conceivable medicines are growing there. There resides the incarnation of the speech of the Medicine Buddha, all of the choicest jewels, the brightness of whose marks of perfection and beauty is shining in the ten directions. All his attendants are spiritual heroes and ḍākinīs. Remember he is excellent and remembering him, pray!

Five hundred dpag-ts'ads to the north, there is the medicine mountain Gaṅs-chen with a jungle of sa-mchog sandalwood, and Gentiana chiretta or Chirayata, Melia Azedarachta, aloewood and all other medicinal plants driving away diseases caused by heat are growing there. There resides the incarnation of the action of the Medicine Buddha who came out of water-crystal with his marks of perfection and with his excellent ability to exert himself for the sake of beings. All his attendants are gods and goddesses. Remember it and pray!

Between the three mountains Ri hBegs-byed, Ri Gaṅs-chen and Ri sPos-ṅad-ldan the ground is covered with red sandalwood, and all kinds of medicine grow there. The distance between Ri hBegs-byed and Ri sPos-ṅad-ldan is three hundred dpag-ts'ads and eight rgyaṅ-grags; between Ri hBegs-byed and Ri Ma-la-ya there is a distance of five hundred dpag-ts'ads and twenty-five rgyaṅ-grags; between Ri Ma-la-ya and Ri Gaṅs-chen six thousand five hundred dpag-ts'ads; and between Ri Gaṅs-chen and

Ri sPos-ṅad-ldan five thousand six hundred dpag-ts'ads and ten rgyaṅ-grags. Each mountain consists of a thousand rocks made of jewels. Also in North and South India and China white and red sandalwood jungles with medicinal plants in them are ripening; and also in Tibet, Nepal and Khotan grow a certain amount of plants. By reason of Yid-hphrog-ma's prayer and the result of the karma of all beings plants that could not grow in one place grow in another but certainly there is a place for them to grow. I gave the blessing and poisons were made into medicine, so there is nothing that cannot become a medicine; there is nothing that is not a medicine for diseases. Still, remember me, the paṇḍita Khrus-kye sDoṅ-po! Go to the four medicine mountains and have your wishes fulfilled. I went to the four medicine mountains, and there is no mistake about the Medicine Buddha's speech, it is not an illusion, it is real. By remembering his wisdom my faith has been growing deeply. Future beings will be cured from diseases, Yid-hphrog, your wishes will be fulfilled, so be happy!' Then she was very happy getting all her wishes fulfilled and she offered a thousand sraṅ gold to the paṇḍita. Then she said: 'Incarnation who has the signs of perfection, who saw lTa-na-sdug and the successful growing of the medicinal plants in the four mountains, who above all actually has met the Medicine Buddha and who has had from him prophecies and instructions, great saint, fulfiller of our wishes, once again we ask you to protect us.' Then the great minister Much-gold said: 'Incarnation of wonderful Yid-hphrog Lha-mo, with a face beautiful as an opened lotus flower, holding a bowl in the right hand, in the left hand a flute, and a medicine bag containing nectar over her shoulder, goddess of bDud-rtsi-ma who drives away the diseases caused by the three poisons: look with mercy upon beings suffering from diseases and give us the blessings of the genuine nectar medicine!' Then the king asked her: 'Who are the eight medicine goddesses?' Yid-hphrog-ma replied: 'The goddess of bDud-rtsi-ma, the goddess of Grub-pa'i Lha-mo, gZe-brjid Lha-mo, 'Od-ljaṅ, sMug-bsel, gDoṅ-khra-ma, mDaṅs-ldan, Rigs-byed-ma, we are these eight goddesses.'

Then king dGah-ba'i bLo-gros said: 'My bodies and my minds have grown, celestial Mother, who has been appointed to be the goddess of medicine, the goddess bDud-rtsi-ma who increases the power of medicines, the protector of those who suffer from diseases, give me the blessings which enhance the teachings of medicine and which will enable me to improve them.' Yid-hphrog-ma promised to do as requested by her son. Then queen bDe-byed-ma said: 'With your charming and smiling face, adorned with beautiful ornaments, you who has lovely eyes like open lotus flowers, you who has an equal mercy towards all beings, please look with your mercy upon all who suffer from diseases. Please, protect beings and give your blessings and change medicines into nectar!' Then minister bLo-gros Chhen-po said: 'Yid-hphrog-ma who are the goddess of deathlessness, the three rishis and brahmins who have appeared by the glorious power of the Three Protectors: look with your mercy upon all of us who have become disciplined by your teaching, and give me the blessing so that my mind becomes inseparable from yours.' Then the minister and Yid-hphrog-ma immediately turned into the light of a rainbow and they sank into the Medicine Buddha's chest.

XI THE QUEST FOR FERTILITY

Then queen dPal-gyi Khrims-mdzes-ma bore to king dGah-ba'ibLo-gros a prince, Pad-ma dPal, whose queen became Lha-mo dPal-sgron. They had no son and asked the soothsayers who prophesied that in the Ri sPos-ṅad-ldan there was a hare* with a turquoise topknot. They should invite him to their palace, then they would have a son. Then the king asked the soothsayers: 'Who can invite the hare?' The soothsayers replied: 'In the Five-pointed Mountain in China there lives a black-clad rishi Chu-shiṅ Hkhar-ba-hdzin who can invite the hare.' The king asked: 'Who can invite the rishi?' 'The minister Seṅ-ge-stobs-ldan can invite him.' Then the king asked the minister Seṅ-ge-stobs-ldan: 'You are a hero with great knowledge and great strength. We have been looking for signs whether we would get a son and heir, and the soothsayers said: if we invite a hare with a turquoise topknot living in the Ri sPos-ṅad-ldan who can be invited by the rishi in black Chu-shiṅ Hkhar-ba-hdzin, we shall have a son. Will you, please, go and bring him here?' Then he went as the king said. He came near the bank of a big river. He could not cross the river and prayed to the rishi. Then a red man came along the bank of the river carrying a book on his back and a sword in his hand. He said: 'I am going to invite the great rishi but I cannot cross the river.' The red man said: 'If you offer me a gift I can help you across.' The minister had a turquoise called dKar-chen 'Od-hphro in which his life was residing and which he offered to the red man. Then the minister went with the man in red, and when arriving in front of the Five-Point Mountain the red man said to the minister: 'The Five-Point Mountain is like the five fingers raised. On the right-hand point Avalokiteśvara is staying, on the secondTārā, on the left Pha-dam-pa, on the other the black brahmin Chu-shiṅ Hkhar-ba-hdzin, on the middle point Mañjuśrī. Today they are meeting on the

* In Tibetan folklore the hare is regarded as very wise.

middle mountain and making a sacrificial offering. So let us go there.' And they went towards the middle point. They could not enter because of fog and the reflection of rainbows in it. Then he said: 'Great rishi, protect me with your mercy and bless us and fulfil the king's wishes,' and he prayed deeply. Then the fog dispersed and he reached the gate of the middle point mountain. Then the red man came again and said: 'I requested the permission to enter the palace. So come with me!' And he went with him. There was a beautiful translucent palace where there was everything you could wish for. In the palace were Mañjuśrī, Tārā, Avalokiteśvara, Pha-dam-pa and the red man who turned into the black brahmin Chu-shiṅ Hkhar-ba-hdzin and was wearing the turquoise which the minister had offered to him. Then Mañjuśrī asked him: 'Great minister, where are you going?' And the minister told him all about it. Then Mañjuśrī said to the rishi: 'Please, go to India to fulfil the king's wishes.'

The minister and the rishi rode in the sky on a palmyra tree stick. And they flew to the palace of king Pad-ma dPal. He offered the rishi a thousand jewels and told him about his plight. The rishi replied: 'Prepare a chalice made by a thousand jewellers of a thousand jewels, and a handful of white rice with blood of the king and a bag of white rice with blood of the queen* sprinkled by each of them'. Then they offered a chalice, and the blood was drawn with a thorn from a palmyra tree and was sprinkled on a handful of rice by the king and a bag of rice by the queen. Then the rishi said: 'Minister dPa-bo gDoṅ-drug-pa, we need the help of the minister Seṅ-ge sTobs-ldan and Vajrapāṇi, Ambika the king of hunters (reincarnation of Hayagrīva), and the bird with great strength in his wings (celestial appearance of four-handed Avalokiteśvara). We five must go and get the milk of a white lion to feed the hare with.' Then the king offered him ten thousand jewels and said: 'My good fortune is wonderful indeed that you have appeared before me, you who have great miraculous power and strength. Please protect and bless me so that my wishes will be fulfilled. Give us what we wish for! There is no other place for us to turn to. Look upon us with mercy!' Then the rishi put the rice bag and the chalice on the minister's back and they flew on the palmyra tree stick to lTa-na-sdug. There the Medicine Buddha told them about the plants on the mountains as he had told the paṇḍita Khrus-kye sDoṅ-po. In addition, they, but not Khrus-kye sDoṅ-po, heard the prophecy: 'On Ri Gaṅ-chen Vajrapāṇi is staying and Ambika the king of hunters; and on Ri Ma-la-ya gShog-brgyans-chen, the king of the birds; and on Ri hBegs-byed the king of the lions, called Lha-la sGra-sgrogs

* The Lhasa Shol edition has: king, queen and others.

and his female from whom he had always milk. On Ri sPos-ṅad-ldan there is the hare with the turquoise topknot. Moreover, on that mountain there is the deathless nectar of the gods and the human nectar which gives happiness and the demons' nectar which raises the dead.' The Medicine Buddha prophesied where they were to be found on those mountains. The rishi and the minister went to the four mountains and invited Vajrapāṇi, Ambika the king of the hunters, and the king of the birds gShog-brgyans-chen, to accompany them. Then they exchanged the bag of rice with the king's and queen's blood sprinkled on it against a chalice of milk from the king of the white lions. Then they invited the hare from the sPos-ṅad-ldan. They all went to king Pad-ma dPal's palace. Then the six great saints prayed for the fulfilment of the king's wishes. The king offered a hundred thousand jewels to each. Then they went back to their own places. After some time the queen was pregnant and prince dPal-ldan Phun-ts'ogs was born.

XII BIRTH OF BI-BYI DGAH-BYED

Some time later when prince dPal-ldan Phun-ts'ogs had fallen from the palace roof, the minister Seṅ-stobs-ldan brought the demons' nectar for raising the dead and instilled it into him. He was revived. King dPal-ldan Phun-ts'ogs and his queen dbYaṅs-kyi Lha-mo had two sons, one of whom was prince sDoṅ-hdum sKes, married to Rol-rnyed-ma, the daughter of dMar-rgyan, the queen of the rakshas; Rol-rnyed-ma had two sons, king rṄa Chen-po and king Legs-pa'i bLo-gros. The former was a devotee of Tārā, and she prophesied to him: 'If you live with Gaṅ-ga'i Lha-mo, the daughter of the drum maker, she will bear you a son called king Bi-byi dGah-byed who is going to improve the science of medicine like lightning in the country of darkness—Tibet.' King Rṅa Chen-po lived with Gaṅ-ga'i Lha-mo and they had a son Bi-byi dGah-byed. At the same time, the daughter of a brahmin bell-maker was born. Her name was Be-lha dGah-mdzes-ma (fair joy calf-goddess). The prince and the daughter were of very poor health and unintelligent and thin and ugly. Then the daughter of the drum-maker made ten big drums. She offered the drums at Bodhgayā to the ten directions, and the daughter of the bell-maker made ten bells and offered them at Bodhgayā in the same way. The prince and the daughter changed and their skin became beautifully white and they became charming and attractive to look at, their movements and strength were those of Bodhisattvas, and their knowledge increased. King Bi-byi dGah-byed and the daughter Be-lha dGah-mdzes-ma were friends from childhood. They requested their parents' permission and went to the son of a brahmin rGyun-shes-kyi Bu to study medicine. After having acquired a thorough knowledge of all medical texts they returned home. Then these two spread the medical teachings throughout North and East India, China, Khotan, and Nepal. At Rājagiri there was a great doctor Ts'o-byed gZhon-nu who was a saint with a hJa-lus (rainbow body), and prince Bi-byi dGah-byed met him there. He was instructed by him in the Outer, Inner, and In-between Teaching. Then they practised as doctors and were called by the people doctor Bi-byi dGah-byed and doctor Be-lha dGah-mdzes-ma. Then they became devotees of bDud-rtsi sMan-grub (Turning Medicine into Nectar) and attained the blessing of immortality. Even now they are staying in the sandalwood jungles of India.

XIII THE INTRODUCTION OF MEDICINE INTO TIBET

When staying at Bodhgayā, Bi-byi dGah-byed and Be-lha dGah-mdzes-ma were told by Tārā to go to Tibet. This was the time when Tibet was ruled by Lha-tho Tho-ri sNyan-shal, an incarnation of Kun-tu bZaṅ-po. They implored Tārā: 'Great Goddess, by your leave, Tibet is a country of wild men who have faces like rakshas, abounding with demons harming people, and the people are more foolish than cattle and do not acquire merit. They do not know what should be done and what should not be done. Whatever is said to them, they understand the opposite of it. They requite good with evil and they do not know the teachings of medicine. They are committing sins. That is not a country where the teachings of medicine can be furthered. Please, give us leave not to go!' Tārā replied: 'It has been prophesied by the Buddha about the country of Tibet, and all the Buddhas have discoursed on Tibet, and Avalokiteśvara was made the special protector of Tibet. Avalokiteśvara is the chief protector and I am helping him. When you go to Tibet you will teach the people medicine, in the way the Buddha comes with his teaching. There is no doubt of success. Go quickly, and I shall look after you with my merciful eyes. And wou will have the blessing of Avalokiteśvara and great results. By the strength of your former prayers the teaching of medicine will be kept up by the lineage of your families. Be of good cheer and go to Tibet!'

Then the two set out and reached Tibet without a mishap. They came to a district of Tibet where they saw a twenty-year-old girl with the mark of a Dākinī* carrying an old lady out of the door of her house. The two doctors asked her: 'Why have you taken this lady out of this house?' She replied: 'She is my mother but she is sick.' Then they said: 'She is your mother and also she is sick. You should not turn her out of doors. Take her back into the house.' She said: 'This is the custom in Tibet. If she stayed in the house the smell of the disease and the infection† would reach us, and the god of the house would not be pleased.' Then the doctors asked her: 'Do Tibetans have a Guru?' She replied: 'We have Avalokiteśvara.'‡ Again the doctors asked: 'Do you have the Buddha, the Dharma, the Saṁgha, protectors, the science of medicine, and doctors who can cure?' She replied: 'We have the Buddha sNaṅ-ba mTha-yas,§ the Dhamma: Oṃ Maṇi Padme Hum, the Saṁgha of Bhikshus, for a protector the king, for the science of medicine diet prescriptions and enough to know how to stop the blood flowing from fresh wounds with melted butter, to cure us we have the parents.' Again the doctors asked: 'Is it a Tibetan custom that all sick people are taken out of doors?' Then she said: 'If son and daughter are ill the parents will not turn them out.' Then the doctors felt great compassion and thought: 'Tibet is indeed a dark country, where people are capable of behaving like cattle and doing things like that', and they said: 'Listen to us, Rin-chen 'Od-mdzes, who is attentive and beautiful and has the mark of a Dākinī: the country of Tibet is dark and a jungle, and the people are more foolish than cattle because of their lack of merit. You cannot turn sick parents out of the house. This is the custom of barbarians. One's parents, the sick, and the Three Jewels are objects of respect. The Guru, the Buddha and the Saṁgha are your protectors. The teachings of religion and the science of medicine are newly arrived here but there is no proper knowledge of them. We shall kindle the light of the teaching in Tibet, so be happy and announce it to the people!' Then she took her mother back into the house and did as the doctors told her and nursed her back to health. She offered a thousand sraṅ of gold to the two doctors and said: 'You two doctors, full of mercy, incarnations of the Medicine Buddha, who have come to Tibet as prophesied by Tārā for the improvement of the teaching of medicine and to drive away pain and suffering: you are most certainly incarnations of the Speech of the Medicine Buddha, and it is wonderful and fortunate for the king and the people of Tibet that you have

* The yang-yin sign on the forehead or a conch shell sign on the cheek or other marks.

† hgo-ba 'to infect', originally 'to soil'.

‡ Being a dākinī she knew about Avalokiteśvara but generally the people of Tibet did not yet know of him. There also was no Saṃgha of monks at the time.

§ The Buddha Amitābha.

arrived here.' She announced it to the country: 'There are two new healers who have arrived here from India.'

XIV THE KINGS AND THEIR COURT PHYSICIANS

King Lha-tho Tho-ri sNyan-shal heard of the fame of the two doctors introducing medicine into Tibet and he invited them to the palace of Yum-bu lBa-mkhar. He asked them to be seated on thrones made of nine jewelled cushions piled on top of one another. He presented a hundred thousand sraṅ to each. He showed his respect by putting the doctors' feet on his head while kneeling before them, and said: 'O you two excellent doctors, born from compassion, kings of the doctors (Medicine Buddhas) who came to Tibet for the sake of beings! This is a glorious event and a happy day is dawning over Tibet. It is wonderful and my good fortune that you have appeared to me. Please, take the Tibetan people across the lake of sickness to the other shore, and make the teaching of medicine in Tibet as bright and shining as the sun! For the sake of king and subjects I hope you will stay here for ever and will look upon us with mercy.' And he presented Lha-chhen Yid-kyi Rol-chha to Bi-byi dGah-byed. The two doctors replied: 'We are well aware that you are the Incarnation of the Bodhisattva Kun-tu bZaṅ-po appearing as Your Majesty, the King, working for the increase of the teachings, for the sake of beings, and ruling over the country of Tibet. We are happy you have presented Lha-chhen Yid-kyi Rol-chha to us, and we shall stay in Tibet for some time as you requested. Then we shall go back to India, and I shall hand the teaching down to the physician-saint, and his following will grow and increase.' They stayed in Tibet for some time.

Then Lha-chhen Yid-kyi Rol-chha had a son whose name was doctor Duṅ-gi Thor-chog-chen. The two doctors taught him how to diagnose by the pulse, the rules of diet, how to mix medicines, and the surgery by moxa and bloodletting, the dressing and healing of wounds, and texts and commentaries of medical works with their introductions and divisions into theory and practice.

Then the two doctors went back to India. Doctor Duṅ-gi Thor-chog-chen became court physician to king Lha-tho Tho-ri sNyan-shal and to his son, prince Khri-sNyan gZugs-chen. Each descendant of king Khris-nyan gZugs-chen down to king rJe-dPal hKhor-bTsan, had a descendant of doctor Duṅ-gi Thor-chog-chen for his court physician. This is how the kings and doctors became connected: During the earlier part of king Khris-nyan gZugs-chen's life, Duṅ-gi Thor-chog-chen was his physician, during the latter part of it Duṅ-gi Thor-chog-chen's son bLo-gros Chhen-po became his physician. The name of bLo-gros Chhen-po's mother was Ts'angs-pa'i Glu-len-ma. The son of Khri-sNyan gZugs-chen, prince hBroṅ-snyen lDe'u had for a physician the son of bLo-gros Chhen-po, called bLo-gros mTs'uṅs-med. His wife was called dGah-ba dPal. lTag-re gNyan-gzegs, the son of hBroṅ-snyen lDe'u, had bLo-gros Rab-gSal, the son of bLo-gros mTs'uṅs-med, for his physician. His wife, dPal-gyi gZi-brjid-ma, had a son, bLo-gros rGyal-mdzod. He was the physician of king gNam-ri Sroṅ-btsan. bLo-gros rGyal-mdzod's wife was called bLo-gros bZaṅ-mo, and their son was called bLo-gros bShes-gnyen who was the physician of king Sroṅ-btsan sGam-po. bLo-gros bShes-gnyen and his wife dKon-mChhog bZaṅ-mo had a son called hDre-rJe rGya-gar Vajra Chuṅ who was physician to king Guṅ-sroṅ Guṅ-btsan and king Maṅ-sroṅ Naṅ-btsan. He and his wife dGah-skyoṅ-ma had a son called Khyuṅ-po rDo-rje (Eagle Vajra). He was the physician of king hDus-sroṅ Maṅ-po rJe-rluṅ gNam-hphrul-gyi rGyal-po. Khyuṅ-po rDo-rJe's wife was called rGya-sachhos sGron, and the son born to them was gYu-thog Yon-tan mGon-po. He lived for one hundred and twenty-five years and was the physician of king Khri-sroṅ lDe-btsan and his father, king Mes-'Ag-Ts'om. gYu-thog's sons hBum-seṅ, dPal-hBum, and dGah-dgah, were the physicians to the kings Mu-sTegs bTsan-po, Mu-ni bTsan-po and Mu-khre bTsan-po. These three were able to keep up their father's great reputation. Their wife Lhamo dPal-ldan had a son, gYu-thog hGron-mgon, who was the physician of king mṄah-bdag Ral-pa-chan and gLaṅ dar-ma. During their time the teaching of medicine increased but king gLaṅ-dar-ma was trying to destroy religion and the rules of the Discipline. gYu-thog hGron-mgon's wife was Jo-hjam Nor-bu bZaṅ-mo and she had a son called gYu-thog Jo-sras dPal. He was the physician of mṄah-bdag 'Od-sruṅs. With him there was another king who was called Yum-brtan, but it is clear that Yum-brtan was not really of the lineage of the king so that there is no need to talk further about him. gYu-thog Jo-sras dPal and his wife Jo-mo Phun-ts'ogs Nor-bu had a son gYu-thog Byams-pa Thugs-rje. He was the physician of king mṄah-bdag dPal-hkhor bTsan.

Up to now the lineages of the kings and of gYu-thog were linked together. mṄah-bdag dPal-hkhor bTsan had a son sKyed-bde Nyi-ma mGon, and his son was brTa-shes-lde. At the same time as the descendants of the Elder gYu-thog, there lived Byams-pa Thugs-rje's son Byams-pa dKon-mchhog bDe-legs and his son Byams-pa bDe-legs. Up to Byams-pa bDe-legs the lineage was called that of gYu-thog Nyiṅ-ma (Turquoise-roof the Elder). After that it was called the descent of the Younger gYu-thog. But the history of this is explained in the Younger gYu-thog Yon-tan mGon-po's Life Story.

XV HOW THE GYU-THOG FAMILY RECEIVED THEIR NAME 'TURQUOISE ROOF'

Amongst the Elder gYu-thog's lineage there was a very learned man called hDre-rje rGya-gar Vajra (Indian Vajra, Lord over Demons). Since his time the family had the name of gYu-thog-pa. Why are they called gYu-thog-pa (Turquoise-roof) and why Lord-over-demons and why Indian Vajra? The first reason, that is why they are called Turquoise-roof: Once when he was staying at sTod-luṅ sKyid-sna (Happy-place in the Upper-Valley), looking constantly after the sick and accumulating the two kinds of merit: that of learning and that of moral conduct, he was going to revisit an old patient at the Upper-Valley Bridge, when he encountered a beautiful lady, and she asked him to visit her country. He replied: 'I bow before the Medicine Buddha Vaiḍūrya. It would be against my doctor's vow if I did not visit the old patient. If I did not keep my appointment this would make him very sad and unhappy, and those nursing him would abuse me behind my back, and I would be punished by the lineage of my teachers. Beautiful spirit-girl, don't be annoyed and go back to your country.' She said: 'You, Skyid-sna-ba,* King of the Dharma of the Three Worlds, your name is Beneficial Presence, you Bodhisattva, who has conquered the three worlds. Your power has overcome the three worlds by your knowing Śūnyatā. You have perfected your meditation, and the eight demons are at your beck and call. You are well protected by your tutelary deities, and they are showering on you the fulfilment of all your wishes. You have become master over gods, over human beings, and over ghosts, therefore your name is "Master of gods", "Master of human beings", and "Master of ghosts". Therefore your mind is like the sky and does not discriminate between beings because (you know that) all beings have been your parents. Your Excellent Reverence who has no equal, my master, the king of the Nāgas is suffering from a serious illness, so please come for a short while to see him.' He asked: 'Where is your country?' and she pointed to a very dark big rock and said, 'My country is over there.' He said, 'This is very far away, we cannot reach there tonight, I'll come tomorrow.' She said, 'Please, come on this roll of cloth,' and spread it out. When he put his feet on it he reached immediately a country with people in it which he had never seen before. There was a black-coloured magician with a top-knot as big as one man and a body as big as three people, who was lying groaning with pain and suffering in a big castle on a steep mountainside which was decorated with gold and

* Man from Happy-place.

turquoise and other jewels and filled with inconceivable objects of enjoyment. At the head of his bed there was a throne consisting of three layers of cushions piled on top of one another and made of silk, jewels and black antelope's skin whereon he was asked to be seated. The magician addressed him: 'Learned Saint, you who are the best of all the best! That which is able to dispel all bodily pain is the best medicine. He who knows how to mix cooling and warming medicines in the right way is the best doctor. He who knows how to heal wounds is a sure guarantee of happiness. He who can distinguish between hot and cold diseases is the best of the learned. A sweet voice is the best cause of happiness. You have the greatest wisdom and deepest insight. You are one from whose sight everyone benefits and who leads those who follow him into Nirvāṇa. Please, free this evil Nāga from diseases and sufferings!' He replied: 'From what causes have you been afflicted with these diseases?' He said: 'I harmed the crops in such a country, and those who protect the crops from hail put a spell of enchanted mustard seeds on me and they have hit me in a disastrous manner.' He said, 'So this is it, then show me your body!' When he showed it to him he saw mustard seeds in his skin, in his bones, in his veins, and in his flesh. He gave him tablets made of culled khyuṅ-lṅa* and quicksilver to be taken internally, and applied an rgyan-hkhor ointment externally, and immediately the malignant Nāga recovered. Then he said: 'You are a very harmful malignant Nāga born from a raksha father and a nāga mother. Formerly you committed sins and took the breath of people and killed them. In your next life you will be born in the three lower worlds, and I am sorry for this malignant nāga. By the blessing of the Medicine Buddha and the lineage of the teachings your ferocious mind will be cleansed and you will, along with other beings, have powerful enlightened minds and shall be able to be in lTa-na-sdug.' Now the malignant nāga and his attendants conceived faith and offered their lives with the promise to support the followers of the lineage of the teachings. Then he offered many wishing jewels amongst other articles. Then the beautiful girl who had invited him spread the roll of cloth, and when he stepped on it immediately he was transferred back to the place at the bridge. She said to him 'I also want to present you with something, so please come tomorrow at this time to this bridge.' She whirled round like a storm and dissolved into the rocky mountain. Then he went to visit his old patient and returned to his place. The next day he thought: 'Gods and ghosts always are very punctilious in keeping their word,' and went to the bridge. There was thunder and lightning, and heavy rain was falling, and he saw a dead woman's body whose upper part was covered with gold and jewels brought

* Pain-relieving tablets compounded of five medicinal herbs.

on by the river and it did not float on but stayed there in a whirlpool. He thought, 'This is my present which she had told me about yesterday and now she has committed such a great sin for me.' He kept the ornaments and left the body in the river. He put the gold and turquoise on the roof of his house, and a shepherd saw it and said: 'The Lord of beneficent Presence has a turquoise roof', and since that time he was called Learned gYu-thog-pa (Turquoise Roof).

Then he went to India to search for the teachings which turn medicine into nectar, and for the Essence of the Explanation of mGo-thig Rin-chen gNad-ghGrel (Measuring of the Head) written by Nāgārjuna (mGon-po kLu-grub). First he went to dPal-gyi Ri (in South India). He met Nāgārjuna and offered a thousand gold sraṅ, and requested him to teach him the mGo-thig-chen gNad-hgrel. Nāgārjuna taught him the mūla (text), the commentary, and the accompanying instruction as requested. Then he went to Pad-ma'i gLing, and there in a market place he met a brahmin of a majestic appearance who asked him: 'Where are you coming from and for what purpose?' And he told him all about it. The brahmin said: 'Oh, then you are my relative! I am sMan-ba (Doctor) Bi-byi gDah-byed.* If you want to learn the teaching of bDud-rtsi sMan-grub (Turning-Medicine-into-Nectar) go to the Southern Sandalwood Jungle and pray to me and the Medicine Buddha, which are one and the same. He prayed as he was told, and first of all came the Medicine Buddha and taught him the whole of the Turning-the-Medicine-into-Nectar and its explanations. Then the eight goddesses of medicine and the three rishis and brahmins taught him on the same subject. Then came His Reverence Doctor hTs'o-byed gZhon-nu (Young Life-giver) and also taught him about it. Then he returned to Tibet and the teaching was handed down (up to the present time).

XVI GYU-THOG KHYUṄ-PO RDO-RJE

He married dGah-skyoṅ-ma, the daughter of the district governor, and a son was born to them whose name was gYu-thog Khyuṅ-po rDo-rje. Even from the earliest age he had a deep faith and a sharp brain and was very diligent so that he soon became the best of the learned. Then he practised the teaching of Turning-medicine-into-Nectar, and at that time the eight goddesses of medicine and the brahmin teachers of the lineage appeared to him. Since then, whenever he looked at a sick person, he was able to see

* Though he and hTs'o-byed gZhon-nu are not hDre-rje Vajra's contemporaries they are able to appear to him because of their miraculous powers.

their inside from top to bottom, just as one can see an olive on the palm of the hand. He said to his father: 'It is due to your blessing, O Incarnation of the Medicine Buddha, that I have a general knowledge of medicine. I have applied my mind to the practice, and thus have achieved the essence of medical lore which is all I had wished for. As I have learned by the excellent method of propitiating the Medical Buddha how to find the essence of the hearths of diseases and by going the rounds of my patients have gained experience of the actual practice, I have no fear of diseases or pain. This perfect fulfilment of the needs of all the sick is the result of the blessing of the Medicine Buddha, the lineage of the brahmin teachers and the goddesses of medicine. I, Khyuṅ-po rDo-rje, am feeling happy and cheerful now, and I am going to send a letter of dismissal to hot and cold diseases, and if the diseases should show any further inclination to harm people, my medicine will simply not allow them to do so. By taking people's pulse I shall find out their diseases, by making dietary prescriptions I shall drive the diseases into a tight corner, by my medicines I shall shoot the diseases like with a lightning arrow. By bleeding and cauterization and by surgery I shall put the diseases into the lawcourts. I shall visit my patients lovingly and humbly. However tired I may be I shall disregard all discomfort and go on visiting my patients. I shall treat my patients without discrimination, without considering rich or poor, high or low, or gifts. I shall be giving my medicines to sick beings, without stint. A doctor who does not do what he has promised to is a wretched doctor. It is wretched too of a doctor to be insincere and tell lies. If a doctor is given to lazinesss and drunkenness he is a wretched doctor too. An ignorant doctor who thinks he knows all is also unworthy of his profession. If a doctor tries to manipulate other people's lives without knowing much about them this, too, is despicable. Nor is he a good doctor who lacks knowledge but explains and gives much advice without having the relevant experience. A doctor who does not know the right time for balancing the treatment of hot and cold diseases is no good either. One who treats hot diseases with remedies for cold and vice versa is a quack. It is a mistake for a doctor to advise conflicting dietary prescriptions and activities. A doctor who cannot make a prognosis for the disease and does not know how to bleed or cauterize does not deserve the name. A doctor who does not practise what he preaches is not a good doctor. A doctor who likes "poison-water" (alcoholic drink) is a fool. A doctor who cheats and likes to commit sins is a fool. A doctor who runs after high personages and is unkind to poor ones is a foolish doctor. A doctor who likes women and distractions too much is a fool. A doctor who is susceptible to meaningless flattery is a fool. A doctor who does not know how to mix medicines is also a fool.

'A person who has learned all the texts and has a wide horizon, is a doctor indeed. A person who knows well how to practise from the instruction, is a good doctor. A person who can distinguish between (mere) words and their meaning is a good doctor. A doctor who gives exactly the right medicine against each disease is a good doctor. A doctor who attacks the diseases at the right points is a good doctor. A person who has the Bodhisattva Mind is a good doctor.'

Then his father was delighted to hear this and said: 'Son, who has strength of knowledge and wisdom, you are young but you have perfect knowledge. Entering the gate of the teaching of medicine, you know perfectly how to mix the medicinal plants for cold and hot diseases, and you are well versed in bleeding and cauterizing and in the healing of wounds. You are becoming the most learned of the learned, my son. You will increase the teaching of medicine even further, and it is my good fortune that you were born. There will be a son better than his father, called Yon-tan mGon-po (Excellent Protector). And just as the son will rise, the teaching of medicine will rise during that time. He will keep up the medical tradition of the gYu-thogs. The diseases of all beings caused by the three poisons will he drive away. He will become the physician of Khri-sroṅ lDe-bTsan, and Vairochana will request the paṇḍita, his Excellency Chandra, to teach Yon-tan the dPal-ldan rGyud-bzhi (Glorious Four Treatises). You will translate it into Tibetan. gYu-thog Yon-tan mGon-po will expound clearly the words and the meanings of the rGyud-bzhi. Moreover, he will write the Supplement to the rGyud-bzhi and many essential instructions on medicine. Nine foreign doctors will be offering their homage to him and regard him as their head. Among nine learned Tibetans he will be the most learned.' And he prophesied: 'He will become the master of all the teachings of medical science.' gYu-thog Khyuṅ-po rDo-rje received this prophecy from his father.

XVII BIRTH OF GYU-THOG YON-TAN MGON-PO

Then gYu-thog Khyuṅ-po rDo-rje married rGya-sa Chhos-kyi sGron-me, and they had a son called Yon-tan mGon-po, the great ornament of the world, whose name became known as far and wide as the sun and moon.

When he was entering his mother's womb she had a dream that a white-robed man cut her belly open and put many medical texts in and asked her to look after them carefully. In another dream a white-robed man said to her: 'The Medicine Buddha is staying in your belly.' In another dream he said: 'hTs'o-byed gZhon-nu is staying in your belly.' In another dream: 'Mañjuśrī is staying in your belly. Look after him well', and so on. Especially in the night of the tenth day of the fourth month of the monkey year, when she was slumbering for a while, there appeared a light in a thousand colours rising from the East and it all sank into her chest. After that, eight ladies with leather medicine bags appeared and three rishis holding leather bags led the procession of the Medicine Buddha surrounded by seven other Buddhas, eight Bodhisattvas, Rishi Rig-pa'i Ye-shes, rishi Yid-las-skyes and the doctors Dar-byed Kun-tu Grags-pa* and Dar-lugs practising fifty-seven different systems, surrounded by Brahmā, Indra, and the twelve masters of demons and the loka-pālas of the ten directions and seventy-five different mahā-kālas and ten Bodhisattvas appearing in their wrathful aspect and sixty other protectors. Also many protectors of the Buddhist teachings, surrounded by their warrior attendants, spiritual heroes and countless Dākinīs and a host of medicine brahmins and many other famous protectors of the religious life and nāgas gathered together here. They said to the mother: 'This being is the protector of all beings generally, but specially the protector of the sick. Look after him well, we will help you.' Then the mother asked: 'What is his name?' The Medicine Buddha replied: 'This is the Incarnation of my speech and his name is Learned gYu-thog Yon-tan mGon-po. He is going to establish the teachings of medicine in Tibet.' When the mother awoke her mind was exceedingly serene and her body felt healthier than ever before. After ten months† had passed, on the fifteenth day of the monkey month he was born to the music of pleasant sound, during thunder and lightning and rainbows and an earthquake and many other good omens.

XVIII GYU-THOG YON-TAN MGON-PO'S EARLY CHILDHOOD

When he was three years old he sat on his mother's lap and exclaimed: 'O mummy, pity, pity!' Then his mother asked him: 'To whom are you saying this?' And he replied: 'Sick people, sick people!' After that, when he was sitting on his father's lap, he said: 'There, there!' Then his father asked him: 'Who is there?' He replied: 'The Medicine Buddha, the lineage of brahmins, the goddesses of medicine, and the doctors practising fifty-seven different systems came here for the sake of sick people,' and he started praying: 'You who are able to drive away the diseases caused by the three

* Fifty-seven doctors everywhere famous for furthering the science and teaching of medicine.
† Moon months consisting of twenty-eight days.

poisons, who have achieved the five kāyas* and excellent wisdom! Just by seeing you all the fetters of sickness are destroyed and just by hearing your name all the obstacles are removed. Just by remembering your mind one is able to reach the Path of Bodhi.† Please, preserve me and the beings of the six worlds with the hook of your mercy and bless me so that I shall be successful for the sake of beings!' His father now had exceeding faith and said: 'My son, the merit you have acquired before has now ripened. The result of the karma you have practised has now manifested. We are very fortunate indeed that you who are the Incarnation of the speech of the Medicine Buddha who is of the intrinsic nature of the Three Jewels have been born voluntarily in this snow-fenced land of Tibet for the sake of us beings so that you can proclaim and make clear to us the heritage of those learned forbears of ours in Tibet who were as numerous as the stars. Now you had better learn to read.' 'Listen, my dearest parents! You have given me my body and my mind and looked after me with love, for instance, carrying me about and keeping me clean from excrements and urine, and giving me useful advice, and so on. I have not forgotten how to read and because the practice and the profound instruction are still clear in my mind I have no difficulty with the Scriptures on the science of medicine. I have no need of a teacher because my former knowledge of the instructions and the practice is still with me. I am more learned in writing, preaching and debating than the others. The truth of this will become apparent when I practise.'

Then his father discussed with him his reading and the medical texts, and in this way he became perfect in reading and he became the most learned in the science of medicine. His father thought: 'Even though he is only three years old and did not learn how to read in this life, as a result of learning it in former lives, he has a perfect knowledge of all medical texts and so on. I had better send him with a faithful servant to visit patients.' He said: 'My son, you have not learned reading and writing in this life, but as a result of having increased your learning in past lives you are now able to read, write, and understand the medical texts. So now, for the sake of sick beings, take your leather medicine bag and practise medicine!' The father gYu-thog Khyuṅ-po rDo-rje gave his pupil dGe-ba rDo-rje to his son Yon-tan mGon-po as a servant and put him to work as a doctor for the sick. Since then gYu-thog Yon-tan mGon-po did great work for the sick, and the people of Tibet called him Yon-tan mGon-po, the Second Medicine Buddha. His father thought:

* (1) chhos-sku (Sanskrit: Dharmakāya); (2) loṅs-sku (Skt. Saṁbhogakāya—bliss body); (3) Emptiness as the Buddha's mind-consciousness; (4) Separation from defilement in the Buddha's mind-consciousness; (5) sprul-sku (Skt. Nirmāṇakāya—the body resembling a human body in which a Buddha or Bodhisattva appears on earth).

† Enlightenment.

'This my son Yon-tan mGon-po will definitely become a learned saint. What a deep faith he has in his Guru and his parents!' He looked at him with his prophetic insight and he knew that he would disobey one of his own orders and that, as a great punishment of this fault, he would be falsely accused. So he told him: 'Medicine Buddha and lineage of the teachings, look upon my son and give your blessings to Yon-tan mGon-po! Listen, young Incarnation, my son, you have become a well-known learned doctor but you will disobey one of my orders, and as a result of the punishment of this fault a false accusation will be brought against you. So, therefore, don't disobey your Guru and father and meditate with compassion on beings and with praying to the Medicine Buddha. There is no doubt that you will get the supreme consummation of wisdom, and don't forget my advice! Keep it in your heart!' 'I bow before my kind father and Guru and the lineage of the teachings, I have a deep faith in your remembering the power of the wisdom which is like the ocean. Please, give me the blessing that I will not disobey the order of you, my kind parents. It is generally foolish of a person who knows the law of cause and effect to act carelessly without regard to results. It would be better if I were killed than that there should be a person called religious who disobeyed an order of his Guru. Please, tell me all about it!' Khyuṅ-po said: 'As a result of your disobeying my word once in this life, you will be born the thirteenth in the gYu-thog family lineage and then also be called Yon-tan mGon-po. At that time the Paṇḍita Me-lha Phyag-ldum will come to Tibet and you will enjoy a good teacher–pupil relationship because of a Karmic concatenation in a past life. At that time nine learned men will appear in Tibet, the followers of eight learned Tibetans, and one of your followers. The followers of the eight learned Tibetans will falsely accuse Me-lha Phyag-ldum, and the ill-report of this will reverberate on all of you.' Then he asked: 'My father, will the great paṇḍita Me-lha Phyag-ldum and the followers of the nine Tibetan doctors be connected by a teacher–pupil relationship or not? Why are they going to accuse him and will they be successful?' He said: 'If paṇḍita Phyag-ldum and the nine learned men had had a teacher–pupil relationship, there would not have been an accusation. As it is, they will commit many sins but the connections of their black and white karma between them will make an end to their Saṁsāra. The reason why they will commit sins is: an evil demon called Gnyan-mkhar-na* (poisoning people's minds) is sitting in their heart. Because of gNyan-mkhar-nag's influencing them the nine will accuse the paṇḍita. Afterwards, for their satisfaction, Me-lha will create an

* An evil demon believed to be living in an eddy of the Tsangpo river near mNyes-thaṅ in the vicinity of Lhasa.

illusion to make them believe Me-lha Phyag-ldum is running away from them. Then he will meet two fortunate persons, followers of Braṅ-ti and gYu-thog. He will give them a thorough instruction, as powerful as heavy rain. Then he will return to India.' Then gYu-thog asked: 'Please, tell me, who are the two followers of Braṅ-ti and gYu-thog who will meet the paṇḍita? To whom will Braṅ-ti and gYu-thog entrust their teachings?' Then the father said: 'Braṅ-ti rGyal-ba bZaṅ-po and the Younger gYu-thog Yon-tan mGon-po. Braṅ-ti will be entrusted with the study of the Gold-bre (measure) and the Silver-bre, and gYu-thog-pa with the sDe-sKor (Divided Sections) Outer, Inner, and Inbetween Teaching.' Then Yon-tan mGon-po was overjoyed and asked his parents: 'I am going to make a sacrificial offering to both of you, my parents. In which place shall I make it?' The father said: 'In the Black-Ghost Valley in sTod-luṅ on the Poisonous-Touch Rock.' The mother said: 'Wouldn't it be better to do it here? I could not have all the necessary objects carried there.' But the father said: 'Perhaps Yon-tan mGon-po may have all the objects?' Then the mother said: 'Are you teasing a son who is only between three and four years old? And if parents cannot fulfil their child's wishes, who will do it?' The father said: 'In general, parents should fulfil their children's wishes. But this is a very surprising boy, and I should like to watch what is going to happen. So leave it to him to find the objects!'

Meanwhile Yon-tan mGon-po made the following obeisance: 'Through the overwhelming kindness of Buddha, Dharma, Saṁgha, and my Parents who have sustained me with their love and compassion, also of the Medicine Buddha who is always benefiting those who have established a link with him, I, Yon-tan mGon-po, shall succeed in whatever I shall begin. In whatever way I shall do it I shall always be happy. The fulfilment of all my wishes will be showered upon me as the result of merit accumulated in former lives. My parents, please, go now to the Poisonous-Touch Rock in the Black-Ghost Valley in sTod-luṅ sKyid-sna. The objects for the sacrificial offering I shall get without effort.' And they went there. And whatever they needed came like a shower from all the four directions. The good news of the son making a sacrificial offering to his parents was spread far and wide, and from everywhere people came to assemble there.

At that time he saw the mantra of the Medicine Buddha in the sky and he was so happy that he jumped with joy, and wherever his feet touched the rocks a footprint remained as if it had been mud. His parents also jumped with joy and they too left footprints. Then he bowed down before his parents and he left two hand prints and two knee prints. Then everybody believed in his saintly power. His father, Khyuṅ-po rDo-rje thought: 'This my son is very learned and saintly, and there is no doubt that he will work diligently for the Buddhist religion in general, and specially for the teaching of medicine, for the sake of sick people, wearing the clothes of love and compassion. Who is his tutelary deity with whom his former life was linked?'

XIX GYU-THOG'S TUTELARY DEITY

On the twenty-ninth of the first month, just after midnight, the Medicine Buddha appeared to him as the king of the gods in his terrifying form in smoke colour, surrounded by a blaze of fire in a black storm brandishing the sword in the sky with his right hand, and with his left hand throwing the black noose like an arrow. He was very fat and standing on eight Nāgas as his cushion. On his head was a reddish-black horse's head. United with him was his black coloured Śakti rDo-rje Phag-mo Vajra-Vārāhī, holding in the right hand a crooked dagger and in the left hand holding a skull filled with blood, and from their union came hot molten metal flowing through the chest of the enemies, and the horse was neighing, and on the Śakti's head was a sow's head, and both were reciting aloud this mantra: 'Om vajra maha krota [sic] hayagriva hu lu hu lu hum phat niritri shatrun samaya hum phat.' They said: 'Your son, Khyuṅ-po rDo-rje, is the son of the Medicine Buddha, and therefore he should know the Medicine Buddha as his tutelary deity and pray to him deeply, and his achievements will be great.' Then the father made a goodly offering to the king of the terrifying gods and his śakti, and he said: 'You, O Medicine Buddha, appearing in the terrifying form called rTa-mGrin Nag-po (Black Horse's Neck), for the purpose of expelling evil spirits! Please, drive away the enemy and obstruct the demons!'

'In the same way as the two of you, I, too, shall be born entering my mother's womb without desire for her. Please, give me the instruction, so that I know when I die and am reborn whether I should dismiss the tutelary deities* in my body or whether I should ask them to stay where they are, for ever.' One attendant god, holding a club, said: 'Listen, you man of little faith, practising the desireless union as a path to Nirvāṇa without instructions means committing a sin. One should meditate on Bliss and Emptiness, oneself turning into rDo-rje hChhaṅ and the Śakti into rDo-rje Phag-mo. In meditation one should turn the male organ into a blue letter *hūm* and the female organ into a red letter *hrī* (pronounced *shi*) and over them the letter *pha*. When these three letters meet one should think of oneself offering

* There is a meditation by which one can turn parts of the body into tutelary deities.

pure bliss to the tutelary deities and the Buddhas in the body. One should recognize the four states of happiness and meditate on Emptiness and Happiness united without desire. The four states of Happiness should be identified with Emptiness. When the semen sinks into the Śakti one should keep one's mind quiet without a discursive thought. One should concentrate on what the eyes see and should look at the sky without thinking of past and future.' Then he disappeared.

When gYu-thog was five years old his exceptional learnedness was talked about everywhere. One night his mother saw in a dream a black man in a terrifying form with six arms and with four attendants who told her: 'Many people talk about your son. If he takes the consecration of Turning-medicine-into-nectar from his father and prays deeply to the Medicine Buddha and the lineage of the teachings and the goddesses of medicine he will see the Medicine Buddha face to face and will get instruction from the Medicine Buddha.' Then his father gave him the consecration of Turning-medicine-into-nectar and granted him instruction in the method of propitiating the Medicine Buddha, the lineage of the teachings and the medicine goddesses. When he prayed to them the Medicine Buddha appeared to him with a smile and instructed him with the full explanation on how to meditate on the maṇḍala of the Medicine Buddha situated in the body.

XX GYU-THOG AND KING KHRI-SROṄ LDE-BTSAN

When he became ten years old, King Khri-sroṅ lDe-btsan, the incarnation of Mañjuśrī, was also ten years old. Both were born in the Earth Monkey year. King Mes Ag-htsom heard about gYu-thog's fame and sent the minister Tarag-chen who was well disposed towards Buddhism as a messenger to invite him to his Court. Then gYu-thog Yon-tan mGon-po went with the minister Tarag-chen to the bSam-yas Monastery. Then the king and his son asked gYu-thog to debate with the doctors Braṅ-ti and rGyal-gnyen, mKhar-bu and other Tibetan doctors. gYu-thog replied: 'Don't you remember the time when you had become the king of Pad-ma rGyal-bhi mDzod in Sham-ba-la in the North and I was called doctor Pad-ma-hdzin, and here I am called Learned gYu-thog Yon-tan mGon-po. Do you not remember how you recovered when I treated you many times? As king Mes Ag-htsom, you were the incarnation of Vajrapāni. The prince, when he was in Sham-ba-la, was called king Padma dPuṅ-pa. Do you not remember how your life was renewed when I treated you when you were king Pad-ma dPuṅ-pa in Sham-ba-la? At that time I was doctor Padma Me-'od-chan and treated you many times and preserved your life. Do you remember these things? Here you are the incarnation of Mañjuśrī and called Khri-sroṅ lDe-btsan. In Tibet there is no umpire to judge my debating with anyone. I have gone beyond the ocean of the science of medicine and I can answer any questions quite easily. The practising of medicine is like a thunderbolt which can penetrate wherever it is thrown. Therefore nobody can answer if I debate. Under Lha-tho Tho-ri Gnyen-btsan the science of medicine had just arrived and under king Sroṅ-btsan sGam-po the practice of medicine was introduced. Now the teaching of medicine is reaching its flowering period and you, Khri-sroṅ lDe-btsan, are the only god of Tibet.'

Then the king and his son conceived great faith. gYu-thog-pa was at that time court physician under Khri-sroṅ lDe-btsan. The king replied: 'You, the Incarnation of the Speech of the Medicine Buddha, full of mercy, are in India called doctor hTs'o-byed gZhon-nu (Kumārajīva). In Sham-ba-la you are called Padma-hdzin and Me-'od-chan. In Tibet you are called gYu-thog Yon-tan mGon-po. It is our good fortune that you are here. We are appointing you as the head of all the doctors. May, through your increasing mercy, the science of medicine increase in Tibet!'

Then nine learned Tibetan doctors took him as their teacher and showed their respect to him, and they received instruction from him.

XXI GYU-THOG'S TREATMENTS

Once in bSam-yas a man was sick. And the doctors Braṅ-ti, rGyal-gnyen, mKhar-phu, and others treated him in different ways but in vain. One day the king and his attendants and gYu-thog-pa and other doctors went out riding. The king saw him being carried past and asked him what was the matter with him. He said: 'No one has been able to improve my condition though many doctors have treated me. Please, help me, great king!' Then the king called: 'gYu-thog-pa, gYu-thog-pa.' gYu-thog examined his pulse and said: 'Great king, if you want this patient to recover, then, please, lend me your horse!' Then the king dismounted from his horse and lent it to gYu-thog. Then gYu-thog bound the patient's hand with a rope. Holding the other end of the rope in his hand he rode off on the horse's back. Then the patient recovered and the king was astounded and asked him: 'This patient was suffering from sickness, how is it that he could be cured by a running horse?' gYu-thog said: 'His lung was sticking to his rib, and through racing behind the horse it was separated.' They all were greatly surprised, and the king offered gYu-thog his horse and his saddle. Then gYu-thog went back home and presented the horse and saddle to his parents.

At that time there was a doctor called Kun-rgyug living in his country who showed great jealousy of gYu-thog. gYu-thog felt great pity for him thinking: 'I am working for sick people. Why is this foolish doctor committing such a great sin?' The doctor had one daughter who was a nun but who was filled with desire and she fell very ill because of that. Her father tried to treat her in many ways but she was not able to recover. The daughter said: 'Let us ask the gYu-thogs, father and son, to come here.' Her father said: 'I am not going to ask those liars even if my daughter should die.' Then mother and daughter discussed the matter and asked gYu-thog, father and son, behind the father's back. But gYu-thog's father had heard all about it and refused to go and stopped his son also from visiting them. The son gYu-thog Yon-tan mGon-po told his father: 'If patients, doctors and nurses could not face calumnies this would be against the professional code of a doctor whose duty it is to work for the sake of sick patients, treating them with compassion. If one wants a good life in the next incarnation one should requite evil with good. I will think of all sound as empty like an echo. Forms are visible but empty of selfhood. Mind is able to range far and near, but in reality it is empty. Keeping this in mind I shall do my work,' and he did not listen to his father* and went off. Doctor Kun-rgyug said: 'The value of this daughter is greater than that of a son. Please, make her well, and I shall offer you her value in money.' gYu-thog asked: 'Didn't you treat her?' He said: 'Yes, I did my best but I could not help.'

When the daughter had gone out to fetch water she had seen two donkeys copulating. This increased her desire and she hit herself on her female organ and fainted. After some time she saw two pigs copulating and put a radish into her vagina, and the radish broke and little animals started to irritate her.

Then gYu-thog treated her with rdo-ts'va (smoke salt) and burnt it under her seat so that the radish came out but she was not yet recovered. The little insects still caused her trouble. Then gYu-thog recommended that she should sleep with a man and she thenceforward lived no longer as a nun and was cured. Then Kun-rgyug bowed at gYu-thog's feet and offered many gifts to him and he became his follower. He requested him for instruction, and gYu-thog gave him instruction in Nyams-yig.†

When gYu-thog was fifteen years old king Khri-sroṅ lDe-btsan had trouble with his eyes and he called gYu-thog who said: 'You will get worse diseases than this in your eyes because horns will be growing from your knees.' The king said: 'gYu-thog-pa, please, do something for it!' gYu-thog-pa said: 'Make your knee bones smooth by rubbing them with your hands.'

* This seems to be the occasion when gYu-thog disobeyed his father.

† The result of his own experiences in meditation.

The king did as gYu-thog told him, and his eyes recovered because he did not touch them with his hands.

Once the king had trouble with his teeth. gYu-thog said to him: 'You will get an excrescence on your palate and will be unable to talk.' Then the king said: 'Please, do something so that it does not grow!' He said: 'You have to rub the tip of your tongue against the roof of the mouth.' His tongue did not touch the teeth, and he recovered.

XXII GYU-THOG'S SONG OF WISDOM

Once there was an incarnation of Vajravārāhī at bSam-yas whose name was mChhim-phu, and gYu-thog went to see her. She told him: 'You, great gYu-thog-pa, Incarnation of the Speech of the Medicine Buddha, you are indeed doctor Ts'o-byed gZhon-nu (Kumārajīva), you have worked continuously for the sake of the sick, and therefore this time even those whose only connection with you is that they have given you a little food will be, when you become the head of lTa-na-sdug, born amongst your attendants.' She said: 'Your incarnation is an excellent one, so please, tell me, how did you acquire your understanding and wisdom?' gYu-thog sang about his acquiring wisdom:

'I bow before the jewel of My Mind.
Amongst the best remembrances is to remember the Guru's excellence;
So I am happy there is no hail-and-farewell with my Guru.
I am happy that I am getting the fortunate consequences of my good deeds
As the result of merit accumulated in former lives.
I am happy I have obtained the six ingredients* of the noble body (dal-hbyor).†
I am happy that I have met the Essence of the Teaching

* Necessary for meditation: the four elements capable of being transmuted, the veins and semen.

† Right juncture of opportunities. The eight *dals* (opportunities) are: (1) not to be born in hell where one has no time to meditate; (2) not to be born as a hungry ghost who cannot meditate; (3) not to be born as an animal; (4) not to be born as a god because their happiness will end; (5) not to be born deaf and dumb; (6) not to be born in a country where they have *asuras* (enemies of the gods); (7) not to be born a heretic; (8) not to be born as an uncivilized man. The ten *hbyor-pas* (attainments) are: (1) to be born as a human being; (2) born in a central country (that is where there are four kinds of attendants of the Buddha: monks, nuns, male and female novices; (3) all five senses intact; (4) not having committed the five great sins (parricide, matricide, killing a Saint, wounding a Buddha, schism in the monks' Order); (5) having faith in the religious Teaching; (6) being in a country where the Buddha has been; (7) in a country where the Buddha has been teaching; (8) where the Teaching has an unbroken tradition; (9) where there are followers of the Buddha; (10) where the Teachers have great compassion.

Because of good works done in connection with the Dharma.
I am happy I can see everything as purity, without distinction.
I am happy in having great love and great compassion towards beings,
Knowing that all of them have been my parents.
I am happy to be working for the Dharma for the sake of all beings
In the knowledge that their lives will come to an end so quickly.
I am happy that I can stay alone in the mountain solitude,
Knowing that my home town is like a city in a mirage.
I am happy that I have given up completely
Personal love towards relatives and friends,
Knowing that they all are like guests at an inn.
I am happy I have cut off the root of desire,
Knowing that one who has servants and attendants
Has to leave them behind because they are like groups of birds sitting on a tree.
I am happy I have given up desire for wealth and have given it to others,
Knowing that it is like bees collecting honey.
I am happy understanding that all glory is like a kingdom in a dream,
Useless and untrue.
When the ignorance of thinking "mine" and "thine" has gone,
All fame and ambition are like an echo or like bubbles in the water.
I am happy that I understand their impermanence.
To the imperfect mind all objects appear as self-existent:
I am happy to know that they are not so.
All intention of turning my mind towards meditation has left me,
Meditating naturally from the beginning without separation.
Thus I am active in the world while my mind is composed for meditation:
I am happy practising the best method of destroying selfishness, the root of Saṁsāra.
I am happy I am gaining experience in my own meditation.*
I am happy I am always confident in the profound religious instruction.
I am happy to know there is neither obstruction nor need for propitiation
Because all appearances are Emptiness.
I am happy I resolved that all merit
Acquired in the present, the past and the future
Should be the cause of Enlightenment for all beings
As my gifts were given with a pure motive.
If I, gYu-thog-pa, the man without religion,
Make any mistakes when practising these nineteen kinds of happiness

* Besides book-learning.

In the house called "Fortunate House" by the gods
In the district of bSam-yas, please, forgive me!
May my merit be the cause of glory and happiness for all beings.
I bow before the Guru.
The purified vision has been growing within me
Which sees all without distinction as the Dharmakāya.
This is the prayer of a madman without religion:
Having gained unwavering faith he sees no distinction
With a mind become as pure as the Dharmakāya.
This is the meditation of a madman without religion.
The interference by hypocrisy has been broken up,
The three means of expression, (body, speech and mind) have been liberated;
This natural flowing forth of action is the activity of a madman without religion.
All signs of hope and fear have disappeared,
Saṁsāra and Nirvāṇa are mingled into One,
The Trikāya has ripened in me:
This is the fruit reaped by a madman without religion.
Indeed, O great joy!
I bow before the spirit of the Guru of the wisdom within:
To your Reverence, the Jewel of a Guru who has bestowed on me three great kindnesses.
It is fortunate to be able to pray deeply and earnestly, not just superficially.
Decidedly, you are the best of protectors!
It is fortunate to practise on nectar-like oral instructions
And not to throw them to the winds of laziness and unsteadiness.
It is fortunate to study and practise to one's whole satisfaction,
Feeling reverence, making effort and having excellent knowledge.
Seeing that all beings in the six worlds have been one's parents
It is fortunate to love others more than oneself
And not to use discrimination between enemies and friends.
We should not give in to the fabrications of our ordinary mind
Which presents as self-existent the objects we see,
Knowing Emptiness which is naturally self-existent.
It is fortunate to see with a purified mind the real nature of things
And not to give credence to the outward appearance of objects.
Saṁsāra and Nirvāṇa, both, are of the nature of mind.
It is fortunate to have made the resolution to liberate oneself from worldly existence
While knowing that all the worlds and Nirvāṇa are of the nature of Mind,

Without having imperfect views and without taking the phenomenal world to be real.
It is fortunate to remember from one's heart
Meditations which are useful for the next life
Knowing that what is born is of the nature of death
And is not unchangeable as we imagine,
And to have given up laziness and preoccupation with the business of this life.
It is fortunate to have unwavering repentance,
While seeing all might and glories as the kingdom of illusion
Knowing by wisdom without pride or conceit how futile they are.
It is fortunate to know, whether you are praised in various ways or blamed,
All of it as an echo and to hear it in a mantra.
Seeing that many people cannot recognize the Dharmakāya
Because their imperfect mind has become their enemy,
It is fortunate to know that the nature of the diverse appearance of mind
Is that of the Dharmakāya.
His Reverence, gYu-thog Heruka sings of his feelings in experiencing spiritual growth:
The Blessed Lord Hevajra is the absolutely purified mind of the Self-Existent:
That is self-emptiness but not actual emptiness in the Perfect Mind.
I understand that those who have been meditating in stages,
Were not knowing the state of absolute inactivity of mind
And were meditating imperfectly with an imperfect mind.
No longer does he see a distinction between meditator and object of meditation:
The meditation on wishing to meditate is hidden by meditation itself
When you know that there is no meditation:
Then all things appear as meditation.
Ordinary people's knowledge is bounded by themselves,
In a nal-hbyor-pa* the five poisons appear as an ornament.
The reality of the essence of things of no arising and no cessation
Is what the learned people do not know and ask the dumb and deaf
Nor do the dumb and deaf know and they ask the dead bodies in the cemetery
And what the dead bodies explain is of the nature of the Dharma.'†

Then she was very pleased and she gave him the ritual of a rJe-btsun Ḍakinī with the essence of its practice. Then the great gYu-thog said to her:

* Yogi.

† One cannot say anything about the nature of the Dharma. Conceptual thought about it is impossible.

'Birthless and unobstructed is the Dharmakāya,
The inseparable intrinsic nature of the three kāyas is the Saṁbhoga Kāya,
For the sake of teaching beings the Nirmāṇa Kāya appears in accordance with their wishes.
By the bliss of possessing the perfected five kinds of divine wisdom,
You are the fulfilment of all wishes.
Self-liberated you have appeared in the form of a body
By wisdom resulting from experience.
Till I reach Enlightenment I shall never be separated from you
Even for a short moment:
My mind and your mind are mingled.
Please, bless me when I die
And let me be reborn with you.'

Then she replied and said to him:

'You have been enlightened before all the Buddhas
But you have appeared as an ordinary person
And entered into the gate of the teaching of medicine out of compassion with all beings.
I bow before you, the spiritual son of all the Buddhas.
When you appeared as a bodhisattva your name was Kar-ma Dri-ma-med
Who when he became enlightened was Vaiḍūrya, the Medical Buddha.
The Incarnation of the Speech of the Medical Buddha
Is gYu-thog Yon-tan mGon.
I bow before you, the Preserver of the Teaching of Buddhism,
The Incarnation of the Action of the Medicine Buddha is Mañjuśrī
Who has appeared as Padmasaṁbhava
[printing error: Padmasaṁbhava who has appeared as Mañjuśrī].
The Incarnation of the Mind of Padmasaṁbhava
Is gYu-thog Yon-tan mGon.
I bow before you who are inseparable from the intrinsic nature of all the Buddhas.
The Incarnation of the Wisdom of the Medicine Buddha
Is gZhon-nu hJigs-med Grags,
The Incarnation of his Speech is Nāgārjuna,
Of the intrinsic nature of the Medicine Buddha, of hJigs-med Grags and of Nāgārjuna
Is gYu-thog Yon-tan mGon-po.
I pray to you, king of all the *kāyas*.*

* See p. 189.

Now you have kindled the light of the teaching of medicine,
All the sufferings of beings have been weeded out with the root.
You are protecting them from the fear of birth, old age, sickness and death.
I pray to you, exalted King over human beings,
You, gYu-thog Yon-tan mGon-po, are the head ornament of all Tibetan and Indian learned men.
You are an excellent guide for those who follow you to Nirvāṇa.
You are the most excellent gate to the happiness and glory of all beings.
I pray to you who are the all-glorious fulfilment of wishes!
Intensified by the power and purity of prayers in a former life
Even one word from you will attain that
For which all the Buddhas have been praying in the past.
I pray to you who by disciplining yourself have gone beyond.
You will work for the sake of beings to the age of one hundred and twenty-five years
In the snow-fenced land of Tibet.
I pray to you, future head of lTa-na-sDug, the city of medicine.
When the people will cause great sufferings to themselves by their behaviour,
In the degenerate age, the worst part of the kalpa,
You will appear in countless forms.
I pray to you, the ornament of beings,
That I may from now till Enlightenment
Never be separated from you,
Your Reverence, even for a short moment,
To be able to see your face and to get instruction
And to mingle my mind with yours.
I pray to you whose kindness is unwavering.'
At that moment all the skies were filled with rainbows and lights
And the air resounded with music and it rained flowers.
There was no dust on the ground, the wind was still and the warm sun was shining.
When gYu-thog looked up he saw the Medicine Buddha
In the sky surrounded by a tent of rainbows and lights,
And he prayed.

The Medicine Buddha said: 'You greatly fortunate man, you should get the blessings of the Medicine Buddha, of the brahmins, of the goddesses, of the saintly doctors of the teachings of medicine,' and he said, 'Cherish this instruction, the essence of all the teachings!' And he gave him the instruction called *The Rosary of Turning Medicine into Nectar* and the *String of Five divisions of Explanation of the Medical Devotional Practice of Turning Medicine into Nectar* with practical instructions.

XXIII GYU-THOG AND THE FOREIGN DOCTORS

gYu-thog and king Khri-sroṅ lDe-btsan were of the same age. When they were twenty years old, they invited nine foreign doctors, and gYu-thog debated with them. Then the Chinese doctor Stoṅ-gsum asked gYu-thog: 'Are there doctors in Tibet?' Then gYu-thog told him the history of Tibetan doctors from king Lha-tho Thor-ri gNyen-btsan and his doctor Duṅ-gi Thor-chog to king Khri-sroṅ lDe-btsan and his own story. Then the Indian doctor asked him: 'How was the task of bringing medicine to India, China, Nepal, Khotan, and Tibet fulfilled?'

gYu-thog replied: 'The Indians have made a special study of the *Rig-pa Ye-shes rGyud* (the Tantra of Wisdom). In China they excelled in prognosis by means of astrology and other methods, in Nepal they specialized in the mechanical arts, in Kashmir in chemistry, in Mongolia in bloodletting, in Garlog in cauterization, in Taxila in the treatment of poisoning, in Khrom in the examination of the urine, in Zahor in cupping with a horn, in Kesar in healing by means of mantras, in Shanshung in curing by purging, in Uḍḍiyāna by vomiting, and in Tibet by the four remedies. The Bon-po system lays the greatest stress on curing by means of heating, balneology, and the use of ointments. The titans had the system of spell-binding diseases, the system of Brahmā is the *Medical Science in a hundred thousand ślokas*, the Bodhisattva system follows the text of *The Mercy of Self-release*, the Rishi's system is the *Tsaraka sDe-brgyad*, the non-Buddhist system is the *Mahādeva Tantra*, the Buddhist system the Rigs-gsum mGon-po rGyud.'*

Then the Nepalese doctor asked: 'How many different founders of systems are there?' gYu-thog said: 'There are two kinds of systems. The systems of the nine foreign doctors and those of the nine Tibetan doctors. For the curing of diseases in general there is a text called *bDud-rtsi Chhu-rgyun* by the Indian doctor Shranti Garbha. The system of the Chinese doctor Tungsum Kangwa is contained in the *Chhuṅ-chhe dPyad Nyi-ma'i 'od-gser* for the curing of children's diseases. In the system of Mahādeva the women's diseases are cured. It is called *Zla-ba'i Khyil-khor*. In the system of Dharma-Buddha the diseases

* From each of these texts systems of Meditation were evolved.

caused by demons are cured. It is called rDo-rje Pha-lam. In the system of the Nepalese doctor Dānaśīla the cure of old age is taught. It is called gNad-kyi mzub-ts'ugs. The Kashmiri doctor Khu-na Vajra follows the system of curing poisonous diseases called *Rus-sbal-gyi hGyur-hgros*. The special skill of the Mongolian doctor Na-la Shan-di-pa was the curing of old age according to the text called *Yan-lag bChhud-kyi rGya-mts'o*. The doctor from Dol-po called dGah-bde hPhel-byed used the system called *Kyo-ma Ru-rtse* for increasing vitality. The doctor from Gru-gu called Seṅ-ge 'Od-chan hPhel-byed was the founder of the system called *Ro-skra hPhrul-gyi Me-loṅ* about anatomical measurements.

The prince of bTsam-pa Shi-la, the son of Mu-rje The-khrom, the king of Khrom, taught the teaching of *Khrom-gyi dBye-ba Drug-pa*.*

The system of the nine Tibetan doctors will gradually come into being in the following manner: Through the system of doctor Bi-Byi which is called *Po-ti Kha-ser* and that of doctor 'Ug-pa which is called *Lag-len gSal-sgron* to the system of doctor Chher-rje which is called *Zin-thig* and that of doctor Braṅ-ti called *gSer-bre Daṅ dÑul-bre* and the system of doctor Mi-nYag which is the *rDo-spyor Chhen-mo* to the system of gYu-thog-pa which is the *Bu-don nYam-yig Khrid rGyud-kri Chha-lag bCho-brgyad*, to the system of gNyah-pa which is *hGrel-pa dri-med 'od-zer hphros-pa dbaṅgi-rgyal-po* (Explanation of the Clear Light Sent forth from the King of Initiations), to the system of sToṅ-sman which is *sToṅ hgrel-gzi'od hbar-ba* (Explanation of the Thousand Splendours of the Blazing Light), to the system of mThah-bzhi which is *bsTan bchos-lam-gyi sgron-me* (Doctrine of the Torch on the Path of Healing)'. This is what he prophesied.

Then the Kashmiri doctor asked him: 'Why are you prophesying the future of the nine Tibetan systems?' gYu-thog replied: 'There will be many learned men, like the essence of butter, in the lineage of the renowned nine Tibetan doctors. I have prophesied the kind of instruction in each one's system of teaching before they are to appear.' Then he asked: 'What are the names of the nine? Will they come all together or one after another?' gYu-thog replied: 'These learned men will appear one after another. Bi-byi Legs-mgon, 'Ug-pa Chhos-bzaṅ, Chher-chhe Shig-po, sMi-nyag Roṅ-rje, gYu-thog mGon-po, Braṅ-ti rGyal-bzaṅ, gNyah-pa Chhos-bzaṅ, Stoṅ-sman Grags-rgyal, and mThah-bzhi Dar-po. These nine will further the science of medicine in Tibet in general, and specially the study and practice of the rGyud-bzhi (Four Treatises).' He asked him: 'Where is the *rGyud-bzhi* at present?' gYu-thog said: 'At the moment it is with the paṇḍita Tsan-dra De-ba (Chandra Deva). From him the translator Vairochana

* This text enumerates ten systems instead of nine.

will take it and give it to king Khri-sroṅ lDe-btsan. He will gradually give it to the Tibetan learned men. Also fifty-seven dar-byed kun-tu grags-pa (famous doctors) will come and cause medical science to flourish in Tibet and make it as clear as daylight. He asked: 'What are the fifty-seven* means of increasing medical science and what is their name?' Then gYu-thog taught him and told him the prayer of the lineage of the rishis called *Victorious Gem.* On this text, the summary, the detailed explanation, and the conclusions I could write, but this text, with its commentary, has been written down elsewhere.

Before saying this prayer to the lineage of the rishis, one should, as in all other rituals, take refuge to the Three Jewels and direct the mind towards Enlightenment. Then one should meditate on the subject of everything being self-emptiness. Out of that emptiness rises the letter *bhrum* [pronounced dum]. It is turning into a wide throne made of various jewels supported by eight great lions; on that is the letter *pam* which turns into a lotus flower, the moon and the sun respectively. Above that is the letter *hūṁ* which turns into a (blue) vajra which has the letter *hūṁ* in the middle. The vajra is of the nature of one's Guru and appears in the form of a blue victorious Vajradhara holding vajra and bell in his hands which are crossed over the chest, with his śakti rDo-rje Phag-mo of dark-blue colour holding a crooked dagger and a blood-filled skull (in her hands) embracing him as her consort. Both are adorned with ornaments made from bones and jewels. From their united bodies flows a nectar which gives inexhaustible bliss to all beings. In the Vajradhara's crown of the head (one should visualize) the letter (*Oṁ*), in his throat the letter (*ah*) and in his chest the letter (*hūṁ*). Above him one should invite all the saintly lineage of rishis in the sky and then pray. It is more efficacious with all prayers and rituals if one takes the Bodhisattva vow† beforehand, and at the end one should say twenty-one times: 'I bow before the Victorious Tathāgata Arahat Sa-hdzin rGyal-po.' It is mentioned in the sūtras that if one repeats this twenty-one times the outcome of the prayer will be definitely successful.

Then a Mongolian doctor asked: 'What is the very first origin of the science of medicine, generally speaking?' gYu-thog said: 'Five hundred and fifty great kalpas after the external world had come into being, gradually beings with the internal world came into existence. In India there was a brahmin named Hala Mig-yaṅs. His wife was the brahminī gSal-ba'i Nyi-ma, and after some time her body caused her sickness. She said to her

* Printing error: five.

† The vow taken in front of the Buddhas and Bodhisattvas to undertake what a Bodhisattva does and to refrain from what a Bodhisattva does not do.

husband: 'You have achieved the miraculous powers resulting from a constantly truthful speech. Please, expel my sickness!' Then the brahmin spoke, and by the strength of his truthful words the cry GSO-BA RIG-PA (science of medicine) came from the sky. Then the brahmin went out to search for gSo-ba rig-pa. One day he met a brahmin called gSo-rigdPal who asked Mig-yaṅs: 'Where are you going, Mig-yaṅs?' He said: 'I am trying to find gSo-ba rig-pa.'

Then Mig-yaṅs went into the jungle dGah-ba ts'al (Happy Forest) and he saw a naked rishi holding in his right hand a Myrobalan plant and in his left hand the bowl of the Victorious Medicine filled with nectar. With him were the goddesses and the lineage of saints and also many other sprul-skus (manifestations). The brahmin Mig-yaṅs asked him: 'Where is the king of medicine, Kar-ma Dri-ma-med-pa staying?' One very beautiful woman asked: 'What is it you want?' He said: 'I want to learn the teaching of gSo-ba rig-pa.' Then she pointed to the naked rishi. The brahmin (Mig-yaṅs) bowed before the rishi and presented him with a piece of unwrought gold and told him all about his wife's illness. The rishi said: 'Bee-gyel Bee-gyel' and made the threatening gesture into the sky. In the sky appeared, surrounded by lights and rainbows, the Medicine Buddha and said: 'First the external world existed and then, for the sake of the welfare of beings, the gSo-ba rig-pa (science of medicine) came into being. Then the *gSo-dpyad hBum-pa* (Hundred thousand philosophical analyses of medicine) and then the *dPal-ldan rGyud-bzhi* (Glorious Four Treatises), then the *Yan-lag brgyad-pa* (Eight Branches). Then gradually all the different systems of instruction in the practice of medicine by many learned doctors will arise. Be happy and study them!'

Then the divine system containing fifty chapters of the Medicine Sūtra, a hundred chapters on the subject of mixing medicines (pharmacology), a thousand chapters on the pulse, twenty-five chapters on bleeding, moxa and acupuncture, one hundred and ninety chapters on curing wounds, and twelve thousand short instructions (aphorisms) on other matters came from the sky. Then doctor Kar-ma Dri-ma-med said to the brahmin Mig-yaṅs: 'The heaven of Yaṅs-pa Chen was situated countless trichiliocosms above. You, Ha-la Mig-yaṅs who are the fountainhead of the science of medicine are the incarnation of the Buddha Mar-me-mdzad (Sanskrit Dīpaṁkara), and were called Great Brahmin. There is no doubt that the brahminī gSal-ba'i sGron-me who is appearing as the incarnation of the goddess Sarasvatī will be instrumental in spreading the light of the teaching of medicine in all the ten directions.'

Then he disappeared. The brahmin took all the texts and brought them to his own country. Then the brahminī said to him: 'Because of your constant truthfulness in the past you have become one whose words always come true and have found those medical texts and have been prophesied to by Kar-ma Dri-med. You are successful in finding medical texts for yourself and other beings. The Yaṅs-chen-ma (Sarasvatī) in the prophecy is me.'

Then Lord Ba-nu-ma came to see the brahmin Mig-yaṅs and taught him: 'You, good brahmin, incarnation of Mar-me-mdzad who has obtained a prophecy from Kar-ma Dri-ma-med, you are the glory of beings who are founding the science of medicine which has never been established before, and you are increasing its number of followers. Please, teach me the science of medicine.'

'Dam-pa Tog-dkar (the Venerable Śveathetu, name of Gautama Buddha while he was waiting in the Tushita heaven), You, Master of the heaven Sum-chu-tsa-rtsan-gsum, the protector of beings, were born in India for the sake of beings, in the great country of Pad-ma-gliṅ. You took the brahminī Chhos-kyi bLo-gros to wife and, for the sake of beings, two sons were born to you: rDo-rje Thog-hbebs and Shes-rab Ral-gri. You have become the founder of the teaching of medical science, and to your hands I will entrust all the texts of the science of medicine. And he told him the early history of medicine and gave the texts to him. Ba-nu passed the teaching on to Shes-rab Ral-gri who passed them on to king dGah-ba'i bLo-gros who passed them on to king Pad-ma dPal. He gave them to king dPal-ldan Phun-ts'ogs. He gave them to king sDoṅ-sdum-skyes. He passed them on to king sṄa-Chhen-po. From him they were passed on to Bi-Byi dGah-byed. From him to doctor Duṅ-gi Thor-chog-chan. From him to gYu-thog's family lineage in Tibet.' Then the doctor from Dol-po asked gYu-thog: 'What are the eight branches of medicine and what are the eight kinds of diseases called?' gYu-thog replied: 'The eight kinds of medicine are: Curing, healing, expelling, pharmacology, application of oil, reciting mantras, surgery and regeneration. The eight kinds of diseases are general diseases of the body, children's diseases, women's diseases, diseases caused by demons, lack of sexual power, wounds caused by weapons, diseases caused by poison, and old age caused by the diminishing of the elements.

Now we come to the treatments of these eight kinds of diseases: although there are many diseases between the top of the head and the soles of the feet, their totality can be divided into two kinds: hot and cold. Although there are many divisions of medicine, one can distinguish two main divisions: those with a cooling effect and those with a heat-producing effect. Although there are many ways of dealing with diseases, their totality can be divided into four principal ones: medicine, treatment, diet, and regulation of activities.

Then the Gru-gu doctor asked: 'Who were the first doctors and under which kings did they introduce medicine into the different countries like China, Nepal, Kashmir, Mongolia, Dolpo, Grugu and Khrom and so on?' gYu-thog replied: 'The brahmin Hala-mig-yaṅ during the reign of king Ta-mchhi-chan in India, in China doctor Hala-dhara under king Seṅ-pags-chan, in Turkestan doctor Hbi-gu-ta during the reign of king hBa-ga-dur (Bahadur), into Nepal doctor Ra-rtsa-na during the reign of king Ra-hdzu-ge, into Kashmir doctor hDzu-ge-dpal under the reign of king dPal-'od, into Mongolia doctor Bha-ya-ha under the reign of king Ba-ri-ta, into Garlog doctor Ha-ri-sna under the reign of king Ga-ga, into Tazig (Persia) doctor Ra-si-rta (Rhazes?) under the reign of king Bha-ri-bha, into Khrom doctor dKar-sna-skas-ri under the reign of king Sag-shu, into Gesar doctor Rigs-bzaṅ-bu under the reign of king dPah-bo, into Uḍḍiyāna doctor Bho-ya-rta-ye under the reign of king Za, into Zhaṅ-zhuṅ doctor Hzi-ra-sna under the reign of king gYuṅ-druṅ-dpal, into Tibet doctor Bi-byi dGah-byed under the reign of king Tho-tho-ri gNyan-btsan.'

Then the nine foreign doctors said: 'It is truly astonishing that in Tibet excellent teachers like you exist.' And they praised him in the following manner:

'We bow to you who is renowned as a Saint.
Yours is perfected knowledge acquired through study and merit,
Accumulated in former lives,
Who are the great protector of innumerable helpless beings,
You who are called gYu-thog-pa, the most learned amongst the learned,
Above all, you are the very life of medical science,
The only protector of all the sick,
You are the sun of Tibet who has dispelled the clouds of darkness there,
We bow at the feet of the great gYu-thog.'

Then they chose him to be their protector. The king and his attendants were astonished when they saw the nine foreign doctors bowing before gYu-thog and praising him and they conceived great faith.

Among the foreign doctors, the Chinese doctor requested him: 'Please, teach us the method of treating gZah (Rāhula) paralysis, and khyi (dog) and bya (bird).' gYu-thog replied: 'They are very harmful.' They said, 'Do you know how to propitiate Rāhula, dog and bird?' gYu-thog said: 'I do not know it. Please, teach me.' The Chinese doctor said: 'The treatment of paralysis is called the Wheel of Life. The treatment of Bird is called the Wheel of Signs. The treatment of Dog is called the Wheel of razors.' He offered them to gYu-thog who, with the three rituals, learned to propitiate the three gods causing the diseases.

In the 29th night since he started Śrī Vajrapāṇi, the Treasurer of the Secret Teachings, leading a white man with a crystal staff in his hand and a red man with a bird's head and a black man with a dog's snout, said to the three: 'You three, offer each one of you to the learned gYu-thog instruction in the method of treating your disease! If you do not offer it I shall banish you to the other side of the ocean.' The three answered: 'If he gives us a cake offering and keeps us as protectors of his teaching we will give it to him.' Then gYu-thog promised to do as they requested, and they offered him their instruction in the ritual for the treatment of their respective diseases. Since then gYu-thog's disciples and followers have to offer sacrificial gtor-mas to the three, Rāhula, Bird and Dog, and keep them as their protectors, and especially they keep as their protector Rāhula who has promised to fulfil all their wishes.

Then gYu-thog asked the Chinese doctor: 'Where is the Ārya Mañjuśrī staying at present?' The Chinese doctor said: 'He is staying here,' and cut his trunk open, and simultaneously with him all the nine foreign doctors showed each one their miraculous power. In the Chinese doctor's chest Mañjuśrī was clearly discernible; in the Indian doctor's chest the Buddha Śākyamuni, in the Nepalese doctor's chest Avalokiteśvara, in the Kashmiri doctor's chest the goddess Tārā, in the Mongolian doctor's chest Vajrapāṅi, in the Dol-po doctor's chest the Medicine Buddha, and in the Gru-gu doctor's chest the five Dhyānī Buddhas. And they said: 'We bow before the Guru and the Tutelary Deities. If one can look with the eye of faith at us nine foreign doctors one can see that we are definitely manifestations of Those who are beyond the nature of ordinary people. Anyone showing disbelief in us will fall down into hell. If anyone prays to us he will get our blessing. If your Excellency gYu-thog-pa would like to see a spectacle, then see this!' Then gYu-thog conceived great faith into them and exclaimed: 'Oh, how wonderful are these nine foreign doctors who are real Buddhas and Bodhisattvas. They are the great Protectors of all beings. Whoever can pray to them they will lead undoubtedly to the abode of bliss. They are merciful and contact with them always brings benefit. I put your feet on the top of my head and am offering you my whole person. Give your blessing to me and to all sick people. We will not be separated from you in this life and all other lives. Our minds are mingled,' and he bowed to them. At that moment the king also conceived great faith into gYu-thog and the nine foreign doctors. Then the foreign doctors gave gYu-thog and the king a great number of medical texts and many instructions by ḍākinīs. Then they went back to their own countries.

XXIV GYU-THOG'S FIRST JOURNEY TO INDIA

At bSam-yas when king Khri-sroṅ-lde-btsan had been five years old, his father and himself had invited Śāntiraksha and Padmasaṁbhava (from India) to Tibet. They laid the foundations of bSam-yas Monastery which was completed when Khri-sroṅ lDe-btsan was fifteen years old.

One day, when gYu-thog was twenty-five years old, he went to visit a patient. A woman holding a lance adorned with ribbons and a mirror in her hands appeared to him and said, 'gYu-thog-pa, go to India,' and then she disappeared. Then gYu-thog decided to go to India and procured a great amount of gold, and the king and others tried to dissuade him but he did not listen. On his request he received mantras and talismans from Padmasaṁbhava and went to India.

In Nepal he met doctor Dānaśīla who welcomed him very warmly and introduced him to the Nepalese. He said: 'This is the great Teacher, the Tibetan doctor gYu-thog-pa.' Then he stayed in Nepal for a few days and looked after the sick. Dānaśīla presented him with the Nepalese instruction in the treatment of sun stroke and rṅam-ru sti-ba (cupping).

At the mountain Kun-tu rGyu on the border between Nepal and India, he met the translator Vairochana who said to him: 'Where are you going, gYu-thog-pa?' gYu-thog replied: 'I am going to India to get instruction in the medical and allied sciences.' The translator said, 'I know how to translate, and especially I have received the rGyud-bzhi with complete instructions from the paṇḍita Chandradeva who said to me: "Pass this teaching on to the king and to gYu-thog-pa," and so let us go to Tibet!' 'bLo-tsa-ba, keep the rGyud-bzhi as a hidden treasure in the central pillar rising out of a chalice in the central temple on the middle floor of bSam-yas Monastery,' said gYu-thog; and afterwards the interpreter and the king did as gYu-thog had said.

Then gYu-thog went to visit the paṇḍita Chandradeva as the interpreter had indicated to him and requested instruction from him. The paṇḍita gave him the supplementary instruction to the rGyud-bzhi and asked him, 'Have you and the king of Tibet received the translation of the rGyud-bzhi by Vairochana?' Then gYu-thog told him about his meeting and converse with Vairochana. Chandradeva also taught him a great number of different instructions in medicine. Because of this gYu-thog became a little conceited and he said: 'Having accumulated both, much learning and much merit in former lives, I, the Tibetan doctor gYu-thog Yon-tan, am able to meet the great Guru-Saint and Protector and to display the great treasure of instructions. In the past I was the only one to spread the teaching effectively, and now there is none greater than me.' After that he received many more teachings and returned to Tibet. The king was greatly pleased and had gYu-thog's exploits announced publicly far and wide.

XXV GYU-THOG'S SECOND AND THIRD JOURNEY TO INDIA

One night, when he was thirty-five years old, he had a dream that a white man said to gYu-thog: 'gYu-thog-pa, go to India.' Then gYu-thog took much gold and went to India. He went to see the paṇḍita Chandradeva and he received many instructions. He also met the learned Me-dbaṅ from whom he received a hundred instructions, and returned to Tibet. Then the king asked him: 'Wouldn't it be a good thing to take the rGyud-bzhi now from its secret hiding place?' Then gYu-thog said: 'Still I have to go to India once more. Until then, please, do not take it out!' And (later on) again he went to India and he met a hundred gurus and he received many instructions on astrology and many Buddhist and non-Buddhist sciences, and especially the explanation of words with a hidden meaning different from the manifest one in the rGyud-bzhi, with annotations. Then he returned to Tibet. gYu-thog made the following speech to the king and his attendants and the assembled nine learned Tibetan doctors: 'Your Royal Highness and doctors gathered here together, for the sake of the sick, my disciples, and my son, I, gYu-thog Yon-tan mGon-po, have been to India three times and have met some Guru-Saints and have received instructions like a king's treasury. I have learned all the eighteen sciences, Buddhist and non-Buddhist, and the *Inner, Outer and Secret District* text. I know a thousand explanations of the rGyud-bzhi and countless other instructions and the one hundred and ninety-one thousand instructions of the dMar-hded and countless Aphorisms. I know the anatomical text *The Magic Mirror*, I know the text called *How to Find the Empty Spaces Between Important Organs in the Body*,* I know the *Essence of the Key to Thur-dpyad* (a tube to be put into different organs), *The Magic Wheel, the Perfect method Gained from Taking the Pulse*, I know *The*

* Where one can apply moxa and acupuncture.

Reckoning of Astrological Charts, I know the *Jewel Lamp of The Diagram of Body Measurements*, I know *The Astrological Computations on Favourable Times for the Rites for the Dead*, I know *The Working Out a Horoscope from the Nativity*, I know the *Perfect Explanation of the Relation of Saṁsāra to Nirvāṇa*, I know the *Astrology for Shattering Mountains to Atoms*, I am the foremost one in the science of medicine, specially the *Guide to the rGyud-bzhi* and the explanatory notes on its obscure terms, I know the Supplement and the Index to the rGyud-bzhi, I know the Instruction in the system of the rGyud-bzhi. I know how to apply moxa, the black method of stopping bleeding, I know the perfect practice of bleeding, I know how to give emetics (Pulling Upwards like a fish hook), I know how to give purgatives like hurling stones down from a mountain, I know notes whose sight is helpful, I know one hundred and eight commentaries (on the rGyud-bzhi).'

The king said: 'All connection with you is auspicious, victorious prince of doctors, gYu-thog, who has the knowledge of protecting beings, great hero and protector, able to dispel diseases, who has an abundance of mercy and love. You went to India three times by the power of your prayer and ripened former karma and brought with you a host of essential instructions for the sake of many beings and a few pupils. You dispelled the darkness in Tibet and specially established the teaching of medicine. You are kindness itself, gYu-thog-pa.' He presented three districts to gYu-thog: Dags-po, Koṅ-po, and Khyuṅ-po. Then the nine Tibetan doctors said together:

'The profound jewelled teaching of the Buddha is difficult to probe.
Long live gYu-thog-pa Yon-tan mGon-po
Who holds the life-tree of the teachings and the science of medicine
In the country of Tibet
Guided specially and protected by Avalokiteśvara.
For the sake of many beings and pupils
You went to India three times to get the Dākinīs' instruction.
Specially you brought the medical texts and their commentaries
From India and spread them throughout Tibet.
In the snowfenced country you kindled the lamp of happiness and bliss.
You are the most excellent one who can drive away the diseases caused by the three poisons.
You are the most learned one able to mix medicines to balance hot and cold.
It is wonderful that we have a protection.
You are the great guidance of doctors and the ornament of beings;
It is wonderful to have a protection.'

Then they bowed at his feet and put them over their heads. Then gYu-thog Yon-tan mGon-po taught them in day-time the five sciences* and at night-time the essence of the instruction in the science of medicine. His disciple Byaṅ-chhub rDo-rje said: 'This side of the Brahmaputra river there is probably nobody more learned than you who is good and wise.' gYu-thog replied:

'Listen, my faithful disciple Byaṅ-chhub rDo-rje!
This is the early history of me, the learned Yon-tan mGon-po:
I am the manifestation of the speech of the Medicine Buddha
And the manifestation of the mind of Mañjuśrī and the manifestation of the body of hTs'o-byed gzhon-nu.
I am Yon-tan mGon-po who is learned, conscientious and good.
He who is in contact with me will benefit by it.
I am free from cares.'

Then Byaṅ-chhub rDo-rje asked him: 'Where is Me-hla Phyag-sdum staying at present?' gYu-thog replied:

'The great Me-hla Phyag-sdum stayed in India for eight hundred years,†
Then he lived in Tibet for fifty years,
After which he lived in India for two hundred years,
Then he went to lTa-na-sdug.
I have heard this from him himself
When I met him during my stay in India for the second time.
The details of this have been told in Me-hla's own story.'

XXVI THE MYROBALAN TREE

Then the disciple hJam-dPal Seṅ-ge said: 'The planting of medicinal plants by the goddess Yid-hphrog-ma has been explained before, but what about the planting of the myrobalan [Arura]?' gYu-thog replied:

'Continually the Saint came back into his lineage like a string of pearls:
I bow before my famous ancestors gYu-thog Khyuṅ-po and hDre-rje.
How it happened that Arura was first planted
By sKyes-pa'i Yid-hphrog-ma
Was that Queen bLo-gros bDe-byed-ma presented her with an arura tree and said:

* Astrology, Grammar, Medicine, Dialectics, Mechanical Arts.

† Being a great Saint he was able to live for a very long time.

"Listen to me, Yid-hphrog-ma!
This flourishing arura tree, the excellent medicine,
Beautifully formed and of perfect qualities,
The excellent medicine tree of arura
I am presenting to you.
Please, accept it with compassion on me.
Please, pray and plant this for the sake of future beings.
There is no doubt good results will ensue."
Then Yid-hphrog-ma went again to Bodhgayā
And planted with the following prayer:
"By the kindness of the Guru and the Three Jewels,
By the power of the sincerity of my mind,
By the strength of the truth of karma and its result,
May what I pray for be successful!
May this Arura rNam-rgyal tree with its nectar
Grow in the eastern mountain Spos-ṅad-ldan
And may its root, stem and branches
Drive away diseases of the flesh, bone, skin and limbs!
May its blossoms drive away the diseases of the five sense organs
And its fruit those of the internal organs!
May five kinds of Arura grow on the top of (mountain) trees
Which have six different tastes
And eight actions
And seventeen good qualities,
With digestive effects and driving away all traces of diseases
And specially the four hundred and four!
Beautiful king of medicine with a pleasant fragrance,
Surrounding you grow the five perfect aruras.
May arura become the chief ingredient
Whenever a medicine is compounded!
Planted at the Eastern celestial mountain of sPos-ṅad-ldan
Which can be reached only by the elect,
May therefore the five aruras be successful everywhere.
The excellent medicine of arura and other plants,
May it be spread all over the suffering worlds!
May all the sufferings of beings be driven away
By doctors skilfully mixing compounded medicines!
The arura planted by Yid-hphrog-ma with her prayer
Grew in the sPos-ṅad-ldan mountain
Exactly as it is mentioned in the *rTsa-rGyud*

About the arura rnam-rgyal.'*
This is what gYu-thog said.

When gYu-thog said this hJam-dpal Seṅ-ge's faith increased greatly.

Then his disciple dKon-mchhog asked him: 'What marks of distinctions has the arura?' gYu-thog said: 'There are five marks: 1. By their origin.

* The arura rnam-rgyal is a rare species of arura. It is also mentioned in the *gSer-'od Dam-pa Sūtra* which says: There is arura rnam-rgyal and five other aruras. They have six tastes. In the *Zur-rdol* it says:

The rNam-rgyal tree bears the deathless nectar.
Its root drives away bone diseases.
Its stem drives away diseases of flesh and blood.
Its branches drive away diseases of veins and nerves,
Its bark drives away skin diseases
And its leaves drive away diseases of the five sense organs.
Its fruit drives away diseases of the inner organs.
In the top of the tree also five aruras grow.
They have six tastes and eight actions and seventeen good qualities.
The excellent medicine of deathless nectar
Has an influence on the three parts of digestion.
Smelling its pleasant scent drives away four hundred and four diseases
In the centre of the arura rnam-rgyal tree.
In the east it grows the hJigs-med, in the south the Sha-thub,
In the west the hPhel-byed zlum-bu,
In the north the sKem-po sul-maṅs.
The arura with the excellent action grows in sPos-ṅad-ldan in the east.
Through the power of Yid-hphrog-ma's prayer
Aruras similar to the rnam-rgyal may grow in other places.
That medicine tree has eighteen good qualities,
Other aruras have good qualities,
But not as good qualities as the arura rnam-rgyal.
The learned men and Saints who mentioned the good qualities of the arura
Always meant the arura rnam-rgyal.
The uneducated and those with corrupted knowledge
Say that the four other aruras have the rnam-rgyal's good qualities.
This is the system of the yokel, and the learned will laugh at it.
To say that all aruras have the good qualities of the rnam-rgyal
Is like saying the ignorant have the qualities of the learned,
How can one assume that the value of gold and brass is equal?

The *A-tsa-ra'i sDe-skor* mentions an arura with six tastes and eight good qualities and three effects on the digestion etc.: 'that is the arura rnam-rgyal'. hTs'o-byed gZhon-nu's text *sMan-gyi sDe-sbor* dealing with medicinal compounds says:

India is a pleasant land and its people fortunate:
By the blessing of the perfect Saints and by Yid-hphrog-ma's prayer
Arura rnam-rgyal, the king of medicines, grows in the sPos-ṅad-ldan mountain in the east.
Wherever the Saints are present there is no disease.
There is a miraculous medicine by the blessing of the Medicine Buddha.
Khotan, Nepal, Tibet and other countries did not grow it.
Inferior aruras grow in the other countries through Yid-hphrog-ma's prayer.
Their action is only helpful in some measure.

2. By the way of planting them. 3. By the way to recognize them and the place where they grow. 4. By distinguishing fifteen qualities and forms. 5. By the genus to which it belongs.

1. In olden times the nectar of the gods dropped down into this world. It was believed that arura grew from these drops. Or else, the gods and titans churned the ocean and obtained nectar in this way. Rāhula stole it from them and fled. But a brahmin threw his wheel at him and cut off his head which dropped on the ground and from this grew arura.

2. Planting medicinal herbs in general and specially arura. Yid-hphrog-ma, the Incarnation of the goddess bDud-rtsi, who has the gift of the soothsayer, invited many gods and saintly rishis and went to Bodhgayā. There she planted medicinal plants and specially arura, as mentioned before. The seed was presented by queen bLo-gros bDe-byed-ma to Yid-hphrog-ma who planted it and prayed.

3. The arura rnam-rgyal grows only in sPos-ṅad-ldan. But the other four aruras can grow anywhere.

4. The arura rnam-rgyal has eighteen distinctive qualities, and the other aruras have fewer good qualities and in some measure only. But among the other four aruras those called hphel-byed or gser-mdog are said to be better.

5. The shape of the fruit of the arura rnam-rgyal looks like a kul-ba's tail, that of the arura hjigs-byed is like a five-sided pyramid, the nectar arura is thick and yellow, the sha-hthug arura is like a round chalice and is also called shugs-su nag-po, the skem-po is narrowed towards the top and has many folds and the fifth species is the hphel-byed or gser-mdog which is yellow and pointed like a lemon. The hjigs-byed is black, the bdud-rtis or nectar arura yellow and the sha-thub black.'

When he had expounded these things, they conceived great faith in gYu-thog. Then all disciples thought they would like to start the ritual for making a quicksilver solution.* gYu-thog sent dPal-ldan hBum-seṅ and his son dBus-pa Phyug-gtsaṅ and a few other disciples to (the district of Koṅ-po to bring khyuṅ-rgod-ma (kind of mercury). They found fifty-five khals of quicksilver.

Then they went to Kashmir with five hundred disciples. There they met the paṇḍita Nyi-ma Rab-gsal. gYu-thog disputed with him on grammar and on the system of veins (misprint 'root circle'). gYu-thog won in the discussion. Then the king of Kashmir and others present conceived great faith. Then the paṇḍita said: 'You have won in the word battle. Now we shall have a real contest.' Then he cut his trunk open and showed that all his veins were

* Accompanied by the recital of mantras the quicksilver is mixed with other substances and pounded and diluted in water.

in the form of letters. He asked gYu-thog: 'Now, show me your miraculous power!' Then gYu-thog exclaimed: 'Look here!' and turned his body inside out. Then all his veins looked exactly as gYu-thog had expounded before. The king and the paṇḍita were astonished. The paṇḍita said: 'You are as learned and as saintly as a Kashmiri paṇḍita!' Since then the people called gYu-thog the Kashmiri paṇḍita.

Then king hDzum-ha-ri of Kashmir fell sick with lupus and gYu-thog gave him a quicksilver mixture and the instructions on how to use it. And the king was cured. He offered gYu-thog twenty-five khals of pearls and many other jewels, saying: 'Gracious doctor, you have protected me from a mortal disease. Please, tell me about the origin of quicksilver, how it is found and how to dilute it, boil it and wash it and how to pound it.' Then gYu-thog explained it. After this, gYu-thog and his disciples returned to Lhasa. There he had twenty-five silk hangings made for the Jo-bo Temple ornamented with five khals of the pearls. He offered hanging ribbons to Avalokiteśvara. And to Raṅ-byuṅ lṄa-ldan* he offered hanging ribbons ornamented with five khals of pearls, and to the goddess Ma-gchig dPal-lha he also offered silk hangings with one khal of pearls. To the poor in Lhasa who numbered about five thousand he gave one month's food and other necessities of life.

XXVII SALT, BEER, SUNLIGHT AND WOMEN

One day king Hadharu was sick with a cold fit of ague (shaking palsy?) and he asked gYu-thog to his bedside, who came with some disciples. There he met the Nepalese doctor Śrī Siṁha. The two doctors examined the king's pulse, and gYu-thog said: 'You Nepalese diagnose this disease as a fever, but we Tibetans regard it as a cold ague. When the king was ill before you stopped him from taking salt with his food, therefore his ague has gone down to the lower part of his body. So now, give him salt again, little by little.' Then the Nepalese doctor said: 'Salt does not agree with any disease. A patient should keep away from four poisons: 1. Salt harms his bones. 2. Beer harms his flesh. 3. Sunlight harms his skin. 4. Women harm the strength of his body. If someone makes do without these four, his strength and happiness will be increased and he will recover soon. His life will be as long as that of sun and moon, his strength will be greater than that of a wild man of the woods, and his movements will be faster than the wind. Think of our history, when king Ratna-tāla was sick with graṅ-ba skya-rbab (cold dropsy), doctor Ratna-vajra and other doctors treated him in different ways

* Famous image in the gTsug-lag-khaṅ temple in Lhasa.

but without success. Then the king propitiated the goddess Tārā and he received the following prophecy from Tārā: "Listen, king Ratna-tāla of Nepal! The sickness of your body is caused by the cold ague. The graṅ-ba skya-rbab is like a leather bag full of air. There is not the slightest fever in your disease, only cold. Your treatment should be to give up staying in hot sunlight for a long time, salt, beer, keeping a woman, onion, garlic, radish, goat's meat, mushrooms, rul-sum ser-chhen (anything tasting rancid and rotten). Give up eating too cold food and the eighteen kinds of food difficult to digest, getting too cold, getting too hot, and eating raw vegetables. Especially partaking of the sunlight, salt, and beer [and women] can bring fever even to one who suffers from a cold disease, e.g. rheumatism, just as clouds will suddenly appear in a cloudless sky. Also many texts have stated that these four poisons should be given up. Therefore, I, too, am of the opinion that salt does not agree with this disease."' Then gYu-thog replied: 'In general, the literal meaning of the words of physician-saints is as you said but they say them on purpose because of circumstances, and there are also objections against this advice in exceptions to the general rule. Please, listen to my instruction for the practice which is sealed by the ḍākinīs.' Then he told them the instruction of the practice of Purifying the Gold: 'I bow before my Guru and my father to bless the destruction of the false beliefs maintained by heretics. You are very famous, Śrī Siṁha, follower of Dānaśīla, and you other Nepalese doctors, who are very conceited indeed. When a learned doctor speaks he is always concerned with the state of health and the state of mind of his patient, and there are underlying motives and reasons why something is said, and the envisaging of logical consequences in learned speech and your way of debating with words only without knowing these things would make scholars laugh. I, gYu-thog Yon-tan mGon-po, went to India three times for the sake of driving away diseases and searching for the essence of instruction in medicine, and I met the great learned Me-dbaṅ and Pan-chhen Chandra and hundreds of trustworthy scholars. From each one of them I heard the same opinion: that the medical texts prescribing for sick people the giving up of these four are right in general, but in exceptional cases the practice is like this: when a patient has only fever caused by blood and bile he should give up eating hot, sour, sweet, or salty things, but he should always have bitter things. If you have too heavy and too fat food there is the danger of getting high blood pressure, bilious diseases, pulmonary diseases, and cold ague caused by phlegm mixed with air. Then one should eat hot and sour and salty food and give up bitter and sweet food. If one eats too much light, cool and cold food, then the heat in the stomach will be extinguished, and a tumour or a swelling will grow, or the patient will get dropsy. Therefore one should first find out what proportion of salt should be used in each disease. If it is a cold disease one-third of the usual amount should be given. If it is a mixed hot and cold disease only very little salt. If it cannot be recognized whether it is a hot or a cold disease two-thirds of the usual amounts should be given. If too much salt is eaten a slow lingering fever may ensue. Eating no salt causes a lingering cold disease.

Therefore one should know what is the right quantity of salt to be taken. This is the key to the understanding of the relation of salt to diseases. But if someone is used to eating much salt or very little salt from childhood doing suddenly the opposite can also cause disease. But if people are habitually ailing this effect of sudden change does not apply to them. I know this by practice and experience.

Beer is said to be poison to the flesh but thin people grow fat from it. Sunlight is said to be harmful to the skin but in winter skin chapped from the wind gets smooth through the sunlight. Salt is said to be poison to the bones but broken bones can be mended and pus be dried by salt. To have intercourse with a woman is said to be poison to health but a man with stricture of the urethra should have intercourse. This instruction is the mouth-to-ear teaching like pure gold which I am giving you, Śrī Siṁha, you conceited doctor.

There is an ancient* story about a brahmin who lived at the monastery called "Jungle Monastery" who never ate a grain of salt or drank a drop of alcohol, who looked upon woman as an enemy and who, since he lived underground, never saw the sun any more. After some time he became quite emaciated and very feeble. His skin was very rough and he suffered from air diseases and his semen became as hard as stone preventing him from urinating. His five limbs became swollen like a head, and when he bent down or stretched himself he suffered pains as if his bones were broken. He propitiated the goddess Rigs-byed-ma, and she appeared to him. He asked Rigs-byed-ma: "What is the cause of these my diseases? What is the additional cause of them? What is the treatment for this?" Then she said: "Because you did not drink alcohol you have become so emaciated and you have developed dropsy, therefore your limbs are swollen. You have not been in the sun, and this has caused nervous complaints because of the *rluṅs* not coming at the right time of day and not at the right speed.† You have not eaten salt, therefore your bones are not solid enough. You have not used women and have contracted a stricture of the urethra." Then he used the

* In the Vedas.

† A different rluṅ (wind or air) is prevalent in the body at different times of day or night.

four poisons and recovered from his diseases. Have you heard of this?' said gYu-thog. Dr. Śrī Siṁha said: 'I don't believe all this poppycock. There is one doctor with the appearance of a rishi who is meditating at the temple of hPhags-pa Shiṅ-kun in Nepal. Let us go there to ask him! What he says I shall believe.' Then gYu-thog and he went to see the rishi and they told him everything. The rishi said: 'gYu-thog is right,' and then he disappeared. Thereupon Dr. Śrī Siṁha conceived great faith in gYu-thog and bowed to him, put his feet on his head, and said: 'gYu-thog Yon-tan mGon-po, you doctor from Tibet, I feel ashamed and deeply sorry confessing, as I must, that I had not known that you were like a second Medicine Buddha, and am asking your forgiveness for having always opposed you in debates with a self-opinionated and jealous mind. I believe that there is no birth or death for your body which is unchangeable like a *vajra*. I believe there is no impediment or shrill note in your melodious voice. I believe your mind is as wide as the sky, as perfect, as immeasurable, and as inexhaustible. We shall be following you in this life and in other lives until we are enlightened. Please, look upon us with your wisdom eye and protect us!' Since that time Śrī Siṁha followed gYu-thog as his disciple wherever he went, and people called him 'the second gYu-thog'.

XXVIII HDRE-RJE VAJRA'S JOURNEY TO INDIA

Doctor Śrī Singha asked gYu-thog: 'How many members of your lineage have been to India?' gYu-thog said: 'The beginning of my lineage came from Heaven to India. Then it came to Tibet. From Tibet my ancestor hDre-rje Vajra went to India once. I, gYu-thog Yon-tan mGon-po, went three times and endeavoured to achieve a great purpose.' Śrī Siṁha asked him: 'Please, tell me what it was like when you and your ancestor went to India?' And gYu-thog said: 'My ancestor hDre-rje Vajra is the lord over demons, gods and human beings, and especially he is close to the tutelary deities and has miraculous powers. Therefore his journey was not arduous. His only difficulties were encountered when he was searching for the teachings. He went to Lho-phyogs dPal-ri (Glorious Southern Mountain) to visit Nāgārjuna who was to teach him the *mGo-thig Rin-chen gNad-grel*, *rTsa-thig gSer-gyi Thig-le*, *Yan-lag gNad-kyi mDzub-brtsugs*, *Sha-thig Rin-chen Shags-pa*, *gSaṅ-thig-skar Khuṅs-phye-ba*, *gNad-hgrel gChig-shes Kun-grol* texts. He offered Nāgārjuna a thousand sraṅs of gold and prayed to him: "You are the second Buddha, preserving the teaching of the Buddhas. You are very learned and you are the Master of the teachings of the Sūtras and the

Tantras. You are the source of the Dharma and have achieved all the perfections. I bow before Nāgārjuna who is lord over the Nāgas. I, the Tibetan hDre-rje Vajra, came to India in search of the teachings, for the sake of curing the Tibetans of their diseases. I am taking your feet on my head and am offering you these thousand gold srań. Please, accept them and give me the essence of the teachings." Nāgārjuna said: "You Tibetan disciple, your present is not very big but it is cash and not goods for bartering. We Indians like gold, so if you have more, give it to me." hDre-rje thought: "I have a lot of gold but I shall need it when looking for other teachers. But if I do not offer more this time it may be an evil portent," and he offered five hundred srań requesting Nāgārjuna to teach him. Nāgārjuna said: "This is not a place to teach you. I am going to Brag-dmar sKe-ts'ań (Red Rock Forest), you come there!" Then he disappeared. hDre-rje Vajra crossed many empty valleys in search of him until he came to a terrifying place where tigers, leopards and bears and other wild animals were running about and fighting. There his food supplies gave out and his boots were torn to shreds. His suffering was like that of a blind man put suddenly onto a plain who does not know where to turn, yet he could do nothing about it. He began to pray to the Medicine Buddha asking him for protection from the wild animals that they should not eat him. Then a horrible black bear came and lay down to sleep at his feet. He was so frightened that his heart seemed to leap right out of his mouth. Then he imagined the Medicine Buddha situated on his head and kept very still. After a little while a tiger came and lay down at his right-hand side. Later a leopard came and lay down at his left-hand side. Then a poisonous snake came and lay down in front of him. Then a man-eating red bear came and lay down there. All these animals growled angrily. Then he thought: "Now I am definitely going to be eaten by these wild beasts but I cannot do anything and I have no protection. When I die, may I be born in the realm of the Medicine Buddha!" And he prayed very deeply. Then he fell asleep. When he woke up the next morning the sun was shining brightly, and there was no sign of the animals. Then he got up and continued his search of Brag-dmar sKe-ts'ań. On the way he met a black man holding a spear. He asked him: "Where are you coming from?" The black man said: "I come from Nāgārjuna at Brag-dmar sKe-ts'ań. Now I am going to Lho-phyogs dPal-ri." hDre-rje Vajra felt as happy as if he saw Nāgārjuna himself. He requested him: "Please, be merciful and take me to Nāgārjuna!" The man replied: "One who has not conquered the devil of selfishness and whose pride is growing is not entitled to any mercy. If someone cannot give up too great a fondness of his body and is incapable of facing the dangers of one night or of keeping a steadfast mind, how can he reach Brag-dmar sKe-ts'aṅ? There is no question of Nāgārjuna looking at him with his merciful eyes." Then he disappeared. hDre-rje Vajra did not know where to go and he felt quite dejected and he remembered all his relatives and he cried for a long time. On the other hand he thought: "If I go as far as I can go I may reach the border of the country," and he went in the Eastern direction, going by the sun in daytime, and in the evening he looked at the Pleiad. Then, on a river bank, he saw a woman washing cotton clothes. He went to her and she said: "When the cotton clothes are made ready for laundering to be trampled on by the feet, a small man should keep to the fire place." Then she pursued him. He was so frightened that he was nearly ready to jump into the water. She caught him by the scruff of the neck and said, "You, the one and only Tibetan disciple, coming to India with great courage: if you want to take the essence of the teachings you should not be overfond of your body and your life. If you want to search for Nāgārjuna you should meditate on every appearance as your Guru. Whatever you find comes from your karma. Take it as a method of gaining Enlightenment." Then she disappeared. He thought: "Whatever appears to me is just an aspect of my Guru but I did not recognize him." There was a grass or straw hut and he went in. There he saw a monk killing goats and sheep and laying out the steaming hot viscera on his robe. The monk gave him an old female buffalo and told him: "You kill this! If you cannot kill it I'll kill you." Then he said: "I am a healer, I cannot kill her." Immediately the monk put the robe round his neck and killed the buffalo. Then he said: "There is no victim and no slayer. So there is no distinction between victim and slayer. Therefore, when I am killing, yet I have never killed. This is the method of Nāgārjuna. You, Tibetan disciple, cannot find Nāgārjuna when you search for him. Pray to him. If you achieve perfect compassion then immediately you will be able to see him." Then he disappeared like a rainbow. hDre-rje Vajra continued his search with a very deep prayer to Nāgārjuna and the Medicine Buddha. On the road he saw a sick man who was hungry and naked. Then very deep compassion grew in him. He said with a loud voice: "O Medicine Buddha and lineage of the teachings please, look with mercy upon this unprotected being, naked and hungry," and as he cried he found himself at Brag-dmar Ske-ts'aṅ. Then he seized Nāgārjuna's robe and cried. Nāgārjuna said: "You and I: there is no distinction and no separation between you and me. But your sinful karma is greater, therefore you did not see me." Then hDre-rje Vajra told him: "Because of my sinful karma I did not recognize you when you appeared to me and because of this I saw you as fearful and terrifying manifestations. That is why I did not see you as you are. But tell me, what is the cause that I can see you now?" Nāgārjuna said: "The good reason for your reaching Brag-dmar sKe-ts'aṅ and seeing me came into operation when perfect compassion grew in you when you saw that sick man and you prayed a deep prayer to the Medicine Buddha and me. These wiped away your sinful karma." Then hDre-rje knew that the wild animals, too, were manifestations of Nāgārjuna and he thought that specially that sick man was really Nāgārjuna. Then he offered five hundred sraṅs and requested him again to teach him. Then Nāgārjuna said: "Before, you felt much pride, so in order to break that and to wipe away the rest of your sinful karma I put so many obstacles in your way." Then he said, "I bow before the Buddha Śākyamuni, you Tibetan disciple who has much gold and strength of faith and courage. You came to India through virtue accumulated in your former life, and I, Nāgārjuna, played a little trick on you to test you. By my testing you your sinful karma has been wiped away. I hope your wishes will be fulfilled." And he taught him all the instructions mentioned above and also many other texts.

Then Nāgārjuna told him: "Today, Tibetan disciple, go to visit the big market." hDre-rje went there, and in the centre he saw a brahmin shining with great splendour who looked him up and down. hDre-rje started screaming like a calf, and the brahmin asked him: "Where do you come from? For what purpose have you come here?" Then he told him his story. The brahmin said: "You are my descendant. I am doctor Bi-byi dGah-byed." Then he asked hDre-rje: "Have you got the teaching of the bDud-rtsi-sman-hphreṅ and dDud-rtsi-sman-grub?" He said: "I do not have the first one. Please, give it to me!" Then the brahmin said: "In the Southern Sandalwood Jungle bDud-rtsi-ma with the other seven or fifteen* goddesses are residing. Go there." hDre-rje said: "Now I realize that you are my ancestor. Please, give me your instruction!" Then Bi-byi dGah-byed gave him the Nad-bsreg-pa Me-hi Rgyud (Disease-burning Fire-treatise), and Nad-dkrug-pa rLuṅ Rgyud (Disease-churning Air-treatise), the Nad-hkhrud-pa Chhu-hi Rgyud (Disease-washing Water-treatise), and the Nad-hdon-pa Sa-hi Rgyud (Disease-expelling Earth-treatise). He gave him instruction in these four destroyers of disease.

Then hDre-rje went to the Southern Sandalwood Jungle and during his journey reached the border of a great kingdom. In the interior of the country he saw a big crowd and he begged for his food. The people said: "This man is a spy for the Central Kingdom.† Let us dig a pit filled with vermin for him." Some said: "Drive him out of the country!" And some said, "It is

* There are two ways of counting them: eight or sixteen.

† The centre of India.

better to keep him imprisoned." Then they put him into prison. hDre-rje thought: "These foolish people who do not know about karma and its results are keeping me imprisoned without any fault on my part." And compassion for them grew in him. The jailer asked him: "Have you got any gold on you?" He said: "I have no gold. I am a little Tibetan student. I came here in search of the teachings." Then the jailer said: "You are Tibetan. And moreover you are coming in search of teachings. Then you must surely have some gold and hide it!" And he searched him and beat him. hDre-rje suffered so much pain as if his last day in this incarnation had come. Then he thought: "I do not think I shall ever be able to escape from this gaol. Please, bless me, Nāgārjuna and Bi-byi dGah-byed, so that I, in my next life, for the sake of beings, may achieve the knowledge of the Medicine Buddha and the lineage of the teachings." One night Nāgārjuna appeared to him and told him: "Be joyful! Soon you will escape from this prison, and pray to the Medicine Buddha and to the lineage of the teachings!" Immediately he woke up. He was so happy that he sang and danced as follows:

"I bow before Nāgārjuna, the Protector.
Please, bless this Tibetan and help him
To escape from his suffering!
By the Guru's and the Tutelary Deities' power of mercy,
By the blessing of the Medicine Buddha and the rishis,
By the strength of his virtues, and good deeds,
May this Tibetan escape from this prison!"

One day they opened the trapdoor at the top of the dungeon and let the ladder down and asked him to come up. He climbed up the ladder, and at the top stood a girl, about fifteen years old, decked out with her ornaments, and asked: "Where do you come from and where are you going?" He said: "I come from Tibet and I am going to the Southern Sandalwood Jungle." She said: "What a pity that an innocent man should be thus imprisoned!" Then he said to her: "I suppose, you are the king's daughter, so please, help me to escape from this prison." She said: "Run as far as you can." He said: "Please, tell me the way!" She said: "Today it is my duty to look after you, tomorrow the minister Gar-bdud Nag-po will kill you. Go immediately to that lake over there and pray to the Medicine Buddha whose action is so swift that I am sure somebody will come and escort you." He changed into royal attire and ran away. The people said: "The prisoner has killed the king and now he is escaping," and they pursued him. At that time a terrifying red Garuḍa came out of the middle of the lake. He stood with outstretched wings before hDre-rje who bestrode him, and the garuḍa brought him to the Southern Sandalwood Jungle. Then hDre-rje went in search of the goddess bDud-rtsi-ma. In the Southern Sandalwood Jungle he saw eight beautiful ladies making medicine tablets and practising the Turning-of-Medicine-into-Nectar. Then he said:

"O merciful eight manifestations of the Medicine Goddesses,
In the Southern Sandalwood Jungle,
Who, practising Turning-medicine-into-nectar,
Have achieved power over life and death:
This little Tibetan is very fortunate
For to meet you is as rare as a star in day-time.
Please, think of all beings with your mercy
And give me the teaching of the bDud-rtsi-sman-hphreṅ
And the teaching of the bDud-rtsi-sman-grub!"

Then the goddess bDud-rtsi-ma described to him the bDud-rtsi-sman-hphreṅ and gave him the complete instruction. Then he said: "Now, please, give me the bDud-rtsi-sman-grub." She laughed and said: "The teachings which are the essence of the Mind of the past, present and future Buddhas, the instruction how to achieve immortality, the ability to achieve the perfect method of Enlightenment, the hammer which destroys diseases and evil demons, the oral instruction of the Ḍākinīs are beyond your range of vision", and disappeared. Then hDre-rje thought: "I do not think anybody else has this profound and perfect teaching. Therefore I had better go on searching for those goddesses", and he went into the jungle to look for them. Then he saw all the goddesses standing by a white sandalwood tree. He requested them to give him the teaching. The goddess bDud-rtsi-ma said: "Tibetan disciple, if you have the gold for the consecration I shall give you the instruction." Then hDre-rje said: "I once had two thousand sraṅs but I have given all of them to Nāgārjuna. Now I have none left. But I am offering you my body, speech and mind." The goddess said: "There is no need to tell me so proudly that you had a lot of gold. If you have gold then bring it along." Then she disappeared. hDre-rje searched for her everywhere but could not find her. He thought: "Even if I found the goddesses now, having no gold I shall not get their instruction. Now I am going to see Nāgārjuna and then return home to Tibet and try and find new gold there with which to come back to India." And he went back.

In a wild country there was a trader called Zla-ba Phun-ts'og. He was very ill and hDre-rje went to his home and met Zla-ba Phun-ts'og's daughter Pad-ma Khrom-mdzes. She said: "Do you know how to heal sickness?"

He said: "Yes, I know it." She said: "My father is sick. So, please, stay here for some time." Then she went in. After some time she came back and asked him to come in. Then the trader said: "I contracted a fatal disease. Please, help me! If I recover I shall offer you five hundred sraṅs in gold." Then hDre-rje stayed with them and treated him with the Four Destroyers of disease. And soon he recovered. Then the trader offered him five hundred sraṅs of gold. He said: "Many famous disciples of great Indian doctors have put me on one side like a dead body. You, hDre-rje rGya-gar Vajra, well-known as sKyi-sna-pa* have protected my life. In order to return your kindness I offer you these five hundred sraṅs in gold. It is my good fortune that this is my beloved daughter, Pad-ma Khrom-mdzes, who loves me dearly, who is the incarnation of Nor-rgyun-ma. She is fit to be a queen. I offer her to you as a wife. Please, stay in India." Then hDre-rje said: "I came to India from Tibet to search for the teachings, disregarding all the obstacles on the way. All my gold I have offered to Nāgārjuna. With no gold left I would not get any further teaching. I am therefore accepting your gold but I shall not take your daughter from you. If I had stayed in India I should have felt pity for the sick amongst the Tibetans, that is why I shall be going back to Tibet." He took the five hundred sraṅs of gold and returned to the Southern Sandalwood Jungle. He searched for the goddesses and found them in a Sa-mchhog Sandalwood Jungle. He offered the five hundred sraṅs and asked bDud-rtsi-sman-grub-ma for the instruction. The goddess said: "You Tibetan disciple, did you lose your faith when I refused to give you the consecration for which you had no gold?" hDre-rje said, "I only thought this was caused by my bad fortune but I did not distrust you." She said: "It was sufficient for you to offer your body, speech and mind but it was not the right time for teaching you, and also I intended to show you the value of the Dharma. Now the time is ripe and I shall give it to you. Rejoice! We do not need the gold but we are taking it to complete your merit. You will see for yourself if this is not so." She made the threatening gesture into the four directions. Then everything appeared to him as gold. He was very surprised. Then he asked: "Give me the instruction!" She gave him the whole of the instruction and told him: "Now you should practise the ritual of bDud-rtsi-sman-grub." And he practised it. After seven days the Medicine Buddha appeared to him and gave him the same consecration and instruction. After a fortnight three rishis came and gave him the consecration and instruction. After twenty-one days hTs'o-byed gZhon-nu also gave him the same consecration and instruction. Then he received the instruction on the bDud-rtsi-sman-grub from each one of the eight goddesses.

* His other name: 'the man from sKyi-sna'.

Afterwards he made a sacrificial thanks-offering for the success of his instruction. Then he went to Lho-phyogs dPal-ri to meet Nāgārjuna. He bowed and put his feet over his head and inquired after his health. Nāgārjuna said: "You, Tibetan disciple, are you satisfied?" He said: "I bow before Nāgārjuna and Bi-byi dGah-byed and other Gurus. This little Tibetan is very fortunate having received the teaching of the science of medicine and the essential teachings of the Dharma. I have an exquisite present to take back to my people in Tibet, the teaching of the science of medicine. The sun of medical science will rise over Tibet. I shall be famous and wealthy. This is due to your kindness. I am singing this aloud out of happiness!" Nāgārjuna said: "I will protect you from all obstacles on the way. You shall establish the teaching of medicine in Tibet. A grandson of yours will be greater than your son. He will certainly further the teaching of medicine in Tibet." Then hDre-rje asked him: "Please, look after me always with your mercy!" And he made his parting bow to him. Nāgārjuna said: "There is no separation between you and me at all. But whether you are receiving my blessing is dependent on your faith. It is quite a number of years now since I died but we are connected through karma, and by the strength of your faith I was able to appear to you and to teach you the essence of my teachings. If you pray to me deeply and sincerely, with compassion in your heart, you can see me whenever you want to, wherever you are. My compassion knows no discrimination nor does distance make any difference." hDre-rje had gone to India during the Dragon year and returned to Tibet in the fourth month of the Monkey year. On his return from India he became very renowned.

After some time hDre-rje Vajra surrounded by a few disciples and many lay supporters celebrated Nāgārjuna's anniversary. At that assembly mKhas-grub Khyuṅ-po Do-rje asked: "Father, you reached India without difficulties and stayed there for many years. What instructions have you had from which gurus?" hDre-rje told him all about the adventures that befell him between Tibet and India and the difficulties he encountered in order to get instruction, and from whom he finally received the Teaching and the detailed story about all this. Then he said: "I bow before Nāgārjuna, Bi-byi dGah-byed, and the other Gurus. I am a descendant of Dam-pa Tog-dkar-po. By my good fortune and through the merit accumulated in past lives I was able to go to India, the Āryan country and reached Lho-phyogs dPal-ri without encountering difficulties on the way. I met the Second Buddha, Nāgārjuna. I made an offering of a thousand gold sraṅ. I asked him to give me the *mGo-thig Rin-chen gNad-hgrel*, *rTsa-thig gSer-gyi Thig-le*, *Yan-lag gNad-kyi mDzub-brTsugs*, *Sha-thig Rin-chen zHags-pa* and the *gSaṅ-thig Skar-khuṅs Phye-hdra gNad-hgrel gChig-shes Kun-grol.* Nāgārjuna said to me: "I shall not give you the teachings here. Come to the Brag-dmar ske-ts'aṅ." On the way I nearly lost my life. I was frightened by wild beasts and was nearly killed by them, also I was afflicted with hundreds of sufferings, and then Nāgārjuna favoured me with the teachings and his protection. I made an offering of a thousand gold sraṅ, and he gave me the treasure of the essence of the Teaching, and then he asked me to go to the market. When I went there I met Doctor Bi-byi dGah-byed who also taught me the treasure of many essential teachings and asked me to go to the Southern Jungle to get the bDud-rtsi sMan-grub and the bDud-rtsi sMan-hphreṅ and other teachings from the eight goddesses. I went to those goddesses and requested them to give me instruction but bDud-rtsi-ma replied: "I shall not give you instruction if you have nothing to offer for it." Then I said: "I will offer you my body, speech and mind!" But she did not give me instruction and disappeared. Then I searched for the goddesses but could not find them and then I grew very weary and gave up the search. I went to find something to give as an offering for the consecration, and then a trader named Zla-ba Phun-ts'og, in return for my having saved his life, offered me his daughter Pad-ma Khrom-mdzes and five thousand* gold sraṅs. Again I went to the Southern Jungle. I searched for the goddesses and offered them five thousand† gold sraṅs. I went down on my knees, folded my hands and implored for the teaching. Then the goddess gave me the perfect teaching. Then my wish was fulfilled.

I went to Lho-phyogs dPal-ri and requested Nāgārjuna to teach me. Again he opened the treasure house of his instruction to me. Then I went back to Tibet and reached it without difficulties. I am happy to meet my disciples and lay supporters in this assembly, and this is a very happy time." Then all of them felt admiration for him and that they had met the very Medicine Buddha. (It was prophesied that among the five most famous descendants of gYu-thog the third gYu-thog Yon-tan mGon-po would come.)'

XXIX GYU-THOG'S FIRST JOURNEY TO INDIA TOLD BY HIMSELF IN DETAIL

Then Doctor Śrī Singha told him: 'It was admirable of your ancestor to go to India once. But you yourself, gYu-thog Yon-tan mGon-po, most

* Should read five hundred.

† Five hundred.

learned protector of all beings, have been to India three times. Please, tell us all about it!'

Then gYu-thog replied: 'I have already told about my three journeys to India. But if you want to hear it in detail it is like this: the first time I went to India I took a hundred gold sraṅs and went to Bodhgayā to see the paṇḍita Chandra Deva and I offered twenty-five gold sraṅs and requested from him the rGyud-bzhi with all the additions and supplements. Then the paṇḍita said: "You and Khri-sroṅ lDe-btsan have received the rGyud-bzhi from Vairochana. Now, if you want to have the additions to the rGyud-bzhi it is like this." And he told me. Again I offered twenty-five gold sraṅs, requesting him for the supplementary teaching to the rGyud-bzhi. Then he gave me the supplementary *Mu-thig hphreṅ-ba* and a contents list of the rGyud-bzhi called *gSal-ba'i sGron-ma.*

Then one day I went to Bodhgayā circumambulating the temple from outside and saw a female leper with her hands and feet gone, with a cataract in both her eyes, with thick patches all over her skin, with worms growing in her brain, with pain in the whole upper part of her body and mucus issuing from it, and the lower part of her body shaken by a cold fit of ague. The interstices of her joints were filled with lymph, and her whole body was swollen with dropsy. She was unable to speak because she was dumb. When I saw her I was seized with deep compassion and prayed a fervent prayer to the Guru. Then I saw a bluish-coloured lady with a moustache and honey-coloured eyebrows with white hair coming down to her heels. She said: "What has happened to you, Tibetan disciple, with all your tales of woe?" I thought, "This lady is definitely a Ḍākinī" and I told her, "I saw a leper woman who suffered very much and I conceived deep compassion and prayed to the Guru", and the Ḍākinī replied: "Prepare a sacrificial offering! I shall give you instruction." Then I created in my meditation the image of my skull taken off and stood on three human heads like on a tripod, and my body cut into little pieces, and I blessed them so that they turned into the five kinds of flesh and the five kinds of nectar. Of this I made a sacrificial offering, and the Ḍākinī sucked it with the hole in her tongue. Then the Ḍākinī said: "You should not only dispel the leper's physical suffering but also her mental suffering." And she taught me the teaching called *gSal-byed lṅa-bchu-pa*. Then she disappeared.

I went to Rājagiri in Magadha to the learned Me-dbaṅ and offered twenty-five gold sraṅs for the teaching of the three yogic books of Āchārya, inner, outer, and in-between, and the Commentary to the rGyud-bzhi comprising one thousand and one *ślokas*, and the one hundred and eighteen *dMar-hded*, and the *Ro-kra hphrul-gyi me-loṅ*; the *Byaṅ-khog gSaṅ-dbye mDzub-*

btsugs; the *Thur-dpyad gNad-kyi lde-mig*; *mṄon-shes gnad-kyi hkhrul-hkhor*; *gSaṅ-thig Rin-chen sGron-ma*; *Maṅ-ṅag Phan-byed* and the *gNod-byed*; and many other small instructions. Then I offered twenty-five gold sraṅs, and Me-dbaṅ gave me all these teachings as I requested, completely. Then I reached Tibet without any difficulties.'

XXX GYU-THOG'S SECOND JOURNEY TO INDIA TOLD BY HIMSELF IN DETAIL

Doctor Śrī Siṁha asked him: 'Please, tell us of your second visit to India!' gYu-thog said: 'When I went to India I met the paṇḍita Chandra Deva and the learned Me-dbaṅ. By the kindness of those two I received the above-mentioned teachings and specially the profound instructions directly out of the mouth of the Ḍākinīs, from mouth to ear. I opened the sealed oral teachings and taught them to my disciples and lay supporters who have a deep faith and a keen intelligence. Nor did I keep the secrets from energetic sick people, I gave them to all these; especially the supplements to the rGyud-bzhi, inner, outer and in-between. I completed my teaching with the sayings of the Saints and paṇḍitas of earlier times. I wrote it down for the disciples of the future, and with this I have spread the teaching of medicine in Tibet just as the sun spreads its rays.

The enemies of religion became jealous, especially the minister gLaṅ-sna Chan who was inspired by devils and caused great suffering to all learned people in Tibet, and I was imprisoned. I declared before the Protector, the six-handed Mahākāla, that I was free from blame; and gNod-sbyin Kshetaphala, the attendant of Mahākāla, tore the minister's heart out of his chest and he dropped dead. Then people said it was through gYu-thog's black magic, and I was deported to Klo-kha Khra under the reign of king Mi-tsa Yo-khur. He wanted to test me and was fond of eating human flesh. He asked me: "Where do you come from? For what purpose have you come? What can you do? What is your name? Our place is very savage. Those who are here one evening will no longer be here the next morning." Then I told him my whole story. "I am a doctor who preserves life, I dispense the nectar of life." The king said: "If you are like this look at my diseases." I replied: "This is not a time to take the pulse. Tomorrow morning when the sun rises over the highest mountain I will take your pulse." The king agreed. The next day the king put indigo on the right side of his mouth and on the left side red ochre. He bound up the places where the veins are prominent with threads and asked me to take the pulse. I said: "Your Majesty is not sick but you want to eat human flesh. If you wish to eat my flesh, please listen to this song." Then I sang of my fearless confidence.

"I bow before Vaiḍūrya, the Medicine Buddha
Who has the auspicious marks.
You, the king of Klo-kha Khra,
Because you want to eat human flesh,
Are using deceit and cunning
And are pretending you are sick.
The blue-green phlegm coming from your mouth
Is caused by indigo and ochre.
The pain and discomfort in your veins
Is caused by your own binding them up in prominent places.
If you do not know who I am:
My name is gYu-thog Yon-tan mGon-po.
To me all the learned scholars come for wisdom.
I am the lord of life who gives it to others,
I am the excellent nectar which revives;
I am the incarnation of the speech of the Medicine Buddha.
Those trying to test me will get as tired
As those who are trying to measure the sky by finger lengths.
They will be hated by those with wisdom eyes.
The people are vicious in this evil country.
Please, bless them to dispel their ferocity!"

Then the king said: "I will cut your body into pieces of flesh and separate each drop of blood." I was surrounded by all his attendants and his whole army who were wearing full armour and brandishing their weapons. Then I said: "The weapon of bad kings turns against them," and made the threatening gesture. At this moment they began to fight each other, with heavy casualties. The king said: "Now we are even fighting amongst ourselves, this is caused by gYu-thog's black magic!" Again they surrounded me, and I meditated on the body maṇḍala in the protection wheel. One man amongst them said: "Where is gYu-thog? In the maṇḍala surrounded by fire is the Medicine Buddha and round him are the Lineage of the Teachings." And he went back. I thought: "I had promised my guru to preserve life and to answer harm with kindness, and now I have acted contrary to this. I have committed a great sin. Now I shall help these suffering people," and I went amongst the wounded and spit on their wounds and stroked them, and they recovered immediately. When the evil king saw me again he said: "This is an enemy whom I should chase and kill!" Then I put the invisible-making charm on so that they could not find me, and I went back. Then, with a purified mind, I prayed deeply to the Lineage of the Teachings of medicine that this king and country without religion should become converted. After some time the Medicine Buddha and the Lineage of the Teachings appeared before me in the sky and they all said in unison:

"You have a famous name, gYu-thog-pa.
There is no comparison with you, Yon-tan mGon.
Yours are the qualities of all the Buddhas.
You, valiant hero, are the incarnation of the Medicine Buddha
Who drives away the three poisons of diseases.
If you go to the excellent Āryan country
Three times, your wish will be fulfilled.
You will receive the essence of the excellent
And especially the mouth-to-ear instructions
From Saints and Paṇḍitas such as the great learned Me-dbaṅ
And the Paṇḍita Chandra Deva.
You are the sun of the science of medicine
In the dark country of Tibet,
You will have hosts of pupils and your work will flourish.
Just as ducks flying to the lotus lake cannot be intercepted
Countless pupils will flock to you like bees to the lotus flowers.
The evil minister gLaṅ-sna was very jealous
And has sent you to this barbarian country.
Through the king's cunning you nearly lost your life.
By your miraculous power you have conquered the king and his minister,
You disciple, it is wonderful
For this barbarian country to be converted.
One should see the Guru as the real Buddha
With constant deep faith just as the thought of a mother.
By having power over veins, airs and mind
You will perform miraculous feats of a physical nature.
Having recognized the five poisons as the five wisdoms,
One should have compassion together with the knowledge of śūnyatā.
If anyone has these knowledges
He can conquer this barbarian country."

Then he disappeared. Then I thought:

"If anyone is pious without having given up selfishness
And without compassion together with the knowledge of śūnyatā,
It is like a rope of yak's hair round one's body.

To understand the true meaning of Śūnyatā is difficult
Because it is very profound.
To give up selfishness one should not have desires of the body,
As so many Sūtras and Śastras have said.
Now, for the sake of the conversion of this barbarian country
I should act regardless of my falling sick or dying,
Without attachment to worldly things."

While he thought these thoughts he dwelled in the sky where Queen Kha-kra Mdzes-ldan-ma who had the mark of a Ḍākinī was staying.

"I bow before Vaiḍūrya who is able to see clearly the past, present and future
And I am the learned gYu-thog Yon-tan mGon-po.
I have the strength of love and compassion.
I will convert this barbarian country into a religious country.
Having the power over veins, airs, and mind,
I can make hundreds of thousands of bodily appearances.
Now my wheel of the throat vein has been opened
I can sing the rDo-rje Song with perfection.
As a result of many lives' meditation
I can see the three periods of time quite clearly.
Having the knowledge of Śūnyatā and Compassion
My useful activity for all beings has increased in the ten directions.
You, Queen Kha-kra mDzes-ldan with the mark of a Ḍākinī,
Your mercy and the strength of your compassion work swiftly.
This evil king of this barbarian country is very sinful.
In his next life he will go down to the three lower worlds.
I feel sorry for him; please, look upon him."

The queen and her attendants thereupon conceived great faith and invited me to their palace. They offered five hundred gold srańs and said:

"Victorious gYu-thog Yon-tan mGon-po
Who is inseparable from the Medicine Buddha,
The power of your blessing is like a cloud in the sky of your grace
And the rain of your instruction improves all the fields
And your disciples are ripened like excellent crops.
Your good deeds are spreading in all ten directions.
Please, exhibit your splendid miraculous powers
In order to conquer this barbarian country by religion!
Please, make the king virtuous by the teaching of religion!"

Then the minister Kha-kra Nag-po got jealous and sent a man to the queen and me who bound us together with a cotton cloth and knotted a stone into it which was as big as a yak and then threw it into the mThso-nag rBa-rlabs-chen lake (black high wave lake). Then immediately I blessed the lake, and it turned into a lake of jewels. I and the queen became beautifully feathered sea-birds singing with marvellous voices and teaching the beings in the lake. Then the king and his attendants were very astonished. And I escorted the Queen to the palace.

Somewhere in the country was a big black rock near which tigers, bears, snakes and other wild animals had their abode. This place harboured powerful ghosts and devils. People avoided the place because they were too afraid even to look in that direction. I went to sit on that stone and meditated there. The king said: "gYu-thog-pa was not harmed by the lake, now he is doing harm to our gods." Then his warriors surrounded me; but I appeared in the form of a terrifying deity with numerous attendants, riding the black stone like a horse. Some of the warriors fell unconscious, some became petrified, and some very frightened. Then I took the king and the minister by the feet and swung them round and said: "I am going to throw you into the lake." I scared them. The king and his minister said: "You are an Enlightened One in the form of a human man. We confess that we have often spoken against you and antagonized your body, speech and mind. Please, forgive us! From now on we shall do whatever you say. Please, preserve our life!" "Do you agreee with the four propositions: 1. All component things are impermanent. 2. The imperfections of the five skandhas* are the cause of suffering. 3. In reality all things are self-emptiness. 4. Parinirvāṇa is the Final Peace. Are you going to take refuge in the Three Jewels?" Then the king and the minister said: "We are not going to reject the essence of your speech which is like the anther of a lotus flower." They promised to do whatever I would say. Then the king invited me to the palace, and he and his ministers and attendants made a splendid offering, and they requested me for my teaching and received instruction about the good fortune of having acquired a human body and the eighteen blessings that go with this, which are so difficult to attain, and about the inevitability of death, and about karma and its fruit, and about the faults of saṁsāra. After this, by and by, the country became like an Āryan country.

In the meantime the Tibetan king talked about me with his minister and sent two messengers to the barbarian country, who reached there and took me with them back to Tibet. Then king Sad-na-legs received me in the palace and put me on a nine-cushioned throne and he made an offering of jewels.

* Aggregates: body, feelings, perceptions, mental habits, consciousness.

"You excellent chief of doctors,
Of the intrinsic nature of all the Buddhas of the past, present and future,
Inseparable from the Medicine Buddha,
You, gYu-thog Yon-tan mGon-po,
Having achieved much merit in past lives,
You are famous for your learning, your morality and your kind heart.
May your glory increase daily in all the ten directions!
It is wonderful that you have converted the barbarian country
Where you showed your diverse miraculous powers.
Any being, in whatever relationship to you, will benefit thereby.
In the snow-fenced country of Tibet
You have furthered the teaching of medicine,
Having driven away the suffering caused by diseases.
I shall make you and your descendants the court physicians of the kings of Tibet
And the document awarding you this rank I am offering respectfully."

Then I said:

"The Medicine Buddha who can drive away the three poisons of diseases
And the lineage of the teachings
By the blessing of the activity of whose grace
I have been ripened and by my former good karma.
I shall (on the whole) go to India three times
For the sake of sick beings
They shall learn the general inner, outer and in-between science
And its doctrines,
Especially I shall bring the essence of the science of medicine
Like curds in the milk to Tibet, and increase it there,
Hurrah, I, gYu-thog Yon-tan mGon-po,
By the blessing of the lineage of the teachings!
Most assuredly I shall fulfil my destiny.
In the country of the barbarian Kha-kras
Like in Māra's country, there is not a sound of religion
And by the committing of sins its people are accumulating bad karma.
The minister gLaṅ-sna-chen carried Māra's curse in his heart
And had me deported to the barbarian country
Where now religion is fully thriving."

Then I saw five bone ornamented ladies coming to tell me:

"You, Lord of beings, who benefits all coming in contact with you,
gYu-thog Yon-tan mGon-po,
Guide on the path to deliverance,
You have converted the barbarian king and country into a religious one
By your spiritual and miraculous power.
It was truly excellent and wonderful!
You should go to India three times
And search for instruction on the teachings
For the sake of countless beings.
We, the Ḍākinīs, shall support you."

Immediately I woke up I prayed to the Medicine Buddha and the Lineage of the Teachings for success in going three times to India. I took a thousand gold sraṅs and went to India. On the way I stayed in Nepal for six months, at the city of Yeraṅ, where I met two brahmins who told me they, too, were going to India, in search of teachings. Then I went in their company. I asked them: "Who is the most learned, moral and kind-hearted paṇḍita in Eastern and Western India?" The brahmins said: "At Nālandā there is the paṇḍita dPal-ldan Chos-skyoṅ (Śrī Dharmapāla)." Then I went to Nālandā and I made an offering of fifty gold sraṅ to the paṇḍita and received the teaching of Hevajra, the Guhya Samāja and the Chakra Saṁvara and Vajra Bhairava and Mahāmāya as I requested. At the Padma sPuṅs-pa'i sKe-ts'al (Happy Lotus Garden) the paṇḍita Prawahasta was living. I went to see him and offered him fifty gold sraṅs. I requested from him the teaching of the *rDzogs-pa Chen-po* (the Great Perfect Teaching) and other early Tantric teachings; and also I received from the Ḍākinī Seṅ-ge gDoṅ-chen (Great Lion Face) the oral teaching of the Ḍākinīs for which I offered a hundred gold sraṅ. To the paṇḍita Rig-pa'i Khu-byug I offered fifty gold sraṅ and requested from him the eighteen sciences and the five esoteric sciences. I offered a hundred gold sraṅ to Saraha who is the most excellent of all the Saints and received the *Phyag-rgya Chhen-po Brda'i-skor, dBu-phyag Zuṅ-hjug rDzogs-phyag Zuṅ-hjug, Rig-pa'i Ral-skor lÑa.** Then I visited the great rishi gZhuṅ-skyes. I offered a hundred gold sraṅ and received the *sKar-rtsi Ri-bo rDul-hbebs Nag-rtsis hKhor-ldas gTan-hbebs* and one hundred and one different esoteric teachings, especially the *hBras-rtsis Shiṅ-rta'i Srol-hbyed.* Then I went to the learned Me-dbaṅ, offered a hundred gold sraṅ, and received the medical text containing one hundred thousand ślokas called gSo-dpyad hbum-pa (One hundred thousand Verses of Philosophical Analysis of Medicine) and the following medical texts: the *rGyud-shel-gyi me-loṅ*

* All these texts explain the true nature of existence.

(Crystal Mirror Treatise) and the *bsTan-bchos So-ma Rah-dza* (Doctrine begotten by Sōmarāja) with appendices and supplements. Then I went to the paṇḍita Chandra Deva and made an offering of one hundred gold srań and received the one teaching of the rishis of *bsTan-bchos Yan-lag brGyad-pa* (Eight-branched Healing Doctrine). I also met many other well-known learned men, pleased them with gold, and received many beneficent and maleficent instructions, especially those to dispel evil influences, increase good influence, to obtain respect, to keep devils under control, to exorcise devils and to drive them far away, and to summon devils, to reduce devils to helplessness, and so on. Especially from the Ḍākinī Rus-pa'i rGyan-chan (Bone Ornamented) I learned this.

Then I went to Bodhgayā and there I encountered a lady holding a mirror in one hand and carrying a leather medicine bag over her shoulder. She said to me: "O learned gYu-thog-pa! If you want to see the city of lTa-na-sdug, please, come with me!" Then I said: "Please, take me there. I should like to see the city of lTa-na-sdug." She replied: "Now then, we both ought to pray to the Lineage of the Teachings of Medicine." While we were praying we reached the city of lTa-na-sdug. All the pavements in the city of the Medicine Buddha were made of blue Vaiḍūrya as flat as the palm of the hand. There were no pebbles or other imperfections in that city. The city was large and its ground plan was square. Rays of light were always shining, so there was no difference between day and night. The whole ground was resilient and the city was constantly pervaded by the fragrance of incense. In the four directions there were the four medicine mountains. Between the mountains were charming valleys with various beautiful flowers and lakes and pools with water having the eight good qualities: coolness, sweetness, lightness, softness, clearness, purity, harmlessness to the throat, harmlessness to the stomach. The mountains were thickly covered with jungles of medicinal plants. To improve the medicines celestial birds and wild animals lived there joyfully without harming each other. The sweet sound of divine music was heard everywhere, and the city was decorated beautifully with umbrellas and flags and many different religious banners. In the middle there was a four-cornered palace with four gates made of gold, silver, red and black pearls, blue lapis lazuli, and five other kinds of jewels. The palace was decorated with ornaments made of the five kinds of divine jewels.* The roof was covered with beautifully made chequered tiles. On the top of the roof the victorious banner was made of bodhisattvas' jewels. Sixteen thousand pillars and beams were made of the blue celestial jewels called mthon-ka. (When people suffer from the heat, water with the eight good qualities

* Gold, silver, turquoise, coral, pearls.

flows down from this octagonal jewel, and within eight dPag-ts'ads from it diseases are never mentioned. Rays of a scintillating light in various colours issue always from the jewels.) The palace was transparent.

When I reached the palace gate the lady said: "Please, stay here, I am going to get the permission for you," and disappeared. Then a doctor came in a bhikshu's robe. He carried a bunch of saffron in his hand and said: "Please, come in. I came to fetch you," and as he said it he went in. In the centre of the palace was a throne made of jewels. On it was a cushion made of white lapis lazuli. There sat the Medicine Buddha with all the marks of perfection shining in all ten directions. At his right hand sat doctor Kumārajīva, hTs'o-byed gZhon-nu, at his left sat my ancestor and his son. In front of the Medicine Buddha there was a jewelled throne, and I was motioned to sit there. The Medicine Buddha addressed me thus:

"Excellent gYu-thog who has achieved Enlightenment,
Whose wisdom is as vast as the ocean,
Whose action has reached the utmost perfection!
By using various methods
Such as dispelling sufferings, increasing growth,
Controlling and exorcising devils,
You have converted the three worlds into a happy land.
Your name 'gYu-thog Yon-tan mGon-po'
Is as well known as sun and moon.
You are the salvation of all beings, Yon-tan mGon-po.
There are three medicine cities:
External, internal, and in-between.
The external city of lTa-na-sdug is in India,
In Uḍḍiyāna, 'Og-min, Ri-rab-rtse (the king of the mountains),
And many other earthly places.
This excellent celestial city can be seen
By fortunate people when they pray.
Wherever one is staying is the internal lTa-na-sdug
When one is the Medicine Buddha.
The In-between lTa-na-sdug
Is the wheel of bliss in the crown of the head.
One should visualize one's mind
Turning into Vaiḍūrya,
The Medicine Buddha—residing in that wheel.
One should think that the Enjoyment Wheel
At the throat is the Ma-la-ya Mountain.

The Wheel of the Dharma
Is the mountain of sPos-ṅad-ldan, at the heart.
The Wheel of Imaginative Creation
At the navel is the mountain of hBigs-byed.
The private parts Wheel of Preserving Happiness
Is the mountain of Gaṅs-chan.
Go to visit the four mountains
And find out what benefit they bring,
How the medicines are growing there!
Go to India to obtain
The essence of the medical teachings
And increase medical science in Tibet!
You will live for the sake of the people of Tibet
To the age of one hundred and twenty-five years.
There is no need for you to doubt
You will definitely return
To lTa-na-sdug and lead the Saints
And spiritual heroes assembled there."

Then Ts'o-byed gZhon-nu said: "You are successful for yourself and others, and the sky of your grace is filled with the clouds of your wisdom and your deeds. The rain of your profound teachings is covering the earth, and the minds of beings are ripened so that they can go beyond suffering and saṁsāra. You, gYu-thog Yon-tan mGon-po, are of the intrinsic nature of all the Buddhas. You are the Bodhisattva who has attained the eighth stage of the Great Vehicle. You will never return to Saṁsāra by the law of cause and effect, you are at the head of those well versed in the practice of the Tantra. For the sake of beings you should go to India three times. There you should obtain the teachings and with them benefit the people in Tibet."

Then my grandfather hDre-rje Vajra and my father Khyuṅ-po Do-rje spoke in unison: "You, Yon-tan mGon-po, the Second Medicine Buddha, are descended from the line of the gYu-thog, excellent protector of beings, go from here to Phu-la-ha-ri and perform the propitiation of the essence of the rDud-rtsi-sman-grub (sNyiṅ-po Don-gyi) for seven days. You will pass beyond sickness and obstacles caused by demons, and achieve miraculous powers and foreknowledge, and will attain spiritual power. Then you will be called to Tibet in order to help the sick. There you will increase the science of medicine."

Then I prayed a deep prayer to the Medicine Buddha and his Attendants. As the Medicine Buddha had prophesied I went in search of the four mountains. At the Eastern mountain sPos-ṅad-ldan I found myrobalan and a climber (ba-le-ka) and all other medicinal plants growing as a thick jungle. On the top of the mountain was a palace made of sandalwood. In that stayed a white emanation of the Medicine Buddha, with all the marks of perfection, in shining brightness and splendour. All his attendants were bodhisattvas. Ordinary people and those following the Lower Vehicle were not able to see him. At the Southern mountain hBigs-byed grew pomegranate flowers and black pepper (pi-pi-liṅ) and other medicinal plants curing cold diseases. On the top of that mountain was a palace made of sun crystal. In it there was an emanation of the wisdom of the Medicine Buddha. His colours and attributes were not definite because they were changing. His marks of perfection were clearly visible. All his attendants were rishis. On the Western mountain, Ma-la-ya, there was a fabulous kind of sandalwood, gor-shi-sha, and the six good things: nutmeg, cloves, saffron, cardamom, camphor, and sandalwood, and all kinds of mineral medicines such as stones and earths. There was a palace made of jewels. In that was the emanation of the speech of the Medicine Buddha, with the marks of perfection, and its rays shining into the ten directions, attended only by spiritual heroes and ḍākinīs. At the Northern mountain, Gaṅs-chan, there grew yellow sandalwood (sa-mchog) and gentian (tig-ta) and Cajanus Indicus (nim-pa) and aloewood (a-ka-ru) and other medicinal herbs able to drive away hot diseases. There was a palace made of water crystal. In that there was the emanation of the action of the Medicine Buddha. He had all the marks of perfection and was shining very brightly, and excelled in benefiting all beings. He was attended by gods and goddesses. Then I went to Phu-la-ha-ri, and there I propitiated bDud-rtsi-sman-grub (sNyiṅ-po Don-gyi) for seven days. During this many auspicious signs occurred, and I gained excellent spiritual powers, and the Medicine Buddha appeared to me with four disciples and surrounded by a thousand Buddhas. Therefore I recognized my own mind as the Dharmakāya.

Then I went to the gate of a big city at the border, and an attractive woman came, and I asked her to give me a night's lodging. The woman replied: "Yes, follow me." I did as she said, and there was an assembly of about a thousand women who offered me many kinds of meat and beer. I said: "I am living on the three white things: curds, milk and butter. I do not want meat and beer." Then they offered me a lot of the three white things. That night I slept on the sky-light in the roof. Then one woman said: "Tonight you should fulfil our wishes." I asked: "What is your wish?" They said: "You should stay with us and empty your blood until your blood is gone completely. If you do not do it we shall kill you by cutting your flesh in little pieces and sucking your blood drop by drop." Then I thought: "Now I have fallen into the hands of harlots," and prayed to the Medicine Buddha. I said: "Now I shall use the method of increasing the semen and will fulfill all of you." The women said: "Now he is going to escape," and they surrounded me and some guarded the door. Then I prayed a deep prayer to the Medicine Buddha with compassion for these women. Immediately I flew through the sky-light and stayed in the sky and said: "I bow before the Guru who has overwhelmed me with his kindness, and the Tutelary Deities. I am the Tibetan doctor gYu-thog Yon-tan mGon-po, and hundreds of teachers have favoured me out of compassion, and the Medicine Buddha has appeared to me, therefore I have these miraculous and spiritual powers. If one wants to display powers gained by propitiating it is like this: If any one wishes to see a spectacle, let him look at this one!" Then I took ten billions of Ḍākinīs as śaktis, and some of those above-mentioned women cried, some fainted, some fell to the ground and some tore their hair out.

Then I went to a big non-Buddhist country and there was a Guru of the non-Buddhists, who was called sMra-ba zLa-med. sMra-ba zLa-med asked me: "Where do you come from? For what purpose? Whom do you ask for protection?" I replied: "I am from Tibet. I came to search for teachings for the sake of beings. I take refuge in the Three Jewels." The heretics put handcuffs on me and threw me into a poison lake, and I broke my handcuffs as if they were a piece of thread, and then turned the poisoned water into balls of fire. Then they tried to burn me in a sandalwood fire, and I turned the flames into water. Then they showered weapons on me who blessed them and thereby turned them into a flower rain. Then sMra-ba zLa-med said: "You and I are now going to debate. If I win you will have to become my follower; if you win I become yours." Then I said: "Yes, it is all right." Then we debated. I won and beat the victory drum seven times. After this I was called "Seven Times Victory Drum Tibetan". Now a paperman riding a paper horse came to debate with me. I imagined fire, and this burned horse and rider. Then the god Pra-babs took possession of sMra-ba Zla-med and debated with me who made the threatening gesture and sMra-ba zLa-med fainted. Then sMra-ba zLa-med turned into a sparrow and flew away. Then I became a falcon and pursued him. While I pursued him sMra-ba zLa-med turned into a fish and jumped into the lake. Then I turned into an otter and swam after him and caught him. Then sMra-ba zLa-med was helpless and could not find any method of escaping and panted with fear. Then I said: "Do you remember your proposition now?" sMra-ba zLa-med said: "Please, do not kill me. I shall take you as my teacher." Then I took sMra-ba zLa-med with me to Bodhgayā. There I met the learned

Me-dbaṅ. I told him all about it. Me-dbaṅ was delighted and told me to offer sMra-ba zLa-med to him. I offered him as he said. Later sMra-ba zLa-med embraced the Buddhist religion. In the course of time he was called "the paṇḍita sMra-ba zLa-med" and "the unquestionably learned one".

East of Bodhgayā there is a large market place Nor-bzaṅ gÑas. Many people were assembled there, and there stood a man wearing nothing but a bloody skin over his shoulder holding a spear, and flesh was lying in front of him. In his other hand he held a red gTor-ma. He wore a hat of red copper. He took many dharmapālas to witness and specially a powerful evil demon. I became frightened and ran away. Then I encountered a white man hiding his face* and I told him what I had seen. He said to me: "In general, there are two oaths. One kind is conflicting and the cause of harm, and the other consistent. This one is the conflicting kind." Then I asked him: "Where do you come from? Tell me, how can one distinguish between a consistent and a conflicting oath?" The man said: "I am the patron god of this place. I have come here to judge which is true. This man is not truthful and so I shall take his heart. This is how to take a conflicting oath as you have seen here. In addition, there are two kinds of consistent oath: one just words from the mouth and one from the heart. The first one is taken in a place where the three jewels are worshipped and the two people (concerned who are confirming an agreement) take to witness the wordly gods† with linked ring fingers before an altar or shrine when they take their oath. For the second one, the two people come wearing new and good clothes and ornaments and sit on good high cushions or thrones; they should make a good offering and they should prepare many kinds of food and drink and enjoy themselves dancing and singing, and to witness they take only the Three Jewels inviting the Buddhas and Bodhisattvas whom they can trust to support the success of their wishes." Then he disappeared.

Then I went to the learned Me-dbaṅ and told him all about this. Me-dbaṅ said: "If someone breaks the unacceptable oath he will become a murderer, and in his next life he will be born as an attendant of the god he had asked to witness. If someone swears an acceptable oath taking to witness a god recognized as powerful in the world or a demon, he will help him but not sincerely, and in the end take his life. If someone swears an oath taking the Three Jewels to witness they will sincerely protect him, and in the end they will lead him to Enlightenment. If somebody breaks his oath through the

* Showing his disapproval.

† Gods who have not yet achieved the āryan stage: they are recognized as powerful in the world, such as Mahādeva, Rāhula, etc.

influence of sinners whom he has been friendly with, he can be purified from it by the four blotters-out of sin,* as the Buddha said."

Then I asked him: "How should one call the Three Jewels to witness?" Me-dban replied: "First of all the Three Jewels ought to be really complete. If all Three are not possible, one should have at least an image of the Buddha, a text, a stūpa, and a member of the Saṁgha in monks' robes keeping the rules. If even that is not possible one should at least affirm the Three Jewels as protectors." Then I asked him: "If someone swears an oath taking the Three Jewels to witness, will they commit a sin or not?" Then Me-dbaṅ replied: "The Three Jewels can be witness if they are taken to witness by somebody with an acceptable purpose. For anybody who does not despise the law of karma, the Three Jewels when taken to witness will certainly have the effect of witnesses. If anyone takes the Three Jewels to witness, be his action good or bad, the action can be turned into a good one."

On the return journey to Tibet I met Pha-dam-pa. I requested from him the Teaching of *sDug-bsṅal Shi-byed* (The Destruction of Suffering), and the *dKar-nag Khrag-sum-gyi mKhyud-spyad* (The Vessel with the Three Kinds of White and Black Blood), and the *rTen-hbrel brGyad-chu* (The Eighty Water Auspices), and received them. I reached Tibet without obstacles on the way. Now my name was very famous because I had returned safely from India twice and had received the excellent teaching of the Ḍākinīs fresh from their mouth. The lay supporters and disciples made a great sacrificial offering in gratitude for the success of my undertaking.'

Amongst the assembly a Nepalese, Doctor Śrī Singha, asked: 'gYu-thog-pa, please, tell us about your safe journeys to India and back and how you met the Teachers! How did it come about that you received these profound teachings?' Then gYu-thog, after having told them all about his journeys in detail, said: 'I bow before my royal Guru. May I receive the blessings of the Teachings and the brahmins! Listen carefully and lend your ears, you lay supporters and disciples, gathered here together! I, Yon-tan mGon-po, passed easily through all the dangers and difficulties on the journey, and without fear. At the Nālandā monastery I received from the paṇḍita dPal-ldan Chos-skyoṅ the Hevajra teaching and the Yoga Treatise and the Guhya Samāja and the Śrī Chakra Saṁvara, Vajra Bhairava and the rGyud Mahā-Māya, and I offered fifty gold sraṅ for it. In addition I received from the Ḍākinī Seṅ-ge gDoṅ-chan the oral teachings and I offered a hundred gold sraṅ. I received the Buddhist and non-Buddhist sciences

* (1) Repentance; (2) reading Scriptures and praying, reciting mantras, circumambulating stūpas; (3) and most important: good resolutions for the future; (4) prayers in front of the Guru, Buddhas, Bodhisattvas or images.

from the paṇḍita Rig-pa'i Khru-byug and offered fifty gold sraṅ. From the great brahmin Saraha I received the *Phyag-rgya Chen-po brDa-yi Skor* and the *dBu-phyag rDzogs-phyag Zuṅ-hjug* and specially the three *hDu-ba* teachings. I offered for them a hundred gold sraṅ. From the great brahmin gShuṅ-skyes I received the *Skar-rtsis Ri-bo rDul-hbebs* and the *Nag-rtsis hKhor-hdas gTan-hbebs* and the *hBras-rtsis Shiṅ-rta'i Srol-hbyed* and many other astrological teachings, and I offered a hundred gold sraṅ. From the learned Me-dbaṅ I received the *gSo-dpyad hBum-pa* and the *bDud-rtsi Shel-gyi Me-loṅ* and the *bStan-bchos Sōma Rāja* and many other essential teachings. I offered a hundred gold sraṅ. From the paṇḍita Chandra Deva I received the brahminic oral teachings on medicine and the *bStan-bchos Yan-lag brGyad-pa*. And I offered a hundred gold sraṅ. I also pleased many renowned teachers by offerings of gold, and I received many magic formulas, black and white, and specially from Rus-pa'i rGyan-chan I received the instruction for the rituals of the *Shi-rgyas dBaṅ Drag-po* and the *mNan-bskrad dGug-gzir*. I propitiated her with sacrificial and other offerings. I went to lTa-na-sdug. I received a prophecy from the excellent doctor hTs'o-byed gZhon-nu (Kumārajīva) and from my father and grandfather. I went to the four medicine mountains and then I happened to get to the town of the prostitutes and I displayed excellent miraculous powers, and then I engaged in a contest of magical powers with some heretics and with my great power I defeated them. I converted sMra-ba Zla-med to the Buddhist philosophy. On the way back to Tibet I met Pha-dam-pa Saṅs-rgyas and received the teaching of the *sDug-bsṅal Shi-byed* and the *Man-ṅag dKar-nag Khra* and the *rTen-hbrel brGyad-chu*. I delighted him by a sacrificial offering. Then I reached Tibet safely. I am glad and happy you have gathered here faithfully,' he addressed them. Then the lay supporters and disciples conceived great faith and admiration.

Then the spiritual heroes and ḍākinīs said to gYu-thog in unison:

'We bow before the father, the protector of beings,
The Three Jewels and the excellent Protection one can rely on.
To you, gYu-thog-pa, we are offering this song:
Listen and lend your ears,
Gods and human beings assembled here.
When we, gods with the wisdom-eyes,
Look at the learned gYu-thog Yon-tan
We see countless attainments.
You have excellent qualities, externally and internally.
Your spiritual knowledge is immeasurable.
We have seen these excellent qualities in your body:

The bliss wheel in the crown of your head
We have seen as the city of lTa-na-sdug.
It is external and internal.
From it branch off thirty-five external veins
And thirty-two internal ones.
In the middle external wheel
Is the Medicine Buddha seated
And on the thirty-five branches thirty-five Buddhas are seated.
On the thirty-two veins branching off from the internal wheel
Are seated thirty-two Gurus of the Buddha family,
United with their thirty-two śaktis,
Ḍākinīs of the Buddha Family.
From their union flows nectar
And we have seen how it ripened beings,
Bringing them to liberation.
We have seen the wheel of enjoyment in the throat
As the Ma-la-ya mountain
And there are two wheels, one external and one internal.
From the external wheel a thousand branches issue
On which there are a thousand Buddhas of this fortunate kalpa.
In the middle is the emanation of the voice of the Medicine Buddha.
The internal wheel has sixteen branches.
On each of them sits a Guru of the lotus family.
They are emanations of the voice of the Medicine Buddha
United with their sixteen Ḍākinīs of the lotus family as śaktis.
From their union flows nectar
And we have seen how it ripened fortunate beings
Bringing them to liberation.
We have seen in the chest the wheel of dharma
As the sPos-ṅad-ldan mountain.
It is external and internal.
On the external branches eight Medicine Buddhas are seated.
In the middle is the emanation of the mind of the Medicine Buddha.
On the internal branches there are one hundred and five Gurus of the Vajra family,
Emanations of the mind of the Medicine Buddha,
United with one hundred and five Ḍākinīs of the vajra family as their śaktis.
From their union flows nectar,
And we have seen how it ripened faithful beings,
Bringing them to liberation.

In the navel the wheel of imagination
Seen as the mountain hBigs-byed.
It is external and internal.
On the seven external branches there is the succession of the Seven Great Buddhas.
In the middle is the emanation of the knowledge of the Medicine Buddha.
The internal wheel has sixty-four branches.
On them are sixty-four Gurus of the Jewel family
United with sixty-four Ḍākinīs of the jewel family as their śaktis.
From their union flows nectar,
And we have seen how it ripened fortunate beings,
Bringing them to liberation.
The wheel of preserving happiness is at the genitals.
We have seen it as the Ri-bo Gaṅs-chan mountain.
It is external and internal.
The external wheel has eight branches
And eight Bodhisattvas are seated on them,
In the middle the emanation of the Medicine Buddha's activity.
From the internal wheel come seventy-two thousand branches.
On them seventy-two thousand Gurus are seated,
Emanations of the activity of the Medicine Buddha,
United with seventy-two thousand Ḍākinīs of the karma family as their śaktis.
From their union flows nectar
And we have seen how it ripened faithful beings,
Bringing them to liberation.
On your toes ten Lokapālas are seated,
On your eight joints of the lower part of the body there are eight great Nāgas,
On your ten fingers there are the ten deities appearing in the terrifying form,
On the eight joints of the upper body are the eight great gods.
On the nine openings of the body are the nine great planetary spirits,
On the five sense bases are five Ḍākinīs,
In the six viscera are the six Pāramitās,*
The form of your body is the five Buddha Families.
The constituents necessary for healthy life (chyle, blood, fat, muscle, bone, marrow, semen)

* Perfections: Generosity, Morality, Patience, Energy, Concentration, Wisdom.

Are the seven Rishis.
On the twenty-eight vertebrae of the spinal column
There are the twenty-eight lunar mansions
And on the twenty-four ribs
There are the twenty-four holy countries of the Ḍākinīs
And on the thirty-two teeth are the thirty-two holy places of Spiritual Heroes and Ḍākinīs.
On the eight functions of the mind
Are the eight great cemeteries.
On the hairs of the head
Are the twenty-one thousand Spiritual Heroes,
On the hairs of the body
Are millions of countless Ḍākinīs.
In you, gYu-thog-pa, the incarnation of the Medicine Buddha,
We have seen innumerable excellent qualities.
It is wonderful, O gYu-thog-pa!'

Then they disappeared. Since the day when Spiritual Heroes were gathered together thinking of this everyone thinking of gYu-thog has been conceiving great faith and seeing him as a Buddha.

XXXI GYU-THOG'S THIRD JOURNEY TO INDIA IN DETAIL

One night when gYu-thog was in a trance a woman ornamented with bones appeared to him and said: 'gYu-thog-pa, ask the five dzam-bha-las* for gold and go to the following five places: Bodhgayā and the great river Nairañjanā (falling into the Ganges in Magadha, now Nila-dyan), the great holy place Sārnāth, the Bodhi-tree in Magadha, and Kushinagara, and pray to, supplicate and entreat [the Buddha]!' Immediately after this he awoke. gYu-thog thought: 'Now I should propitiate the five dzam-bha-las as the Ḍākinī said,' and then he propitiated them. The dzam-bha-las offered him a thousand gold sraṅ and the king of Tibet, too, offered him a thousand gold sraṅ. From turning the offers of his disciples and lay supporters into gold he obtained another thousand gold sraṅ. In addition he made great efforts to get more gold and finally had seven thousand gold sraṅ. He took them

* Sanskrit Jambhalas, gods of wealth.

with him and appeared as a Garuḍa bird as big as a horse and flew to Bodhgayā. He was thinking: 'At which place should I pray a prayer first?' Just then a white-robed man came and told him: 'Start from Bodhgayā and proceed from there!' Then gYu-thog began praying in front of the principal statue of the Buddha at Bodhgayā. Then the statue addressed him as follows: 'O you wonderful, excellent man, who are the incarnation of the speech of the Medicine Buddha, full of mercy, and protector of beings, who has strength to guide the beings of the three worlds to liberation, called gYu-thog Yon-tan mGon-po, who drives away the three poisons of diseases: You have come to India three times as the Ḍākinī has prophesied. Your prayers and your former karma have ripened and come to fruition now. You have achieved great success. Melt down the five thousand gold sraṅ and make a statue of the Founder of the Dharma! It will be fashioned by Avalokiteśvara. And I, the living principle of this statue, will give it its initial blessing. And it will be looked after by Tārā. May your success and the number of your disciples increase!' gYu-thog thought: 'Now I shall entrust this gold to the charge of the Buddha and go to find some goldsmiths and custodians and one who can give the rab-gnas (initial blessing).' And he left the gold in front of the statue and said: 'O you who can emanate millions of appearances, who are able to destroy the five poisons and the miseries of beings, the colour of your body is that of pure gold. O emanation of the speech of the Buddha from the Śākyan clan, whose knowledge is immeasurable like the ocean, whose wisdom eye discerns knowledge, protector of beings, please, look after this gold which is destined for a great purpose. I am going to find a goldsmith who can make this statue.' Then the statue of the Buddha answered: 'gYu-thog-pa, you faithful man, by searching you will not find one who gives the blessing, a goldsmith or a custodian. But if you pray a prayer you will find them.' Then gYu-thog prayed a deep prayer.

On the fifteenth day of the fourth month a white-robed man came and melted the gold down and made a statue the height of a man's body. Then gYu-thog thought: 'That it was possible for the five thousand sraṅ to become this statue is really due to the blessing of Avalokiteśvara,' and offered him a thousand gold sraṅ. The white-robed man melted it down and put it on the crown of the statue's head, and immediately it grew as high as a three-storied house. Then a bhikshu equipped with the thirteen necessary things came and gave the statue an initial blessing, and gYu-thog offered him a thousand gold sraṅ. The bhikshu told the goldsmith: 'You excellent goldsmith, melt this gold down and put it on the crown of this image!' The goldsmith did as the bhikshu said. Then the statue became five stories high, composed of many different jewels, shining with great brightness and majesty, and the rays radiating from it had a circumference of ten dpag-ts'ad (miles), and the image acquired all possible excellences. Then gYu-thog was astounded and sang:

'By the blessing of the mercy of the Lord of the Teaching
And the blessing of the excellent Bhikshu
And the Handiwork of Avalokiteśvara
Have these seven thousand gold sraṅ
Become as high as five stories!
Moreover it has many wonderful properties!
I am offering my song to the Three Jewels.'

At that very moment came a woman wearing a turquoise ornamented cloth holding an eight-petalled lotus flower in her right hand and in her left hand a blue lotus rosary and she said: 'I am the custodian of this image.' Then she was absorbed into the image. Then the white-robed man too was absorbed in it. Then the bhikshu was absorbed in it. Then a dharmapāla came and was also absorbed in it. Therefore the image was later called 'the five-fold Buddha'.

Then gYu-thog prayed prayers and supplications and entreaties in front of the image for three months. Then he prayed for seven days at each of the following places: Nairañjanā, Sārnāth, under the Bodhi-tree in Magadha and Kushinagara. Then he met the hundred gurus and Saints that he had met before and prayed and supplicated and entreated, and said:

'I take refuge in the Tutelary Deities and in the kindest Guru.
I, the Tibetan gYu-thog Yon-tan mGon-po,
By the kindness of the Medicine Buddha
And the Lineage of the Teachings
Have seen my former prayers coming to fruition
So that I could make the principal image in Bodhgayā.
As prophesied by this image,
I prayed prayers at Nairañjanā, Sārnāth,
The Bodhi-tree in Magadha, and Kushinagara.
I met the learned Me-dbaṅ and a hundred Gurus,
Who showed great kindness towards me.
I prayed prayers, supplications and entreaties.
Now all my wishes have been fulfilled.
Now I, the Tibetan disciple,
Am going to Tibet.

May I have the protection
Of the Three Jewels and the Guru.
May the Tutelary Deities receive me graciously
And the Dharmapālas support me on my journey.'

And he went to Tibet.

On the way he met a white-robed man who said: 'I come from South India and was sent after gYu-thog by the learned Me-dbaṅ.' Then gYu-thog said: 'I have nothing except these little stones (mineral tablets). What do you want to eat?' Then the man said: 'I will offer you food. Please, do not eat these pebbles!' Then gYu-thog said: 'Well then, regale me with a meal!' 'What would you like?' gYu-thog said: 'I eat lion's meat.' 'O yes, then I am going to search for lions', and he went. After some time he brought a dead lion and said: 'gYu-thog-pa, eat now!' Then gYu-thog replied: 'I do not eat meat, only the three white things. Take the lion to its den where you got it from!' Then the man recited a mantra over the lion, and the lion was resuscitated and went back to its place. Then gYu-thog accompanied the white-robed man and somewhere on the way they encountered nine robbers. Then the white-robed man turned into a terrifying six-handed man. He took into each hand one robber and squeezed him, one he put into his mouth, and one he drew in through each of his nostrils. gYu-thog thought: 'I'll find out what sort of a man this is.' One night they stopped at a place without water, without wood or shelter, and he asked that man to find water and wood. Immediately he stamped his feet on the ground and all they wished came. Then gYu-thog thought: 'This is definitely a white Ratnamahākāla sent by Me-dbaṅ as a protector for me and my followers.' He said: 'All my future disciples, you should make an offering to him and ask him for success.' gYu-thog reached Tibet without difficulties.

Then there was much talk all over Tibet, and everybody was filled with admiration for gYu-thog-pa who had been to India three times, and the disciples and lay supporters came to see him. Among the assembly Doctor Lha-yi rGyal-mts'an said: 'gYu-thog-pa, our peerless protector, please, tell us about your journeys and stay in India!' Answering this request, gYu-thog first told them all in detail and then he said:

'I take refuge in the Medicine Buddha and the kindness of the Gurus.
I, gYu-thog Yon-tan mGon-po, went to the Āryan country.
At the great, holy place of Bodhgayā
I prayed to the principal image of the Buddha Śākya Seṅ-ge.
I received a prophecy and had five thousand gold sraṅ molten
Into an image of the Lord of Teachings

By Avalokiteśvara as its goldsmith.
The initial blessing was performed by the principal image
And Tārā has promised to watch over it
And the goldsmith and the others were absorbed into the image.
It received the name of the Five-fold Buddha.
It is about five stories high and has innumerable excellences.
I prayed in front of it for three months,
Then I prayed for seven days
At the river Nairañjanā
And the great holy place of Sārnāth
And under the Bodhi-tree of Magadha
And in the town of Kushinagara.
I met one hundred and one Gurus;
Especially the learned Me-dbaṅ.
I received Ratna Mahākāla as protector
And reached Tibet without any mishap.
I gathered round me all faithful disciples.
Now, my disciples, gathered here,
You can be happy because my work is done.'

Then a lay supporter called Nor-bu bZaṅ-po said: 'The lineage of the gYu-thogs is more admirable and better than that of others, and you specially, great Teacher, have increased the teaching of medicine in Tibet. You have converted the barbarian Kha-kra into a religious country. Moreover, you were able to travel three times to the Āryan country. Therefore there is no doubt you are a Saint.' Then he asked: 'How old are you now? At what age did you go to India and how long did you stay there?' Then gYu-thog replied: 'When I was twenty-five years old I went to India for the first time. In India I stayed for three years and my journey took me one year. I went to India for the second time when I was thirty-five years old. I stayed in India for a year and on the journey I was for eight months. When I went to India for the third time I was thirty-eight years old. I stayed there for four years, and spent eight days on my journey. Now I am forty-two years old.' Then he sang:

'Listen attentively, lay supporter Nor-bZaṅ.
I, the learned gYu-thog Yon-tan mGon-po,
Went to India when I was twenty-five.
I stayed there three years and spent one year on my journey.
I went to India when I had reached thirty-five,
I stayed there for one year and on my journey eight months.

When I was thirty-eight I went to India
And was staying there for four years
And spent eight days on my journey.
Now my age is forty-two.
Be happy and commit it to your mind.'

Then gYu-thog propitiated the Medicine Buddhas for three weeks at sMan-luṅ. On the fifteenth day of his propitiation suddenly in the early morning a white rainbow appeared in front of him in the sky and came towards him from Vaiḍūrya's palace in the East. In the middle of the rainbow sat the Medicine Buddha with a crown and ornaments. At his right hand sat the Bodhisattva Nyi-ma lTar-rnam-par sNaṅ-byed, and at his left Zla-ba lTar-rnam-par sNaṅ-byed surrounded by rishis and the lineage of the Teachings and the medicine goddesses and many saintly doctors, and they said to him in unison:

'You are the spiritual son of all the Buddhas and Bodhisattvas
And an excellent protector of beings.
You are the excellent eye that looks after suffering and misery,
You, Yon-tan mGon-po, a descendant of gYu-thog,
Respected and worshipped and forever victorious.
Whoever ponders over your story will find it
As unfathomable as a whirlpool in the ocean.
Your excellence is as infinite as the sky.
Your grace is like a heavenly treasure,
Your deeds are innumerable and ineffable.
Whoever comes in contact with you, gYu-thog Yon-tan mGon-po,
Will reap the benefits.
Look after suffering beings with mercy and grace!
Between you and me there is no separation
And no distinction even for a moment.
To the eye of the faithful disciples,
Contemplating you in the right way,
There is no difference
Between you and the Medicine Buddha.
Meditate deeply and pray
For the sake of others and yourself!'

Then gYu-thog praised the Medicine Buddha in those truthful words:

'My mind filled with faith and respect, I take refuge
In you, the Lord and Protector, O Medicine Buddha
And your Attendants, of the intrinsic nature of all the Buddhas.

I and all those who have been my mothers
Wish for your blessings until we achieve Enlightenment
So that your mind mingles with my mind
Not to be separated for a moment.
May I be infused with your grace
And by it be able to help other beings.
May I reap the fruits of all the prayers you have ever prayed.
Look with your merciful eyes on me and sick beings!
Look after me and sick beings
And drive away all diseases
And sufferings caused by devils
And dry this ocean of Saṁsāra!
Your blessing is as swift as lightning
If anyone is able to pray to you.
Whoever remembers you for a moment,
His desires and evil thoughts are immediately transformed
Into the wisdom mind like the change of a galaxy.
If anyone remembers you for a moment
Who has been suffering from poverty
He will enjoy happiness and glory
Without fraudulent acquisition.
If anyone remembers you for a moment
When suddenly befallen by an unwished-for calamity
All disasters and obstructions dissolve at once.
He will obtain the fulfilment of his wishes
And achieve the accomplishment of supreme consummation
And the lower eight siddhis.
I can definite declare
That there is no better protector than you.'

While gYu-thog sang this song the Buddha and his Company disappeared.

The gods saw gYu-thog's innumerable excellences and his successful return from India and said to gYu-thog in unison the following:

'We bow before you, wonderful gYu-thog-pa.
When we look with our eye in the right way
We see innumerable excellences.
You are one person with many different names,
Called the most learned amongst the learned,
Learned gYu-thog-pa who has achieved perfection,
Learned, good and conscientious gYu-thog-pa

Who is experienced in giving instruction,
gYu-thog-pa the skilful with perfect practice,
gYu-thog-pa well-versed in treating hot and cold diseases.
gYu-thog learned in balancing hot and cold medicines in the right way,
gYu-thog-pa learned in preaching, discussion and writing,
Learned in philosophy and meditation and perfect in action,
gYu-thog-pa the incomparable,
gYu-thog-pa, protector of all gods and humans.
May we never be separated from you for a moment
Until we reach Enlightenment!
Please, look upon us with your merciful eyes!'

Then they disappeared. At that time all disciples and lay supporters were very happy.

XXXII GYU-THOG CURES THE NĀGA QUEEN

From now on the great gYu-thog spread the teaching in day-time surrounded by a huge number of disciples by preaching, discussion and writing. At night he was meditating and stayed in samādhi. While he was thus working incessantly day and night for the benefit of the sick, one day a lady came to see him whose upper part was human and the lower part that of a snake. She was ornamented with a wishing gem on the crown of her head and said to gYu-thog: 'This victorious wishing gem I am offering to you, gYu-thog-pa, for having returned three times successfully from India. My elder sister is sick. Please, come to my country,' and she bowed before him and circumambulated him. Then gYu-thog asked her: 'Where did you come from and what is your name?' She said: 'I come from the Nāga country and we are three sisters. My elder sister is called Nāga queen lTa-sdug mThoṅ-dgah, and the second lTa-sdug mThoṅ-legs, and the next one is I, lTa-sdug mThoṅ-mdzes. My elder sister, lTa-sdug mThoṅ-dgah, has pains all over her body. Please, come at once!' Then gYu-thog said: 'What do you three sisters do?' 'We three sisters are queens of the Nāga king,' said she. 'We wait upon the Nāga king. We make offerings to the Buddha dBaṅ-gi-rGyal-po. We keep the harmful nāgas in subjection.' gYu-thog said: 'I do not know anything about your country and I cannot be your physician or that of the nāgas. And listen to my song:

I bow before the rishis
Who have achieved the six foreknowledges
And are in the possession of the five eyes.

I, gYu-thog Yon-tan mGon-po, am the physician of the human body
Which is the best among the six realms.
You Nāgas are full of ferocity and spite
And do not know how to give them up.
As a result of ignorance you are sleeping too much.
Your race is one of dull and stupid beasts.
I cannot play the physician of the Nāgas.
Please, go back to your own country!'

She said:

'The spiritual son of the Medicine Buddha,
Who has performed perfect deeds
And is constantly increasing his success,
You who are called gYu-thog Yon-tan mGon-po,
I bow before you.
You are the protector of gods, human beings and devils,
Therefore they call you Lord of Gods, Human Beings and of Devils.
Please, drive away the disease of the Nāga queen.
You are the Lord of the Nāgas, Yon-tan mGon-po.
Though the race of the Nāgas is harmful
There is no reason why they should hurt you.
Please, do not say you are not coming
And come at once!
Please, do it for my own sake, lTa-sdug mThoṅ-mdzes,
And for the sake of the Nāgī mThoṅ-dGah.'

Then she took off the wishing jewel and presented it to him. gYu-thog said: 'In order to help the Nāgī mThoṅ-dgah I have to go to the Nāga country. You, Nāgī mThoṅ-mdzes, show me the way.' Then she offered him a silver mirror beset with many different jewels. She said: 'Great paṇḍita, please, look here!' He looked into the mirror as she said and he saw the attractive and beautiful Nāga palace containing all that one could wish for before him, and as he looked into it he reached the palace. A very attractive and beautiful sick Nāga girl was lying there, breathing heavily because of her disease, in a bed at whose head there was a big jewelled throne with nine silk cushions on it and a tenth covered with the skin of a black antelope, and gYu-thog was asked to stay there. Then Nāgī lTa-sdug mThoṅ-dgah said: 'I bow before you, gYu-thog mGon-po, the Lord and Protector appearing in human form. I, the Nāgī lTa-sdug mThoṅ-dgah, am sick because those practising the Tantric teaching are not keeping their vows and monks lose their morals, people break their oaths, women are not keeping their bodies unsullied, and yogis are chattering nonsense, therefore the powerful guardian gods became angry. They sent steam from their mouths like mist and sent the Nāga disease phol-hbras (bubonic plague) to the people and a swelling in the throat (diphtheria) and lumbago and dropsy, and specially ha-la lchog-hgyal (falling sickness?) and a disease fatal after six or seven days. If I recover from this disease the other people will also recover. Please, save me from this disease!' gYu-thog washed her with saffron water and made an oblation of water offerings to the Nāgas and buried a mineral Nāga chalice at their place and gave her the consecration of bDud-rtsi-sman-grub. He compounded a mixture of dṅul-chhu rin-chen sbyor-ba (jewel quick-silver preparation) and gave it to her. Then she recovered. lTa-sdug mThoṅ-dgah-ma presented him with a turquoise umbrella and lTa-sdug mThoṅ-legs offered a jewel increasing wealth according to one's desire. Then lTa-sdug mThoṅ-mdzes presented him with a prayer and a wishing gem and the Nāga king offered him a nine-pointed vajra of eight fingers' breadth, made of gold, and countless other jewels. And gYu-thog looked again into the mirror and reached his own place again. Since then, wherever he stayed, he always held the turquoise umbrella over his head. Therefore people called gYu-thog-pa 'Holder of the Turquoise Umbrella'. Whenever he put the bsam-hphel (wishing gem) on the head of a sick person he was able to see all the diseases inside and outside the body, and so people called him the Second Medicine Buddha. When he prayed with the wishing gem all his wishes were fulfilled, wherefore people called him gYu-thog-pa, God of Wealth. Whenever he displayed the gold vajra all devils were dispelled, and people called him 'gYu-thog the King of Those Who Appear as Terrifying Gods'. Whenever he looked into the mirror he was able to go wherever he wanted to, therefore people called him Saint gYu-thog. Then gYu-thog's fame covered the earth because he had returned from the country of the Nāgas.

XXXIII GYU-THOG AND THE RGYUD-BZHI*

When gYu-thog was forty-five years old it was prophesied to him that he would unearth the treasure of the *rGyud-bzhi* and that he would write Supplements to the *rGyud-bzhi* and many texts on medicine. Then he wrote the eighteen Supplements to the rGyud-bzhi and many other medical works. For the details of these see the *Catalogue of the Medical Works of gYu-thog*.

* This chapter is extant only in the Zhol-par-khaṅ block print, not in the sDe-dge edition.

When gYu-thog was fifty-five years old he took his disciple bDe-ba dPal with him and they went to Koṅ-po, and then about three hundred disciples gathered around him. He told them the *rGyud-bzhi*, its Supplements and its oral Completion. From hearing this about fifty doctors achieved the title hBum-rams-pa or Druṅ-rams-pa, a doctor title, and about fifty received the title of Rab-hbyams-pa (of widely spread learning), Doctor of Philosophy. About a hundred received the title of dKah-bchu-ba (Having Overcome Ten Difficulties). He stayed at Koṅ-po to the age of sixty-five. For the hBum-raṁs-pa degree the requirement is to learn the text of the *rGyud-bzhi* and its Commentary with Supplements and Completion and all the medical texts translated by the nine doctors from the North, and all books written by the nine learned Tibetan doctors and the text of *Soma Rāja* by Nāgārjuna and the *bDud-rtsi Bum-pa* by Padmasaṁbhava, the summary of the essence of the *Yan-lag brGyad-pa* by sLob-dpon dPah-bo and the ear-to-mouth teaching by the rishi dPal-ldan hPhreṅ-ba and the *Ts'i-gdon Zla-zer* by the paṇḍita Zla-dgah and its Commentary and Supplement. Those should be learned by heart and their meaning understood.

A rab-hbyams-pa should know the Index of the rGyud-bzhi, its Commentary and Supplements and all the texts by the nine Tibetan doctors and the *Soma Rāja* and the *bDud-rtsi Bum-pa* and its commentary and supplements. For the doctor title of dKah-bchu-pa the Index of the *rGyud-bzhi* and its Commentary and Supplements are required, for the doctor title of bsDud-ra-ba the three Commentaries to the *rGyud-bzhi* and the Supplements to it and the oral Completion with Index. Those disciples who know only one or two Supplements ought to work as assistants to the doctors and cooks.

One time, while they were discussing the rGyud-bzhi some disciples of gYu-thog's contracted a fever epidemic and gYu-thog saw in a dream a bone ornamented ḍākinī coming and saying: 'Teach the secret rGyud-bzhi but do not have it discussed and do not reveal it to unsuitable disciples. Before you give the instruction of the secret rGyud-bzhi you should prepare the disciples by giving them the eight *sNod-sruṅ-brgyad* (Vessel Protectors) and the consecration of the *bDud-rtsi-sman-grub* and the ritual of propitiating the goddesses of medicine and the rishis. If they are taught the instructions of the secret rGyud without the consecrations they are punished for the blood of our heart is poured out.' Then gYu-thog did as the ḍākinī prophesied and went to Dar-rtse-mdo in China. There he saved the life of the Emperor of China and many other people came with him to Koṅ-po sMan-luṅ where he founded a Medical College called lTa-na-sdug.

There they were all learning and discussing medical problems. It was the place where there were self-evolved statues of the eight Medical Buddhas and the Lineage of the Teachings and the doctors of Dar-byed Kun-tu Grags-pa, and because of their presence any visiting student progressed quickly with his studies and became a good doctor.

XXXIV MINERAL SPRINGS

gYu-thog and his disciples stayed at the monastery of sMan-luṅ in Koṅ-po. gYu-thog was teaching his disciples at night, according to their different capacities. In day-time he was only caring for the sick, and he cured many sick people. One evening a red man* holding bow and arrow appeared to him and said: 'gYu-thog-pa, to the South-West from here there is a cave called sKyed-hphraṅ bDud-rtsi Phug-pa. If you propitiate bDud-rtsi-sman-grub there for six months you will reap great benefit.' Then he disappeared. gYu-thog sent all his disciples home to their own places and went without a retinue in search of the cave. He searched for five months and eight days without success. Tired and worn out, he fell asleep in a narrow gorge difficult of access. Then a black lady† came with a pig's head on her head and said: 'gYu-thog-pa, your cave is on this mountain. Search for it,' and disappeared. gYu-thog searched everywhere but did not find it. He sat down on a big flat stone and thought: 'For many lives my Tutelary Deities were Rig-sum mGon-po. If I pray a prayer to them now I shall definitely find it,' and he prayed:

'My Tutelary Deity
Whom I have been propitiating for many lives,
Victorious Rig-sum mGon-po and Attendants,
Please, look well upon me with merciful eyes!
Please, help me to find the bDud-rtsi Phug-pa cave
For the sake of future beings!'

Again he searched, and there was a reddish rock under which there was the mouth of a cave facing north where the sun never reaches. There was water in it. There he propitiated bDud-rtsi-sman-grub. After six months had passed, one day he heard the sound of six letters (Oṁ Ma-ṇi Pad-me Huṁ) like thunderclaps. The cave and the earth were shaking. gYu-thog thought: 'What is this?' He saw a white yogi‡ with a medicine bag over his shoulder holding two rosaries in his hands and twirling them, who said: 'gYu-thog-pa, now you have gained power as a result of your propitiation. Now perform the initial blessing with care!' gYu-thog thought: 'Is this as the Tutelary

* An incarnation of Mañjuśrī.
† Vajravārāhī.
‡ Incarnation of Avalokiteśvara.

Deities had prophesied or is this an obstruction from the Māras?' On that evening came a black man* riding a monkey and he swallowed gYu-thog. When this happened gYu-thog found himself immediately in a beautiful palace. In the centre was a vaiḍūrya throne on which the Medicine Buddha in the form of the Saṁbhoga Kāya was seated. He put his hand on gYu-thog's head and said:

'gYu-thog-pa, second Medicine Buddha,
In the Sum-chhu rTsa-gsum heaven
You were called Dam-pa Tog-dkar.
In India, the Āryan country,
Your name was Kumārajīva.
In the mountain of Ri-bo rTse-lṅa in China
You were the rishi Chhu-shiṅ hKhar-ba-hdzin.
At hPhags-pa Shiṅ-kun in Nepal you were the Second Buddha, Nāgārjuna.
In the dark country of Tibet you are the learned gYu-thog Yon-tan mGon-po.
You are one man with many names,
O wonderful Incarnation!
This is the fruit of six months' propitiation
Of bDud-rtsi-sman-grub in the cave of bDud-rtsi Phug-pa.
Air, phlegm and bile diseases,
Each causing a hundred thousand diseases
And from their mixture one hundred thousand diseases
And from each two combined one hundred thousand diseases
And from the three combined one hundred thousand,
Altogether seven hundred thousand diseases
Are driven away by the waters sprung up in this cave
By your propitiation of bDud-rtsi-sman-grub.
The healing power of this water
Is like that of seven hundred thousand different medicines.
O excellent Incarnation,
Perform the blessing of this healing water
For the sake of future beings!
This healing nectar well is mChhog-gi Sprul-sku's medicinal water (i.e. the Buddha's).
No longer will those drinking its water
Ever again suffer from diseases and evil spirits.
They will be born in a land purified from misery (Dag-pa'i zhiṅ)'

* Incarnation of Vajrapāṇi.

While he was saying this he woke up. Then immediately gYu-thog went to search for this spring. On that mountainside he found that there were one hundred and eight springs and he blessed the springs with a rab-gnas (initial blessing) to remain there forever for the sake of future beings. He said:

'I bow before Vaiḍūrya,
The excellent chief of all deities.
Produced by the current of the water of your grace
This nectar spring is growing.
It possesses the power of seven hundred thousand different medicines.
Seven hundred thousand different diseases
It can definitely drive away.
On this jewel mountainside
By my success in propitiating bDud-rtsi-sman-grub
Seven hundred thousand springs will grow
Of the excellent medicine nectar
Which can drive out constipation with great strength.
I heard this from your, the Medicine Buddha's, mouth.
Therefore it is called the Spring of Seven Hundred Thousand Powers.
This is the water possessing the eight good qualities:
Lightness, clearness, coolness [this print has: lukewarmth], softness,
Purity, sweetness, stomach-soothingness, cure for all diseases;
Preventing air diseases, driving away bile diseases,
Phlegm diseases and with a purifying effect.
It cures high blood pressure and drives colic away,
It preserves the balance between the three humours,
Curing air and phlegm diseases which push upward (arthritis?) by its emetic effect
And other kinds of rheumatism and dropsy, wherever they are, will be cured.
It preserves the warmth of the digestive fire, the basis of a healthy constitution.
Therefore this is the king of medicines.'

Then gYu-thog put a Nāga demon there to guard the springs and he inscribed a stone pillar as high as a man with a description of the springs. Then he said:

'Buddhas and Bodhisattvas of the ten directions!
Holy Teachers, specially my Guru,
O Medical Buddha, look down upon me
And bless me that my prayer may be successful:
May this spring

Containing the concentrated power of all medicines
Which came into being through the blessing of the whole Assembly
Of Saints and Supreme Teachers
Allay the suffering of all those beings
Who will use it!
May even one drop of this precious nectar,
When passing through the body,
Equalize the elements
Externally and internally,
Bringing happiness, health and strength.
May anyone sprayed by this spring
Or smelling it, at the same moment
Be victorious over untimely death
And the darkness of diseases and evil demons!
May those who set out from home
Even with one step on the way to the spring
And those thinking of it
Calm the waves of birth, old age and death
And achieve the siddhi of deathlessness.
May anyone hearing of this spring
Or thinking of it and remembering
Or drinking the water of the streams as which it continues
Achieve happiness, health and power in this life
And at the end achieve the state of rDo-rje Byaṅ.
May the power of all the nectar
And all the medicines in the world
Be increased and drive away
All the suffering caused by diseases.
May all the doctors in the world
Be learned in the mixing of medicines,
Balancing hot and cold in the right way
For the sake of suffering beings.
May doctors not treat them superficially
And cure their patients to their satisfaction!
May all the sick be obedient to doctors'
And to their attendants' orders
And be cured of the sufferings
Caused by hot and cold diseases
And not be sick in their future lives!
May all the sick-attendants

Have so much love and compassion
That they do not leave the sick.
May they speak gently and lovingly
To the sick and work for them
Diligently and keep them clean!
This will gladden the heart of the sick
And they will recover speedily.
May whatever they wish
Be showered effortlessly on the sick
And may all the sick-attendants' wishes be fulfilled!
May they be free from diseases
And be wealthy in riches of every kind!
May the power of this my pure prayer
Make me and all others pass
Through the whole of the stages of the Path at once
And may we reach Enlightenment in this life!'

Then he returned to the cave.

One evening a bone-ornamented lady came and she said: 'gYu-thog-pa, Southwest from here there is the place of the future Mi-la-ras-pa bShad-pa rDo-rje, reincarnation of the paṇḍita hJam-dpal bShes-gnyen, a place called La-phyi Gaṅs. Go and open it up to future worshippers and clear the place from all evil influences!' Then she disappeared. Then gYu-thog went, to open the entrance of the holy place, to the mountain-pass of Khra-bo-la. He looked down to the South and saw the valley filled with a lake. At the foot of the mountain there were some scattered hamlets and only few people travelling. He asked everyone he met where was La-phyi Gaṅs but they all said: 'I don't know.' Then gYu-thog thought: 'I cannot find it now. I shall pray to the Medicine Buddha and ask for a prophecy.' Then he prayed. Somewhere on the road he met a woman who looked like a Southerner and said: 'Are you the learned gYu-thog Yon-tan mGon-po?' gYu-thog replied: 'Yes, I am.' She said: 'I have been sent by the Medicine Buddha to show you the way.' Then he went with her. They came to a narrow and deep valley which looked bare and dark, covered with clay and slate. She took him there and said: 'This is the entrance to the holy place.' Then she disappeared. gYu-thog thought: 'I do not know in what way this place could be opened up. I will pray to the Medicine Buddha.' And he prayed. Then the same woman came back and said: 'You stupid lamenter! Do you have to ask the Medicine Buddha's help for your cooking? What right have you got to ask the Medicine Buddha?' gYu-thog replied: 'Guru, Medicine Buddha and

Lineage of Guiding Gurus and Tutelary Deities, Bodhisattvas and Āryas, please, stay always above the crown of my head and bless me to enable me to work for sentient beings. Please, listen, emanation of Vajra Vārāhī, appearing as a Mon woman: I, gYu-thog Yon-tan mGon-po, during all my lives, have never forgotten the Supreme Medicine Buddha for even a moment. I have prayed from the depth of my heart and have seen him and received his blessings and siddhis. Therefore I felt greatly entitled to ask him. Do you understand, you, in the form of a Mon woman?' Then she laughed: 'Ha-ha, forgive me, I have teased you. This is the entrance to the holy place. Go up this valley!' Then she disappeared. gYu-thog walked up the valley, meditating on the body maṇḍala of the Medicine Buddha and praying deeply. He did not harm any of the wild animals. Then two poisonous snakes, one as long and thick as a beam and another one as long as a yoke of oxen, obstructed his way. Then came from gYu-thog's shoulder the goddess Khros-ma Nag-mo who devoured the big snake which passed right through her and left her body again. From the back of his head came the ḍākinī Seṅ-ge gDoṅ-chan and devoured the smaller one in the same way. The two ḍākinīs sank again into his left shoulder and the back of his head. The two snakes disappeared.

Then he went up the valley and there was a white rock which looked as if it was leaping into the sky, and he approached close to it and stayed there. The ghosts and demons became angry and caused snow to fall for a month uninterruptedly. gYu-thog could find no shelter there, so he began to meditate on fire, and within a stone's throw round him the snow melted so that the black earth could be seen. After twenty days had passed he thought: 'The snow cannot do me any harm but what can I do to find food?' Then he began to think: 'The Medicine Buddha has the power to give all earthly goods and even to give Enlightenment in this life. So I should pray to him,' and then he prayed deeply. After some time the Mon woman came again and said: 'It is wonderful that you are still alive. Who melted this snow? And who gave you food and drink?' gYu-thog replied:' 'I meditated on the heat of fire. That is why the snow has melted. Instead of eating and drinking I prayed to the Medicine Buddha.' She said: 'In what way did you pray?' He said: 'Dwelling in Emptiness, I created a space of love and compassion around me, and faith and sincerity were my cushions. I rode the horse of god-identification (bskyed-rim*) and I was ornamented with the Stages of Perfection (rdzogs-rim†), and with the two of them together I reined the horse in. I stayed in a state of complete Nothingness.' She said: 'Dig, either

* bskyed-rim: Meditations with an outward object, such as a maṇḍala or an image of a bodhisattva or god, aiming at identification with that object.

† rdzogs-rim: Inward practices during the state of identification.

to make a cave in the rock or to let a spring come forth!' gYu-thog said: 'You dig a cave in the rock, I will dig for a spring.' Then she cut the rock as easily as it if was clay and made a cave from it, and they gave it the name 'Mon-mo Cave'. gYu-thog invited the Lord of the Water, and a spring welled forth which they called 'gYu-thog Spring'. He said: 'Now fortunate people can definitely find this cave.' He spent three months clearing the place from evil influences, blessing it, and subduing the ghosts and demons.

One day five beautiful ladies came bringing many medicines, many dainties and many jewels of different kinds and gYu-thog asked them 'Who are you?' They said: 'We are called the Five Ḍākinī Sisters', and disappeared. After three years and three months he returned home.

His disciple dKon-mchhog dPal-bzaṅ said: 'Where have you been, Your Reverence, these three years? We have been searching for you but could not find you.' Then gYu-thog told him what had happened during those years, in detail. Then he said:

'I bow before the Medicine Buddha
Who has the five divine eyes and the six super-knowledges.
Listen to me, dKon-mchhog dPal-bzaṅ, faithful and wise!
By the power of propitiating bDud-rtsi-sman-grub for six months
In the nectar-cave of Skyed-hphraṅ (Happy Narrow Path)
Welled up the healing nectar spring.
It contains the power of seven hundred thousand medicines
And can cure seven hundred thousand different diseases.
It is called "Seven Hundred Thousand Healing Waters".
Along the mountainside of the Skyed-hphraṅ cave
Seven hundred thousand medicinal plants are growing.
Medicinal waters are springing forth on that mountain face
Which are called hBum-tso gDoṅ-gi healing waters.
Then I received the prophecy from the Ḍākinīs:
I went to the place called La-phyi Gaṅs
Where a future Saint is going to reside.
It is as hallowed and blissful as Bodhgayā.
There I spent three months to open up the place
And to clear it from evil influences.
Having achieved great benefit I returned home.'

XXXV SACRIFICIAL OFFERINGS

Then, taking his disciple dKon-mchhog with him, he went to Central and Northern Tibet until they reached sTod-luṅ sKyid-sna. There all his lay supporters and disciples were assembled and they made an offering of meat and beer and other foods. Then gYu-thog said: 'I will not partake in ordinary meat and beer', and his lay supporter rDo-rje rGyal-mts'aṅ said to him: 'Please, bless it and turn it into a sacrificial offering and do partake of it!' Then gYu-thog blessed only his and dKon-mchhog's portion and no other, and the beer was boiling and turning into nectar. Into this he threw meat and everybody saw the meat melting completely. Then rDo-rje rGyal-mts'aṅ said: 'Please, give me a little of your food!' gYu-thog replied: 'It is said that from sacrificial offerings one will get siddhis but I do not know where the unfaithful and insincere are, so it would not be right to give it.' Then rDo-rje rGyal-mts'aṅ said: 'We have seen your good qualities and have come to see you with faith.' Then gYu-thog said: 'The insincerity does not have to refer to this life, it may refer to a former life.' rDo-rje rGyal-mts'aṅ replied: 'If we had failed in our relationship to our Teacher in a former life we would not be born as teacher and pupils in this life.' Then gYu-thog said: 'By the power of prayers and karma it is possible for us to be born here even though a fault was committed in the teacher–pupil relationship in the past. So one cannot be certain. Now you all look at me at what you can see.' Then all of them looked at him, and some saw Pha-dam-pa and some saw the emanation of Māra, some saw a demon and some saw gYu-thog Yon-tan mGon-po as he usually is, one of them saw a dead dog and one of them saw a snake, one saw a flame of fire, rDo-rje rGyal-mts'aṅ saw him as the crowned Medicine Buddha, one saw him as a dung beetle. Then gYu-thog gave them holy food. Those who had seen him as a dead dog, a snake or a dung beetle, saw it as pus and blood, those who had seen him as Māra or demon, saw it as foul water, those who had seen him as gYu-thog saw meat and beer, and from the hands of the person who had not seen anything when looking at him the food disappeared. Those who had seen the flame of fire saw the nectar of human bliss, and those who had seen Pha-dam-pa saw it as the elixir of the Asuras, and he who had seen him as the Medicine Buddha saw it as the deathless nectar of the gods. gYu-thog said: 'He who saw pus and blood, his bond of devotion with me, his teacher, has been impaired in two lives: one in the past and one in the future. Those who saw foul water have either had an impaired bond with their teacher or their will had been paralyzed. The bond of the people who saw me as gYu-thog was unimpaired. Those who did not see anything are not connected by faith with their teacher. Those who saw the flame of fire and Pha-dam-pa have kept and are keeping the connecting link with me in the past life, in this life, and in a future life they will keep it pure.' Then the lay supporter rDo-rje rGyal said: 'How are things turned from their ordinary state into a sacrificial offering?' gYu-thog replied: 'There should be an assembly of those linked by pure devotion, and spiritual heroes and ḍākinīs and brahmins and they all, in order to be able to know how to turn food and drink into nectar, should know that a brahmin, a dog and an outcast are of one and the same nature. Each must be able to see the whole assembly as one of beings of the nature of spiritual heroes and ḍākinīs and gods and goddesses. And the place they must see as 'Og-min (Akanishtha Heaven) or a celestial palace. In short, all ordinary appearances should be kept out, and a pure vision should be practised with regard to everything, otherwise their original moral faults will be multiplied like a shower. Where there is great benefit there is also great danger.' rDo-rje rGyal said: 'gYu-thog, Your Reverence, it is not a pure or perfect sacrificial offering when it is only made before an assembly of spiritual heroes, Great Teachers.' gYu-thog said: 'There is one kind of sacrificial offering where only spiritual heroes are present and another sacrificial offering made by only ḍākinīs. Both can be called a sacrificial offering. If one wishes to make a sacrificial offering the head of the assembly should meditate on sToṅ-nyid zuṅ-hjug,* and spiritual heroes and heroines should meditate on perfect heroes and heroines. A brahmin should meditate on a brahmin who has foreknowledge, and one should think of an outcast, a hunter and a butcher, a beggar, a leper, a sinful person, a dog, a pig, and any other unclean being. And one must know that there is no distinction between their natures. One should not see them with an impure vision and see them all as pure. And one should be able to keep out all ordinary appearances and see all the males as gods and spiritual heroes and all the females as goddesses and heroines.'

Then they gave up all distinctions and enjoyed the offerings, and there was no discord between them and they knew that one should recognize one's mind as the Dharmakāya. One should dance, sing and rejoice without thinking of oneself.

Then the ascetic Byams-pa dPal said: 'Please, give me the instruction for not getting disturbed in the performance of my religious duties!' Then gYu-thog said: 'Don't keep any outward sign of a religious person. Don't commit sins, look at your mind whether you get happiness or suffering, and when your mindfulness grows introduce it to the Dharmakāya. Try to see everything with a pure vision. Go and live in a country with no people in it and meditate without people knowing. Then you will become one whose contact is beneficial to anyone he meets.'

Then the disciple Sha-kya bZaṅ-po asked: 'Please, would you give me the consecration of the Eight Medicine Buddhas!' gYu-thog said: 'Listen

* Emptiness and Bliss as two aspects of the same Reality.

my son. When I was young I received many consecrations such as bDud-rtsi-sman-grub and so on, and I gave many consecrations too. Later on I did no longer want to take the consecration of kun-rdzob (object consecration) or to give it.' Then Sha-kya bZaṅ-po said: 'Please, tell me the meaning of the outer, the inner and the in-between mystical consecration?' gYu-thog said

'I bow before the Medicine Buddha
Who knows with perfect clarity the past, the future and the present,
My faithful and wise disciple,
Sha-kya bZaṅ-po, listen carefully to me!
The consecration of persons and of articles and the conventional consecration,
These are the outer consecrations.
The inward consecration introduces
The mind to Bliss and Emptiness.
There is really no other dBaṅ
Than the inner consecration.
The consecration is the means
Of knowing Emptiness with perfect vision.
There is no self-existence of the giver,
The receiver, or the object in the consecration.
There is no self-existence of a goal
Or of one who achieves a goal.

By training one's mind one should become capable of gaining that knowledge. This is the path of clarifying the practice of the consecration. He who knows the meaning of this will receive the Consecration. The Buddha introduced the consecration by objects.* But I have no use for it. If anyone wants to practise let him practise what leads to inward consecration!'

XXXVI THE GODS IN THE BODY

Another disciple dPal-ldan Dar-po asked: 'Under how many main diseases can you put the four hundred and fifty-four† diseases?' Then gYu-thog said: 'Listen, my faithful dPal-ldan Dar-po: there are many diseases, but if you put them under main headings you find two only: hot

* For instance, a chalice or water being consecrated.
† The number in the rGyud-bzhi is four hundred and four.

diseases and cold diseases. The different indications of diseases are not reliable because sometimes the symptom of fever can indicate an air disease, and the symptom of an air disease can indicate a pestilential disease. The symptom of a pestilential disease can indicate a cold fit of ague. The symptoms are similar but one may easily make a wrong diagnosis. For this you need the "Practice-clarifying Lamp".' Then the disciple said: 'Please, teach me the *Practice-clarifying Lamp* for the sake of us disciples and all the sick.' Then gYu-thog said: 'After having recognized diseases from their various symptoms one should know what medicines cure what diseases.' And he composed the Lag-len-gSal-sGron (*Practice-clarifying Lamp*).

Then the disciple Nam-mKhah lHa-dbaṅ said: 'Please, tell us what is the purpose, essence or importance of visualizing and meditating on the gods of the bDud-rtsi-gman-hphreṅ consecration.' Then gYu-thog said: 'You have the good fortune to get the essence of the instruction. I will tell you its meaning, and do keep it in mind! There are three divisions: 1. Transforming yourself into a god, 2. putting the gods into the body and meditating on them, 3. how to recite a mantra and how many times a mantra should be recited for the propitiating of Tutelary Deities. The first one, of turning oneself into a god, should be practised as mentioned in the ritual of the body maṇḍala of the Medicine Buddha. In the case of the second one, putting sixty-four gods into the body: in general, the gods in the body are innumerable because the nature of the body is divine. This shows where to put the sixty-four principal gods into the body: one should meditate on oneself as the Medicine Buddha, and in the crown of the head rDo-rje hChhaṅ (Vajradhara) with the Śakti Vajravārāhī giving the impression of enjoying bliss. In rDo-rje hChhaṅ's chest Amitāyus, in Amitāyus' chest Grub-pa'i rGyal-mo surrounded by the Lineage of Teachings. In the chest of the śakti Vajravārāhī is Ri-khrod Lo-ma Gyon-ma (Sanskrit Parṇaśabarī), the dhāraṅī protectress against epidemics,* in Ri-khrod-ma's chest rNam-pa rGyal-ma (Sanskrit Vijaya), and other places in the body where the Tutelary Deities are to be put.' He explained thoroughly and in detail how one should imagine them and how one should recite their mantras.

Then gYu-thog and his disciples went on a pilgrimage to hPhags-pa lBa-ti bZaṅ-po.† He made an offering of five hundred khal (i.e. two thousand six hundred and fifty-six pounds) of butter lamps, and with four gold sraṅs he painted the images in the temple, and he offered a butter lamp container made of eighteen gold sraṅs and prayed, whereupon in the fifteenth night of

* At the Tantric Colleges in Lhasa tablets against epidemics were made and sold. Those about to travel bought some and took some with them to far-away places where they were much appreciated.

† A sanctuary in Nepal.

the first month the Medicine Buddha came in the guise of the Nirmāṇakāya, and in front of him were the rishis, Buddhists and non-Buddhists. On the right-hand side were sixteen medicine goddesses surrounded by many other goddesses. On the left-hand side were the three sages (rishis) Ser-skya, dMar-skya and sṄo-skya surrounded by many other sages. On the right and left there were many young godlings making offerings. Above the Medicine Buddha was the Buddha Śākyamuni and at the right and left sun and moon. The Buddha Śākyamuni was surrounded by the translator (Vairochana?), the paṇḍita (Padma Saṁbhava?) and the bodhisattva (mKhan-chen Śāntirakshita?) and the excellent five healers and fifty-seven Dar-byed Kun-tu Grags-pa healers.* And in the Medicine Buddha's chest was Mi-gyo-ba. In Mi-gyo-ba's chest was Phyag-rdor (Vajrapāṇi). In Phyag-rdor's chest was rTa-mGrin (Hayagrīva). On the Medicine Buddha's right shoulder was Mi-hKhrugs-pa. In Mi-khrugs-pa's chest was Spyan-ras-gzigs (Avalokiteśvara). In Spyan-ras-gzig's chest was the guru Padma. On the Medicine Buddha's left shoulder was Kun-rig rNam-snaṅ, in his chest sGrol-ma, in sGrol-ma's chest Khros-nag, in Khros-nag's chest dBaṅ-sdud dMar-mo. In the Medicine Buddha's forehead was hJam-dPal dKar-po, on hJam-dPal dKar-po's right side was hJam-dpal dmar-ser, and on hJam-dpal dKar-po's left hJam-dbyaṅs sṄon-po, in hJam-dpal dKar-po's chest hJam-dbyaṅs Nagpo. At the back of hJam-dpal dKar-po's head was the Buddha Śākyamuni. In the Buddha Śākyamuni's chest was Seṅ-gdoṅ-ma. On the crown of hJam-dpal dKar-po's head was rDo-rje hChhaṅ with the śakti rDo-rje Phag-mo giving the impression of enjoying the highest bliss, and in rDo-rje hChhaṅ's chest mGon-po Ts'e-dpag-med (Amitāyus). In his chest the ḍākinī Grub-pa'i rGyal-mo. In rDo-rje Phag-mo's chest Ri-khrod Lo-ma Gyon-ma. On the crown (of the Medicine Buddha's head) was (Jambhala) Zam-bha-la Nag-po. In the (Medicine Buddha's) throat was Zam-bha-la dMar-po. In the (Medicine Buddha's) chest was Zam-bha-la dKar-po. In the (Medicine Buddha's) navel was Zam-bha-la Ser-po. In the (Medicine Buddha's) genitals was Zam-bha-la lJaṅ-gu.† Each of them was surrounded by eight rNam-sras rTab-dag. On their right was the Lord of Wealth, the great king of the Nāgas, on their left the great lBa-ru-na (Varuṇa). Above them the gracious instructing gurus sitting above one another and surrounded by the Lineage of the Teachings. On the right-hand side the Tutelary Deities, on the left-hand side bodhisattvas and arhats. In front Yum-chen-mo surrounded by the Buddhas of the ten directions. Behind the line of gurus were the volumes of Scriptures in the form of leaves

* See above, p. 188.

† The colours of the Five were respectively white, black, red, yellow, and green.

between boards like rocks heaped one upon another. In the East Rin-chen hByuṅ-ldan, in the South Mya-ṅan-med-pa'i dPal; in the West Rin-chen 'Od-hphro, in the North rGyal-ba'i dBaṅ-po. In the North-East was Tiṅ-ṅe-hdzin-gyi dBaṅ-po, in the South-East Pad-ma Dam-pa, in the South-West Nyi-ma'i-dBaṅ-po, in the North-West gDugs-dam-pa. Above dGah-ba'i dPal, below Pad-ma dPal. In the East of all the gurus were Yul-khor-bsruṅ, in the South hPhags-skyes-po, in the West sPyan-mi-bzaṅ, in the North rNam-thos-sras. In concentric circles, in the front of the Medicine Buddha was the six-handed Mahākāla with his attendants guarding the propitiators. In the outside row were the Mahākāla Gur-mgon lCham-dral and other powerful Dharmapālas sitting. Beyond that row were twelve thousand spiritual heroes and one hundred thousand Ḍākinīs, and there were the twenty-four great countries and thirty-two holy places and the eight cemeteries, and beyond that Brahmā, Indra and the twelve chief demons and other demons. Beyond that were the Ḍākinīs of above the earth, below the earth, and on the earth, and the Protectors of the temples, and demons, gods and nāgas with faith in the Teachings, and outside there was a wall of fire filled with defensive weapons, and the ground was made of vajras and above was a vajra canopy and it was surrounded by a curtain of vajras so that all formed a protective vajra wall. Then gYu-thog prayed:

'O Medicine Buddha, refuge without falsehood,
Majestically looking protector of beings,
The blessings of whose grace issue forth swiftly,
Who has achieved the four kāyas:
And is of the intrinsic nature of them all.
That you have appeared to me
Is wonderful, and I am truly fortunate!
It is wonderful and I am fortunate
That you appeared in your divine form and beauty,
Adorned with the thirty-two marks of a Buddha
And the eighty physical perfections.
Your melodious Brahmā voice is fearless
And you have the wisdom of perfectly knowing the two truths.*
It is wonderful and I am fortunate
That you appeared in the four directions and those in-between
Surrounded by Spiritual Heroes and Ḍākinīs.
Beyond their circle is the circle of flame of wisdom fire.
It is visible but without substance, like a rainbow.

* Conventional truth and sublime truth.

It is wonderful and I am fortunate
To see the gods who appear in their angry form
Frightening the spirits with their scornful laugh.
By the song of the Spiritual Heroes diseases
And evil spirits are driven away.
By the dance of the Spiritual Heroines
All obstacles are removed.
May you with your grace take me and all beings
from Saṁsāra to the bliss of Heaven
And to Nirvāṇa and to the pure Beatitude of mKha-spyod
and to the celestial city of lTa-na-sdug!'

A bone-ornamented woman said:

'The powers of all the Buddhas combined are in you,
The grace of all the Buddhas ripened into one,
The blessings of the Three Jewels together are upon him
Who is called gYu-thog Yon-tan mGon-po.
By the meeting of former merit and karma you are fortunate
Having manifestly seen the essence of the Medicine Buddha's secret teaching:
It is as incredible as the existence of a lotus flower in the sky.
He who meditates on this once has as much benefit
As the person who has read for a thousand times
The bKa-hgyur and the bsTan-hgyur which, like two lotus trees,
Come out of the lake of the Buddha's speech.
Think of this diligently!'

Then she disappeared. gYu-thog prayed the following prayer to hPhags-pa:

'You who have great power, hPhags-pa lPa-ti-bzaṅ,
Lord and hero, who has great power of love,
Tārā, who has great power of grace,
Medicine Buddha who has great power of wisdom and mercy,
And Buddhas and Bodhisattvas, look upon me!
All beings, immeasurable as the sky,
Fortunate in every respect now here and healthy and living a long life,
To be born in your place
In the end, after having passed through all the stages:
Please, bless us to enable us to imitate all your deeds
And purify us from the sins we have committed in the past.'

While gYu-thog prayed suddenly rays of white light issued from hPhag-pa's chest and sank into gYu-thog's chest, and hPhag-pa spoke to him as follows:

'Victorious Yon-tan mGon-po
Who is inseparable from the Medicine Buddha,
Who has arisen for the welfare of beings,
Who has achieved the knowledge of the Medicine Buddha,
You, gYu-thog-pa, contact with whom brings always benefit
Are guiding to Nirvāṇa those who have seen you
And who think of you and remember you.
You have achieved great knowledge of all that exists
And have specially become the ancestor of medical science,
The protector of all sick beings,
gYu-thog-pa endowed with the Bodhisattva Mind.
Furthermore you should meditate on Śūnyatā for the sake of beings
And should be learned in teaching, discussing and writing
In order to increase the Buddhist doctrine.'

Then gYu-thog and his disciples prayed a final prayer turning over their merit to all beings.

XXXVII THE QUEST FOR INSTRUCTION ON PARALYSIS AND RABIES

And they went to Grum-pa rGyaṅ. There they prayed. At that time Doctor Don-yod bZaṅ-po, a descendant of Braṅ-ti-pa, asked: 'gYu-thog-pa, you are famous and learned. So please tell me: What is the meaning of the following mnemonic verses in the bShad-rgyud about the length of the seasons and other measures of time: summer, the rainy season and autumn: each of these lasts two months. He quoted eight verses from the bShad-rgyud about the division of time into days, seasons, etc. and asked about the meaning of the verses.

gYu-thog replied: 'Your versions, one from the bShad-rgyud and one from the Phyi-rgyud, are corrupt.'* He said: 'What is wrong with my version? And what is the correct version?' gYu-thog explained and quoted what was wrong in his version and then gave him the correct version, explaining it in detail. From the correct text 'Time, one day and night, and then a month, then a year,' he explained in detail. After that he really

* It is possible that the issue was intentionally confused when the Indians debated on the subject of time with the Tibetans.

conceived deep faith in gYu-thog and he praised him in the following manner:

'gYu-thog-pa, the most learned amongst the learned,
Conscientious and good,
Among doctors you are the very Medicine Buddha.
You are a wish-fulfilling gem for all beings,
Indeed you are Buddha in reality but I did not recognize it',

and he praised him very strongly and placed gYu-thog's feet on the crown of his head and prayed extensive prayers.

Then gYu-thog and his disciples went to Koṅ-po sMan-luṅ. There many villagers, men and women, came to see gYu-thog and they told him: 'We have been thinking of you very much. Seeing you today is like meeting someone believed dead who has been revived.' One girl among them with the marks of a Ḍākinī felt elated and started singing:

'Happy, happy, joyful and happy!
I am happy to meet the great learned Saint!
The sound of the Spiritual Heroes' song is resounding,
Clearly visible is the dance of the Ḍākinīs.
Distinctly can the sound of their singing *huṁ* be heard
And the sound of *phat* and the symbolic signs appear
And the sound *bhyo* is booming
And the threatening sound of scornful *ha-ha*'.

gYu-thog with his vision saw a blue-clad lady holding a lance adorned with coloured ribbons, with head and body ornaments, dancing and swaying, calling 'gYu-thog, gYu-thog, sMan-hphreṅ, sMan-hphreṅ (turning medicine into nectar), gYah-bzaṅ, gYah-bzaṅ (place name), propitiate, propitiate. Subject Rāhula and great benefit will accrue to you!'

Then she disappeared. On the mountain of gYah-bzaṅ the great gYu-thog propitiated bDud-rtsi sMan-hphreṅ. One day gYu-thog went to fetch water and when he returned to his place he saw a smoke coloured man with nine heads whose lower part of the body was in the form of a coiled snake. gYu-thog meditated on the body maṇḍala of the Medicine Buddha and while he was absorbed in meditation the being disappeared like a rainbow. gYu-thog thought: 'That creature is an emanation of Rāhula,' and gave him a gtor-ma. After some time the sky was filled with dust, and horrible sounds could be heard issuing from it. He looked up at the sky and saw him smoke coloured and nine-headed as before, in the same shape, but as huge as to cover half of the four worlds. gYu-thog thought: 'Oh, by the power of prayer and karma he was born with this body!' And he felt great compassion with him.

One day Rāhula came to him in his own form and offered him the wheel for protection against paralysis (gza-hkhor) and an excellent instruction for the treatment of paralysis very beneficial to beings and said: 'Great paṇḍita, I offer you this instruction. Do not try to beat me or kill me but keep me as your protector and give me a gtor-ma.' gYu-thog agreed to this. After that gYu-thog was also called gYah-bzaṅ-pa.

Then gYu-thog went to Lhasa and circumambulated the statue of the Buddha Śākyamuni a hundred thousand times for seven days. Then he stayed there praying. He saw approaching him a bone-ornamented lady and a yogi holding a brass trumpet. They said: 'Learned gYu-thog-pa, if you want to learn the excellent teaching how to treat rabies ask the Ḍākinī living in that fence over there!' Then these two disappeared. When he awoke he prayed deeply to the Medicine Buddha and Lineage of the Teachings and went in search of the Ḍākinī. In a fence he saw an ugly lady who smelled of sweat and was lame with sores all over her body and blind. gYu-thog asked her to give him the teaching. She said: 'Teaching?' And showed her female organ. gYu-thog thought: 'Perhaps this is not the Ḍākinī. Perhaps it is another one,' and when he thought this five Ḍākinīs sang this to him in unison:

'Oh, ignorant beings! The principal cause of involvement in Saṁsāra
Are ignorance and faithlessness.
While you find a mine of jewels
You are returning empty-handed.
Sure to achieve Enlightenment in this life
We are sorry for your having spoiled it.
Still, if you wish to get the instruction
Do not be incredulous and search for it!'

Then they disappeared. While gYu-thog was listening to the Ḍākinīs' song he did not notice where that lady went. He thought: 'The rGyud brTag-gnyis says: 'Beautiful appearance and ugly appearance are both mind-made. Therefore one should not make a distinction between them. I did not understand its meaning and that is why I failed. Even if she is in India I am going to search for that lady for the sake of the teaching,' and he searched but did not find her.

He went to see the statue of the Buddha Śākyamuni in the temple at Lhasa. He saw that lady sitting in front of the statue. Then gYu-thog said:

'May I request you for your Teaching?' When he said that she turned into light and sank into the chest of the statue of the Buddha Śākyamuni. Then gYu-thog thought: 'Now I have lost the opportunity of seeing her. But I shall pray a deep prayer to Śākyamuni,' and then he prayed. When he prayed the statue said smilingly: 'Those who do not recognize their own mind will not find the Ḍākinī they are searching for. Those who will not see an instruction in everything that appears to them will not find the Teaching they are searching for. Those who cannot recognize that the true nature of their ordinary mind is the Pure Wisdom Mind will not find this Mon-woman. Those who make distinctions between "I" and "others" will not receive blessings. The prayers of those who do not feel abhorrence of Saṁsāra and have no faith will not be fulfilled. Those who have not given up selfish thoughts and partiality will not prosper in their work for other beings. He who understands the meaning of what I have said will be a truly learned person. If you persist in searching for the Mon-mo you will find her. May you, gYu-thog, father and son and your lineage be blessed and successful in the work you are doing for the sake of beings!'

Then gYu-thog went to Koṅ-po in search of the Mon-mo and he asked everyone he met whether they had seen a Mon-mo and described her. Amongst them was one woman with the marks of a Ḍākinī and she said: 'If she is the daughter of the Koṅ-po Don-yod rDo-rje she is now drawing water.' gYu-thog said: 'She is not able to do this being blind, lame and with crippled arms.' The lady said: 'She is a Ḍākinī and sometimes she appears lame and blind and sometimes as a rich, attractive woman holding a jewel spindle. On the back she carries a jewelled case. All her body is ornamented with jewels.' Then gYu-thog waited at the well, and a very attractive lady came, and gYu-thog seized the hem of her dress and implored her for the teaching. She said: 'Don't be so greedy. If you do not eat meat when it is cooked you cannot bite it when it is frozen. Leave me alone. If you hold me all Koṅ-po people will be jealous and surely they will kill you.' He said: 'I do not care if they kill me. I will not let you go unless I receive the teaching.' Then she said: 'You are stupid and persistent. I will get the permission from my father.' gYu-thog followed her. When her father Koṅ-po Don-yod rDo-rje saw him he recognized him and asked him to come in and gave him a warm reception, treated hin hospitably and with respect, and said: 'I have given my daughter here to Gyad-pa Do-med. Please, don't touch her,' and gYu-thog replied: 'I am a bhikshu and will not have a woman or drink alcohol.' After some time, though there was no fault in the behaviour of gYu-thog and the daughter, there were many rumours spread abroad. Then Gyad-pa Do-med heard about it and he put gYu-thog into a box and threw it on the river. The box came to rest on an island with sand dunes. A fisherman went fishing there, found the box and opened it, and out came gYu-thog as fresh as a daisy in the morning dew. The fisherman asked: 'What wrong have you done?' And gYu-thog told him the whole story. The fisherman said: 'You have probably been sleeping with the wife of Koṅ-po Gyad-pa,' and he dug a hole in the ground and buried him and took the box away. Then cattle was driven to pasture on the island, and the shepherds and cowherds were digging in the sand and found gYu-thog. When he came up from below they said: 'He is a rising corpse,' and collected wood to burn him. But the fire did not burn him, and his countenance remained as dewy as before. They they said: 'This is a ghost,' and they ran away. Then gYu-thog went in search of the teaching and met Koṅ-po Gyad-pa's daughter. She said: 'Great gYu-thog, I can see you have power over the four elements,' and gYu-thog requested her to teach him. And she said: 'Go to Koṅ-po Gyad-pa's place; it will be of great benefit to you.' gYu-thog went to Koṅ-po Gyad-pa's place. Koṅ-po said: 'You are my enemy. Let us see if you can stand up to me!' And he shot an arrow at him which cut gYu-thog's body into pieces. Then his wife called: 'Koṅ-po Gyad-pa! That monk is sitting in our home!' And he went in to see and saw gYu-thog in the house. He took hold of him and threw him down from the ninth floor of the house. Then gYu-thog sat in the vajra posture in the sky and exclaimed:

'Protectors of beings, Buddhas of the past, future and present,
Look upon this faithful beggar with gracious eyes!
Koṅ-po Gyad-pa, you sinful man,
Covered with a thick layer of ignorance,
Shedding the blood of your faultless servant,
Me, gYu-thog Yon-tan mGon-po,
Ornamented with the three moral vows,
Who observes the rules of the Vinaya
And who never enjoyed even the smell of alcohol and women.
Through your lack of faith you have contracted a bad karma.
Me who committed no fault you threw into the water,
Then you buried me in the ground.
You burned me with the hot fire
And then cut my body into pieces.
You threw me into the abyss from the ninth floor:
You killed gYu-thog but he did not die.
If you want to show miraculous powers do it this way!
If you want to ask for forgiveness do it now!'

Koṅ-po Gyad-pa said:

'Lord gYu-thog-pa, most learned amongst the learned,
Your lineage is like a beautiful string of pearls;
One after another came the Saints.
Excellent is the whole of your descent.
I have produced bad karma by the sins of faithlessness and desire.
You are a Saint but I did not know it.*
When I contemplate all your excellences
A thrill runs through my whole body
And, as I am moved by deep faith, tears run down my face.
I offer you a herdsman with a hundred mdzo (cross between yak and bull)
And a hundred horses with saddles
And a hundred bales of cotton and a hundred bales of silk.
And all my gold and turquoises and jewels
I request you to accept as a sign of your forgiveness.'

And gYu-thog forgave him.

Then gYu-thog went to the Mon-mo Ḍākinī and requested the teaching from her. She replied: 'I have the treatment of rabies, the teaching with rapid and thorough results. Even the people who bark like dogs when they are bitten need not fear: they will be cured. You are a suitable disciple for this teaching; Be happy for I shall give it to you from mouth to ear!' Then she gave him the teaching on the treatment of rabies called Bye-maReg-gchod. Again she said: 'Spiritual son of all the Buddhas of past, future and present! Excellent Incarnation appearing in human form, who is called gYu-thog Yon-ton mGon-po whom I revere: to you alone I have given this instruction how to drive rabies away, for the sake of future beings. Do not forget it and hide it in your heart!'

Then gYu-thog came to Lhasa and to the Buddha Śākyamuni image and to that of Avalokiteśvara and he put eight fathom long banners there made from his silk and a turquoise as big as a pig's head, and one hundred and eight small ones and one khal of pearls, and he made from them the eight auspicious symbols. And Avalokiteśvara's image spoke to him:

'Listen carefully, Yon-tan mGon-po,
Inseparable from the Medicine Buddha
And the most learned of the learned,
The successor of your father gYu-thog-pa!
From here towards the West

* In the sDe-dge edition a few lines are inserted here.

There is a mountain called Ri-bo bKra-bzaṅ
This is its ordinary appearance.
In truth is is a celestial palace
Miraculously sprung up from the ground
Secretly called the palace Pad-ma 'Od-zhiṅ.
Propitiate there for seven days:
Assuredly a great aim will be achieved by you.'

And he propitiated at Pad-ma 'Od as Avalokiteśvara had said. Early in the morning, after seven days had passed, a naked bone ornamented lady appeared, with the right hand beating a drum made of Acacia catechu wood, in the left hand holding a silver bell, attended by five Ḍākinīs. She said: 'gYu-thog-pa, you are saintly and learned. Do you know how to use your imagination to drive away diseases?' Then gYu-thog requested: 'Please, give me the teaching!' She said: 'Prepare a sacrificial offering!' Then gYu-thog turned his body into a huge wisdom skull and he blessed his entrails and they turned into the five kinds of meat and five kinds of nectar. And he regaled the Ḍākinī and her attendants by his offerings. Then she gave him the excellent teaching called Dug-gsum Hchhiṅ-ba Raṅ-grol which drives away a great diversity of diseases through the use of imagination.

XXXVIII GYU-THOG'S CONTEST WITH THE MṄĀ-RIS DOCTOR

Then gYu-thog and about two hundred disciples went to mṄā-ris and an incalculable number of sick benefited from their reciting mantras, administering medicines and using their imaginative faculty during meditation and many other methods of healing. While they were thus occupied a mṄā-ris doctor, called mThu-chhen rGyal-po, became jealous and sent his disciple Ṅan-sṅags bDag-po to debate with gYu-thog. He said: 'gYu-thog-pa, we have heard you are learned, conscientious and good and of your great strength and miraculous powers. I wonder therefore if you could answer this question for me: there is no medicine in Tibet, with a pleasant taste, a good curative property and which retains its distinctive quality after digestion, whose flavour has an effect on disorders of the stomach. There are so many different poisons growing in the soil, which amongst them are medicines? How do you diagnose a disease from feeling the pulse as being bad blood pumped through empty veins together with the breath? Diseases are driven away by countermeasures, how then can taking the pulse cure them?

gYu-thog, give me the answer to this contradiction.' Then gYu-thog replied: 'Please, listen to me, firmly dependable King of Medicine, and Tibetan doctors! How did it come about that you ask this undoubted question? Who is the conceited person using such a method of arguing? It is just laughable for a learned man to be asked such a question. If I do not answer my opponents' anger will burn their innate goodness.

If there is no medicine with a pleasant taste, a good curative property and which retains its distinctive quality after digestion there can be no arura in Tibet. There is nothing on earth which is not a medicine. Each disease and its antidote exist together like the body and its shadow. In the soil grow a great many poisons but if you know how to use them they are the best medicines. The twelve veins of the viscera* enter the main artery distinctly one after the other like waves on a lake so that they can be distinguished in feeling the pulse. The beating of the pulse is caused by air and blood. But they call it examining the pulse though, in fact, they examine the air and the blood because vein, blood and air always go together. When a disease is cured by a medicine we say it is good for the disease. But in fact it destroys the disease. What is really meant is that the medicine is good for the person suffering from the disease.

For our achieving Enlightenment it is not important to know black magic and evil spells for even if we know them well they will cause our downfall and that of others. Therefore it is better to remain without knowledge of these things. Mine, the learned gYu-thog Yon-tan mGon-po's special virtue is meditating diligently with love and compassion for the sake of beings. This is my special qualification'. 'If you have a turquoise roof show it to me now!' 'Is this any good to you?' asked gYu-thog and caused everything to appear as if made of turquoises. He said: 'You have a lot of turquoises.' gYu-thog said: 'I have not only turquoises but I have plenty of other precious possessions.

During all my lives I have propitiated my tutelary deity:
Coloured bluish, the Vaiḍūrya Buddha.
One face and two hands, sitting cross-legged.
The two hands holding arura and medicine bowl;
Head ornament, ear ornaments and garland rosary.
Jewelry ornamented armlets and anklets.
With a beautiful and high nose,
With very clear and long eyes,

* Heart, lungs, liver, spleen, kidney, gall-bladder, stomach, small intestine, large intestine, urinary bladder, spermatic vessels (uretus in female). See p. 38.

With a plaited top-knot of dark-blue hair
Majestically looking, emitting rays in all the ten directions,
With the Buddha Akshobhya seated on the crown of his head,
In his rainbow body, the Saṁbhoga-kāya.
If you remember him just for a moment
All your wishes will be fulfilled.
Just hearing his name once drives away diseases,
Dispels demons and removes all obstacles.
Anyone praying deeply to him will get all his blessings
And his sins will be washed away.
Vaiḍūrya, Medicine Buddha, Guru, Protector, all in one!
Before I reach Enlightenment may I be spared
All obstacles from evil demons
And be granted the supreme and the ordinary siddhis.
Please, protect me from the fear of birth, old age, sickness and death
And take me beyond the ocean of the suffering of Saṁsāra,
And forgive me the sins I have committed and wipe all bad karma away.
Listen to me, sorcerer-doctor,
I am the wealthy gYu-thog Yon-tan mGon-po,
Wealthy in having the Medicine Buddha as a tutelary deity,
Having the six-handed Makākāla as a protector,
Having the protection of the Three Jewels,
Having Ḍākinīs and rich gods as companions in the Dharma.
My wealth consists in immutable faith in the Guru.
My wealth is having the seven Treasures* of a Saint
And having gods, humans and ghosts as lay supporters
And having dBus and gTsaṅ and Dags and Koṅ as my neighbours.
I am rich possessing the Teachings of Medicine:
The wealth of my property is inexhaustible.
If you want to be rich then follow me!'

When the sorcerer-doctor heard these things he conceived deep faith and said:

'I did not know you had such an undisputed knowledge.
I have been casting evil spells
And kept people in subjection by black magic
But from now on I shall follow you
And shall do whatever I can for the sake of beings
According to the precepts of Religion.'

* Faith, morality, sense of shame and good resolutions, humility, learning, generosity, wisdom.

And he remained with gYu-thog as his follower. When he heard this, doctor mThu-chhen rGyal-po became very angry and said: 'You wicked gYu-thog-pa, you try and stay there, I will show you within the space of time of three days.' Then, day and night, he prepared a magic spell. His disciple Ṅan-sṅags bDag-po heard about it and became very frightened and went to gYu-thog and told it to him: 'Doctor mThu-chhen-po's spells', he said, 'are very potent: when he ends one with *hūṁ* his victim is killed, and when he ends it with *phat* he is cast down to the ground. We have to avert it by a counter-spell.' Then gYu-thog said: 'The whole of the external world is like a dream and an illusion. Therefore his magic spell cannot harm me. But if you are as myopic as all that and remain suspicious I can work a counter-spell like this.' In the evening he performed the ritual of the counter-spell of the Ḍākinī Seṅ-ge-gdoṅ-chan, at midnight the ritual of the counter-spell of the Prajñāpāramitā, in the early morning that of the black Mañjuśrī, in the morning that of gTsug-tor dKar-mo, at noon that of gTsug-tor hBar-ma, in the afternoon that of gTsug-tor Ṅag-mo. He said: 'This is called the Six-watches Counter-spell.' Thus doctor mThu-chhen-po's spell could not harm gYu-thog, and people pronounced gYu-thogs counter-spell greater than his gYu-thog said: 'Where is mThu-chhen's counter-spell?' And he disappeared.

XXXIX GYU-THOG RECEIVES INSTRUCTION FROM AN INCARNATION OF MAÑJUŚRĪ

Then gYu-thog went to the market place of T'son-hdus hDiṅs-ma through South La-stod. When he arrived there the fair had not yet started. In a cave a brahminī was meditating, and gYu-thog went to her but she said: 'You greedy Tibetan, you will commit a sin if you disturb somebody's meditation.' He said: 'Please, listen, Ḍākinī in the form of a Brāhminī: the meditation of him who meditates continuously, even through the changes of the watches, is the best one. Meditation without knowing the Self-existent will be mixed with desire.' She said: 'In reality it is as you say but if there is no conscious wish to meditate then activities happen in the ordinary way without distinction between meditation and non-meditation.' He said: 'The conscious wish to meditate on Śūnyatā is like the activity of purifying gold.' She said: 'It is not from birth onwards that every appearance is an occasion for meditation. It needs practice.' gYu-thog said: 'You are a Ḍākinī. Please, give me a siddhi!' Then she said: 'Prepare a sacrificial offering and I will give you a prophecy together with a siddhi.' Then gYu-thog turned his body into five-coloured nectar. The Brāhminī changed into the Ḍākinī Khros-ma Nag-mo surrounded by Ḍākinīs, one of each of the five families, enjoying the sacrificial offering. She gave him a rNams-naṅ hBo-zan (lump of meat). Then gYu-thog turned it into five-coloured nectar and drank it. It was excellent and delicious and its scent was exquisite. Then gYu-thog said: 'Now I request you to prophesy.' The brahminī said: 'From here to the North in the cave of hJam-dbyaṅs in Sakya there is an Incarnation of Mañjuśrī called doctor Yon-tan bZaṅ-po. Ask him to teach you!' And she disappeared.

Then gYu-thog went in search of the district of Sakya and he reached Chhu-hdus. He encountered a cowherd and asked him: 'Where is the Sakya hJam-dbyaṅs Cave?' And he said: 'I don't know. Ask someone else.' gYu-thog went to search in the northern direction as the Brāhminī had said. On a mountain pass he met a group of traders and he asked them. All of them said, 'We do not know', but one said, 'Is it sBa-skya Luṅ?' gYu-thog asked 'Is in sBa-skya Luṅ any cave called the hJam-dbyaṅs Cave?' He said: 'There is a cave but for the hJam-dbyaṅs ask someone else!' Then gYu-thog went about like a madman roaming in a waste land searching for the cave. But he did not find it. Then gYu-thog prayed a deep prayer to the Medicine Buddha and immediately he saw a white woman with a full milking pail made of conch shell. She said: 'I was sent by the Medicine Buddha to guide you. Drink this milk!' Then gYu-thog followed her. She said: 'Thick wood can be made into a beam, medium wood into a stick and very thin wood into a spear shaft.' After a while she said: 'This is the palace of the Nāgas. Over there is the hJam-dbyaṅs Cave.' And she disappeared.

gYu-thog went there and searched for the cave. In a cave facing South there was a bhikshu well versed in science and medicine called Yon-tan dPal-bzaṅ. gYu-thog said: 'Are you the incarnation of Mañjuśrī, the tutelary deity, in the form of a bhikshu propounding the doctrine of the Vinaya, king of the doctors? For the sake of myself and beings, please, rain the refreshing rain of your profound teachings on me!' Then the bhikshu replied: 'You spiritual son of the Medicine Buddha, the most learned of the learned, Yon-tan mGon-po:

Learned and well-grounded are you
In the essence of the Ḍākinīs' teachings.
Yet many a treasure not to be found in a king's treasury
Can be found in a poor man's hand.
A teaching not known to the learned, received by an unlearned man
Is only just possible like a star in day-time.

If I have any teaching you have not received
I will gladly offer it to you.
Today is a day in the month of miraculous powers,
The great festival when the Buddha showed his miraculous powers,
From the first of the year to the fifteenth day:
Especially the great festival of the rGyud-bzhi
Taught by the Medicine Buddha.
In the excellent palace of the Nāgas
From now to the fifteenth the three Bodhisattva Protectors
And Tārā and many Indian Saints and paṇḍitas
Are discussing and clarifying the teaching.
Let us now go and see it!'

And both went there.

In the Bra-phon the Bodhisattva Protectors and Tārā and many Indian paṇḍitas were holding a discussion. gYu-thog and Yon-tan dPal-bzaṅ prayed a very deep prayer. Then Yon-tan dPal-bzaṅ said: 'In the future a descendant of the great hKhon* will found a monastery here, and it will become the Tibetan Bodhgayā.' Then gYu-thog requested: 'Now, please, teach me!' The bhikshu replied: 'Make a sacrificial offering. I will give you the teaching.' Then gYu-thog, by his blessing, changed the external world into a jewellery pot and the internal world into nectar. The bhikshu said: 'Your offering is good. I will give you the essence of the teaching.' Then he taught him the text called *sByor-hphreṅ* by Mañjuśrī and other texts, one hundred in all.

XL THE SIX QUALIFICATIONS OF A GOOD DOCTOR

While gYu-thog went on a pilgrimage to the Khā-hu sKyed-lhas Cave, he met doctor dKon-mchhog rGyal-mt'san who offered him a horse and saddle and equipment and four gold sraṅ. He requested gYu-thog to teach him. gYu-thog said: 'You should offer this horse and gold to that incarnation of Mañjuśrī and request him for the teaching. He is the most excellent teacher on earth and above and below.' He replied: 'He is excellent but I should like to request you to teach me because I am connected with you by our past karma.' gYu-thog said: 'As doctors we ought to learn the six qualities

* Founder of the Sa-skya lineage.

of doctors as described in the Bodhisattva chapter [in the text in the bKa-hgyur].' Then he quoted: 'The fortunate person gifted with the six qualities of a doctor can be taught the rGyud-bzhi by the great rishis.

The first requirement for becoming a good doctor is deep knowledge which can be acquired with the help of a discerning mind. The second requirement is an all-compassionate mind. The third requirement is remembering the six precepts at all times. The fourth requirement is to return kindness with kindness. The fifth requirement is to carry out one's duties diligently and be skilful in worldly activities.

The first requirement—a discerning mind—can be divided into three: 1. a comprehensive mind able to know the meaning of all the religious texts; 2. a firm, unswerving mind; 3. a sharp and careful mind.

The second requirement—an all compassionate mind—consists of two qualities: the conventional bodhisattva mind and the virtue of transcendental Bodhisattva knowledge. The first one consists of two: the latent Bodhisattva mind in abeyance and the bodhisattva mind in action. The Bodhisattva mind in action is divided into five kinds: 1. Love, 2. compassion, 3. the resolution to help others in their release from suffering and towards their attaining happiness, 4. a mind filled with repentance caused by disgust with worldly matters, and 5. the firm resolve to attain Enlightenment for the sake of all beings.

The third requirement consists in keeping six precepts in the mind: 1. He should have reverence for his teacher in the same way as for the Buddha. 2. He should regard his teacher's word as a medical scripture. 3. He should love his fellow disciples. 4. He should have love and compassion for suffering patients. 5. He should make his mind like that of a dog or pig, and not regard his patients' urine, stool, blood, etc. as dirty. 6. He should practise religious morality, worldly morality, and combine the two.

The fourth requirement—returning kindness—can be divided into three: returning it by body, speech and mind.

The fifth requirement—carrying out one's duties diligently—can be divided into two: carrying out duties for others, and 2. carrying out one's own duties.

The sixth qualification is morality of which there are three kinds: 1. to be well-versed in religious morality, 2. social morality, and 3. combining the two.

The result of having, with a kind heart, made one step towards a sick person or having dispensed one portion of medicine or having given any other treatment will be inexpressibly great. As the Sūtra says: "To give one portion of medicine or any other treatment or to walk one step forward towards a sick person completes the merit acquired by virtue for this life and completes the merit acquired by metaphysical insight in the next life. In the life after the next one he will attain Enlightenment." In an old story the king of Central India, called Chandra, who had never taken refuge to the Three Jewels cared only for the sick and later in the same life he became enlightened. So you should work only for the sick. There is no greater instruction than this in the world.'

'That is indeed the real instruction but in this degenerate age infections, demon-caused diseases, dropsy, lupus on the legs, gall bladder complaints, poisonous diseases are increasing, therefore I request you to teach me how to cure these by the teachings fresh from the Ḍākinīs' mouth!' Then gYu-thog said: 'These diseases are increasing in this degenerate age, and there are many diseases which are not mentioned in the rGyud-bzhi, so you doctors, be careful!' Then the other one said: 'You are indisputably very learned, you are a true pioneer [leader] in the Teachings, the doyen of all the learned. Whatever deep teaching you think is best for me, please, teach me that!' gYu-thog said: 'I have the essence of the heart of the teaching of Padma-Saṁbhava fresh from the Ḍākinīs' mouth, the Teaching of the Chalice of Nectar. The text of the rGyud together with its explanation which she gave me in detail, and I will give it to you. Be happy and help the sick!' Then he made the following praise of the teaching:

'Spiritual son of the Buddhas, Padma Saṁbhava, O Victorious One,
Forgive me for handing on your instruction
Which is like purified gold
To others, for the sake of the sick and the teaching.
Bless this faithful dKon-mchhog rGyal-mt'san
To become a most excellent benefactor of beings!'

XLI GYU-THOG'S MARRIAGE*

gYu-thog had been a monk since his early youth and had been wearing his monk's robe. At the age of eighty-five he went with a few disciples to Koṅ-po rTsa-ri (Foot of the Koṅ-po Mountain). One evening a bone ornamented lady came in actual waking life holding a mirror and an astrological chart and carrying a leather medicine bag on her shoulder. She said: 'Incarnation and doctor in the form of a monk, your age is now eighty-five. We are offering you the Ḍākinī of Wisdom as your śakti in order to preserve your lineage for the sake of beings. If you do not obey the Ḍākinī's

* In the sDe-dge edition this chapter appears in a different place, block-print p. 121.

words you will be punished. If you obey them it will cause you to achieve siddhis.' And she disappeared. After completing his stay at Koṅ-po rTsa-ri he went to the sMan-luṅ Medical College. One day a naked bone ornamented lady brought a fifteen-year-old beautiful young girl with a gold and turquoise ornamented top knot with clothes and ornaments indicating human riches and gave her to gYu-thog telling him: 'Take her as your śakti!' Then she disappeared. Then gYu-thog asked the girl: 'Where do you come from? Whose daughter are you? What is your name?' She replied: 'My country is the great holy place rTsa-ri. My father is rTa-mGrin (Hayagrīva), my mother is rDo-rje Phag-mo (Vajra-vārāhī). I am the Ḍākinī of Secret Wisdom.' Then gYu-thog said: 'You have the mark of a ḍākinī but you ought to work for the sake of beings by secret means, and I shall give you the name of rDo-rje hTs'o-mo.'

When gYu-thog was about ninety years old his son hBum-seṅ (Hundred Thousand Lions) was born. When he was ninety-six dGah-gaṅs (Joyful) was born.

XLII THE FIRST JOURNEY TO UḌḌIYĀNA

Then gYu-thog preached to many disciples the Teaching of the Great Vehicle and of the Lesser Vehicle, and specially he opened to them the treasure of the medical teachings and profound instructions, according to his pupils' capacities and wishes. At that time he taught, at the request of dPal-hbum, the *Miṅ-don brDa-sprod.* While gYu-thog was propitiating bDud-rtsi-sman-grub, a bone-ornamented lady came and said: 'Great gYu-thog Yab-yum (and wife), please, come to Uḍḍiyāna ('U-rgyan) in the Northwest', and then she disappeared. Then gYu-thog-pa Yab-yum went to the Pad-ma 'Od palace, and a lady with a medicine bag on her shoulder came who held in her right hand a sandalwood wishing tree with three roots, nine trunks, forty-five branches, two hundred and twenty-four leaves, five flowers, each of them having three ripe fruits, and molten gold dropping from root, trunk, branches, leaves and flowers. In the left hand she held a Bodhi-tree with seven hundred and twenty leaves. She said: 'gYu-thog Yab-yum, look attentively at the two wishing trees which I am holding. You will see a spectacle and gain benefit from it.' Then gYu-thog Yab-yum looked at them carefully. On the one the Medicine Buddha was teaching the *rTsa-rgyud sDoṅ-hgren* (Analysis of the rTsa-rgyud) to two Bodhisattvas and other attendants. On the other tree Pad-ma hByuṅ-gnas (Padma-

Sambhava) in the form of a doctor was teaching the Analysis of the bShad-rgyud.* gYu-thog Yab-yum received the explanation in detail. At the end Pad-ma hByuṅ-gnas sank into the Medicine Buddha's chest. While this happened the Medicine Buddha said: 'Son, Yon-tan mGon-po, you have been incessantly propitiating bDud-rtsi-sman-grub and performing rituals and meditating and praying to me deeply. On the strength of that you were able to go to Uḍḍiyāna and also were able to see Pad-ma hByuṅ-gnas and to receive instructions; specially you have achieved the great power to pray great effective prayers. Pray to Pad-ma hByuṅ-gnas and me, regarding us as inseparable and as one. To the person who prays to me Pad-ma hByuṅ-gnas will definitely come as well. At the time when people in Tibet will reach an average life expectancy of sixty, the emanation of your speech, called Luṅ-stoṅ sMyon-pa, will come to Tibet, who will have the great power to keep the three worlds in subjection, able to rule over gods, human beings and demons. He will then also come to Uḍḍiyāna. You should pray the great effective prayer to Pad-ma hByuṅ-gnas again which you have prayed before. The strength of that prayer will drive away the kalpa of diseases, the kalpa of wars, the kalpa of famine.' Then gYu-thog Yab-yum prayed the following prayer to the Medicine Buddha:

'Wherever we are born and stay in our lives,
May we never be separated from you,
The Medicine Buddha who drives away
The three poisonous diseases.
May we accumulate merit
And may our sins decrease
And may we be able
To look upon your face
And to receive instructions
And may we soon achieve
Medicine Buddhahood!'

Then they returned to their own country. gYu-thog Yab-yum became very famous all over Tibet for having been to Uḍḍiyāna.

His son dPal-hbum thought: 'My father has been three times to India and to Uḍḍiyāna in the West. He must be an Incarnation; anyway, I am going to examine this.' gYu-thog knew his thought and turned his body into a rainbow. Therefore the disciples did not see him. Some of them said: 'Perhaps he has gone to India', others said: 'Perhaps he has gone to Uḍḍi-

* Tabulating the contents of the two treatises.

yāna', and they all became agitated. His son dPal-hbum prayed to the rainbow, and in the sky appeared five goddesses and said in unison:

'I bow before the Medicine Buddha Vaiḍūrya.
Please, bless the disciples that they may attain the perfect vision.
He who can look in the right way at gYu-thog Yon-tan-mGon-po
Sees that he is of the intrinsic nature of all the Buddhas
And the Medicine Buddha himself has come down to him.
His grace has enveloped all beings.
He can drive away the disease of cause and effect in one moment,
He is victorious over all disasters.
Whoever comes in contact with him
Will get the benefit, be he good or bad.
Whoever prays to him will receive a blessing.
He is the wishing gem of all fulfilment.
Whoever cannot see him this way will fall down into hell,
The place where there is no escape.
Do you understand this, you disciples?
The Buddha is appearing in the human form;
There is no need to examine this.
I feel pity for your committing sins.
This clear mass of rainbows and gYu-thog—there's no difference.
Do not differentiate between those two
And pray to them as one!
May you be blessed to achieve the perfect vision
And see in the right way in this life and in all others.'

And then they disappeared. Then his Yum (wife) rDo-rje hTs'o-mo prayed:

'I bow at the feet of gYu-thog Yon-tan mGon-po
Contact with whom beings benefit to good and bad.
I assert that people insusceptible to religion
And those whose karma has not yet been purified
Are not believing in the Saints and Superior Persons
And are committing grievous sins.
The Buddha said that the sin committed
By not seeing the Guru as a Buddha
Cannot be purged even by confession.
I, Shes-rab-ma, who am the cause of growing happiness
Am offering you inexhaustible bliss.
The son is praying to you.
Please, bless him and look upon him with your merciful eyes!'

Then gYu-thog suddenly appeared with a smiling face and said: 'Haha, I was testing those faithless people.' Then his son bBum-señ said: 'Great father, you are able to turn your body into anything. But please tell us about how you were born for the sake of beings!' Then gYu-thog said:

'I pray to the Father, the Medicine Buddha.
Please, bless us so that we may attain the perfect vision!
I am gYu-thog Yon-tan mGon-po.
When I first caused myself to be born
I became Kar-ma Dri-ma-med.
The second time I was called hTs'o-byed gZhon-nu.
Now I am called gYu-thog Yon-tan mGon-po.
From here I shall go to lTa-na-sdug
And shall be the head of the rishi-Saints.
After that I shall be in India
And be called Me-hla Phyag-rdum.
Then in the snow-land of Tibet
As the son, descendant of the gYu-thogs,
Be called the Younger gYu-thog Yon-tan mGon-po.
Then I shall not be reborn again
And most surely I shall be Enlightened
In the city of lTa-na-sdug
By the power of my former prayers.
Those who pray to me, there is no doubt,
Shall be as swiftly as a shooting star
Born in the city of lTa-na-sdug.
My nature is that of the Medicine Buddha.
Pray and harbour no doubt!
Vajra Vārāhī, rDo-rje Ts'ol-ma is the Ḍākinī.
Pray from the centre of your heart!'

Then the son hBum-señ and all the others were gladdened.

XLIII A PILGRIMAGE TO CHINA

Then gYu-thog and his disciples went to Koṅ-po, and the Koṅ-po doctor Khams-gsum Zil-gnon offered him a horse with saddle and other equipment and ten bales of cotton and five bales of silk and ten cases of tea and eighteen gold sraṅ. He said:

'I bow before the Medicine Buddha
And before the Five Families of Buddhas
And before gYu-thog, father and son.
Victorious Ones, bless me and purify my mind
And make me capable of benefiting beings.
When I remember your good qualities
Through my faith the hairs of my body stand on end.
In your presence the whole of my mind
Is transformed from deep within me.
Your voice is a living demonstration
To me of the sound of an echo and illusion.
You are incomparable, gYu-thog-pa. With mercy
Look upon me and open to me
The treasury of your teaching!'

Then gYu-thog replied: 'I bow before Vaiḍūrya, the Medicine Buddha. Listen, Khams-gsum (Three-elements) Zil-gnon (Resplendent conqueror)! Your actions agree with your good name (Resplendent Conqueror of the Three Elements) as a doctor. I feel sorry for the six kinds of beings turning purposelessly round and round in Saṁsāra. You should purify your bad karma and guide beings to the Way of Liberation. Look after the unprotected sick with compassion! And benefit beings without distinguishing between them! Give up covetousness and dispense medicines freely! And practise your religion diligently without laziness! Put ambitions for this life behind you and devote yourself wholeheartedly to the teachings of religion! Having this attitude, you do not even regret it if you are born in hell.'

Then gYu-thog and his disciples went on a pilgrimage to Ri-bo rTse-lṅa (Five Mountain-tops) in China. Because of fog and damp weather they were unable to cross the mountains. His disciple Rin-chen Grub-pa said: 'Now we cannot go to Ri-bo rTse-lṅa. Therefore it would be better if we prayed a prayer here and then returned.' gYu-thog said: 'Whatever obstacle my, gYu-thog Yon-tan mGon-po's, bad karma should bring me, even if my flesh dries up on my body and goes rotten I shall go to Ri-bo rTse-lṅa (Five Mountain-tops).' And he climbed up the montain in the dark, and after some time fog and dampness dispersed. Then he reached the entrance to Ri-bo rTse-lṅa. His disciples had been unable to continue and had gone back. Then gYu-thog knocked at the palace door, and a lady with a turquoise ornamented top-knot came and she recited 'Tāre Tārī Hūṁ' and with a snap of her fingers she turned into Tārā and ushered him in to meet Mañjuśrī. Mañjuśrī said: 'O you brave man shining with intelligence, all obstacles are removed from whoever hears your name. They acquire faith whenever they look upon your face. All sufferings are driven away whenever they hear your voice, you who is called Yon-tan mGon-po. I pay my respects to you who drives away the three poisonous diseases. Whoever is connected with you in any way shall benefit by it. In this life you should help sick beings and in your next life you will, without leaving your body, be the head of the rishis and saints in lTa-na-sDug. So be happy!' And he gave him the *sByor-ba'i-hPhreṅ-ba* and *Byaṅ-khog Don-hgrem* and he sang other excellent teachings. While Mañjuśrī instructed him in this way he made the threatening gesture, and immediately gYu-thog returned to Tibet.

XLIV GYU-THOG TEACHES DURING THE JOURNEY TO BYA-YUL

Then gYu-thog Yon-tan mGon-po and his disciples went to Bya-yul (Bird Country). A lady looking like a yoginī came to him with a white mdzo (cross between a bull and a yak) laden with two bales of woollen cloth. She said: 'My name is mDa Mi-dman bTsun of Bya-yul. My father died when I was five years old and I studied medicine like my father before me. gYu-thog, you singularly learned man, please, reconcile for me the contradictions in the rGyud-bzhi!' Then gYu-thog said: 'In general, a woman's fate is to marry, and they have less aptitude for studying and becoming doctors. But compassion and love, intelligence and effort will count for more than any other attainments. So you should not marry. The text treatise mentions that arura has six tastes. But the explanatory treatise says it has five tastes and does not mention the salty taste. The difference of the explanation lies only in the expression: one is explicit and one implicit. In the *bDud-rtsi-snyiṅ-po* and the *Sa-ra dBu-tha-hi rGyud*, its commentary, it is said that the root of the arura tastes bitter, the top is acrid, and the parts between them are sweet to the taste. The marrow is astringent and the skin is sour. From a mixture of them all one gets the salty taste.'

Then gYu-thog said: 'You should pray to the Medicine Buddha and the lineage of the brahmins and the goddesses according to the ritual of bDud-rtsi-sman-hphreṅ. You should consecrate yourself in the ritual of bDud-rtsi-sman and ripen your own mind and that of other people! One can consecrate by action or by imagination; before this you should perform the preparatory rites in your mind with the help of the instruction in the *Ral-skor-lṅa*. You should reduce desires and laziness and increase your generosity and altruism.'

[A passage repeating the subject matter of a dispute in logic in an earlier passage is left out here.]

At Dags-po gYu-thog said to some doctor: 'I bow before Vaiḍūrya, the Buddha of Medicine. Listen, doctor bKra-shis of bDog, when working for the sick you should fulfil your duties conscientiously in the following manner. When you take the pulse it is very important to question the patient. You should recognize the six pulses signifying hot and cold diseases. You should diagnose hot and cold diseases correctly and take the pulse from the six veins and the special vein. When you examine the urine, you should, as the rishi said, diagnose hot and cold diseases correctly from the colour, smell, steam, scum, sediment, phlegm, and the changes in the colour after standing. Also you should recognize diseases by looking at the eyes, tongue, and other organs, the vomited food, colour of the blood, observing the sound of the voice, the hairs of the body, the strength of the animal heat, the constitution, the size of the patient's appetite or lack of it. Treating a disease without recognizing the symptoms is like shooting an arrow without a target. Therefore it is very important that one should diagnose diseases. When one is examining the diseases one should not boast, and one should look carefully at the patient, and if one sees he is getting better one should look well after him, and if one sees he is going to die one should direct him skilfully to accumulate merit. If he does not tell his patient meticulously how to do this there will be rumours about the doctor afterwards. If he cannot distinguish the symptoms he is not different from the beasts of the field.

An old door has many holes because it has been pushed by many fingers. I, the old gYu-thog Yon-tan mGon-po, am not very widely read in the Scriptures but, as the result of much practice, I know the essence. Keep this advice in your heart, my wise sons and disciples!'

Then, on the way to Bya-yul, the great gYu-thog saw a large crowd hunting and some people fishing, others were killing yaks and sheep. And some he saw stealing and robbing. He thought: 'It is a great pity that they should commit such sins after having achieved a human birth.' He prayed a sorrowful prayer: 'O Medicine Buddha! Please, look with your great mercy upon these beings accumulating bad karma', and repeated it many times. Then the Medicine Buddha and his attendants appeared in the sky between bands of light and a rainbow. He said: ('I bow before the) Guru Bee-yil. At first in an early life you were Skar-ma dri-ma-med (Pure Star), in the life in-between you were gZhon-nu hJigs-med Grags (Youth Famed for his Courage). At present you are called gYu-thog Yon-tan mGon-po. From here you will go to lTa-na-sdug and be the head of the rishis and saints. Then, at the time when the five unwholesome states increase, you, the

Incarnation of my Speech, will, for the sake of beings, become the New gYu-thog called Yon-tan mGon-po. You will propitiate bDud-rtsi-sman-grub and practise her ritual strenuously.

My incarnation Me-lha Phyag-rdum
Will also go to Tibet
And increase the Science of Medicine.
These two incarnations of my speech
Will come and they will be of one mind.
Being in harmony with one another.
They will expound their own teachings.
The sun of the Science of Medicine
Will rise in those days.
Your voice calling me
Was like the sweet, long-drawn sound
Of the cuckoo's song moving the heart.
Whoever saw you praying this deep prayer
Imploring me for help or hears of it
Or remembers it or recites it,
Before them we and others with wisdom eyes
Shall appear most assuredly.'

While he was saying this gYu-thog and his disciples were filled with extreme bliss. Then gYu-thog and his attendants returned to their home town and he sent his disciples to their own country. His three sons gave instruction in medicine to all, and he gave up all worldly actions and meditated and prayed, in order to influence his future for the better, day and night.

XLV VOYAGES TO DIFFERENT HEAVENS

During this time he once saw a cloud shaped like a strip of cloth before him in the sky. On it he saw two godlings holding tiaras of flowers in their hands who said in unison: 'Father and Protector of beings and Father of all the Buddhas in the past, future and present, called Yon-tan mGon-po, great scholar, listen to us: in this heaven up on high all the gods are enjoying themselves, not thinking of religious work even for a moment. It does not occur to them that they are going to die and at the end they will regret it. But then it will be too late and they will be unable to prevent it. We godlings saw your excellent qualities and from our deep faith our hairs stood on end, and the gods agreed to send us to ask you to come to our heaven. Please, take hold of this cotton cloth and come on it. Please, do come this time!' gYu-thog said: 'rDo-rje hTs'o-mo, I am going to visit heaven', and he took hold of the end of the cloth. Immediately, as he touched it, he found himself in heaven. Then they took him into a beautiful palace and put him on a high god's throne, and seven young goddesses offered him each a chalice of the deathless nectar of the gods. And they sang in unison:

'O admirable being, whoever seeks your excellences
Conceives deep faith that you are the Buddha.
Please, tell us the story of the time
When you were the doctor hTs'o-byed gZhon-nu!'

gYu-thog said: 'You gods have an abundance of enjoyments. I cannot tell my story here. Come down to the human country if you want to hear it!' Then the god mDzes-ldan appeared as a human son bLo-stobs Chen-po and he received the story. gYu-thog returned to the human country and brought with him the present of the seven nectar chalices. And all the disciples were astonished and all said: 'gYu-thog Yon-tan mGon-po is really a Buddha.' And they conceived deep faith.

Then gYu-thog and his disciples went to Lhasa. And for twenty-five days he propitiated bDud-rtsi-sman-grub in front of the Buddha Śākyamuni's image. On the fifteenth morning the crowned Buddha image said: 'gYu-thog-pa, if you want to go to see Vaiḍūrya's palace, come along!' Then gYu-thog said:

'You are the chief of all the Buddhas
And the Founder of the Teaching
Appearing as the Saṁbhoga-kāya
Majestically looking, emitting rays of light.
Please, take me, in your mercy, in this fleshly body, to Vaiḍūrya's palace
And bless me so that I can see the Medicine Buddha
And can obtain his instruction
And that my heart and soul can be in harmony with his.'

One bone-ornamented lady said to him: 'gYu-thog-pa, go to the celestial palace', and she stretched a white rainbow-shaped arch to him, and gYu-thog rode on it, and all the sky was filled with the sound of music and with rainbows and lightning and divine offerings of flowers and victorious banners and umbrellas, silk hangings and other auspicious signs. Some people said the Buddha image had gone to the celestial palace. But some said it was gYu-thog who had gone. Some said both had gone. So no one believed the other, and king Mu-khri bTsan-po went to see for himself. He saw the Buddha Śākyamuni's throne was vacant and gYu-thog's cushion was also vacant. Then a wave of surprise went through the whole assembly. Some people cried, some laughed, others started praying. The king and his people prayed for ten days. Then the Buddha image and gYu-thog returned riding on a sunbeam. Everybody was astonished. Then the king made an offering symbolic of the universe made of a thousand gold sraṅ to the Buddha Śākyamuni and made a turquoise trough-shaped vessel for gYu-thog and prayed. gYu-thog said: 'Isn't it wonderful that the great Buddha Śākyamuni came to guide me to Vaiḍūrya's heaven?' The king replied: 'It is wonderful that you and the Buddha Śākyamuni went to the celestial palace and then returned here for the sake of us Tibetans. Please, tell us what Vaiḍūrya's heaven looks like!' Then gYu-thog said: 'Listen, great king! The excellent celestial palace is such that nobody can see his fill of it. A thousand tongues telling about it for a hundred thousand kalpas cannot tell all about it. But I shall try and tell you a little. Vaiḍūrya's heaven is very extensive in all directions. It is beautifully constructed as the first treatise of the rGyud-bzhi says about the celestial palace.

In the middle was the Medicine City lTa-na-sdug which looks exactly as described in the *rTsa rGyud*. In the middle of lTa-na-sdug is the beautiful maṇḍala as described in Tantric Scriptures,* endowed with a host of excellent qualities. In the middle of the palace grounds is the sPros-bral Chhos-dbyiṅs (Actionless Dharma Heaven) which is beautiful and has countless good qualities and is exactly as mentioned in the Vajrayāna Scriptures. Round the inner, outer and in-between palaces, in each of the four directions there is a medicine mountain. In the outer palace, on a throne supported by eight big lions there are eight Medicine Buddhas surrounded by many Bodhisattvas and Arhats. In the inner palace, on a throne made of vaiḍurya jewels there is the Medicine Buddha in the form of the Saṁbogha-Kāya attended by Bodhisattvas. In the secret mystical palace, on a throne made of victorious jewels there is the Dharmakāya in the form of the Medicine Buddha attended only by Bodhisattvas who have achieved the tenth stage of Bodhisattvahood.' The king said: 'How shall we do it when we practise meditation?' gYu-thog said: 'You can meditate either on what I told you just now and pray to the Medicine Buddha or on the bDud-rtsi-sman-grub body maṇḍala.' Then the king conceived a single-hearted firm faith.

* A maṇḍala is constructed with four gates, etc. like a palace.

XLVI THE SECOND JOURNEY TO UḌḌIYĀNA

After the completion of the bDud-rtsi-sman-grub ritual on the tenth day of the fifth month of the monkey year, the five bone-ornamented ladies came and said in unison: 'You are fortunate and have accumulated a lot of merit in former lives, you are wise and the son of a generally acclaimed honourable family, gYu-thog-pa, you who are Buddha in reality, victorious Yon-tan mGon-po. Ḍākinī of the intrinsic nature of all the Buddhas, protector of all beings and mother of all the Buddhas, who has achieved countless miraculous powers, whose secret name is rDo-rje hTs'o-mo (Vajra-like Life-giver). The two of you are the emanation of Yab-yum. Today is the tenth, the great festival of Tibet. Tomorrow, in Uḍḍiyāna in the North, Padma-Saṁbhava is going to make an offering for the tenth day festival. Spiritual heroes and heroines, Ḍākinīs, holy sages, rishis and brahmins, yogis and yoginīs gathered together will make a sacrificial offering, dance with happiness and sing the secret mantras of hdzab-bro (mantra dance). You both, come now.' Everybody in the assembly heard it. Then gYu-thog said: 'rDo-rje hTs'o-mo, make a good sacrificial offering, then we go both to Uḍḍiyāna in the North for the Festival of Padma-Saṁbhava.' Then the two mounted a sunbeam and rode to Uḍḍiyāna. On the top of the palace of Zaṅs-mdog dPal-ri (Glorious copper-coloured Mountain) was Padma-Saṁbhava in the form of a holy magician at the head of the gathering of spiritual heroes and Ḍākinīs who were making the offering for the festival of the tenth of the fifth month of the monkey year. gYu-thog and his consort joined the gathering, and Padma-Saṁbhava said to them with a happy smile: 'You two emanated beings yab-yum are fortunate to have come for my festival of the tenth. Anyone celebrating our festival of the tenth will drive away all the sins he has committed during ten thousand kalpas and will achieve the stage of rig-hdzin (holder of knowledge). One who keeps the Festival of the Tenth once will drive the sins committed during three immeasurable kalpas away and will become a chief amongst the spiritual heroes and ḍākinīs. You doctors are well learned and practised in the Sūtra rGyud-bzhi. It is a sūtra but has been given a Tantric name. The Tantric rGyud-bzhi is not yet known in Tibet. After the end of the sacrificial offering for the Festival of the tenth he gave them the profound instruction of the rDzogs-pa Chhen-po (Most Perfect and Complete Instruction). And immediately gYu-thog achieved high spiritual wisdom powers. Then gYu-thog Yab-yum rode on a sunbeam and they returned to their own country.

Then his son hBum-seṅ said: 'It is wonderful that you, my parents, have gone to Uḍḍiyāna twice. Is there any chance for us disciples to go there too?' Then gYu-thog said: 'For anyone to be able to go to the Buddha's Paradise it is necessary to have excellent miraculous powers. If you have those, my son, you can go.' After having heard that gYu-thog Yab-yum had travelled to Uḍḍiyāna without giving up his human body and had returned back to earth, everybody believed that gYu-thog Yab-yum was really a great Saint indeed.

XLVII THE ORIGIN AND LINEAGE OF GYU-THOG'S MEDICAL TEXTS

Then again his son dGah-dGas said to him: 'Now I believe that gYu-thog, my father, is the Buddha in human form and rDo-rje hTs'o-mo, my mother, is the Ḍākinī of Wisdom. Please, tell us, for the sake of us disciples, and the doctors of Tibet, the easily intelligible explanation of bzaṅ-po drug (the Six Good Things). Then gYu-thog said: 'My cherished son dGah-dgaṅs, intelligent and discerning, the most learned amongst the learned, if you want to enter the gate of the teaching of medical science in order to help sick beings then you should understand the perfect instructions and the practice of the text and commentary of the rGyud-bzhi; especially you should know the good and bad qualities of the medicines which cure indigestion, such as the six good things (nutmeg, cloves, saffron, cardamom, camphor, sandalwood), and their taste and actions before and after digestion. Keep the thought of sick beings in your heart and meditate on them with love and compassion. Also you should learn to diagnose hot and cold diseases and how to balance mixtures for hot and cold diseases.' Then gYu-thog wrote a history of the six good herbs and how to distinguish their individual qualities and differences. On this book he gave to his sons and disciples a detailed explanation which made them very happy.

Another disciple called Saṅs-rgyas Yon-tan said: 'Great gYu-thog, the knowledge of us disciples cannot even be compared with one hair of your body but we are intending to work for the sick according to your words. Please, give us a complete instruction on how a doctor should look after the sick!' gYu-thog said: 'Listen to me, my son Saṅs-rgyas Yon-tan and my faithful disciples! When you are working for the sick your attitude of mind should be that of love and compassion, and you should have the earnest desire to cure people and you should pray in the early morning and in the evening to the Medicine Buddha. You should shun the poison of alcohol like a dead body. You should not use cunning and devious ways and you should remain kind-hearted and contented. First ask your patient the question: "How did it come about that you fell sick?" Then ask: "What caused your disease?" One should examine the sediment of the urine without making a mistake. One should not bleed or apply moxa or use surgery before one knows whether a disease is hot or cold. One should give the patient an infusion to drink which will purify the urine to enable one to examine it. The doctor's bedside manner should be impeccable. His reputation should be unimpeachable.'

Another disciple called mDzes-dPal said: 'Kind and gracious gYu-thog, please, tell us how you came to know about the *rGyud-bzhi* and the Index of the rGyud-bzhi and the Supplement to it.' gYu-thog replied: 'Listen, my faithful son mDzes-dPal! I, gYu-thog Yon-tan mGon-po, learned in all the sciences, to whom the scholars flock from all directions, to whom all believers present offerings, I am the lord and protector of sick beings. I know all the Scriptures, Buddhist and non-Buddhist. I know the Index of the *rGyud-bzhi* and its eighteen Supplements.* On moxa I know the *mDo-spyod Nag-po* and I know the *Perfect Practice of Bleeding*, I know the *Gyen-hdren* (Pulling Upward [with emetic effect]) which works like the fish-hook pulling up the fish, the *Driving Down* [with purging effect] like a stone down a mountainside, I know the *Instruction which is of benefit even if only seen.* I know the hundred and one *Aphorisms* on medicine.' Then everybody paid respect to him.

†One disciple called Pad-ma rGyal-po requested gYu-thog to teach him the Synopsis of the *rGyud-bzhi.* Then gYu-thog replied: 'To explain the discussion of the rishis in the *bDud-rtsi sNyiṅ-po Yan-lag brGyad-pa gSaṅ-ba sMan-ṅag rGyud Chhen-po* there are eleven introductory Lectures:

1. The Lineage of its Teaching (Its tradition)
2. Its Superiority
3. Characteristics of the rGyud-bzhi
4. The excellent qualities of the rGyud-bzhi
5. The Meaning of Each rGyud in detail
6. Decisions on the Final Meaning
7. Khog-phug-pa (The Hollow of the Trunk of the Body) The History of the rGyud-bzhi
8. Completion by Word of Mouth
9. Proving the Truth of the rGyud-bzhi
10. Quotations in Support of Statements Made
11. Summary of the Preceding Lectures.

* Written by gYu-thog.

† Passage from here to foot of page occurs elsewhere in the sDe-dge edition, block-print p. 120.

First about the Lineage of the Teachings: when I went to India three times, it was there I first saw the Medicine Buddha at the perfect place called lTa-na-sdug which was situated two dpag ts'ad and two and a half miles north of Bodhgayā, at the excellent time of the first day of the first month, when a religious service commemorated the time when the Buddha exhibited miraculous powers while he was living in the world. There was the Buddha, the excellent teacher, in the form of the Medicine Buddha with countless attendant gods, rishis, Buddhists and non-Buddhists, who were discussing the excellent teaching of the *rGyud-rgyal bDud-rtsi sNyiṅ-po* (Excellent Essence of Nectar Treatise). I also saw them later in my illumination. Now I shall tell how I received the *rGyud-bzhi* from the lineage of the Teachers beginning with the Medicine Buddha, then Rig-pa'i Ye-shes, Yid-las sKyes, Kun dGah-bo, gZhon-nu hJig-med Grags, Nāgārjuna, dPal-ldan dPa-bo, paṇḍita Chandradeva, Vairochana from whom I received it. The Supplement of the *rGyud-bzhi* again I have received from paṇḍita Chandradeva and also its Index and the explanation of the concealed meaning of the *rGyud-bzhi*.

Then the disciple Pad-ma rGyal-po said: 'It was wonderful that you have in your perfect vision seen lTa-na-sdug which is in India. What is the reason for keeping the festival of the Buddha showing his miraculous powers in the month of Khra?' gYu-thog replied: 'Not only we, even the Indians keep the religious service commemorating the showing of miraculous powers by the Buddha in the month of Khra because on the 8th of the miraculous month of Khra in the wood-mouse year, at the excellent time when the Buddha was alive, at the perfect place in the Medicine City of lTa-na-sdug, the excellent Teacher, the Buddha Śākya Thub-pa, in the form of the Medicine Buddha, was absorbed in deep and devout meditation which can drive away four hundred and four diseases, surrounded by excellent attendant gods, rishis, Buddhists and non-Buddhists and so on. As the Buddha was absorbed in deep meditation, thousands of many-coloured rays issued from the Buddha's crown of the head, chest, navel and genitals, in all the ten directions. The rays radiated towards all beings, particularly the four types of attendants and the three protectors of the three classes of beings.* When the rays of light reached the Three Protectors they felt they wanted to ask the Buddha, and they knelt down on one knee, threw their upper robe over the left shoulder and said to the Buddha and the rishis: 'O Lord Buddha, please, tell us the excellent teaching of the *bDud-rtsi sNyiṅ-po* for the sake of the three Protectors, the four types of attendants and all other beings!' Then the Medicine Buddha arose from his former samādhi and entered the samādhi of disciplining all beings. Immediately rays in

* Mañjuśrī, Avalokiteśvara, Vajrapāṇi.

thousands of different colours issued into the ten directions from between his eyes and cut off all beings' doubts and returned to the place between his eyes. Then his emanation, Rig-pa'i Ye-shes, appeared seated in front of the Medicine Buddha in the sky and said: 'Lo, my friends should know that I will speak of the excellent Teaching of the *bDud-rtsi sNyiṅ-po* for the sake of the three Protectors of the three classes of beings and the four types of attendants and all other beings. Keep it deeply engraved in your mind and pass the teaching on!' And he taught this teaching to the three Protectors, and the teaching as handed down from the Medicine Buddha was called the Rishis' lineage.

In the Ri-bo'i rTse-lṅa in China Mañjuśrī appeared in the form of hTs'o-byed gZhon-nu and taught it. At Ri-bo Bya-rkaṅ and Bodhgayā Avalokiteśvara appeared in the form of a Rishi and taught it. In Uḍḍiyāna Vajrapāṇi appeared in Māra's form and taught it.

Then one of gYu-thog's disciples asked him: 'What are the seventeen excellent special qualities of this perfect teaching?' He replied: 'It is the essence of all the Sūtras, it demonstrates the principle of all the Tantric treatises, is the essence of all instructions, the source of all the precepts, the source of the whole art of healing, the source of all the works on pharmacology, the best of all the lower and higher vehicles, the instruction in the practice of medicine, the key to the essence of instructions, the lamp illuminating the darkness of ignorance, the seed of the birth of faith, the essence of the distinction between healing practices, the sword for cutting doubts and perplexity, the hammer for the destruction of all the diseases and evil spirits, the nail to undo the knot of the perfect interpretations of the deep teachings, the jewel of the sources of all excellences, and the root of healing.'

Then the great gYu-thog satisfied all his disciples according to their wishes, opening the treasure chest of his instructions. Then gYu-thog and his disciples went to Lhasa on their way to La-stod gTsaṅ and made offerings of ten golden lamps to the Buddha image (Jo-bo Rinpoche) and he also made a ceremonial offering of three gold sraṅ to Jo-bo Rinpoche. Then he said:

'Lord with the shining golden-coloured body,
With thirty-two marks of great perfection
And eighty lesser marks of perfection,
In your great mercy towards all beings,
You are victorious over Māra's obstacles.
Please, protect the sick with your great mercy
And bless me for success in my work for beings
And bless all medicine to turn into deathless nectar!'

Then the verger made them happy by presenting offerings. And gYu-thog meditated and prayed deeply, day and night, before the Buddha image. On the fifteenth day, early in the morning, he felt elated. Then the Jo-bo Rinpoche image said to him: 'The incarnation of the speech of the Medicine Buddha is Mañjuśrī, and Mañjuśrī's incarnation is hTs'o-byed gZhon-nu. And hTs'o-byed gZhon-nu's incarnation is you, gYu-thog Yon-tan mGon-po. In order to spread the teaching of medicine in Tibet you have been blessed by the Buddhas of the present, the past and the future. There are no medical texts of the Buddha's speech, commentaries or instructions unknown to you. Other people's knowledge is like water contained in a chalice; Your knowledge is as deep as an eddy in the ocean. Conceited men try to compare themselves with you and debate with you but in reality there is no comparison between them and you, gYu-thog-pa. You will live up to the age of one hundred and twenty-five in Tibet as the prince of doctors and healers of the sick, then you will go to the pleasant palace of the Medicine Buddha, and there you will become the head of the gathering.' Again gYu-thog prayed:

'Lord of the Teachers, shining with golden colour,
Perfect and majestically looking,
Rays of light issue from you in all directions.
You are the source of the Dharma.
You are the source of the wisdom of all the Buddhas
And have preached eighty four thousand sermons.
I take refuge in you, my Guru, the reliable Protector.
Please, bless me so that I know the perfect Śūnyatā!'

Then he said: 'It is true that one accumulates more merit by meditating on Śūnyatā than by practising inexhaustible virtues. But which virtue accumulates most merit amongst the exhaustible ones?' The Buddha image answered: 'You accumulate the most merit amongst the exhaustible virtues if you save somebody's life, but specially by protecting the life of the helpless who have no clothes, food or shelter, or by protecting a life which had been hindered in the practice of religious duties. These virtues are excellent beyond compare but the last one is the best and is the basis of the path of the highest vehicle and become the cause of achieving Buddhahood. It is like the sprouting of a crop from a seed, not to mention achieving merit by saving the life of one's father, one's guru, one's mother, that of Bodhisattvas and so on. Even protecting the life of people who hinder others in reaching the different heavens or liberation and who are sinful and cruel, whose minds can only be controlled with difficulty, accumulates immeasurable merit.

One should give up an unprincipled mind, conceit, anger, covetousness and jealousy and devious behaviour and feel love and compassion. One should wear the clothes of modesty, the ornaments of diligence and kindheartedness and hold the weapons of instruction and keep all medical instruments and articles necessary for a doctor. Practising all these whilst having the perfect knowledge of Śūnyatā, you will accumulate unspeakably immeasurable merit. All these are an offering to give joy to the Guru and they are articles to give joy to the Tutelary Deities and a sacrificial offering to the Ḍākinīs. They are a method of achieving Enlightenment without meditation. They are a method of reaching the stage of Bodhisattvahood without walking the Path. This instruction is easy to practise but it will bring great benefit swiftly. This instruction consists of the nine great qualities of the Medicine Buddha and of the seven kinds and four branches of faith. They will put the instruction for the attaining of Buddhahood into the palm of one's hand.'

gYu-thog quoted the Sūtras:

'"Anyone administering to their sick patients
Or to the Guru or Bodhisattvas,
Even though they may not be of āryan (saintly) parents
Will accumulate immeasurable merit."

The text *Spyod-hjug* by Shi-ba-lha said:

"May I be a nurse to all sick beings
And a doctor and a medicine
Until they recover!"

The Vinaya text *hDul-ba Luṅ* says:

"When king gZi-mig Chan
Was practising on the path of Enlightenment
He did not accumulate any other merit
Than to nurse the sick. Because of his late life he became happy and wealthy
And in his next life he passed through all the stages and achieved Enlightenment.
This is what the Buddha said who saw
How important it is to help the sick,
And the results of prayer and karma
Are very certain for the future."

The Sūtra *dKon-mchhog brTsegs-pa* (Amassed Three Jewels) says:

"The Buddha thus addressed rDo-rje Rab-hjoms:
If a Bodhisattva has
Cured a sick person in his dream,

That is the Bodhisattva on the eighth stage.
The karma caused by the defilement of passionate desire
Is much diminished except for demonic influence
Stronger than the defilements.
That one should destroy by the practice of compassion
And by diligent work for others,
Without thinking of future gain.
Therefore, whoever practises this
Purifies all the sins and will assuredly achieve Enlightenment.
If he cures a baby boy he will accumulate merit like a Bodhisattva who has achieved the first stage
And if a boy child the second stage,
If a man the third stage
And a pregnant woman the fourth stage
And a Guru who has made a vow of morality the fifth,
A person suffering from a contagious disease the sixth,
A person suffering from dropsy the seventh stage,
One suffering from a demon-caused plague the eighth,
One suffering from leprosy the ninth
And one suffering from paralysis the tenth,
Suffering from hdug-nad, a composite disease, the eleventh
Suffering from bya-gdon* the twelfth,
One suffering from rabies the thirteenth."

The *Nad rab-tu Shi-ba'i mDo* (Disease Expelling Sūtra) says:

"If anyone takes one step for the sick
As a result, he will get food, drink and medicines,
Clothes and ornaments and riches.
If he gives one tablet or a piece of clothing to a patient
No devil will be able to prevail over him.
If he gives them with compassion
He will not descend into the three lower worlds.
His sins will be purged and he will reach
Gradually the Bodhisattva stage."

The *mDo Dran-pa Nyer-gshag* says:

"If anyone tries sincerely to cure a disease,
Even if he does not succeed he will achieve
The irreversible stage." '

* Fifteen diseases of children caused by demons.

Then gYu-thog stayed for two more days at Lhasa praying to Jo-bo Rinpoche. There were about a thousand of his disciples gathered together. gYu-thog said: 'It is difficult to provide for a thousand people, my disciples at La-stod gTsaṅ', and as his parting words he gave them this advice: 'You should give up selfishness and avariciousness and cunning, and practise meditation with a mind bent on achieving Enlightenment for all beings, and work for the sick! Be not conceited, be not out for profit and tend the sick without looking at their purse or caring whether they are rich or poor, and try to be doctors for all beings without distinction! You should not settle down in one place but should travel to all countries to heal the sick. You should not be personal physicians to the great and should help the afflicted poor with compassion. You should not drink alcohol and should eat only the three white foods. Give up using horses or mules and become the servant of the sick. Do not pretend you know what you do not know. And continue studying even if you are old. Do not judge the other people's way of life. When you do not know a disease tell people you do not know it and do not try to treat it. Try to turn all your actions of thought, speech and body into religious actions. And prepare the way for a good next life!' Then he kept a hundred disciples and sent the others home to their own countries.

XLVIII A VISIT TO THE TI-SE MOUNTAIN

Then gYu-thog said to his disciples: 'I am going to visit the mountain called Ti-se*.' All disciples tried to dissuade him but in vain. His chief disciple bSod-nams rTse-mo said: 'There is no Ti-se in Tibet. That is the imitation of Ti-se which we have up there. So please, don't go.' gYu-thog replied: 'There is the Tibetan Ti-se. In reality, Ti-se is in India. This is the imitation of Ti-se but it will accumulate you great merit if you visit it. It is mentioned in many sūtras. Indeed, when I saw the Medicine Buddha he told me: 'You should visit the Tibetan Ti-se and the other three mountains by the lake. So I will go.' Then he visited Ti-se and the Manasarowar Lake and went to Nepal via Southern La-stod and visited Phag-pa Shiṅ-kun (mountain between Lahoul and Zankar). Then he wandered throughout Northern La-stod (gTsaṅ La-stod) and dBus and many places where he protected lives and cured many sick people, and he specially wrote many instructions there and books on medicine for the benefit of doctors and patients.

Then he came to 'On-ljaṅ rDo'ī temple (Dark green Rock Temple). There four royal physicians requested him to tell them how to recognize

* Sanskrit: Kaitasa.

the king of the veins, their minister, their son and their attendants, and they offered him a case of tea. Then gYu-thog taught them the *Five Sections on the King of the Veins* and the *Six Sections on the Minister of the Veins* and the *Nine Sections on the Queen of the Veins* and the *Ten Sections on the Prince of the Veins* and *One Section on the Attendants of the Veins* and *One Section on the Maidservant of the Veins and Countless Soldiers of the Veins* and he told them about the three principal veins and the substances flowing through them such as blood, semen and air, and the four wheels of the veins and the five palaces of the veins. Then he taught the *rTsa-stoṅ thun* (Empty Veins Substance). Then gYu-thog said to the physicians: 'May the Medicine Buddha bless us. You are learned in the Teaching of Medicine, in texts and commentaries. You also had instruction on how to practise. You also have a lot of pride. To heal the sick one should have the nectar of love and of compassion and be diligent without laziness. One should have the ability to investigate, one should be tolerant with people's moods. One should be capable of working for the benefit of the sick and of keeping them out of harm's way. One should practise generosity without avarice. One should pray for the success of the wishes of the sick. One should have unclouded wisdom. One should know a method of persuading them to lead a good life. One should have the strength of mind not to care about public opinion and ill rumours. One should have courage without slothfulness. One should be mindful of past errors and see to it that they are not repeated. One should feel contented and have a great, deep and acute mind.'

XLIX TREATMENTS

Then gYu-thog met a man whose head was torn into pieces, and he thought: 'A sick man like this will never be cured in the end even if I tried to treat him.' The wounded man said to gYu-thog: 'Please, give me treatment, whatever is good for this affliction so that I should not have to be sorry afterwards if I had not asked you for treatment.' gYu-thog told him: 'I am going to introduce you to another doctor.' He said: 'I do not need another doctor. I would rather die in your hand.' Then gYu-thog operated on his head and gave him many other medical treatments, whatever was suitable for this case. Specially he gave him the treatment for cracked bones called seṅ-bug dal-po (Gentle Lion's Hole), Khad-med hDon-pa (Unimpeded Expeller), Rus mThoṅ dBye-ba Klad-ba (Seeing the Brain Bone Section), bsDoms-pa (Dressing of Wounds), Lha-ba hGugs-pa (Seeing to it that Pus is Gathered), Gro-kha'i hDzebs-chhaṅ (Wheat Beer), rLuṅ-gi The du-bu and other treatments for fractured bones and then the injured man's cracked bones, brain and veins were healed, and he was able to walk on a stick. While he was making a good recovery unfortunately his behaviour turned bad and he was plagued by demons of the upper and the nether regions so that his arms, legs and other parts of the body stiffened, and his mouth, nose and eyes became crooked, he was unable to keep his spittle and could not speak clearly and could not stand up unaided. gYu-thog was asked for help and he said: 'This is not the fault of the head injury but it is caused by the upper demons and I will treat him.' At this time everybody believed it came from the head injury and nobody believed what gYu-thog said. But a divine voice came from the sky:

'You people have been blind with ignorance.
As the result of calumniating this excellent man
With passionate hatred, you will be born
Dumb or deep in hell as the bottom stone of its edifice.
This sick man's life is drawing to its close.
His broken bones have been healed like a cemented pot,
The torn veins are knotted like a thread of cotton.
The marrow has recovered in the skull bones
And his brain has returned to its usual curds-like consistency.
This disease is just caused by upper and nether demons.
I feel pity for those calumniators creating sins and bad karma.
One should repent and confess in four different ways.*
May the dead man be born in Paradise
And may the sinful persons be guided out of Saṁsāra.'

gYu-thog then treated a man suffering from a brain disease for which until then no treatment had prevailed. Under gYu-thog's treatment he recovered. Then the patient circumambulated a temple but his stomach started aching from food poisoning and gYu-thog gave him an emetic and he recovered. Then the patient contracted dropsy, and gYu-thog drew the water out of his body and he recovered but he died from weakness. People said: 'He is an excellent doctor who can remove diseases and poisons from a man's body but in this case the time for his death had come.' gYu-thog had one enemy in that country, who said: 'If anyone wants the sick to die he has only to go to gYu-thog.' Then gYu-thog grew annoyed and said: 'We doctors who work for the sake of the next life need to have escorts to see us off and friends to receive us. There are many streams but they can form a pool. If all the sick recover there will be no dead bodies on the bier. After riding a horse many

* See above, p. 242.

times one can fall from it or stay on. You are beating the tail of the ox and rubbing a donkey's tail in powder. You went hunting in the highlands and fishing in the lowlands and have stolen your neighbour's goats and sheep. You have swindled your master and your father, I feel pity for those who commit such sins.' The gods became angry with the man who had slandered gYu-thog, and that night he suffered from colic and nearly died. Then [one of his household] came to ask gYu-thog to see him. gYu-thog's disciples said: 'Even if we go there the patient will be in danger of dying. But for sinful people it is better not to live a long life', and they did not pass the message on to gYu-thog. The sick man's wife came to implore gYu-thog to forgive him and to save his life. His disciples said to gYu-thog: 'He had been stirring up rumours against you, so please, do not go!' 'In general, keeping a resentment in the mind is against a doctor's vow. Moreover, if you hurt a patient you commit a sin as big as if you killed a human being', and he went to see the man and prayed to the Medicine Buddha and the Lineage of the Teachings feeling love and compassion towards the patient and his relatives and comforted them and gave him the medicine gla-rtsi bdun-pa (musk medicine with seven ingredients) and chhig-thub khan-dra (medicinal plant syrup) in turns. Then the real goddess bDud-rtsi-sma came in and said: 'Give these two medicines and add a cathartic to purge the patient. Give him good food and keep him warm and rub his groins.' After having advised this treatment she disappeared. When the sick man had recovered he offered gYu-thog, from gratitude, a horse with saddle and equipment, a hundred khal of barley, and he confessed his sins. gYu-thog put his hand on his and said:

'I bow to Vaiḍūrya who can drive away the three poisons of diseases.
Please, bless beings so that faithlessness is put to flight.
You faithless fool have suffered from much sickness
And nearly separated the body from your life.
This is just the result of your heedless speech
By which you brought the anger of the gods on yourself.
The Medicine Buddha is the incarnation of Mañjuśrī's speech
And of his mind and of his body.
His emanation is hTs'o-byed gZhon-nu
And I am his incarnation.
I, gYu-thog Yon-tan mGon-po
Know past, present and future clearly:
The cause of diseases, the result of diseases
And the treatment for diseases.

And I know what the outcome is going to be.
I take the pulse and examine the urine.
Whether the patient will die or get better
And the number of veins I can see distinctly
Like an olive on the open palm of the hand.
I ward off death when it comes untimely,
I usher in the jewel of life,
I am the nectar of the medicine of revival.
I am the Guru who gives life.
If you want to be a warder-off do that,
If you want to be an usher-in do that,
Do what you feel makes you happy.
I take no notice of sound because it is like an echo,
I feel no desire for forms because they are like reflections in a mirror,
I do not feel any desire, for mind is an empty movement.
Idle chatter causes you to be born dumb,
So, my spiritual son, do not commit sins!'

The man replied:

'You know the past, present and future quite clearly
By the help of the six miraculous powers.
You are the incarnation of the Medicine Buddha of fore-knowledge and five eyes,
Your word is like a king's order
Which it is impossible to disobey.'

He put gYu-thog's feet on the crown of his head. Then gYu-thog said:

'I bow before Vaiḍūrya, the Medicine Buddha,
I, gYu-thog Yon-tan mGon-po,
I rule the kingdom of medical science.
I am the minister gYu-thog Yon-tan mGon-po
Who gives orders to hot and cold diseases.
I am the queen gYu-thog mGon
Who knows how to mix hot and cold medicines.
I am the prince gYu-thog Yon-tan mGon-po
And am enjoying giving instruction like a son playing with his father's property.
I am the general gYu-thog Yon-tan mGon
And destroy diseases and evil demons with the help of medicines.
I am at the head of all doctors, gYu-thog Yon-tan mGon-po

Who gives advice on diseases and the diet for them.
I am the servant Yon-tan mGon-po
Who waits upon the sick people.
I am the magician gYu-thog Yon-tan mGon-po
Who can throw substances with magic virtues
On swellings, pleurisy and the like.
I am the Bon-po gYu-thog Yon-tan mGon-po
Who secures bDud-rtsi-sman-grub by enchantment.
I am the executioner gYu-thog Yon-tan mGon-po
Killing hot diseases with acupuncture, moxa, and other treatment.
I am the wealthy gYu-thog Yon-tan mGon-po,
Having the jewels of the instruction on the practice.
I am the beggar gYu-thog Yon-tan mGon-po
Who does not feel he has anything even for a moment.
Some people see me as a cunning impostor,
Some see me as a fool who knows nothing.
Some people see me as the Medicine Buddha.
If somebody looks at my mind he sees the real Buddha.
These different views are caused by the karma of former lives
And the magnitude of their sins. I shall work for the sick in this life
And go to lTa-na-sdug in my next life.'

L A JEALOUS DOCTOR

Then gYu-thog examined a patient's pulse and asked him: 'Which doctor has seen you before and what medicines did you have?' The patient said: 'I have been suffering from this indigestion for five months and have had medicines from all the doctors I met, specially from doctor bSam-grub hPhel in this country who knows my disease very well.' Then gYu-thog invited that doctor and asked him: 'What is this patient's disease?' He said: 'First it was caused by indigestion. But now it has become dropsy and a tumour in the abdomen.' gYu-thog said: 'This is not so. It is caused by earth demons, and his fever has not yet completely gone down. His dropsy has turned into feverish dropsy because his régime has not been right.' Then the doctor asked: 'How do you cure it?' gYu-thog said: 'First turn the feverish dropsy into cold dropsy and then give the treatment for dropsy.' The doctor replied: 'Feverish dropsy cannot be cured, only cold dropsy.' Then gYu-thog said: 'The literal meaning of the *rGyud-bzhi* is as you say. But if I turn the wheel of dropsy it will be cured.' Then the doctor said: 'We doctors have decided he will never recover. If someone can cure it it must be an Emanation (of the Medicine Buddha).' gYu-thog told his patient: 'Give everything you have to the Saṁgha', and he did so. Then he told gYu-thog: 'I have done it', and gYu-thog said: 'Now you should give up the worldly life and go to a hermitage', and his patient did as gYu-thog said. gYu-thog treated him with seven instructions on dropsy, one after the other, and he recovered. Doctor bSam-grub hPhel said: 'Your recovery was caused by my medicine, and you have to offer me something to give thanks.' He said: 'My disease was healed by gYu-thog and I am grateful to him but I cannot thank doctors who just go by the name of doctors.' He got angry and said: 'A witch cannot get the siddhis of work done by a Ḍākinī. It is not right that you should return your thanks to gYu-thog while I have cured you. It is possible that later one of your friends will want to be treated by my family and to have his pulse taken.' gYu-thog said to the patient: 'In general, a doctor is indispensable and he is the man with whom people should not be on bad terms. A doctor is the man who attracts many rumours. He is a man who unites three virtues within him. I cured your disease but you offer to him your kind thanks!' The patient said: 'Will you, please, explain about the three indispensable men?' gYu-thog said: 'The doctor, the smith and the chief are indispensable men. A doctor and a scavenger and a tanner are three indispensable men. A doctor and a wicked man and a tanner, three rumour mongers. A doctor, a rich man and an astrologer, three men with the three virtues. A doctor, an artisan and a barmaid, the three men who enjoy themselves. A doctor, a guru and a wise man, the three men who are needed by all people. Doctor, master and chief: three persons with authority. A doctor, a full-grown youth and a strong man, three men who can destroy an army.' The patient made Doctor bSam-grub hPhel happy by a great offering of thanks. Then gYu-thog said to Doctor bSam-grub hPhel:

'I bow before Vaiḍūrya, the Medicine Buddha.
May his blessings destroy mischievousmindedness and desirousness.
You, Doctor bSam-grub hPhel, be not selfish and desirous,
Sit on the cushion of modesty.
Be not jealous or angry
And wear the clothes of faith and reverence.
Be not lazy and stupid
And put on the belt of diligence and prudence.
Be not arrogant and avaricious,
Put on the ornament of compassion and love.

Do not cadge favours or use any cunning,
Ride the horse of wisdom and repentance.
Be not a hypocrite or impious,
Be watchful and mindful and full of repentance.
Do not think of rewards and keep on being benevolent
And think of others.
Do not judge other people's lives
And study the instructions until you have confidence in them.
Do not carry instructions in your mouth but in your heart.
Do not pretend to patients you have the Buddha's wisdom
But see whether or not you have the experience.
Do not seek happiness for this life
And search rather for the happiness in the next life.
Do not treat the patients in a careless manner.
Try to stay the battle of diseases.'

Then bSam-grub hPhel recognized his faults and repented. He said to gYu-thog:

'I bow to gYu-thog Yon-tan mGon-po,
Descendant of gYu-thog-pa, excellent chief of doctors
Who destroys the pain of diseases.
When I consider your excellences
The hairs of my body stand on end with my deep faith
And tears of regret run down my cheeks like a shower.
Please, protect me with your mercy!'

He bowed and put gYu-thog's feet on the crown of his head.

LI TAKING THE PULSE

When gYu-thog reached the age of a hundred years he conferred the ritual of the goddesses and rishis on his sons and disciples and told them to propitiate them. To the disciple dBu-zi the eight goddesses appeared. And to the disciple Phags-pa sKyabs the three rishis* appeared. To gYu-thog hBum-seṅ, hTs'o-byed gZhon-nu appeared. And the Medicine Buddha appeared to gYu-thog himself. Then the Medicine Buddha said: 'gYu-thog-pa and your descendants and followers, there will be a prophecy for you from the goddesses and rishis about your rounds of the patients and about

* sBa-mi-sba, Yan-lag mDah-riṅ and the Black Garuḍa.

taking the pulse.' gYu-thog seized the Medicine Buddha's feet and prayed as follows:

'King of doctors, my Guru, Medicine Buddha,
Who drives away the three poisons,
Whoever comes in contact with you will benefit from it.
King of doctors, protector of beings,
King of doctors whose nature is merciful,
King of doctors, (without you) I have no hope,
King of doctors, (without you) I have no defence.
Look down with mercy and protect me with mercy
So that there is no separation between you and me.
Look upon me day and night.'

After having finished this deeply felt prayer he recited this mantra a hundred times:

'Om namo bhagavati guru ai-be' (Sanskrit evaṁ).

Then the Medicine Buddha said smilingly: 'I am not separate from you, my spiritual son. Pray to me and let all your actions of body, speech and mind be concerned with the sick.' Then gYu-thog prepared offerings to sMan-hla (the Medicine Buddha), the rishis, the goddesses and the lineage of the Teachings, and they appeared to him. And they promised him that whenever gYu-thog would treat the sick they would come and tell him all about what to do.

After some time, when gYu-thog was taking a patient's pulse, the Medicine Buddha and the eight goddesses prophesied to him but he did not hear it because of the noise of people, water, dogs, and so on. From then on he only took the pulse when there was no noise from human beings, water or dogs.

One day a disciple was taking the pulse with some bantering and gYu-thog saw this and said to him:

'My son, whenever you examine a patient
Do not be careless or speak nonsense.
Careless treatment based on one's own ideas
Is harmful to the sick.
It will cause you shame and bad rumours.
Specially when you are taking the pulse,
You should avoid noise from human beings and other obstacles,
You should not be absentminded and should concentrate.
Be not in a hurry and try to understand

The Teachers' speech and the texts of Medicine
And your own experience.'

LII BOOKS WRITTEN BY GYU-THOG

When gYu-thog was one hundred and ten years old, one day, while he was giving the bDud-rtsi-sman-grub to his disciples the gTor-ma turned into light and the light turned into nectar of a hundred tastes and everybody saw it and tasted it. During the ritual of collecting tastes from all over the world there fell a shower of nectar of five and many other colours. Then gYu-thog invited, in the ritual, the Guru, the Buddhas, the Bodhisattvas, the Ḍākinīs, the Dharmapālas, and particularly the Medicine Buddha, the Rishis, the goddesses of medicine and the lineage of the Teachings, and he offered medicine nectar to them, and everybody saw it. Then the Medicine Buddha and the brahmins and the lineage sang in unison:

'gYu-thog Yon-tan mGon,
Whoever comes in contact with you
Shall surely benefit.
Driving away suffering and diseases
You have achieved excellent spiritual knowledge.
Whatever you do with body, speech and mind
Is for the sake of beings and specially the sick
Day and night.
When you gave the bDud-rtsi-sman-grub consecration
The gTor-ma turned into nectar and light
And we have seen the essence of the tastes of the elements of worlds in the ten directions
Enjoyed by the Buddhas and Bodhisattvas.
It was wonderful, my spiritual son!'

Then his disciple dPal-ldan Lhun-grub asked gYu-thog: 'Please, tell me what you have written on medicine as you had been prophesied', and gYu-thog replied: 'I have written thirty-three chapters on the theories of Buddhism and Heretical doctrine, fifty-five chapters on the *sDe-skor phyi-naṅ gsaṅ-gsum* (Three Secret Outer and Inner Divided Sections), a commentary and a supplement to the Eighteen Sciences, one thousand and three hundred chapters on the one thousand and fifty-one commentaries on the *rGyud-bzhi*, countless instructions for curing diseases, and the commentary containing one hundred and ninety chapters on the instruction of *dMar-hded* (Final

Success), and also many less important commentaries, twenty-five chapters on the *Ro-pra hPhrul-gyi Me-loṅg* (Magic Mirror of Anatomy), eight chapters on the *Byaṅ-khog gSaṅ-dBye* (Sections on Moxa and Acupuncture Points on the Inside of the Body), thirty-five chapters on the *Thur-dPyad gNad-kyi hPhrul-hkhar* (Tube in the Heart or Other Organs Treatment), fifteen chapters on the *mÑon-shes gNad-kyi hPhrul-hkhor* (Diagnosis and Prophecy from Taking the Pulse), eighteen chapters on the *gSaṅ-thig Rin-chhen sGron-me* (Lines of Body Measurements and Determination of Points for Moxa and Acupuncture), one hundred and twenty chapters on the *Nag-rtsis hKhor-hdas gTan-hbebs* (Astrological calculations based on the Five Elements), twenty-five chapters on the *hBras-rtsis* (Astrological Scheme), sixty chapters on the *dKar-rtsis Ri-bo sDul-hbebs* (Conquering the Atoms of the Mountain of Astronomy), *Thems-yig* a mnemotechnic guide to the *rGyud-bzhi*, commentary on names occurring in the *rGyud-bzhi* (Explanation of Hidden Names in the *rGyud-bzhi*), supplements, contents list and index to the *rGyud-bzhi*, the *Me-rtsa mDo-chhod Nag-po* (Moxa Text), the *gTur-(gTer-?)kha Lag-len Phyug-med* (Bleeding Text), the *Gyen-hgren lChags-kyus Nya-hdzin* (Text on Emetics), the *Thur-hbebs Ri-bo rBab-sgril* (Text on Laxatives), the *Nyam-yig mThoṅ-ba Don-ldan* (Knowledge from Experience), and one hundred and fifty-one other commentaries, including the instruction useful to doctors for bringing prosperity to the sick and restoring them which is called *bSkrad-pa Lṅa-ldan* (Expelling the Five Evils).'

LIII INSTRUCTIONS

When gYu-thog was teaching a host of disciples the instructions called *Rig-pa'i Ral-skor Lṅa* (Turning the Five Wisdom Swords) on the nature of Mind, the eight goddesses sang to him in unison:

'I bow before the feet of gYu-thog Yon-tan mGon-po
Who holds the sword of wisdom
And sees all things in existence
Clearly distinguishing each thing in Saṁsāra and Nirvāṇa
By means of the sky's beautiful emptiness.
I bow before the second Buddha, gYu-thog Yon-tan mGon-po,
The lord of beings with whom whoever comes in contact benefits.
Whenever you remember him you gain excellent knowledges.
He is inseparable from the Medicine Buddha.
I bow before the king of doctors,
The perfect Jewel who is rich in wisdom and the wealth of Saints

Who works for the spreading of religion
But particularly keeps alive the teaching of medicine.
I bow before the founder of Medical Science
Who is victorious over the enemies,
The Lord who brings happiness to beings
And is the source of all joys and bliss.
I bow before the excellent Teacher.
By the water of the well of your former merit
Is nourished the lotus flower of your wisdom dearest to the disciples
With instructions never given before as its blossoming pistil.
In the palace of wisdom and merit
I bow before the chief of the founders of Medical Science
Whose excellent activity has fulfilled the disciples' wishes.
In the pleasant garden of the Buddha's teaching
Decorated with jewel top ornaments of the good doctrine
Blossoms forth the lotus flower of the buddhī mind and speech.
You give the honey of instruction
Whose sandalwood-scented mercy attracts all the bees.'

Thus they praised gYu-thog and then disappeared.

When gYu-thog was aged about one hundred and twenty the disciples made a sacrificial offering and requested him to teach them the essence of the instruction on the science of medicine. Then gYu-thog said: 'I have told you everything I have heard: the instruction, the sources and the story of their acquisition. Now you should leave me alone.' Then gYu-thog hBum-seṅ said: 'You have often taught us the treasure of instruction before but still we are not satisfied. You have prophesied you will live to the age of one hundred and twenty-five for the sake of beings. But now you are already one hundred and twenty years old, and we do not know when you are going to lTa-na-sdug to become the head of the saints and rishis. Now, please, give us all the rest of your instructions!' Then gYu-thog gave the instruction called *mThoṅ-ba-don-ldan-ma* (He Seeing Whom brings Benefit) which are the essence extracted from all learned medical works of the secret seal of the Ḍākinīs to the disciples. He began as follows:

'O Guru and Medicine Buddha, Vaiḍūrya,
Bless me for the success of this instruction!
Listen, my son, gYu-thog hBum-seṅ, and you disciples:
If you work for the benefit of the sick,
You doctors, acting like bodhisattvas,
Should keep benevolence for others in your mind

With love and compassion, and the lamp of wisdom and concentration
united, carry surgical instruments
And fulfil the wishes of the patients.
First learn what medicine fits what disease,
Then use them properly without mistake.
With a kind heart give the suitable medicines for hot and cold diseases.
If one does not know how to take the pulse and examine the urine
And is incapable of diagnosing diseases,
Then one should give up using moxa or any other treatment,
Otherwise it will cause bad rumours.
Therefore do not treat your patients carelessly
And keep a thoughtful mind on them.
You should notice carefully
When your patients first start recovering,
Otherwise the medicine will not attack the disease
And will antagonize hot and cold diseases.
Asking your patient in carefully chosen words
How the disease arose is important like an instruction,
Otherwise it is difficult to understand his disease,
And one should pray to the Medicine Buddha
To the rishis and to the goddesses of Medicine.'

Then gYu-thog taught them whatever they needed to learn.

LIV GYU-THOG'S PROPHECY ABOUT THE GYU-THOG LINEAGE*

Then he went to Yer-pa and lived in the cave of U-rgyan (Uḍḍiyāna) with some few disciples for five days. Suddenly gYu-thog looked up into the sky and laughed. hBum-seṅ's son rDo-rje Thaṅ-pa asked: 'Why are you laughing?' gYu-thog said: 'Listen, I have something important to say. But you are young and it will be difficult for you to understand even if I tell you.' Then rDo-rje Thaṅ-pa told his father hBum-seṅ who said to gYu-thog: 'You did not laugh without a good reason. Please, tell us about it!' The other disciples asked him too. gYu-thog said: 'Lha-bu Dam-pa Tog-dkar came down from heaven and became known as Ba-nu-ma. From then on up to gYu-thog Byams-pa-dpal it is called the Elder gYu-thog lineage. And the lineage of the descendants of hDre-rje Vajra after gYu-thog Byams-pa-dpal will be called the Younger gYu-thog lineage.' They asked: 'When did hDre-rje Vajra come and for what purpose did he come? And how

* This and the following chapter are not extant in the sDe-dge edition.

many descendants did he have?' Then gYu-thog said: 'In my lineage up to gYu-thog Byams-pa-dpal the instructions on bDud-rtsi-sman-grub will remain uncorrupted like a string of pearls. Then the bDud-rtsi-sman-grub Teaching will get corrupted, and the Younger gYu-thog will reform it. Then hDre-rje Vajra* will go to India and again he will ask the sixteen goddesses of medicine for instruction on the bDud-rtsi-sman-grub. Then he will increase the Teaching in Tibet.

Then, from gYu-thog Byams-pa-dpal's fifth descendant, the five descendants of the Younger gYu-thog will come.' Then hBum-seṅ said: 'Please, tell us how gYu-thog's descendant will come from Byams-pa-dpal's son.' He replied: 'Byams-pa-dpal's son will be Pad-ma 'Od-gser, his son will be Padma rDo-rje, his son Guru rDo-rje and his son Byaṅ-chhub rDo-rje. All these will be studying the Teaching of the Old Tantric School.†

Byaṅ-chhub rDo-rje's son will be called Gaṅs-chan mKhas, a learned Saint in the New and Old Tantric knowledge, especially learned in the science of Medicine.' Then hBum-seṅ said: 'Please, tell me about the five descendants of the Younger gYu-thog's lineage.'

gYu-thog said: 'Listen, my son: the Younger gYu-thog, the head ornament of the learned in the snow-fenced land, will have five descendants as follows: my ancestor hDre-rje Vajra will be born as Gaṅs-chan mKhas's son. He will receive from hTs'o-byed gZhon-nu (in India) the instructions of bDud-rtsi-sman-grub and bDud-rtsi-sman-hphreṅ, and with them he will light up the darkness in Tibet. My father Khyun-po rDo-rje will come back as the grandson of Khaṅ-chhen Kal-pa and I will come back as his son. His son will be dpal-seṅ or hBum-seṅ. gYu-thog hGro-mgon will be born as the son of hBum-seṅ or dPal-seṅ and he will be called Sra-lu. From Sra-lu there will be twenty-one descendants, all surgeons and very learned in medicine.' Then hBum-seṅ asked: 'Please, tell me about the twenty-one surgeons!' gYu-thog said: 'hGro-mgon's son will be Shes-rab bZaṅ-po, his son bLo-gros dPal, his son bKra-shis dPal-ldan, his son bLo-gros Dar-po, his son Nam-mkhah bLo-gros, his son Saṅs-rgyas Lhun-grub, his son rGyal-ba'i hByuṅ-gnas, his son bSod-nams Rin-chhen, his son Chhos-skyoṅ dPal-hbyor, his son Sha-kya dPal-bzaṅ, his son bLo-gros brTan-pa, his son Grags-pa bZaṅ-po, his son Chhos-rgyal bKra-shis, his son Chhos-kyi rGyal-mts'an, his son Byaṅ-chhub Seṅ-ge, his son Nam-mkhah mGon-po, his son Chhos-skyoṅ Don-grub, his son Nam-mKhah Legs-pa, his son Nam-mkhah dPal-bzaṅ, his son Rin-chhen bZaṅ-po, his son rDo-rje rGyal-mts'an,

* Or rather his future incarnation.

† Tantric translations from the Sanskrit up to Rin-chen bZaṅ-po are of the Old Tantric School (Nyiṅ-ma-pa). From then on of the New (gSar-ma-pa).

his son bSod-nams dPal-hbar. The next five descendants will be called masters and have precedence everywhere but the Teaching will not flourish then.' hBum-seṅ said: 'Please, tell us who will be those five whom they will call Jo-jo.' 'bSod-nams dPal-hbar (Jo-bo's) son will be dGe-hdun dPal, his son Lha-btsun dPal-ldan-grags, his son Shes-rab rGyal-mts'an, his son mTs'o-skyes-dpal, his son Ṅag-dbaṅ Shes-rab. One generation after that there will come one who will write my history.' hBum-seṅ asked then: 'Tell us the name of father and son and their work and how he will compose the biography from archives and records.' Then gYu-thog said: 'Shes-rab Rin-chhen will be the son of Ṅag-dbaṅ Shes-rab and his son will be dPal-ldan Lhun-grub and dPal-ldan will learn the science and teaching of Medicine and he will practise Medicine and bDud-rtsi sman-grub secretly for the sake of sick beings and compose my biography.' Then hBum-seṅ asked: 'What descendants will come after that and who will spread your teaching?' Then gYu-thog said: 'Under dPal-ldan Lhun-grub's influence my biography will be started. His son called gZhon-nu will spread it. Then there will be many descendants of average ability.' 'Will the teaching of bDud-rtsi-sman-grub be handed down through the lineage of the Elder or the Younger gYu-thog?' Then gYu-thog said: 'For doctor Ts'o-byed gZhon-nu it is all right to say either. The five pure descendants of the Elder gYu-thog will be the same as the five pure descendants of the Younger gYu-thog. The teaching of bDud-rtsi-sman-grub by the Elder hDre-rje Vajra and the Younger hDre-rje Vajra is the same, both going back to hTs'o-byed gZhon-nu. Moreover, the Younger hDre-rje Vajra's teaching of bDud-rtsi-sman-grub goes back to both, hTs'o-byed gZhon-nu and the sixteen goddesses of Medicine.' Again he asked: 'To whom will the teaching be handed down from gYu-thog Sra-lu?' gYu-thog replied: 'In your next incarnation, hBum-seṅ, your name will be Braṅ-ti rGyal-ba bZaṅ-po and to him will the teachings be handed on.' Then he prophesied:

'I bow before my father and Guru and all those
Who teach the Perfect Way to Liberation.
To lay the foundation of the teaching of Medicine
In eastern and western India, Nepal and Tibet
The young god Tog-dkar-po came down from heaven into India.
He had the brahminī Chhos-rgya bLo-gros for his companion
And thus Shes-rab Ral-gri was born and began
The lineage of the teachers of Medicine.
Specially he was born in the ancestry of gYu-thog in Tibet.
From Ba-nu Jo down to gYu-thog Byams-pa

The line is called that of the Elder gYu-thog.
From Padma 'Od-gser down to the end of the lineage
It will be that of the Younger gYu-thog.
From the Younger hDre-rje Vajra up to the Younger Sra-lu
It will be called the lineage of the five Perfect ones.
From gYu-thog Shes-rab gZaṅ-po up to bSod-nams dPal-hbar
It will be the lineage of the twenty-one surgeons.
From gYu-thog dGe-dpal up to Ṅag-dbaṅ Shes-rab
There will be five masters with good human qualities
But without knowledge in the practice of medicine.
The son of the chief disciple of Ṅag-dbaṅ bZaṅ-po will be dPal-ldan Shes-rab*
Who will learn the Science of Medicine
And will keep up the teaching of gYu-thog.
He will work secretly for the beings suffering from diseases
And he will practise and propitiate bDud-rtsi-sman-hphreṅ in secret.
Specially he will write the biography of gYu-thog
To benefit beings.
His son with the cognomen gZhon-nu will preserve gYu-thog's teaching
And he will spread it.'

LV CONSECRATIONS

Again his son hBum-seṅ asked him: 'Are there three different types of consecration, that is one in great detail, a medium one, and a short one in the Ritual of Turning Medicine into Nectar?' gYu-thog replied: 'In the greatly detailed type of ritual there are twelve basic consecrations. Each of them has ten branch consecrations. So altogether there are one hundred and twenty consecrations. In the medium type there are nine basic consecrations. Each of them as ten branches. So there are altogether ninety consecrations. In the short type there is one basic consecration and ten branches, so there are ten consecrations.' Then the son asked: 'What is the benefit of giving the consecration of Turning Medicine into Nectar?' gYu-thog replied: 'Formerly in India hTs'o-byed gZhon-nu gave the detailed consecration but once, and the person who received it lived one hundred and twenty years longer than his apportioned span of life. My ancestor hDre-rje Vajra gave once the medium consecration to a person who subsequently lived ninety years longer than he otherwise would have done. I have once given to a ninety-three-year-

* His whole name is dPal-ldan Shes-rab Lhun-grub.

old person the short consecration, and he was able to live to the age of one hundred and three.' Again the son asked: 'What preparations are needed for the ritual of Divining by Veins presided over by eight or sixteen goddesses and three rishis?' Then he replied: 'First the five-sword-like methods of reasoning should be used by the teacher to help the disciple to find out the true nature of Mind. Then the consecrations of the bDud-rtsi-sman-hphreṅ and the bDud-rtsi-sman-grub should prepare the ground for propitiating. Then one should start to propitiate. Then the actual ritual of divining by veins should be performed. The Medicine Buddha himself taught this to hTs'o-byed gZhon-nu and my ancestor hDre-rje rGya-gar Vajra, but it has to be performed exactly in accordance with his words. Don't commit a sin by trying to do it your own way or being negligent about it. If you do so you will not get the blessings of the lineage.' Then he gave the instruction of the essence of the practice: 'I bow before my father and the Guru and my ancestors. Listen, my son hBum-seṅ whom I have raised since early childhood, if someone is going to propitiate the goddesses and rishis without performing the preliminary ritual, the propitiation is like an orphan child. First the disciple should be introduced to the real nature of Mind by the explanations to (the text of) the Five Sword Wheels. Then he should be given the blessing of the consecration of Turning Medicine into Nectar, and his mind should be ripened by the conferring of power on him. Then one should propitiate exactly according to the text of the ritual. Do not do it your own way, otherwise you will slide downhill, and do exactly what the text says. You should keep all the precepts with faith.' Then the son asked him: 'What is going to be the life story of our gYu-thog family?' He replied: 'There will be two life stories, that of the Younger gYu-thog and that of the Elder gYu-thog. This is the story of the Elder gYu-thog. Because my ancestor worked so hard on the text of the *mGo-thig Rin-chen gNad-hgrel* and of the *bDud-rtsi sMan-hphreṅ* (String of nectar medicines) and of the *bDud-rtsi sMan-grub* (Turning medicine into nectar) without regard to his own life, you disciples should honour it and spread it. The goddesses and the lineage of the rishis have promised to help with the growth and increase of these teachings, and specially the dharmapālas* have promised my ancestor by an oath to look after these teachings for ever.'

LVI GYU-THOG'S DEPARTURE TO LTA-NA-SDUG

Then one day his consort rDo-rje hTs'o-mo said to gYu-thog: 'I bow before the Gurus and gYu-thog Yon-tan mGon-po. Your learning is widely

* Deities protecting religion.

famed. You kindled the lamp of the teaching of medicine in the snow-fenced land in the North of the world. You have protected many people's lives. For the sake of helping suffering beings and us disciples, great learned gYu-thog, stay and protect us with your mercy!' Then gYu-thog said: 'Beautiful consort who gives bliss, accomplished in wisdom, with the marks of a Ḍākinī, I have understood what you requested but I, the Learned Yon-tan mGon-po, have reached the age of one hundred and twenty-five. Now I will stay no longer and shall go to lTa-na-sdug. You, disciples, give up the worldly mind and be diligent and accumulate merit! For this life it is easy to do it but if you seek great benefit for the next life I shall be content indeed.'

Then gYu-thog was teaching his disciples and many rishis and Ḍākinīs and spiritual heroes and spiritual heroines. They sang in unison: 'gYu-thog Yon-tan mGon-po, second Buddha, until your one hundred and twenty-fifth year you have stayed in the human country and have protected beings. Now your karma for staying in the human country is drawing towards its close. We have come to take you to the excellent place of the Nirmāṇakāya called lTa-na-sdug, the City of Medicine, as the head of the rishis, the Ḍākinīs and the goddesses of Medicine. There is no time to delay, so, please, come now!' And immediately they spread a roll of cloth in the four directions, and then gYu-thog said: 'My son hBum-seṅ and disciples, prepare a good sacrificial offering. I am going to lTa-na-sdug to be the head of the rishis and goddesses.' The disciples were stunned when they heard this and did not know what to do, and a bone-ornamented lady prepared a divine sacrificial offering. Then the great gYu-thog snapped his fingers and said: 'Listen, my son hBum-seṅ and my disciples! I was born but I do not have to show my death. I have achieved this through my Guru's and the Medicine Buddha's kindness. I had meditated on the body maṇḍala of bDud-rtsi-sman-grub and bDud-rtsi-sman-hphreṅ. I have completed the propitiation of these as the Medicine Buddha has commanded. I have become a receptacle for the grace of the Medicine Buddha by having the empowering consecration of bDud-rtsi-sman-hphreṅ and bDud-rtsi-sman-grub. I have identified my mind (sems-ṅo-sprad) with the rig-pa'i ral-skor lṅa (the five methods of turning the five wisdom swords) and for many kalpas I have given protection to the lives of sick beings. Specially I meditated on the meaning of the deathless Dharmakāya and I prayed good prayers and I have achieved fearlessness in the face of death and I am looking forward to it with happy thoughts. You disciples should do as I did and follow me.' His son dPal-hbum said: 'I propitiated the gods of bDud-rtsi-sman-hphreṅ, as you said, father. Now, please, tell me how to practise the meditation on bDud-rtsi-sman-hphreṅ.' gYu-thog said: 'My son, the sign of the completion of propitiating bDud-rtsi-sman-grub is like a crop coming from a well-prepared field. But even now there is still a danger: because it is still a question of whether you or somebody else will reap the results.' His son said: 'Please, tell me how this is.' Then gYu-thog said: 'Having completed the propitiation of these gods one should perform the bDud-rtsi-sman-grub ritual beginning with the taking of the three refuges and ending by sending out words of blessing every day and principally one should recite the Medicine Buddha's name and his other two mantras at least twenty-one times. And one should recite the mantra of his attendant gods at least seven times each. This is the method of the Medicine Buddha and my own.' And he continued: 'The Excellent Protectors, the Three Jewels, will not let down those taking refuge to them. Vaiḍūrya, the Medicine Buddha, is of the intrinsic nature of the Three Jewels, and I am of the intrinsic nature of the Medicine Buddha. My son, dPal-hbum and my disciples, I the old father gYu-thog Yon-tan, descendant of the gYu-thog lineage, will give you the essence of the most important instruction. Do not forget it and keep it in your heart! In general, there are four conditions of propitiating: Omens, right time of day for starting them, number of recitations, and resolute intention. Especially, when the propitiating of bDud-rtsi-sman-hphreṅ and bDud-rtsi-sman-grub have been completed one should start the ritual of bDud-rtsi-sman-grub beginning with taking refuge to the Three Jewels and ending by sending out blessings. One should do this every day, and the name of the principal god and his maṇḍala should be recited at least twenty-one times every morning and the mantras of his attendant gods at least seven times for each. It is very important to do this and one should remember it.' Then his śakti and his son and disciples and faithful donors requested him all of them together: 'O wonderful Incarnation who keeps the teaching of the Buddha alive, source of the teaching of Medicine, gYu-thog Yon-tan mGon! You have achieved the power over birth and death, so please do not go to another world for you must stay in this snow-fenced land for at least another three years, there is no other way! Please, secure for us the permission from the gods and ḍākinīs.' Then these sounds came from the sky: 'The Excellent gYu-thog Yon-tan mGon-po in human form who is really the Medicine Buddha has been working for the sick but you human beings were jealous of the excellent gYu-thog working for the sick, and we gods have regretted this and therefore we are taking him up into lTa-na-sdug in his one hundred and twenty-fifth year. Do you remember how you have slandered him? You human beings are not very reliable and are enthusiastic at the beginning and later become forgetful except those of you who are deeply religious. While gYu-thog was attaining Enlightenment, you have committed sins and been unfaithful to him. Whose fault is this? We cannot believe your pretty speeches. Great gYu-thog, come immediately', and a rope was unwound. Then gYu-thog's disciple mThu-chhen Ṅan-sṅags-kyi bDag-po, the sorcerer, said: 'I am requesting you, gYu-thog, to stay, otherwise I shall cut this rope.'* Then five Ḍākinīs sang in unison: 'Listen, Ṅan-sṅags bDag-po, and you others gathered here: it is impossible to disobey the word of Padma-Saṁbhava. You cut this rope for three months and then we shall come to fetch him. Please, come, great gYu-thog!' Then his three sons said: 'You are definitely going to lTa-na-sdug after three months, father, to be the head of the rishis and lineage, but until then, could you, please, give us instruction.' Then gYu-thog said: 'My sons, disciples and donors who have faith in the Medicine Buddha and me, listen to me carefully. I, the old father Yon-tan mGon-po, have completed my work and now I am no longer going to stay here and shall go to lTa-na-sdug. You should give up anger and jealousy and avoid committing sins. And offer to the Gurus and the Tutelary Deities and also offer to deeply religious persons. Make gifts for suffering beings. Try to accumulate merit little by little and if you pray daily to the Medicine Buddha and me we shall meet in Paradise.' Then his śakti said: 'I will follow you when you go to Paradise.' gYu-thog said: 'It depends on you whether you will be able to go to Paradise. Now I am going to Paradise and prepare a good sacrificial offering.' She did so. Then he addressed her: 'rDo-rje hTs'o-mo, if you wish to go to Paradise you should practise as follows:' He pointed his finger to the sky, and there appeared Vaiḍūrya's palace and in it the Medicine Buddha in the form of the Nirmāṇakāya surrounded by eight Medicine Buddhas. Above it appeared the city of lTa-na-sdug and in it the Medicine Buddha in the form of the Saṁbhogakāya surrounded by the gods of the body maṇḍala of bDud-rtsi-sman-hphreṅ. In the centre of the city was the palace of Spros-bral chhos-dbyiṅs† (Actionless heaven). Above it was the Medicine Buddha in the form of the Dharmakāya attended by gods dancing and reciting *hūṁ* and *phat* and mantras.

Then they all made countless offerings to gYu-thog, some of them gave jewels, some flowers circumambulating him and bowing before him, and some praying to him. They all sang in unison: 'I bow before the Guru and Vaiḍūrya. You faithful rDo-rje hTs'o-mo, if you wish to meditate you should do as follows: visualize for instance the three palaces in the sky one

* The ritual requesting an Incarnation to stay longer on earth when he is not well is carried out by five people dressed as Ḍākinīs. Five coloured scarves are held out from a throne and folded up with a certain ritual. This symbolizes cutting off the Rin-po-chhe's road towards heaven so that he stays.

† See above p. 294.

on another. Meditate on this world as Vaiḍūrya's palace beyond. All beings in it are of the nature of gods and goddesses. The manifold appearance of the mind is the Medicine Buddha in the form of the Nirmāṇakāya. Wherever you live is lTa-na-sdug. The purified mind is the Medicine Buddha in the form of the Saṁbhogakāya. The body is the divine maṇḍala of the Actionless. Absolute Mind is the Dharmakāya. If you look with the eyes of faith then there is no separation between the Medicine Buddha and the Buddha in human form, gYu-thog Yon-tan mGon-po, like between butter mixed with butter or water mixed with water. When you are going to the other world you should avoid desire for this life.

Through the fontanel opening
One should visualize one's mind to be transferred
To the three Medicine Buddhas' chests
In the three celestial palaces,
Straight one after another.
Then palaces and gods should turn into light
And be wafted in all directions
And penetrate all beings of the six worlds
Through their fontanel openings.
After this all beings should be taken up into the sky
As by a powerful garuḍa who takes ordinary birds.
Then all beings from beneath the sky
Should be gathered into the sky.
Then one's own mind should reach wherever the sky extends,
Then they all should turn into light
And sink into gYu-thog inseparably from the Medicine Buddha.'

While gYu-thog and his śakti were enjoying the sacrificial offering the five ḍākinīs sang in unison:

'gYu-thogpa who has achieved all the perfections,
Please, come now into Paradise.
There is a reception for you with offerings and music and banners
And the rope has been stretched out.'

Then gYu-thog said: 'I will show the sign of old age.' Then he made the threatening gesture, and immediately the whole sky was filled with rainbows and lights. gYu-thog said: 'Oṁ na-mo bha-ga-va-ti be-ga-yi-la Vaiḍūrya (I bow before the Guru and Vaiḍūrya).' Then he turned into a mass of rainbows and lights and he went up into the sky to the sound of music and unthinkable miraculous events caused by the rishis and the lineage.

Then his son hBum-seṅ and his disciples and śakti saw this and sang in unison:

'gYu-thog Yon-tan mGon-po, king of the Dharma in the three worlds,
Please, look upon us disciples and your son,
Specially protect rDo-rje hTs'o-mo with your mercy.
To whom shall we turn for protection when you go?
Please, stay for the sake of sick people!'

Then gYu-thog said while staying in the sky:

'Victorious Medicine Buddha who is beautiful with the marks of perfection,
I, gYu-thog Yon-tan mGon-po,
Have made a lamp of the teaching of the science of medicine
In the jungle of the darkness of ignorance in Tibet.
In particular the concealed meaning of the *rGyud-bzhi*
Which is difficult to understand
I explained like a sun beam in the darkness.
Come up, rDo-rje hTs'o-mo!'

And immediately hTs'o-mo turned into light and sank into gYu-thog's chest and everybody saw it and was very astonished. And gYu-thog went to the palace of the Medicine Buddha at sunrise on the 15th of the monkey month in the water mouse year.

Then the sick people heard that gYu-thog had gone to Paradise without giving up his body, and they cried: 'Protector of us sick people, look with mercy upon us!' And a gYu-thog came to each of the sick people and healed them.

The disciples performed funeral rites as magnificent as those for the bodhisattva Kun-tu bZaṅ-po. The air was filled with a melodious sound and the earth was shaking and a five-coloured rainbow filled the sky. Sky and earth were pure, and a flower rain fell for three months. The three sons suffered by the separation from their parents and sang in unison with other disciples:

'I bow before Vaiḍūrya, the Medicine Buddha
Who is full of love and compassion.
gYu-thog Yon-tan mGon-po, Second Medicine Buddha,
Look upon us disciples and your sons.
We three sons have lost our parents and are unprotected
Like a blind man in a big empty plain,

Like the young of a raven left in the fog.
Parents, look upon us three helpless sons.
Please, look upon us, our Ancestors.
Now we shall work for sick beings
But who is going to give us instruction and advice?
Who will protect us in this sorry plight
And who will look after us with love?
Oh, please, look with mercy upon us, our parents and ancestors!'

Then the parents came seated on a white rainbow composed of rays of light and sang in unison to the three sons:

'I bow before Vaiḍūrya, the Medicine Buddha
Of the intrinsic nature of the past, future and present Buddha.
You have suffered, our three sons:
It is in the course of nature that who is born must die.
One cannot stay always with one's parents.
Whenever you remember your parents
Pray to the Three Jewels
And keep the memory of your parents in your heart
And meditate on compassion with beings.
Help the sick with mercy
And give them medicines without looking for reward.
Mix medicines for cold and hot diseases without mistakes
And study how to diagnose diseases and their symptoms
And do not make distinctions between patients
And do not expect offerings from them
And do not become conceited and be humble
And look after the sick.
There is no separation between you and me, my disciples.
Pray, above all for the sick!'

And they disappeared.

Then the three sons and the disciples made, to commemorate gYu-thog Yab-Yum, two human life-size Buddha Statues* and one of Maitreya and of the Three Protectors† and a Myaṅ-hdas mchhod-rten,‡ one story high, a receptacle for the nirmāṇakāya. All these were made from gilt copper. A complete text of the Prajñāpāramitā written in gold was made in gYu-thog's

* Medicine Buddha and Buddha Śākyamuni.
† Mañjuśrī, Vajrapāṇi and Avalokiteśvara.
‡ One of the eight styles in which a stūpa could be built.

memory by his sons and disciples. They also made another myaṅ-hdas mchhod-rten, a reliquary nine stories high, and a long gallery of clay images. His three sons also had a text made of the *Nyi-khri* (The *Prajñāpāramitā* containing 28,000 ślokas) and the *brGyad-stoṅ-pa* (containing 8000 ślokas) and the *rTog-gzuṅs* (Power of Discrimination), and the *gSer-'od Sūtra* (Golden Light) written in gold and silver, and the donors made offerings to the Buddha Śākyamuni's image of butter lamps and golden facings for the rūpa* and gifts of scarves and other great offerings.

Colophon by the author

E ma ho! This is the biography of the jewel treasure,
The great gYu-thog, the Incarnation of the Medicine Buddha's speech.
This excellent life story
Was provided by me, Lhun-grub bKra-shis,
A descendant of the gYu-thog family.
If any part of it is superfluous
Or anything missing
Or any grammatical mistakes
I ask the forgiveness of the learned.

Colophon by the copyist, corrector and printer

As this is the description of the life of the crown ornament of all the teachers of medical science in Tibet in the past and the present and the future, the Great gYu-thog Yon-tan mGon-po the Elder, containing the secret biography of the jewel treasure, the ornament of medical science, I wish sincerely for it to be printed all over the country as a religious gift. I have searched everywhere for a perfect and complete manuscript but until now have not found one. However, by the great kindness of His Holiness,† the incarnation of Avalokiteśvara, who is inseparable from the Three Jewels and the Buddhas and the Bodhisattvas, I have received the original text from a member of the gYu-thog family and I had it copied conscientiously and correctly and printed it to accumulate an immeasurable quantity of merit. It was corrected and prepared by me, Doctor Dhar-mo sMan-ram-pa bLo-bzaṅ Chhos-grags and was copied by my disciples bLo-bzaṅ Don-ldan and Mer-mo bLo-gros Chhos-hphel.

Dedication by the Fifth Dalai Lama

Medicine Buddha, chief of the maṇḍala of Five Families foregathered,
For the sake of protecting beings

* Image.
† The Fifth Dalai Lama.

Nowadays in this degenerate age
gYu-thog's emanations are more innumerable than the sand grains of the Ganges river;
But this is the excellent life story of the Elder and the Younger gYu-thog*
Who were born in dbU-(m)skyid-sna† and in Ru-lag Luṅ-dmar in Tibet,‡
Printed for the sake of those with understanding
By the order of Dhar-mo sMan-ram-pa bLo-bzaṅ Chhos-grags
By the hands of many printers well versed in letters.
By the merit of this printing
May the glory of the Teaching of dGe-ldan-pa
And of the Saṁgha who practises it be increased!
May the Tibetan Government be mighty
And all its administrators thrive!
May the beings in China, Mongolia, Tibet and other countries
Live happily in body, speech and mind
Just as during the golden age.
May the sandalwood-like scent of the teaching of the Medicine Tree
Pervade everywhere and give abundant solace
And destroy the four hundred and twenty-four diseases caused by two defilements.
And the bodies became like those of gods.
May the printer, corrector, donor and attendants
Be wealthy and happy in this life
And in the next be born in the Vaiḍūrya Heaven
And may they become protectors of beings!

This dedication was composed by the Fifth Dalai Lama and written down by the Bhikshu hJam-dbyaṅs Grags-pa.

* The biography of the Younger gYu-thog is a separate work perhaps presented at the same time.
† Birthplace of the Elder gYu-thog.
‡ Birthplace of the Younger gYu-thog.

Glossary

A-ru-ra (Tibetan)—myrobalan
Ārya (Sanskrit)—noble, with regard to ethics and spirituality; has no racial or class connotation
Bhikkhu (Pali)—Buddhist monk
Bhikshu (Skt.)—Buddhist monk
bLo-tsa-ba (Tib.)—translator
Bodhisattva (Skt.)—Saint in the Mahāyāna School of Buddhism
Brahmā (Skt.)—Hindu deity taken over by Buddhist mythology
Brahmin (Skt.)—in the Buddhist context, sage living in organized society
Bre (Tib.)—measure of gold or silver dust
Ḍākinī (Skt.)—female helper on the Path to Enlightenment
dBaṅ (Tib.)—conferment of spiritual power
Deva (Skt.)—celestial being
Devanāgarī (Skt.)—alphabet of Sanskrit letters. The Tibetan letters were derived from its North Indian form called Kuṭila
Dharma (Skt.)—religion. There are other meanings not used in the present volume.
Dharmakāya (Skt.)—Ultimate Reality
Families—five types of emanation from Buddhas: Jewel-family, Lotus-family, Vajra-family, Buddha-family and Karma-family
Garuḍa (Skt.)—fabulous big bird
gTer-ston (Tib.)—discoverer of Scriptures hidden centuries ago
Kalpa (Skt.)—aeon, long period of time comparable to the Golden etc. Ages in Greek and Roman mythology
Karma (Skt.)—law of cause and effect according to which thoughts and actions have a commensurate effect in this and later lives
Kāya (Skt.)—body
Khal (Tib.)—grain measure corresponding to forty pints
kLu (Tib.)—snake, snake god or snake demon (Skt. Nāga)
Lotsava (Tib., spelled bLo-tsa-ba)—translator
Lus-thig (Tib.)—system of body measurements
Mahāyāna (Skt.)—see Vehicles
Mantra (Skt.)—invocation repeated in Sanskrit so as to have magical effect, Sanskrit being regarded as a sacred language, but somewhat changed when rendered in Tibetan transcription
Māra (Skt.)—evil spirit, devil, tempter
mChhod-rten (Tib.)—monument in which relics or sacred objects are kept (Skt. Stūpa)
Nāga (Skt.)—see kLu
Nirmāṇakāya (Skt.)—Transformation body, in appearance like that of an ordinary human being

Nirvāṇa (Skt.)—Existence without suffering, birth or death
Pho-braṇ (Tib.)—palace
Pratyeka Buddha (Skt.)—see Vehicles
Rimpoche (Tib., spelled Rin-po-chhe)—literally 'jewel', a title of honour given to men of high rank and high spiritual achievement
Rishi (Skt.)—sage living in solitude
Samādhi (Skt.)—deep meditation, absorption
Saṁbhogakāya (Skt.)—Bliss body in which Bodhisattvas and Deities can appear
Saṁgha (Skt.)—order of monks; community of Saints
Saṁsāra (Skt.)—the world of birth, death and suffering
sDe-srid (Tib.)—regent
Siddhis (Skt.)—powers; lower siddhis—psychic powers; higher siddhis—spiritual powers
Six realms—realms of six kinds of beings: gods, asuras (titans), human beings, animals, hungry ghosts, denizens of hell
Sraṅ (Tib.)—ounce of gold
Stūpa (Skt.)—see mChhod-rten
Sūtra (Skt.)—discourse of the Buddha
Śakti (Skt.)—consort
Śrāvaka (Skt.)—see Vehicles
Śūnyatā (Skt.)—Emptiness
Tanjur (Tib., spelled bsTan-hgyur)—'Translation of Treatises', collection of 225 Commentaries on Sūtras and Tantras. This is the second part of the Tibetan Buddhist Canon, the first being the Kanjur (spelled bKah-hgyur), a collection of 108 Buddhist Scriptures. Both parts have originally been translated from the Sanskrit but the Sanskrit text has often been lost
Tantra (Skt.)—a system of rituals enlisting the help of personified forces by using images, invocations and ritual gestures
Three Jewels—the Buddha, Religious Doctrine and Order of Monks
Three Poisons—hatred and anger causing excessive bile; greed and lust causing excessive air; ignorance and dullness causing excessive phlegm
Trikāya (Skt.)—Three bodies: Transformation Body, Bliss Body and Ultimate Reality
Vaiḍūrya (Skt.)—precious stone, usually translated as beryl. Name of the Medicine Buddha
Vajra (Skt.)—emblem of power, thunderbolt (Tib. rdo-rje)
Vehicles—different ways of achieving Enlightenment, Tibetan Buddhism is based on the Vehicle of the Mahāyāna School which regards the Vehicles of the Śrāvakas and of the Pratyeka Buddhas, both belonging to the Hīnayāna School, as inferior
Vinaya (Skt. and Pali)—rules of conduct observed by Buddhist monks

Index of Medical Topics